HAWAII ACCESS®

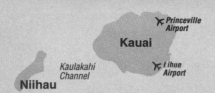

Kauai

✕ *Princeville Airport*

Kaulakahi Channel

Niihau

✕ *Lihue Airport*

Kauai Channel

Oahu

✕ *Honolulu International Airport*

Pacific Ocean

Orientation

Like a giant green comet blazing across the blue Pacific, the 132 tropical islands, reefs, and shoals of Hawaii form a graceful archipelago spanning more than 1,500 miles, yet they are so remote that even the ubiquitous sea gull is unable to traverse the 2,400 miles from the nearest continent. Moving northwest on the back of a lithospheric plate at a rate of four inches per year, the island chain is in a continual state of eruption and erosion, as vast amounts of molten earth emanate upward toward the surface from a stationary "hot spot" on the ocean floor, only to be beaten back down by the merciless elements. After 42 million years of this geologic process, just eight major islands—the Big Island, Maui, Kahoolawe, Lanai, Molokai, Oahu, Kauai, and Niihau—remain, and serve not only as home to more than one million people but also as one of the world's most treasured vacation destinations—Hawaii.

The islands of Hawaii comprise a beautiful, enchanting tropical paradise that put the color in Kodachrome and inspired writers like James Michener and Mark Twain to pen volumes on the majestic volcanoes, golden beaches, captivating sunsets, and lush rain forests. Hawaii altruistically continues to enthrall the millions of tourists who storm the beaches and hillsides every year with its numerous rainbows, magnificent waterfalls, astonishing lava flows, endless summer days, and warm starry nights. It's the unstaged backdrop for such movie classics as *Blue Hawaii* and *South Pacific,* the birthplace of regal humpback whales and playful spinner dolphins, and the home of world-famous surfing sites such as Sunset, Waimea Bay, and the Bonzai Pipeline. It's a playground for golfers, scuba divers, hikers, windsurfers, snorkelers, swimmers, deep-sea anglers, and sun worshipers of all shapes and sizes. In short, Hawaii has something for everyone, whether you choose to sip a cool mai tai under the shade of a palm tree or dive into the depths of the turquoise sea. And, perhaps most importantly, the slow, mellow pace that characterizes the Hawaiian lifestyle tends to ease stress and anxiety, allowing each visitor to return home with something no postcard or souvenir can touch—peace of mind.

Naturally, Hawaii is not without its faults. In an already overcrowded island state where indigenous Hawaiians are becoming increasingly rare (with pure blooded Hawaiians making up less than .0005 percent of the population), an expanding number of immigrants from the mainland and abroad has spurred a rise in racial bitterness, occasionally culminating in violence and, more often, targeted theft. This, combined with a huge foreign investment in precious real estate (the majority of private land, including entire islands,

is owned by foreigners) and a recent surge in ethnic Hawaiian pride, has done little to alleviate the multiracial resentment that has existed ever since Captain Cook set foot on Hawaii in 1778.

As the 20th century comes to a close, however, it marks the beginning of a new age for Hawaii, and after 200 years of pursuing things new, the people of Hawaii are beginning to reassess the value of things old. A Hawaiian Renaissance of sorts is emerging, with renewed interest in ancient crafts, rituals, and dances, and a rekindled passion for the values of traditional island culture, including native art and the Hawaiian language. This Renaissance is nothing short of a necessity, because for Hawaii to prosper in the next century, it must learn from its past mistakes. As Hawaii's Governor John Waihe'e sagaciously observed, "We need to ask ourselves how our ancestors did so much with so little, and why we are able to do so little with so much."

Hawaii—it's the closest thing we have to heaven-on-earth, and a priceless resource worth preserving, for it continually reminds us not only how beautiful the world can be, but also how to appreciate life's simpler things, like lounging by the pool, strolling barefoot down the beach, or just watching the sky change colors as the sun disappears behind the sea.

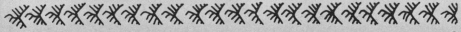

How to Read this Guide

HAWAII ACCESS® is arranged by island so you can see at a glance where you are and what is around you. The numbers next to the entries in the following chapters correspond to the numbers on the maps. The text is color-coded according to the kind of place described:

Restaurants/Clubs: Red   Hotels: Blue

Shops/ 📍 Outdoors: Green   **Sights/Culture:** Black

Rating the Restaurants and Hotels

The restaurant star ratings take into account the quality, service, atmosphere, and uniqueness of the restaurant. An expensive restaurant doesn't necessarily ensure an enjoyable evening; however, a small, relatively unknown spot could have good food, professional service, and a lovely atmosphere. Therefore, on a purely subjective basis, stars are used to judge the overall dining value (see the star ratings above at right). Keep in mind that chefs and owners often change, which sometimes drastically affects the quality of a restaurant. The ratings in this guidebook are based on information available at press time.

The price ratings, as categorized above at right, apply to restaurants and hotels. These figures describe general price-range relationships among other restaurants and hotels in the area. The restaurant price ratings are based on the average cost of an entrée for one person, excluding tax and tip. Hotel price ratings reflect the base price of a standard room for two people for one night during the peak season.

Restaurants

★★★★	An Extraordinary Experience	
★★★	Excellent	
★★	Very Good	
★	Good	
$$$$	Big Bucks	($25 and up)
$$$	Expensive	($15-$25)
$$	Reasonable	($10-$15)
$	The Price Is Right	(less than $10)

Hotels

$$$$	Big Bucks	($225 and up)
$$$	Expensive	($150-$225)
$$	Reasonable	($75-$150)
$	The Price Is Right	(less than $75)

Map Key

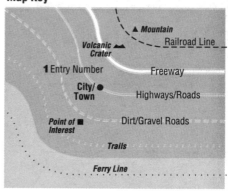

▲ Mountain
Railroad Line
Volcanic ▲ Crater
1 Entry Number
Freeway
**City/ ●
Town**
Highways/Roads
**Point of ■
Interest**
Dirt/Gravel Roads
Trails
Ferry Line

Area code 808 unless otherwise indicated.

Getting to the Islands

Major Airports

On the Big Island:
Hilo Airport..**935.1018**
  Aloha Airlines...935.5771
  Hawaiian Airlines 326.5615
Keahole Airport..**329.3423**
  Aloha Airlines...935.5771
  Hawaiian Airlines 326.5615
  United Airlines 800/241.6522

On Kauai:
Lihue Airport **246.1440**
  Aloha Airlines...245.3691
  Hawaiian Airlines 245.1813

On Maui:
Kahului Airport...**872.3893**
  Aloha Airlines...244.9071
  American Airlines...........................800/433.7300

American Trans Air (only offers chartered flights, but this company usually has the cheapest fares)
....800/225.9920
Delta Airlines....................................800/221.1212
Hawaiian Airlines 871.6132
Island Air 800/652.6541

On Molokai:
Hoolehua Airport (a.k.a. **Kaunakakai Airport**)...........
....**567.6140**
  Aloha Island Air.......................................567.6115
  Hawaiian Airlines 553.3644

On Oahu:
Honolulu International Airport...................**836.6413**
  Aloha Airlines...484.1111
  American Airlines...........................800/433.7300
  American Trans Air 800/433.7300
  Canadian Airlines (from Vancouver only)................
....800/426.7000
  Continental Airlines..........................800/231.0856

Delta Airlines	800/221.1212	Waimea-Kohala Airport	885.4520
Hawaiian Airlines	537.5100	**On Kauai:**	
Island Air	800/484.2222	Princeville Airport	No phone
Northwest Airlines	800/225.2525	**On Lanai:**	
Trans World Airlines	800/221.2000	Lanai City Airport	565.6757
United Airlines	800/241.6522	**On Maui:**	
		Hana Airport	248.8208

Minor Airports

On the Big Island:

Upolu Airport 889.9958

On Maui:
West Maui-Kapalua Airport .... No phone

On Molokai:
Kalaupapa Airport 567.6331

Getting around the Islands

Inter-Island Carriers

Commuter planes fly between the islands with the frequency of a big-city bus service. In some cases, they offer small savings over the major airlines, but the flights generally take longer and enforce stricter limitations on baggage. **Aloha Airlines** (800/367.5250 from the United States), **Island Air** (800/323.3345 from the United States), and **Hawaiian Airlines** (800/367.5350 from the United States), the major passenger carriers, share a terminal at **Honolulu International Airport** on Oahu.

Aloha Airlines and Hawaiian Airlines make regular hops on full-size jets to Honolulu, as well as to Maui, Kauai, and Kona and Hilo on the Big Island. In addition, Hawaiian Airlines flies to Lanai, Molokai, and the West Maui-Kapalua Airport. Island Air flies to Honolulu International, with additional flights to

Waimea-Kohala on the Big Island, Kahului and Hana on Maui, Hoolehua on Molokai, and Lanai.

Air Molokai (834.0043), a small commuter service, offers flights to Honolulu International, Kahului on Maui, and Hoolehua and Kalaupapa airports on Molokai.

For the serious traveler, Hawaiian Airlines offers the **Air Pass,** an unlimited-use ticket valid at eight airports on six islands. You can purchase 5- to 14-day passes, which are also good for discounts on car rentals.

Your hotel will probably be a considerable distance from whichever airport you land at, so try to arrange for transportation ahead of time. Some hotels offer shuttle services, but there are few limousines and no public bus services from any of the island airports except on Oahu.

Ground Transportation

With the exception of Oahu, public transportation in Hawaii is practically nonexistent. Unless you plan to stay put in your hotel or prefer chartered bus tours, you'll have to rent a car on every island to get around.

Buses

Oahu's very efficient bus system, **TheBus** (848.5555), covers the entire island every day for 60¢ one way. It's one of the best deals in Hawaii.

On **Maui,** there is no public transportation, but **Trans-Hawaiian Shuttle** (877.7308) transports people between Kahului Airport and the Kaanapali resort area every hour from 7AM to 6PM; no reservations are needed upon arrival at the airport, but they're recommended for departure from Kaanapali. Trans-Hawaiian's pickups from other hotels in West Maui are available by reservation only. Pickup time for departure is at least three hours before your flight; $13 one way. **Akina Tours** (879.2828) takes passengers from the airport to South Maui, Kihei, and Wailea, leaving the airport every hour and a half from 8AM to 5PM. Reservations are required for departures (use the courtesy phone in the baggage-claim area); $12 per person one way and $10 per person for two or more going to the Kihei/Wailea area ($5 ages 3 to 11; 3 and under are free).

On the **Big Island,** the **Hele-On Bus** (935.8241) runs from 7AM to 6PM from Hilo to Kau, and from Hilo to

Honokaa, Waimea, and Kailua-Kona. This is such a large island that most visitors rent a car.

No matter which island you're on, ask your hotel whether it provides shuttle service; the major resorts offer this transportation.

Car Rentals

Except on Lanai, the largest car-rental companies have booths at the main airports. (The Lodge at Koele and Manele Bay Hotel on Lanai provide shuttle service for their guests, and Lanai City Service provides limited taxi service as well as car rentals; call 565.6780.) The best deals on rental wheels are made in advance through the mainland offices or package deals, and reservations are mandatory during peak seasons. Be prepared for a $2-per-day state surcharge and an optional Collision Damage Waiver (CDW) fee. (Some credit cards and personal insurance policies automatically cover you for CDW, so be sure to check in advance.) Also, many car companies—especially on Maui—don't want their cars on certain roads and will have you sign an agreement. Although they don't actually police these roads, any assistance/insurance coverage is automatically void if you decide to venture onto roads closed to rental cars.

Driving

Traffic jams have become particularly commonplace on the large islands, so try to avoid driving during rush hours, as you'll rarely find alternate routes to the main roads (most of which follow the coastlines). Oahu has the heaviest traffic and is the hardest island to navigate. On Maui, Highway 30 from Kahului Airport to Lahaina can be treacherous during the whale migration season (November through June), when the entire highway becomes a makeshift parking lot every time someone spots a whale spouting or breaching.

Also, keep in mind that it's a major faux pas to pass other cars at high speeds (the locals *hate* to be passed at any speed) or to honk your horn unless it's absolutely necessary. Furthermore, yellow traffic lights are heeded and enforced in Hawaii.

Taxis
Cab service is available on all the islands, but none of them are cheap, so first see if there's a shuttle headed in your direction. You can hail a cab at the airport or look in the yellow pages of the phone book for local taxi services. Fares differ on each island, but in some cases, particularly for long distances, a cab driver may give you a ride for a flat fee. It's supposedly illegal for cabbies to hustle fares, so you're better off calling a cab than trying to hail one.

FYI

Assistance for People with Disabilities
For a nominal fee, **The Commission on Persons with Disabilities** provides a guide with accessibility ratings of most of the Hawaiian islands' hotels, shopping centers, beaches, entertainment, and major visitor attractions, as well as addresses and telephone numbers of support services on all the islands for visitors with disabilities. For more information, call 586.8121.

B&Bs
A new tour de force has swept Hawaii's accommodations market: bed-and-breakfast inns. B&Bs are the same price as, if not less than, average hotels, but they're infinitely more personal and private, with remote locations and complimentary breakfasts, of course. The foremost B&B referral service is Hawaii's **Best Bed & Breakfast,** run by longtime-resident Barbara Campbell. For more information, write to Campbell at: Box 563, Kamuela, Hawaii 96743, or call 885.4550 or 800/262.9912.

Climate
Hawaii has basically two seasons: April through November is the warmer period, with temperatures floating comfortably in the 75° to 88°F range (except during August and September, which are the hottest, most humid months, when temperatures frequently soar into the 90s). The coldest months are December through February, when evening temperatures can dip into the high 50s and 60s; this is also when the heaviest rainfall occurs. The water temperature for all the islands is about 75° to 80°F, lowering about 5° during the winter.

Money
All of Hawaii's banks take traveler's checks, and there is a plethora of multicard 24-hour ATMs scattered throughout the islands (except on Lanai).

Newspapers
The two statewide dailies are *The Honolulu Advertiser* (the morning paper) and the *Honolulu Star-Bulletin* (the afternoon paper). *USA Today* and some other major mainland newspapers are sold in Hawaii a day after they are published.

Telephones
The area code for all the Hawaiian islands is 808. For inter-island phone calls, dial "1" before the number (don't dial the area code). You'll be charged by the minute.

Television
Major TV stations are KGMB/CBS, KITV/ABC, and KHON/NBC—all broadcast from Honolulu, Oahu.

Time
Hawaii does not follow Daylight Savings Time (DST) and is therefore two hours behind the West Coast and five hours behind the East Coast when the mainland states are on DST. When the mainland goes off DST, Hawaii is three hours behind the West Coast and six hours behind the East Coast.

Tourist Seasons
Peak tourist season is from June through August and December through January, when reservations for everything (especially hotel rooms and rental cars) are much harder to come by and more expensive. The rest of the year is off-season.

Visitor Information
The central office of the **Hawaii Visitors Bureau (HVB)** is on Oahu at 2270 Kalakaua Avenue, No. 801, Honolulu, Hawaii 96815; 923.1811.

The HVB's neighbor island offices are:

HVB in Maui, 250 Alamaha Street, Suite N-16, Kahului, Hawaii 96732; 871.8691

HVB in Hilo (the Big Island), 180 Kinoole Street, Suite 105, Hilo, Hawaii 96720; 961.5797

HVB in Kailua-Kona (the Big Island), 75-5719 West Alii Drive, Kailua-Kona, Hawaii 96740; 329.7787

HVB on Kauai, 3016 Umi Street, Lihue, Hawaii 96766; 245.3971

Phone Book

Emergency
Ambulance, Fire, Police	**911**
Directory Assistance	411
Hawaii Visitors Bureau	923.1811
Inter-Island Directory Assistance	555.1212
Weather	961.5582

Local Lingo

In keeping with its cultural diversity, Hawaii has three languages—two official (English and Hawaiian) and one unofficial (pidgin). Virtually all islanders speak English, but it's almost always infused with popular Hawaiian and pidgin vernacular, sometimes to the point of incomprehensibility ("Honey, what did he just say?"). Most of the words listed below are all the Hawaiian the average tourist needs to know, while the rest is pidgin, a hodge-podge of languages originally developed to help traders communicate (for more on pidgin, see "Tongue-Tied" on page 33). However, to avoid becoming the humorous subject of a *pau hana talk-story* session (an after-work conversation among locals), usage probably should be limited to "alohas" and "mahalos."

Aloha (ah-LOW-ha) Hello, good-bye, welcome, and love

Da kine (dah-KINE) Pidgin for "that whatchama-callit" or anything else one doesn't know the word for or location of

Diamond Head The east direction (as in: The library is Diamond Head of Bishop Street)

Ewa (EH-vah) West

Grinds Pidgin for food (also used as a verb, to eat)

Hana (HAH-nah) Work

Haole (HOW-lee) Pidgin for foreigner, normally used to refer to a Caucasian (often in a derogatory sense)

Hawaiian time Pidgin for late (usually about half an hour late)

Heiau (HEY-ow) Sacred temple, place of worship

J.O.J. Pidgin for tourists (stands for "Just Off the Jet")

Kamaaina (kah-mah-EYE-nah) Native-born citizen (but usually refers to any resident or local)

Kane (KAH-neh) Male

Kapu (kah-POO) Keep out, forbidden

Keiki (KAY-key) Child

Kokua (koh-COO-ah) Help, assistance

Lanai (lah-NIGH) Porch, balcony (also an island near Maui)

Lua (LEW-ah) Bathroom

Luau (LEW-ow) Hawaiian feast

Mahalo (muh-HAH-low) Thank you

Makai (muh-KIGH) Toward the sea (used when giving directions)

Mauka (MAU-kah) Toward the mountain (used when giving directions)

No ka oi (no-kah-OH-ee) The best

Ono (OH-no) Delicious (also a game fish)

Pakalolo (pah-kah-LOW-low) Marijuana

Pau (POW) Finished

Pau Hana After work

Pupu (POO-poo) Appetizer

Talk story Casual conversation

Wahine (wah-HEE-nay) Woman or girl

Wikiwiki (WEE-kee-WEE-kee) Fast

Lahaina Harbor, Maui

GEORGE ALLAN

The Big Island

This southernmost isle is formally known as **Hawaii**, although it is commonly referred to as the Big Island to avoid confusion with Hawaii, the state. Despite its relatively enormous size—4,038 square miles—this is Hawaii's least visited major island, with only about 7,000 tourists present on any given day. The low turnout is probably due to rumors that the island is covered by lava, has no beaches, and offers little or nothing to do. The latter may be true for party hounds and searching singles, who will fare much better on Maui or Oahu (a hot time on this island is primarily limited to watching the lava flow at night), but the rest is pure bunk. Lush vegetation covers a vast majority of the Big Island's windward side, and uncrowded white sand beaches line the western coast. Unlike Kauai, you can lose yourself for days here without seeing another soul; unlike Oahu, there are no hordes of tourists or unsavory characters; unlike Maui, nobody will want to sell you time-share deals. And because tourism has such a low impact on the resident population, which mostly depends on agriculture and livestock for income, the locals are particularly warm and receptive.

As any resident will tell you, the islands of Hawaii are vastly diverse in character, and the Big Island is often viewed as the introverted sister, quietly earning recognition yet maintaining an unmistakable distance from the family of isles. Once understood and appreciated, however, the Big Island becomes an easy favorite among romantics, recluses, and adventurers.

The Big Island is frequently described as a miniature continent, with its rain forests lining the windward coasts in the east, immense snowdrifts resting atop **Mauna Kea** volcano, grassy

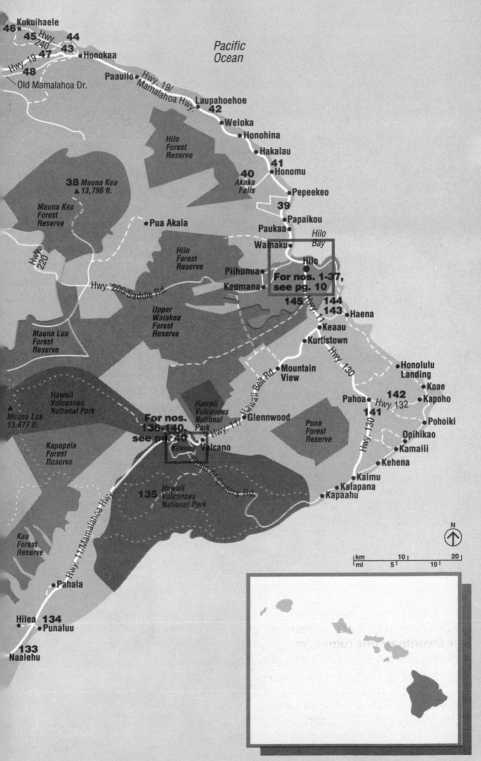

Kukuihaele
46
45 Hwy 44
240
47 43
48 Honokaa
Hwy. 19
Old Mamalahoa Dr.

Paauilo Hwy. 19/
Mamalahoa Hwy.
Laupahoehoe
42
Weloka
Honohina
Hakalau
41
40 Honomu
Akaka
Falls
Pepeekeo
39
Papaikou
Paukaa
Wainaku
Piihonua
Kaumana

Pacific
Ocean

38 Mauna Kea
▲ 13,796 ft.

Mauna Kea
Forest
Reserve

Pua Akala

Hilo
Forest
Reserve

Hilo
Forest
Reserve

Hwy. 200/Saddle Rd.

Upper
Waiakea
Forest
Reserve

Mauna Loa
Forest
Reserve

Hwy. 220

Hilo
Bay

Hilo

For nos. 1-37,
see pg. 10

145 144
143
Haena
Keaau
Kurtistown

Honolulu
Landing
Koae

Hwy. 11

Hwy. 130

Hawaii
Volcanoes
National Park

▲
Mauna Loa
13,677 ft.

Kapapala
Forest
Reserve

Kau
Forest
Reserve

Hawaii
Belt Rd.

Mountain
View

Hawaii
Volcanoes
National Park

Glennwood

For nos.
136-140,
see pg. 40

Kilauea Volcano

Hwy. 11/Mamalahoa Hwy.

Chain of Craters Rd.

Puna
Forest
Reserve

142 Kapoho
Pahoa Hwy. 132
141
Pohoiki
Opihikao
Kamaili
Kehena

Kaimu
Kalapana
Kapaahu

135 Hawaii
Volcanoes
National Park

Pahala

Hilea 134
Punaluu

133
Naalehu

N

km 10
mi 20
5
10

plains stretching around **Waimea**, and miles of desert and lava beds dominating the **Kohala** coast. What's extraordinary about this environmental diversity is that it can all be witnessed in a leisurely two-hour drive from **Hilo** to **Kailua-Kona** (towns on opposite sides of the island) across the wrongfully maligned **Saddle Road** (which is actually a quite pleasant route). Geologically, the Big Island, Hawaii's only island with active volcanoes, is still in its youth. A little more than one million years old, the landscape has become more defined with erosion yet continues to grow with every volcanic eruption. Of the five volcanoes that make up the island, Mauna Kea is the tallest in the world (measured from the ocean floor) and **Mauna Loa** is the world's largest active volcano and last erupted in 1984. But a significantly smaller volcano, **Kilauea** (KEEL-ow-AY-ah), is the one that always steals the show. In a continual state of eruption since 1983, Kilauea has earned its title as the most active volcano in the world. Located within **Hawaii Volcanoes National Park,** which is the island's most popular attraction and the site of more observatories than anywhere else in the world, Kilauea is also home to the Hawaiian fire goddess, a moody spirit known as **Madame Pele.**

HILO

Katwiki Rd.
Wainaku
Hilo Breakwater (no public access)

Hwy. 19

Wainaku Ave.

Puueo 37
Clem Akina Park
Amauulu Rd. (private)
Wailuku River

Hilo Bay

Kuhi Bay

For nos. 21-32, see inset map

Liliuokalani Gardens
7
8 6 Reeds Bay Beach Park
9

Mooheau Park
Bayfront Beach Park
10
11 Banyan Dr.
5 4

Hwy. 19 Hilo Bayfront Hwy.
Kamehameha Ave.
Kamehameha Ave.
Kuawa St.
12 13
14

Kinoole Ave.
Kapiolani St.
Alae St. 33
Haili St.
Wailuku River State Park
34 Rainbow Falls
Hwy. 200 Waianuenue Ave.
← 35 Waianuenue Ave.
Punahele St.

Wailoa Visitor Center
20
Waiakea Pond
Hoolulu Park
Piilani St.

Kaumana Springs Wilderness Park

Hualani St.
19
Wailoa St.
16 Hualani St.
17

Ponahawai St.

Kekuanaoa St.
18

Manono St.
Hinano St.
Kalanikoa St.
Leilani St.
Lanikaula St.
E. Kawili St.

Ainako Ave.
Hwy. 200 Saddle Rd. Kaumana Dr.
Kukuau St.
Hilina St.
Mohouli St.
Kumukoa St.

For nos. 38-145, see pg. 8

36

Komohana St.
University of Hawaii
W. Kawili St.
Kilauea St.
Kinoole St.
Kanoelehua Ave.

Waiakea Schools
Lokahi Park
15 Prince Kuhio Plaza

N

Puainako St.
Kapuaiani St.
Iwalani St.
Nohea St.
Kahaopea St.

km
mi   1/2   1   2
1

To properly tour this island takes about one to two weeks, spending two or three days apiece in its four main regions. An hour's drive apart, each section is astoundingly different in climate and scenery, making it entirely possible to condense several unique vacations into one. Start by exploring the Kilauea volcano and stay overnight in the charming town of **Volcano**. Then pack up and drive to Hilo, a rural city ensconced by beautiful rain forests. Dry out in rustic Waimea, an island anomaly of green pastures, grazing cattle, weathered Hawaiian cowboys, and a few excellent restaurants and shops, and end your tour on the **Kona-Kohala Coast**, poking about the dozens of ancient ruins near the most sun-drenched beaches in the country.

1 Onekahakaha Beach Park With lifeguards, safe swimming (it's protected by a breakwater), white sand, small tidal pools, picnic and camping facilities, and plenty of parking, this is the most noteworthy beach in Hilo. ♦ Off Kalanianaole Ave, 2 miles east of junction of Hwys 11 and 19

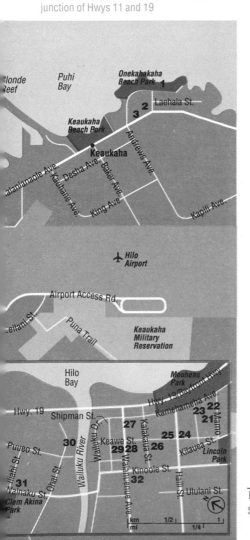

2 Arnott's Lodge $ Although it isn't listed with the American Youth Hostels, Arnott's is mainly a backpacker's lodge. Located in Hilo, close to the beaches, the clean and friendly walk-up offers private singles and doubles, semiprivate singles, and a two-bedroom suite. Budget-conscious travelers will love the fact that free use of the kitchen is included. ♦ 98 Apapane Rd, Hilo. 969.7097, 800/368.8752

3 Hilo Homemade Ice Cream ★$ Endemic ice cream is sold here for a buck a cone. Order the green tea flavor and take a stroll through **Hilo Tropical Gardens** next door. ♦ 1477 Kalanianaole Ave, Hilo. 935.4957

4 Harrington's ★★$$$ Local seafood enthusiasts who come for the chowder, catch of the day, fresh shellfish, and pasta-seafood combinations also get to admire the view of tranquil Reed's Bay. For Hilo, this is as romantic as it gets. ♦ 135 Kalanianaole Ave, Hilo. 961.4966

5 Hilo Seaside Hotel $$ Renovated in 1991, the Seaside's nicer rooms have private lanais overlooking a picturesque lagoon. Nothing fancy here, but the accommodations are pleasant, with A/C, cable TV, and refrigerators. ♦ 126 Banyan Dr, Hilo. 935.0821, 800/367.7000

Within the Hilo Seaside Hotel:

Hukilau $ Having survived four tidal waves, this restaurant must be here to stay. The steak, lobster, crab leg, and prawn dinners are bargains; informal scubawear is optional. ♦ 136 Banyan Way, at Kalanianaole Ave, Hilo. 935.4222

6 Banyan Drive Named for the numerous banyan trees planted here by visiting dignitaries and celebrities during the 1930s, the drive fronts a chain of hotels along Reed's Bay. Plaques at the bases of the trees reveal recognizable names such as **Babe Ruth** and **Amelia Earhart**. ♦ Off Kamehameha Ave, at junction of Hwys 11 and 19

Restaurants/Clubs: Red   **Hotels:** Blue

Shops/ 🌳 Outdoors: Green   **Sights/Culture:** Black

7 Hawaii Naniloa Hotel $$$ The best of the limited choices of hotels in Hilo, the Naniloa commands a fine location on Banyan Drive, with views of Hilo Bay, the beginnings of the Hamakua coastline, and adjacent Coconut Island. Three wings include 325 rooms, a health spa, and a Japanese restaurant. The decor is decidedly Japanese, with lots of pink marble. ♦ 93 Banyan Dr, Hilo. 969.3333, 800/367.5360; fax 969.6622

7 Uncle Billy's Hilo Bay Hotel $$ Uncle Billy Kimi (who also runs the Kona Bay Hotel) believes in keeping prices down at the expense of ambience, hence the video games adorning the lobby. The 156 rooms serve their purpose, but don't expect anything special. They all have TVs, A/C, and phones, and there's also a pool and Polynesian marketplace. ♦ 87 Banyan Dr, Hilo. 961.5818, 800/442.5841 (HI), 800/367.5102 (U.S.); fax 935.7903

7 Hilo Hawaiian Hotel $$ The 285 rooms here were renovated in 1990, making several of them wheelchair accessible. The view from the private lanais is the best in Hilo, and the seafood buffet on Fridays and Saturdays is worth checking out. Baseball legend **Babe Ruth** planted the banyan tree that's in front of the hotel. Accommodations include a pool, restaurant, cocktail lounge, and shops. ♦ 71 Banyan Dr, Hilo. 935.9361, 800/272.5275 (HI), 800/367.5004 (U.S.); fax 961.9642

8 Naniloa Country Club A flat, nine-hole course across from the Hawaii Naniloa Hotel—par 35, 3,156 yards. Starting time is suggested on weekends. The green fees are cheap. ♦ 120 Banyan Dr, Hilo. 935.3000

9 Liliuokalani Gardens Meditation gurus will find solace and harmony in this elaborate 30-acre Japanese garden, a popular picnic site and backdrop for wedding portraits. The usually vacant manicured grounds contain pagodas, stone lanterns, a ceremonial teahouse, bridges, and tidal pools. Follow the footpath to tiny **Coconut Island,** with its palm trees and sweeping view of Hilo Bay. ♦ Northwest end of Banyan Dr, Hilo

10 Nihon Restaurant and Cultural Center ★$$ Although this authentically decorated Japanese restaurant and art gallery serves decent meals, your best bet is a round of sake and sushi at the lanai bar overlooking Hilo Bay and Liliuokalani Gardens. ♦ 123 Lihiwai St, Hilo. 969.1133

11 Suisan Fish Market Early risers can come here to watch Hilo's fishing fleet unload its catch at what old-timers know as **Sampan Harbor.** The auctioneer uses a patois of English, Hawaiian, Japanese, and a bit of pidgin. Set the alarm clock and come experience a thriving bastion of local color. The auction is held every day but Sunday, beginning at 8AM. ♦ Free. Lihiwai St, at the end of Banyan Dr, Hilo

12 K.K. Tei ★$$ Many locals designate K.K. Tei as the Japanese restaurant of choice. If you have more than six people in your party, reserve one of the *ozashiki* rooms overlooking the bonsai garden. Try the sukiyaki or the seafood specialties. Entrées range from good to gourmet, so consult your waiter before ordering. ♦ 1550 Kamehameha Ave, Hilo. 961.3791

13 Ken's Pancake House $$ Located near the airport, this local representative of the California chain is reliable and (most importantly) the only 24-hour restaurant in Hilo. Try the macadamia nut pancakes or one of the wild waffle combinations. ♦ 1730 Kamehameha Ave, Hilo. 935.8711

14 Fiasco's ★$$ The large selection of Mexican, American, Chinese, and Italian food available here covers just about any craving you might have. ♦ Waiakea Sq Warehouse, 200 Kanoelehua Ave, Hilo. 935.7666

15 Prince Kuhio Plaza Fashion is a relative term at this $47.5 million shopping complex, which includes **Liberty House, Sears, Hilo Hattie, Safeway, Longs,** and many other retailers. If you can't find what you're looking for here, try **Puainako Town Center** just across the highway. ♦ 111 E. Puainako St, off Kanoelehua Ave, Hilo

16 Hilo Orchidarium Walk through the quarter-acre tropical garden, filled with exquisite orchids, then purchase an orchid plant of your own at the shop. Some of the varieties are very rare. ♦ Donation requested. 524 Manono St, Hilo. 935.8318

17 Waiakea Villas $$ This former Sheraton hotel, converted into 14 acres of condominiums in 1985, borders the **Wailoa Pond Freshwater Reserve.** Some of the 141 units (from standard rooms to one-bedroom suites) come with kitchenettes. Complete with pool and tennis courts, it's a bargain if you don't mind dark, dank corners and a slightly offbeat location. ♦ 400 Hualani St, Hilo. 961.2841, 800/354.2017

17 Miyo's ★★$ Local Japanese-food aficionados (and Hilo is the town for them) assemble at this popular restaurant at the edge of the Wailoa Pond Freshwater Reserve. The no-smoking dining room overlooks the ponds, with parks and curved bridges in the distance. Specialties include *soba* (buckwheat noodles), *shabu-shabu* (cook-it-yourself vegetables in an earthenware pot), and miso soup with fresh mushrooms. ♦ Waiakea Village, 400 Hualani St, Hilo. 935.2273

18 Dick's Coffee House ★$ In an atmosphere best described as kitschy American with a Hawaiian twist, decent grinds at unbelievably low prices attract a steady following of local residents. Almost all of the breakfast dishes, including the hefty steak-and-eggs plate, go for less than five bucks. It's somewhat difficult to find but worth the effort. ♦ Hilo Shopping Center, 1261 Kilauea Ave, Hilo. 935.2769

18 Restaurant Miwa ★★★$$ One of Hilo's best Japanese restaurants is located in one of the worst locations—tucked into the corner of dilapidated **Hilo Shopping Center.** Miwa's seasonal menu includes fresh Kona crab, Bangkok shrimp, *shabu-shabu,* sake-flavored steamed clams, and sushi. Sweet tooths will flip for the *haupia* (coconut) cream pie. ♦ Hilo Shopping Center, 1261 Kilauea Ave, Hilo. 961.4454

19 Sun Sun Lau ★$$ Standard Cantonese fare is served in a building optimistically designed for droves of customers. Extensive is the operative word here, and it applies to the menu as well as to the selection of "crackseed," a Chinese snack of sorts that's a favorite with local kids. Try the shredded mango or salted lemon seed. ♦ 1055 Kinoole St, Hilo. 935.2808

20 Wailoa Visitor Center Stop by this 10-sided building across from **Waiakea Fish Pond** and ask the friendly staff to set you straight on local activities. But first, check out their well-presented exhibitions on Hawaiian art, history, and culture, including the permanent photographic display of post-tsunami Hilo. It's open every day but Sunday. ♦ Free. 1 Piopio St, Liliuokalani Park, Hilo. 933.4360

21 Royal Siam ★$ A spotlessly clean and unpretentious little restaurant, Royal Siam cranks out consistently good Thai dishes (more than 50 of them) at every spice level from mild to aaaahhhh! ♦ 68 Mamo St, Hilo. 961.6100

22 Hilo Farmers Market Local color abounds at this festive fair, held every Wednesday, Saturday, and Sunday from 6AM to noon. Come early for the best buys on fresh vegetables, flowers and plants, baked goods, and arts and crafts from more than 80 vendors. Truly an ethnic bonanza, the market offers *malasadas* (Portuguese doughnuts), pickled turnips, *warabi* (fern shoots), exotic orchids, winged beans, papayas, corn, and various obscure offerings. A number of well-known Big Island artists got their start right here. ♦ Kamehameha Ave and Mamo St, Hilo

23 Reuben's Mexican Restaurant ★$ When you gotta have it, you gotta have it. Hilo's finest (and only) Mexican restaurant serves classic south-of-the-border fare. Decorated as if every day were a fiesta. ♦ 336 Kamehameha Ave, at Mamo St, Hilo. 961.2552. Also at: 75-5719 Alii Dr, Kona Plaza Shopping Arcade, Kona. 329.7031

23 Cafe Pesto ★★★$$ Pro-tourism Hilo bureaucrats would like to see more of these. A chic yuppie pizzeria, Cafe Pesto comes with all the trimmings, including an open kitchen, wood-fired oven, black and white decor, and an outstanding menu. Try the artichoke pizza with fresh shiitake and oyster mushrooms and rosemary gorgonzola sauce. If you have cause to celebrate, splurge on a bottle of Pesto's Private Reserve (Saintsbury Pinot Noir) with the chipolte shrimp and sausage pasta. ♦ 308 Kamehameha Ave (at Mamo St), Hilo. 969.6640. Also at: Kawaihae Center, Kawaihae. 882.1071

24 Pescatore ★★$$$ Upscale Northern Italian dishes are served here at upscale prices. Start with the *calamari fritti* (fried squid) and then dive into the *fra diavolo* (shrimp, clams, and fresh fish in a garlic and basil marinara sauce). ♦ 235 Keawe St (at Haili St), Hilo. 969.9090

25 Spencer's Fitness Center Has the wet weather put a damper on your jogging schedule? Sweat out your frustration on one of Spencer's treadmills or Stairmasters, then power down some Karrot juice at **Karrot's** (★$) juice bar and health-food restaurant. ♦ 197 Keawe St (at Haili St), Hilo. 935.6191

Kona coffee, named for the region it's primarily harvested in, is the only java grown commercially in the United States. Like Hawaii's sugarcane and pineapple plantations, however, Kona coffee growers are slowly succumbing to cheaper labor costs from overseas. There are about 650 small farms on the Big Island in Kailua-Kona (producing $4 million a year in revenue), but in Napoopoo, where several coffee mills and competing wholesalers used to thrive, only one mill remains in operation (and its entire crop is sold to a wholesale company in Chicago). Because of the high cost of picking the beans by hand and the limited number of places where growing conditions are suitable, connoisseurs anticipating a cup of Hawaiian-brewed Kona coffee may be disappointed to learn that it's relatively expensive, even on the islands.

26 Satsuki ★$ The Japanese-Hawaiian cuisine here has better taste than the interior decorator, but at such low prices, who cares? Always packed with locals (an auspicious sign at any restaurant), Satsuki is a sure bet for oxtail soup fans. Avoid the fish. ♦ 168 Keawe St, Hilo. 935.7880

27 Sig Zane Designs Designer **Sig Zane** takes simple Hawaiian motifs such as ti, breadfruit, or taro leaves and prints them on his fabrics to create islandwear that is both elegant and educational. Each T-shirt, aloha shirt, muumuu, quilted jacket, and *pareu* (wraparound) imparts the spirit of Hawaii. Zane's wife, **Nalani Kanaka'ole,** is a revered hula master, and their son, **Kuha'o,** is launching his own line of children's clothing, **KZD.** Look for their shop with the blue awning. ♦ 122 Kamehameha Ave, Hilo. 935.7077

27 Lehua's Bay City Bar & Grill ★★$$ This is Hilo's hippest gathering place (which isn't saying much) for lunch, dinner, and after hours. The friendly staff serves excellent soups (especially the chicken curry and clam chowder) and burgers. And for dinner there's spinach lasagna, grilled prawns and chicken, fresh fish, scampi, and vegetarian entrées. The nightclub offers live contemporary and Hawaiian music on Fridays and Saturdays. ♦ 90 Kamehameha Ave, Hilo. 935.8055

28 Bears' Coffee ★$ Always bustling, this classic establishment (shown above) offers waffles, eggs, croissants, muffins, and bagels along with espresso and other coffee favorites. You'll be in good company if you choose to begin your morning here. Deli sandwiches and salads are served from 10AM to 4PM. ♦ 106 Keawe St, Hilo. 935.0708

Every four days astronomers atop Mauna Kea on the Big Island are urged to come down to sea level because the thin air at those telescopic heights supposedly makes them more prone to absentmindedness.

---

29 Family Source Everything for the expectant parents, from tasteful maternity dresses to the cutest darn baby toys and books you ever did see (up to age five). ♦ 64 Keawe St, Hilo. 969.3054

29 Roussels ★★★$$$ New Orleans-born brothers **Spencer** and **Andrew Oliver** got together with **Herbert Roussels** and opened this fine French-Creole restaurant in 1985. It's located in the historic **Masonic Temple Building** (meetings are still held upstairs), with 16-foot-high columns and hardwood maple floors. Chef Andrew is a genius with fresh Hawaiian fish, traditional Louisiana gumbo, shrimp creole, and roast duck. The Cajun-style blackened fish is legendary, and the lemon mousse is a must. Dinner only is served. ♦ 60 Keawe St, Hilo. 935.5111

30 Wild Ginger Inn $ A simple, clean, and inexpensive hotel, the Wild Ginger Inn offers 40 rooms, coin-operated laundry machines, and complimentary Continental breakfast. It's conveniently located two blocks from downtown Hilo. ♦ 100 Puueo St, Hilo. 935.5556, 800/882.1887

31 Dolphin Bay Hotel $ Economical and clean, this 18-unit hotel is one of Hilo's best-kept secrets. The rooms are plain but inviting and the grounds are lavishly landscaped with bananas, orchids, ginger plants, and a dense tropical forest. There are four types of units in the two-story walk-up, each with a full kitchen, *ofuro*-type bathtub, TV, and fans (but there's no air-conditioning, and the telephone is in the lobby). You'll love the convenient location, intimate ambience, and friendly banter with owners **Margaret, John,** and **Larry Alexander.** ♦ 333 Iliahi St, Hilo. 935.1466

32 Restaurant Fuji ★$$ A high-ceilinged, pleasant Japanese oasis in a business-person's hotel, Restaurant Fuji offers *soba* (buckwheat noodles), grilled fish, and *nabeyaki* (vegetables and noodles cooked in an earthenware pot). ♦ 142 Kinoole St, Hilo. 961.3733

Restaurants/Clubs: Red   Hotels: Blue

Shops/ 🌳 Outdoors: Green   **Sights/Culture:** Black

Lyman Museum and Mission House

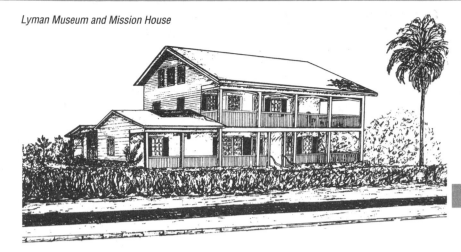

33 Lyman Museum and Mission House
Built in 1839 for the **Reverend David Lyman**
and his wife, **Sarah,** the Mission House
(pictured above) was among the first wood-
frame structures in Hilo. You can still see their
19th-century furnishings and clothing. The
adjoining Lyman Museum, completed in
1973, is one of the least exhausting of
Hawaii's museums. One gallery features a *pili*
grass house, *kapa* (bark cloth), and carvings
and cultural artifacts of Hawaii's ethnic
groups; another displays volcanic and mineral
formations, including land shells. ♦ Admission. M-Sa 9AM-5PM; Su 1-4PM. 276 Haili St,
Hilo. 935.5021

34 Rainbow Falls Early risers can watch as the
sun peeks over the mango trees, forming a
rainbow in the mist of the thundering falls that
cascade 80 feet into the **Wailuku River** gorge.
With an average discharge of 300 million
gallons a day, it's No. 1 in sheer
production/volume in the state. The path to
the left of the parking lot leads to a private
view overlooking the falls. ♦ Wailuku River
State Park, Waianuenue Ave, Hilo

35 Boiling Pots The spectacular collection of
small waterfalls and pools working their way
toward Rainbow Falls are worthy of at least
one picture. Take the short (but steep)
footpath at the right of the point for a closer
look, but resist the temptation to go
swimming—at least one person has drowned
here. ♦ Wailuku River State Park, 2 miles up
from Rainbow Falls on Waianuenue Ave, Hilo

36 Kuamana Caves In 1881 a huge lava flow
from **Mauna Loa** cooled on the surface and
crusted over a flowing tube of molten lava.
When the eruption ceased, the lava tube
drained and these caves (supposedly
radiation-proof) were the result. Seasoned
spelunkers will already know to bring a
flashlight to examine the modern-day
petroglyphs, while the lionhearted timidly turn

around at the mouth of the caves to gawk at
the view looking out. Don't miss this; it's
about five miles from Hilo. ♦ Hwy 200 and
Kuamana Dr

37 Mamalahoa Highway Scenic Drive If
you're not in a rush (and you're not), take this
scenic drive into the past. Beginning at
Wainaku Street on the north side of Hilo,
occasional signs will direct you to the old
wooden-bridged road called the Mamalahoa
Highway (Hwy 19). Pass the ancient surfing
spot of **Honolii,** then turn onto the four-mile
Onomea Bay Scenic Route, overlooking the
bay where sailing ships anchored during the
19th century. This rural road was once filled
with sugarcane trains and bullock carts
passing to and from markets and mills. Before
you get back on the main highway and head
toward **Kamuela-Waimea,** linger at **Akaka
Falls,** a 420-foot waterfall into a verdant gorge
just off Route 220, near the delightfully
archaic town of **Honomu,** once a bustling
center of the sugar industry. Hilo to Waimea is
about 60 miles, approximately an hour and 15
minutes driving time.

38 Mauna Kea A dormant volcano in the
northern half of the island, "White Mountain"
rises 13,796 feet above sea level and is the
tallest mountain in the world (when measured
from the ocean floor). Inactive for more than
4,000 years, its peak now boasts the cleanest,
most rarefied air on earth, which is why nine
countries have observatories here, making it
the largest concentration of observatories in
the world. Each year, the entire northern sky
and more than 90 percent of the southern sky
can be viewed from this spot.

Mauna Kea's uppermost slopes are generally
covered with snow from January through
May. Weather permitting, it's quite possible to
ski Mauna Kea early in the day and return to
your hotel in time for a sunset swim. There's
even an official **Ski Association of Hawaii,**

whose members you'll recognize by their "Ski Hawaii" T-shirts. You won't find ski lifts (or lift lines) at Mauna Kea. Instead, skiers travel 20 miles up a paved road through black lava and cinder cones to reach the snow (which generally starts at 11,000 feet) and then continue up to the start of several runs. Once you've enjoyed one of the three- to five-mile runs, you can hop back into a vehicle and proceed to the top again.

Not only are there no lifts, there's no snow-covered lodge and no après-ski drinking around a roaring fireplace (nor is there biting wind or dangerous underbrush). The gritty texture of the snow is a lot like sand. Veteran skiers compare it to the crisp "corn snow" of New England and locals call it "pineapple powder." The long and fast ski runs are natural, with snow depths generally ranging from five to six feet. Hardly a technical challenge for experienced skiers, Mauna Kea is skied simply because it's there. **Poi Bowl,** a quarter-mile-wide stretch starting at the summit, is excellent for beginners, while the other runs are steeper and more challenging. If you're interested in skiing a volcano, contact **Ski Guides Hawaii** for guides, transportation, and equipment rental (Box 1954, Kamuela, Hawaii 96743; 885.4188).

The **Mauna Kea Observatory** offers tours at the summit on Saturday and Sunday afternoons at 2PM (participants must be at least 16 years of age). Reservations are not required, but you'll need a four-wheel-drive auto to get to the summit. Call **Mauna Kea Support Services** for more information (Monday through Friday from 7AM to noon and 1PM to 4PM; 935.3371). If you don't have a 4WD vehicle, you can still visit the **Onizuka**

Visitor Center at the 9,000-foot level for an evening lecture and a chance to look through a nine-inch telescope (Friday and Saturday at 7PM; 961.2180). ♦ From downtown Hilo, take Waianuenue Ave to Kuamana Dr, which turns into Saddle Rd (Hwy 200). From Kona, take Hwy 190 toward Waimea and turn at Saddle Rd (Hwy 200)

39 Hawaii Tropical Botanical Gardens

For a chance to decide for yourself whether or not this nature preserve and rain forest is the most beautiful place in Hawaii, take the small group tour (offered daily from 8:30AM to 4:30PM). **Daniel J. Lutkenhouse,** a retired California trucking executive who had long been charmed by Hilo's rain forests, formally opened the foundation to the public in 1984. The tours, which last about two hours, provide informative trivia about some of the 1,800 endemic and imported plants, but you can walk around the large lily and *koi* (carp) pond, giant mango trees, pungent guava orchard, or the huge Alexander palms on your own. The exotic plant collection comes from as far away as Fiji, Peru, Madagascar, and Indonesia. Cars are not allowed inside the gardens, so prepare to meander on foot, preferably in comfortable shoes. Tours begin about a half mile from the garden's entrance on the **Onomea Bay Scenic Route,** just off the Hawaii Belt Highway. Parking and restrooms are available, but bring mosquito repellent. ♦ Tour Fee. Onomea Bay Scenic Route, 7 miles north of Hilo. 964.5233

An Island Gone Nuts

A native of Queensland, Australia, the macadamia was originally known as the "bush nut" and was generally considered more trouble than it was worth to eat (primarily because of its tough shell). But when **John Macadam,** an Australian chemist, discovered the pleasure of indulging in roasted and salted macadamias, it became a gourmet treat and was named after him.

The first macadamia seeds were brought to Hawaii in 1881 for the planting of ornamental trees (many species have spiked leaves, similar to holly, that are used as holiday ornaments). By 1921 the commercial potential of the macadamia was realized as it became a popular snack food, and the first plantation was started near Honolulu. Sixty years later, more than 29 million pounds of macadamias were being harvested on the islands annually—almost all for export.

The macadamia tree, a subtropical evergreen that can grow as tall as one hundred feet, is slow to bear its fruit; the first harvest appears in five years,

reaching its peak of productivity after 15 years and yielding an average of 25 to 30 pounds of nuts (in the shell) each season. The macadamia meat is protected by two layers: a green, oval-shaped outer

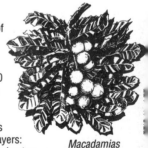

Macadamias

covering lined inside with a shell so tough it's hard to break without crushing the tender nut. The long maturation period and limited supply contribute to the macadamia's steep price, but the crisp, white nut is holding its own among snack-nut competitors.

For a firsthand look at how macadamias are made into various snacks, visit the **Macadamia Nut Factory** in Honokaa on the Big Island. They'll even give you free, freshly roasted samples (see No. 44 on the opposite page for details).

40 Akaka Falls What sets this 420-foot cascade and its 100-foot companion, **Kahuna Falls,** apart from other waterfalls is the lush 65-acre park that surrounds them, an area so beautiful it is celebrated in ancient chants and contemporary love songs. Plants and flowers brought in from all over the world create the dense rain-forest atmosphere: sprays of orchids, bamboo groves, carpets of moss, bougainvillea bushes, gingers, azaleas, ferns, and countless other exotic plants. The moist air and mollifying roar of the waterfalls follow you on the 20-minute walk along the paved circular path. ♦ Rte 220, off Hwy 19

41 Kolekole Beach Park Follow the sign on Highway 19 to Kolekole Beach Park (turn off on the *mauka* side) and your reward will be a cool (make that *cold*) freshwater pond fed by **Kolekole Falls.** A playing field, two picnic pavilions, and camping by permit are also available. ♦ Off Hwy 19, just north of Honomu

42 Laupahoehoe Beach Park This pleasant, grassy peninsula is distinguished by a memorial to the 20 students and four teachers who lost their lives here in the infamous 1946 tidal wave. The park is on the former Laupahoehoe village site, which was wisely moved to higher ground overlooking the point. Picnics and camping are allowed but no swimming. ♦ Laupahoehoe Point exit, off Hwy 19

43 Hotel Honokaa Club ★$ Big Islanders dine at the club (pictured above) when lobsters are in season, since most everything is fresh and inexpensive. The fare is decent and standard—steak and lobster, seafood platters, mahimahi—and the decor doesn't get much fancier than vinyl tablecloths and a TV in the corner. This is not the most chic place (it's a bit weird, and strangely lit), but it's very practical, with loads of local color. ♦ On Hwy 240 (Mamane St), Honokaa. 775.0678

44 Macadamia Nut Factory Watch through the large windows of this willfully nutty processing plant as macadamia nuts are made into various snacks. The kernels are separated from their hard brown shells, roasted in coconut oil, and then packed (unless, that is, they aren't first smothered in chocolate, baked into cookies, or blended into jams). You'll see just how far this designer nut has come since Australian chemist **John Macadam** introduced it to Hawaii in 1881. Free freshly roasted samples. ♦ Free. Daily 9AM-6PM. Lehua St, off Hwy 240, Honokaa. 775.7743

The state of Hawaii boasts the longest life expectancy per resident in the country.

45 Waipio Valley Artworks A remote showcase for Big Island artists, this Kukuihaele shop offers a pleasing amalgam of paintings, native-wood carvings and bowls, sculpture, furniture, and crafts. The bamboo vases, **Marcus Castaing** koa boxes, hand-painted T-shirts, and other works stem from Hawaiian motifs. ♦ Old Village Rd, Kukuihaele. 775.0958

46 Waipio Valley The Hamakua Coast ends at the Big Island's largest valley, with a population of about 35. According to oral tradition, Waipio Valley was once home to 40,000 Hawaiians. Some locals know it as the **Valley of the Kings** and the **Land of Curving Water.** Before **Captain Cook** arrived, Waipio Valley was the cultural and political hub of the island, a pastoral community of taro farmers and fishers. Ancient temple sites, stone terraces, waterfalls, and steep valley walls make this a spiritually inspiring site. The few taro farmers who remain, survivors of the devastating 1946 tsunami, proudly cling to a lifestyle immortalized in the songs and chants of ancient Hawaii. ♦ Hwy 240, just past Kukuihaele

46 Waipio Hotel $ Whether you're a bank executive or a Deadhead, nothing equals the original Waipio Valley hostelry for those who like roughing it. Octogenarian **Tom Araki's** barrackslike "hotel" is a five-room haven for reclusive seekers of a paradise without phones, restaurants, hot water, or even electricity. Bring your own food, flashlights, and towels—everything else is here (which isn't much, but that's the whole point), including taro fields, waterfalls, wild horses, and the pleasure of Tom's company (this alone is worth the stay). ♦ 25 Malama Pl, Waipio Valley. 775.0368

46 Waipio Tree House $$$ Linda Beech's establishment is an exotic offering: a one-room cabin suspended 30 feet above ground in a monkeypod tree (pictured above), with one double and one single bed, a refrigerator, hot plates, electricity, and running water . . . all the comforts of a tree house. A waterfall and mountain pool are just down the trail, and a Japanese hot tub simmers nearby. Standard rental cars can't make it down to the Waipio

Valley, so you'll need to arrange for transportation through **Waipio Shuttle** or Linda Beech. (One warning: For about 10 days every year, the cottage is inaccessible because of high river water. If guests are stranded, their accommodations during the delay are complimentary.) This is a good base for trail rides and wagon and horseback-riding tours that can be arranged in the valley. ◆ Off Hwy 240, Waipio Valley. 775.7160

47 Tex Drive Inn ★$ You'd probably drive right by this place unless you knew what a *malasada* was and how good they are here. These Portuguese doughnut holes from heaven are best eaten hot, so don't procrastinate. If you're still hungry, try the pork plate with mashed potatoes (the meat is so tender you can cut it with a plastic fork). ◆ 191 Hualani St, off Hwy 19 (across from the Old Mamalahoa Hwy exit), Ahualoa. 775.0598

48 Old Mamalahoa Drive If you have some leisure time, take this little-known scenic drive parallel to Highway 19 and pay particular attention to the extreme diversity of vegetation that can be seen in the 12 miles from east to west; a splendid microcosm of the Big Island's organic diversity as a whole. From Honokaa toward Waimea, take the Ahualoa exit, across from Tex Drive Inn.

49 Waimea Checkered with funky-looking buildings, grazing horses and cattle, and the stately homes of the landed gentry, Waimea is a friendly town. It is also a boomtown, growing rapidly (too rapidly for some) into a tourist mecca. Its 2,500-foot elevation provides a cool, crisp climate you may find refreshing after baking on the hot beaches of West Hawaii. **Mauna Kea** looms in the distance, flower and vegetable farms abound, and *paniolos* (cowboys) in boots and hats add a real Western flavor. Volcanic cinder cones long covered by greenery are dotted with livestock. Few people realize that Hawaii's paniolos (a derivative of the word español) predate the American West, having come from Spain and Mexico at the request of **Kamehameha III** in the 1830s to teach Hawaiians how to ride, rope, and herd cattle. Today, Hawaiian cowboys may be Filipino, Portuguese, Chinese, Japanese, or any and all mixtures therein.

Considering the number of signs with the name "Parker" on them—Parker Ranch Shopping Center, Parker Ranch Broiler, Parker Ranch Visitor Center, Parker Ranch Lodge, and Parker School (private)—it doesn't take long to figure out who runs this town. Waimea is cowboy country thanks to **John Parker,** a seaman from New England who jumped ship in 1809, settled on the Big Island, and domesticated a herd of wild cattle that British captain **George Vancouver** had given to **Kamehameha the Great.** The King, who gave Parker some land in exchange for the cattle, had a granddaughter that Parker conveniently married and voilà—the Parker Ranch dynasty was born. Today, the ranch consists of 225,000 acres with more than 50,000 head of cattle. You can tour the ranch, visit its original two-acre homestead, or walk through owner **Richard Smart's** historic home, **Puuopelu,** and his extensive Impressionist art collection (call 885.7655 for more information).

Note: To avoid confusion with the town of Waimea on Kauai, the official post office address for this town is **Kamuela,** which is Hawaiian for Samuel (after **Samuel Parker,** the grandson of John Parker). ◆ From Kona, take Hwys 19 or 190 north (39 miles); from Hilo, take Hwy 19 north (59 miles)

50 Parker Ranch Broiler ★$$ The Parker name is everywhere in this neck of the woods, and since the **Parker Ranch** people own this handsome Western-style restaurant, you'll be cutting into their Big Island beef (not to be ranked with Iowa corn-fed steaks). For a healthy dose of Wild West nostalgia, mosey on up to the red-velvet saloon and sit a spell. ◆ Parker Ranch Shopping Center, Waimea. 885.7366

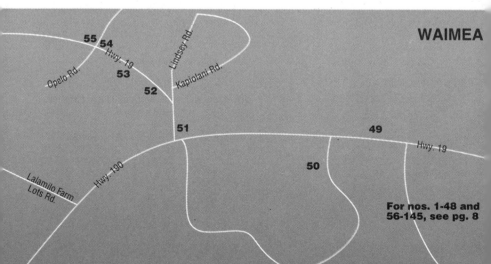

WAIMEA

55 54
Hwy. 19
Lindsey Rd.
Opelo Rd.
53
Kapiolani Rd.
52
51
49
Hwy. 19
Hwy. 190
50
Lalamilo Farm Lots Rd.

For nos. 1-48 and 56-145, see pg. 8

Parker Ranch

50 Parker Ranch Visitor Center and Museum A narrated slide show depicts the history of the 225,000-acre Parker Ranch, the largest privately owned ranch in the U.S. (only the corporate-owned King Ranch in Texas is larger), and describes the life of the Hawaiian cowboys. Parker family memorabilia and photographs are on display. ◆ Admission. Daily 9AM-5PM. Parker Ranch Shopping Center, Waimea. 885.7655

51 Parker Ranch Lodge $$ A small motor hotel with 20 rustic rooms, some with kitchenettes. Of the two hotels in Waimea, this is a definite second choice. ◆ Off Hwy 19 (Lindsey Rd), downtown Waimea. 885.4100; fax 885.7655

52 Edelweiss ★★$$$ German-born chef/owner **Hans-Peter Hager,** formerly of the exclusive **Mauna Kea Beach Hotel,** opened Edelweiss in 1984. It's a small place (only 15 tables) in a *paniolo*-style setting of hewn, open beams, but on any given night, chef Hager offers 14 to 18 house specials ranging from roast duck to venison and a superb rack of lamb basted in garlic, mustard, and herbs. Also recommended are the hasenpfeffer (rabbit stew) and his state-of-the-art Wiener schnitzel. Homemade Bavarian pudding, cheesecake, and fruit pies are worthy finales to the feast. A caveat: No reservations are accepted, so expect long lines. Closed Monday and Sunday. ◆ Hwy 19, Waimea. 885.6800

53 Parker Square Browsing through the shops here without making a purchase is virtually impossible. Start at **Gallery of Great Things** (885.7706), with its wild collection of museum-quality artifacts from Hawaii, Indonesia, Papua New Guinea, and throughout the Pacific, including tribal jade carvings, chopsticks made of exotic woods, Indonesian baskets, koa furniture, coconut-fiber hats, and handmade jewelry. Work your way toward **Bentleys** (885.5565), a shop that specializes in ceramics and tableware (the Christmas display is unbelievable) but also carries gifts and accessories from around the world. Save some room on your credit card for **Waimea General Store** (885.4479), which carries patterns for Hawaiian quilts and needlepoint, as well as pillow kits, yarn, and how-to books. ◆ Off Hwy 19, across from Waimea Park, Waimea

54 Kamuela Inn $$ This is definitely the nicest of the two hotels in Waimea, and less expensive to boot. In addition to standard and deluxe suites, you can choose from executive suites with full kitchens. Cozy rooms, private baths, cable TV, and free Continental breakfast served on the lanai combine to make this inn worth the layover in Waimea. ◆ Off Hwy 19, just before Opelo Plaza, Waimea. 885.4243; fax 885.8857

55 Merriman's ★★★$$$ Owner/chef **Peter Merriman** pioneered the development of Hawaii's regional cuisine, giving new meaning to the word fresh. His innovative use of seaweed, *opihi* (limpets), sea urchin (which he sometimes dives for himself), and Big Island-raised beef, lamb, and veal is legendary. The mahimahi and *ono* are in his kitchen soon after they're caught, the veal is naturally raised in Waimea, the goat cheese is made in Puna, and the strawberries and tomatoes are grown down the road. Specialties include wok-charred *ahi,* Kahua lamb, *lokelani* tomato salad, and for dessert, passion fruit mousse. ◆ Opelo Plaza, Hwy 19, Waimea. 885.6822

Sights from the Saddle

If you want to experience the Big Island's *paniolo* (cowboy) country, there's no better way than to saddle up on a horse. **Ironwood Outfitters** offers trail rides into the pastures and highlands of the Kahua Ranch, a 30,000-acre cattle spread in the Kohala foothills. Owner/operator Judith Ellis will set you up with a fine quarter horse, thoroughbred, or Morgan for the leisurely journey up the 4,000-foot elevation of the Kohala Mountain range. Choose from Ironwood's Top of the Mountain Ride (daily 10AM to 1PM), late-afternoon horseback tours (one- to one-and-a-half-hours long), and private equestrian rides. Make reservations at least a day in advance, especially during August and around Christmas. For more information, call 885.4941.

Waipio Na'a'apa Trail Rides offers horseback tours along a black sand beach. Your adventure begins at the Waipio Lookout parking lot, just outside the town of Honokaa, by hopping into their four-wheel-drive vehicle, which takes you a thousand feet down (on a treacherously steep road) and across the valley to their stables. The two-and-a-half-hour ride follows Waipio Beach. For more information, call 775.0419.

Near the small town of Pahala, you'll find **E-Z Riders Trail Rides,** a friendly horse outfit that takes folks ranging from beginners to experienced on one- to three-hour rides through the beautiful Ka'u countryside. Children ages 6 to 13 have their own special ride available, so there's no getting out of it *this* time, mom and dad. Trail rides by reservation only; call 928.8410.

Restaurants/Clubs: Red   **Hotels:** Blue
Shops/ 🌴 Outdoors: Green   **Sights/Culture:** Black

55 Bread Depot ★★$ Just follow the aroma of freshly baked breads to find this popular venue for cinnamon rolls, caraway rye, *paniolo* (a variation of French sourdough), passion fruit muffins, cheese brioches, deli sandwiches, and homemade soups. If you're planning on clam chowder for lunch, get there early—it goes fast. Desserts are changed seasonally, so if you're here during *lilikoi* (passion fruit), mango, or guava seasons, expect hints of them in the *coulis* and the tropical cheesecakes. For an inexpensive dinner, there's a decent selection of pizzas, salads, calzones, and sandwiches. The seating is limited, but take-out business is brisk. Closed Sunday. ♦ Opelo Plaza, Hwy 19, Waimea. 885.6354

56 Hale Kea Built in 1897, this former Parker Ranch manager's home is now a beautifully restored 11-acre complex with English gardens, a museum, a restaurant, and boutiques. ♦ Kawaihae Rd, Waimea. 885.6095

Within Hale Kea:

Hartwell's ★$$$ A high-ceilinged lodge with a fireplace and several cozy dining alcoves, each with its own character. Ranch memorabilia provides the backdrop for hearty steaks, lamb, *lilikoi*-glazed duckling, fresh seafood, and flapjacks (Sunday breakfast only). ♦ 885.6095

56 Waimea Gardens Cottage $$$ Owner/host **Barbara Campbell** (who worked for more than 20 years at the **Kona Village Resort**) has perfected the art of hospitality and applied it to her lovely B&B overlooking the Waimea hillsides. A longtime resident of Waimea, Barbara has surrounded her immaculate cottage with geraniums, ferns, roses, Easter lilies, and a graceful willow tree in the front yard. Amenities include a full kitchen with a stocked refrigerator, desk, fireplace, and even a small henhouse across the lawn. Although not earmarked for the budget traveler, this is definitely one of the nicest B&Bs on the island. ♦ Off Kawaihae Hwy, just past the 59-mile marker, Waimea. 885.4550, 800/262.9912

57 Kamuela Museum Hawaii's largest privately owned and most unorthodox museum was founded by Big Island native **Albert K. Solomon,** who claims that when he was eight years old his grandmother predicted he would open a museum. It took several decades, but she was right. Opened in 1968 by the former Honolulu policeman and his wife, **Harriet** (they live in the same building), the museum ranks somewhere between an institution and a weekend flea market. Undocumented and unorganized, there's everything from Japanese machine guns to ancient Hawaiian feather money and even an old Model-T tire remover. ♦ Admission. Daily 8AM-5PM. Junction of Hwys 19 and 250, Waimea. 885.4724

58 Ohana Cafe and Pizzeria $ The highlight of this place isn't the flavor of the food, which is just okay at best, but the flavor of its local customers. For a real taste of what life in Hawi is like, grab a bar stool, order a draft and a slice, and watch. ♦ Hwy 270, Hawi. 889.5888

59 Tropical Dreams Gourmet Ice Cream Shop ★$ Tropical Dreams' ice creams and sorbets have a strong following on the island, especially at the finer restaurants, and this is where they're made. Stop in for a passion fruit sorbet or Lava Java Road ice cream (the coconut and macadamia nut flavors are also exemplary). ♦ Off Hwy 270, Kapaau. 889.5386

60 Original King Kamehameha I Statue This statue may have a less dazzling setting than the Honolulu replica across from **Iolani Palace,** but its history is much richer. For $10,000, American sculptor **Thomas R. Gould** was commissioned in 1878 by the Hawaiian Legislature to create a statue of the mighty warrior king in commemoration of the centennial anniversary of **Captain Cook's** arrival in Hawaii. Gould studied a photograph of handsome Honolulu businessman **John Baker,** a close friend of **King Kalakaua** who posed in loincloth, feather cloak, spear, and helmet as inspiration for Kamehameha.

Gould's clay figure was finished in Florence, Italy; sent to Paris for bronze casting; and eventually shipped from Germany to Hawaii. Nearing Cape Horn, the ship burned and sank at Port Stanley in the Falkland Islands, carrying the statue and its nine-ton shipping crate to the bottom of the sea, presumably lost forever. Gould agreed to make another statue for $7,500. This one reached Honolulu intact and was unveiled on 14 February 1883, during Kalakaua's coronation. A few weeks later, to everyone's surprise, the original Kamehameha statue arrived in Honolulu on a British ship whose skipper had bought it for $500 from a salvage yard. The skipper's asking price was $1,500. Since one hand was broken off and the spear was missing, Kalakaua talked him down to $875 and then had the statue repaired and sent to the sleepy town of **Kapaau,** in North Kohala, where Kamehameha was born. The Honolulu statue is more fanciful, but the original is a more honest and appropriate homage to the great Kamehameha. ♦ Off Hwy 27, in front of the Kapaau Courthouse, North Kohala District

61 Keokea Beach Park Located on a cliff overlooking the ocean, this picturesque beach is popular on the weekends but during the week is usually vacant. Picnic and camping (by permit) facilities are available. ♦ Off Hwy 270, 2 miles past Kapaau, Niulii

62 Pololu Valley Lookout and Trail The wonderful view of a classic taro farming valley is surpassed only by the switchback mule trail (a 15-minute walk) through tunnels of *pandani* shrubs to a black sand beach. ♦ End of Hwy 270, Makapala

63 Lapakahi State Historical Park This semi-restored ancient Hawaiian fishing village dates back 600 years. Be sure to grab a brochure and take the casual self-guided tour among the stone-house sites, canoe sheds, fishing shrines, and stone games displayed here. Learn about local legends, fishing customs and techniques, salt gathering, and the prosperous, simple life of Hawaiians centuries ago. ♦ Free. Daily 8AM-4PM. Off Hwy 270, Mahukona. 889.5566

64 Kawaihae Center A great rest stop on your way to Kona or Hawi. Stop by the **Tres Hombres Beach Grill** (★$$) for a margarita and Mexican *pupus* (appetizers) before browsing through **Cactus Tree's** unusual selection of men's and women's clothing, much of it in Indonesian batik. If you're still hungry, grab an ice cream cone at the **Tropical Dreams** outlet. ♦ Off Hwy 270, near the Hwy 19 junction, Kawaihae

65 Puukohola Heiau National Historic Site Measuring 224 feet by 100 feet, this fortresslike structure is the largest restored *heiau* (temple) in Hawaii. It is also a marvel of engineering, with waterworn lava rocks and boulders set together without mortar. Built in 1550 and rebuilt by **King Kamehameha** more than two centuries later, it serves as a powerful reminder of the practice of human sacrifice in the ancient Hawaiian religion. A prophecy of the time held that Kamehameha would conquer and unite the islands if he erected a temple to his family war god on the hill at **Kawaihae,** a prophecy fulfilled after the erection of Puukohola. At its dedication in 1791, Kamehameha invited his arch rival to the ceremony and then offered him up as a human sacrifice. ♦ Free. Daily 7:30AM-4PM. Off Hwy 270, south of Kawaihae. 882.7218

Within the Puukohola Heiau National Historic Site:

Samuel M. Spencer Beach Park A white sand beach with the best and safest swimming along the South Kohala shoreline, as well as good snorkeling and spearfishing. Picnic, camping, and tennis facilities make this a popular spot for families.

66 Mauna Kea Beach Hotel $$$$ On his first visit to this hotel, **Merv Griffin** proclaimed, "Now I know where old Republicans come to die." Built in 1965 by **Laurance Rockefeller,** the Mauna Kea set the standard for super-luxury resorts along the Kohala Coast. And, although its accommodations, service, and dining have bowed slightly to the competition, it still stands out as one of the finest hotels on Hawaii and remains well within the top 20 tropical resorts in the world according to readers of *Condé Nast Traveler* magazine. Its two strongest selling points are nearby **Kaunaoa Beach,** without question the nicest on the island, and the legendary **Mauna Kea Golf Course.** The hotel's classic design gives it a graceful appearance as it recedes from the sea into the mountains, maximizing the ocean views. More than a half-million plants of nearly 200 varieties were brought in from other islands to landscape the spacious grounds and courtyards. The Mauna Kea is literally an art museum without walls, with more than 1,600 art objects from throughout Pacific-Polynesia, Thailand, Japan, Sri Lanka, New Guinea, China, and Hawaii. Choose from the modified American Plan (room rates include breakfast and dinner) and the European Plan (room only) year-round. There are 310 rooms, 13 Plexipave tennis courts, and no TVs. ♦ One Mauna Kea Beach Dr, Kohala Coast. 882.7222, 800/882.6060; fax 882.7552

Within the Mauna Kea Beach Hotel:

Mauna Kea Buddha A 1,500-pound pink granite form, this seventh-century Indian Buddha (illustrated below) sits on a solid block of Canadian black granite in the shade of a *bodhi* tree.

Mauna Kea Buddha

Cafe Terrace ★$$$ The fresh ingredients used for the cafe's breakfast and lunch buffets have made the Mauna Kea a major proponent of regional cuisine and supporter of local farmers, fishers, and ranchers. Many varieties of seafood, island produce, and other specialties share billing with the ocean view. The dinner menu features American cuisine with a Mediterranean touch. ◆ 882.7222

The Batik, The Garden ★★$$$$ In the hotel's most formal setting, the Batik offers Continental cuisine with strong influences from southern France and northern Italy, plus Sri Lankan curries and dessert specialties, including soufflés. The Garden serves Hawaiian regional cuisine, using fresh local ingredients such as Big Island-raised abalone and salmon, Kona coffee-smoked rack of lamb, and *ohelo* berry mousse. ◆ 882.7222

Mauna Kea Luau ★★$$ Hawaiian delicacies (and some non-Hawaiian alternatives) are served on the hotel's grassy oceanside gardens at this very upscale luau. The feast includes *hulihuli* (spit-roasted) pig, *kalua* pig on special occasions, poi, *lomilomi* salmon, and baked taro, as well as steak, chicken, ribs, and crab claws. ◆ 882.7222

Mauna Kea Golf Course Designed by Robert Trent Jones, Sr., this reclaimed ancient lava flow is generally credited (or cursed) as Hawaii's toughest course. Other than a few refinements catering to the fair-weather golfer, the course remains an ego bruiser for even the above-average player and a severe threat to misdirected shots. It is a beautiful layout, with the ocean always in sight. Ranked among America's hundred greatest golf courses and designated "Hawaii's finest" by *Golf Digest*, the course hosts two tournaments annually: the Pro-Am in July and an Invitational in early December. An 18-hole course, par 72, 7,114 yards. ◆ Preferred starting times and rates for hotel guests; expensive green fees. Off Hwy 19. Pro shop 882.7222

67 **Hapuna Golf Course** This brand-new 18-hole public course was designed by **Arnold Palmer** specifically for the **Hapuna Beach Prince Hotel** (still under construction). The environmentally conscious design uses half the land acreage of a regular 18-hole course and is landscaped with native Hawaiian grasses and trees. The Hawaiian birds and waterfowl came pro bono. Expensive green fees. ◆ Across from the Mauna Kea Beach Hotel. 882.1035

With an elevation of 13,020 feet, Lake Waiau, on Mauna Kea on the Big Island, is the third highest lake in the country and the highest in Hawaii. Niihau's Halalii Lake is the largest in the state.

68 **Hapuna Beach State Park** One of the nicest beaches on the Big Island, this long, white sand strip is great for bodysurfing but can border on the treacherous when the currents are especially strong. Although there are lifeguards on duty from 9AM to 5PM, be sure to follow warnings posted when swimming is hazardous; Hapuna has claimed more lives than any other beach park in the state. Sorry, no camping, but the State Parks Department rents A-frame cabins nearby (call 961.7200). Excellent picnic facilities are available, and there's a snack bar open from 10AM to 5PM. ◆ Daily 7AM-8PM. Off Hwy 19, south of the Mauna Kea Beach Hotel

69 **Puako Petroglyph Archaeological Park** One of the largest clusters of petroglyphs in Hawaii, this public park at the south end of the Ritz-Carlton Mauna Lani was officially placed on the State and National Historic Registers in 1982. The Ritz-Carlton established it mainly to protect the petroglyphs (such as the ones illustrated above), which have been subjected to vandalism, theft, foot traffic, and even damage from bulldozers after recent fires in the area. A natural trail system with controlled access is posted with signs leading to the archaeological sites at the **Holoholokai Beach Park,** located at the north end of the resort. Don't step on the stone carvings or make rubbings from them (an area has been provided where you can make rubbings from replica petroglyphs). Damaged petroglyphs are open to public view so visitors can realize the consequences. ◆ Off Mauna Lani Dr; entrance in the Ritz-Carlton Mauna Lani

70 **Francis H. Ii Brown Golf Course** Since the course opened in 1981, these emerald fairways and greens have received worldwide attention, with *Golf Magazine* rating it one of the 12 best golf resorts in America in 1992. Two nine-hole courses have been added to the original **North Course** and **South Course.** Carved out of a 16th-century lava flow, all 36 holes flow bright green through the black *a'a* and *pahoehoe* lava fields, sculptured masterpieces lined by groves of twisted *kiawe* trees. Ocean views are almost secondary. Both courses are par 72, 7,015 yards. ◆ Preferred starting times and rates for Mauna Lani Bay Hotel guests; expensive green fees. Off Hwy 19. Pro shop 885.6655

70 Ritz-Carlton Mauna Lani $$$$  Exceptionally professional and courteous service is combined with an elegant old-world decor—signature cobalt-blue vases (which contrast nicely with the crimson roses the hotel has specially cultivated in Waimea), as well as antique armoires filled with rare china. More than a thousand works of art grace the walls and hallways, with 19th-century English and American paintings setting the tone of excellence that pervades the hotel. The dining rooms and hallways have padded silk brocade wall coverings, koa paneling, Italian marble, and Renaissance-inspired upholstery, with chandeliers of Baccarat crystal (and quartz crystal, too, an unusual touch). The two six-story wings face the ocean, and the large, luxurious rooms have celadon-green walls and marble bathrooms with separate showers and tubs. Outside you'll find a 10,000-square-foot swimming pool adjacent to a man-made white sand lagoon. The 32-acre manicured grounds feature myriad plantings selected for color, cultural integrity, and fragrance. The **Ritz-Carlton Club** tops the Kohala wing with its own lounge, tea service, elevator key, and special privileges. Tennis buffs can choose from 11 courts, and golfers are very near the Mauna Lani's fabled **Francis H. Ii Brown Golf Course.** ♦ One N. Kaniku Dr, Kohala Coast. 885.2000, 800/241.3333; fax 885.5778

Within the Ritz-Carlton Mauna Lani:

The Dining Room, The Grill Restaurant and Lounge, The Cafe Restaurant and Lounge $$$$ Executive chef **Philippe Padovani** brought his considerable talents here from the Halekulani Hotel (and its stellar **La Mer**) on Oahu and lost no time earning a reputation on the Big Island. The Dining Room offers *kiawe*-smoked (mesquite) Norwegian salmon, duck liver terrine, and lamb loin medaillons with artichoke jardiniere. Chocolate Saint Remon and fresh pear tart make for a grand finale. The Grill's clubby atmosphere suits the menu of fresh seafood and steaks—classics with an innovative regional twist. A plush private dining room is available for parties of up to 14 people. The Cafe, however, is Padovani's creative statement, with Asian specialties highlighting fresh seafood and local produce. ♦ Jacket required; reservations recommended in The Dining Room. 885.2000

Inter-Pacific Some of the finest shopping in Hawaii is available right here. The **Giorgio Armani** boutique offers ties, suits, and high-priced sportswear by the Italian designer, with American designs by **Ralph Lauren** next door. Women can choose from **Bottega Veneta, Anne Klein, Nina Ricci, Adrienne Vittadini,** and more. ♦ 885.2000 ext 7162

71 Mauna Lani Bay Hotel and Bungalows $$$$ To make it into the top 100 of *Condé Nast Traveler* magazine's reader's choice awards is certainly commendable, but to rank No. 3 among the tropical resorts in the world is phenomenal. Located on the sunny Kohala Coast, the Mauna Lani (pictured below) opened with a world-class flourish in 1983 and soon began winning accolades and awards for its historic preservation, golf course, and overall excellence. This distinctively Hawaiian landmark combines the highest standards of Hawaiian hospitality:

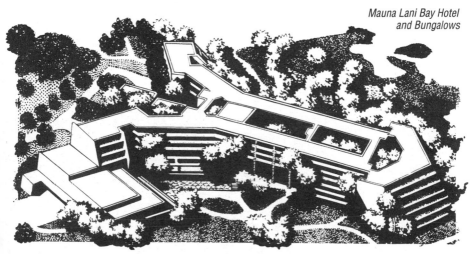

Mauna Lani Bay Hotel and Bungalows

grace, style, architectural excellence, and a charming aloha spirit. Inside the blue-tile courtyard, a waterfall leads to the Grand Atrium, filled with fish ponds and rare orchids. Rooms (built at a cost of $200,000 each) include teak and rattan furnishings, color TVs hidden away in armoires, roomy baths with twin vanities, and private lanais. Almost all of the 345 rooms have ocean views, and 27 of them face the Mauna Kea and Mauna Loa mountains. Deep pockets will enjoy the 4,000-square-foot bungalows with private pools and 24-hour butler service, while families may prefer the luxurious one- and two-bedroom ocean villas.

The grounds feature prehistoric Hawaiian fish ponds and a 16th-century lava flow with shelter caves and petroglyphs. Golfers will enjoy privileges at the nearby 36-hole **Francis H. Ii Brown Golf Course,** and there's also a championship 10-court **Tennis Garden.** Daily activities include windsurfing, canoeing, scuba diving, and aqua-aerobics. All in all, it's an exceptional experience. ♦ Off Mauna Lani Dr, Kohala Coast. 885.6622, 800/367.2323; fax 885.4556

Within the Mauna Lani Bay Hotel and Bungalows:

The Canoe House ★★★★$$$ A rare match of ambience and consistently impressive cuisine fired by the imagination of chef **Alan Wong.** Dine indoors, where a large koa canoe dangles from the high ceiling, or outdoors, where the breaking waves are lit by the setting sun. Specialties include seared rare *ahi* with fern shoots and Chinese sausage, lobster won-ton ravioli, bamboo-steamed mahimahi (flawless), and *poha* (berry-glazed rack of lamb with Big Island sweet potatoes). ♦ 885.6622

Bay Terrace ★★$$$ Pleasant American-Mediterranean dining—three meals a day—with *malasadas* (Portuguese doughnuts) for starters and pasta and sandwiches at lunch. Candlelight and the à la carte menu of international cuisine make for romantic dinners. ♦ Jacket requested. 885.6622

The Gallery ★★$$ The informal dining room serves mostly American fare, emphasizing fresh seafood caught and cultivated on the Big Island. Daily fish selections can be prepared four ways, including sautéed with *lilikoi* (passion fruit) and cilantro beurre blanc. Vegetarian black-bean chili and shrimp phyllo add an international flavor. ♦ 885.7777

Knickers ★★$$ *Soba* (buckwheat noodles), sandwiches, hamburgers, seafood, and steaks round out the luncheon menu. For dinner, the selections are upgraded to bouillabaisse, prime rib, London broil, and sautéed Hawaiian snapper. ♦ Mauna Lani Golf Course. 885.6699

72 Kings Course, Beach Course, Waikoloa Village Golf and Country Club The newest and most challenging of these is the par 72, 7,064-yard Kings Course, adjacent to the Royal Waikoloan. Designed by **Tom Weiskopf** and **Jay Morris,** it opened in 1990 with six lakes, nine acres of water, 83 sand traps, and a 25,000-square-foot clubhouse. The par 70, 6,507-yard Beach Course is also adjacent to the Royal Waikoloan, and the par 72, 6,687-yard Waikoloa Village Golf and Country Club is just six miles north of the hotel. These two courses were both designed by **Robert Trent Jones, Jr.** ♦ Kings Course 885.4647. Beach Course 885.6060. Waikoloa Village Golf and Country Club 883.9621

73 Hyatt Regency Waikoloa $$$$ Described as a Disney-esque enterprise by those who favor more intimate settings, this 62-acre super resort has more than a mile of waterways (traveled by a dozen 24-passenger canal boats), a mile-long museum walkway, and an air-conditioned electric tram. As you walk the endless paths and gardens, it's immediately apparent that developer **Chris Hemmeter** and partners pulled out all the stops with the gargantuan complex. The $360 million hotel is more like a small city, with 1,241 rooms, 2,000 employees, 2 main swimming pools, waterfalls, waterslides, 19 meeting rooms, 8 tennis and 2 racquetball courts, and the largest health spa on the island. The 25,000-square-foot spa offers European herbal treatments, fitness classes, nutrition counseling, steam rooms, saunas, whirlpools, and Jacuzzis. The hotel's eight restaurants include **Imari, Cascades, Donatoni's,** and the **Kona Provision Co.,** but the most popular attraction by far is **Dolphin Quest,** the 2.5 million-gallon home of six Atlantic bottle-nosed dolphins. Guests and visitors are given the chance (by lottery) to interact with the dolphins, with most of the proceeds going toward marine research. (Education, not exploitation, is the key word here.) Even if you have no intention of staying at the resort, drop by and spend a few hours gawking at American opulence at its best. *Condé Nast Traveler* magazine rates it one of the top 20 tropical resorts in the world. ♦ One Waikoloa Beach Dr, Kohala Coast. 885.1234, 800/228.9000; fax 885.5737

The Hawaiian islands are the most photographed place on earth.

Restaurants/Clubs: Red   **Hotels:** Blue
Shops/♠ Outdoors: Green   **Sights/Culture:** Black

74 Anaehoomalu Bay Ideal for windsurfing, scuba diving, walking, swimming, and sunning, this crescent-shaped beach fronts the Royal Waikoloan. The ancient royal fish ponds behind the beach are preserved by the hotel. Parking and public access are available at the south end of the beach. ♦ Off Queen Kaahumanu Hwy, 18 miles north of Keahole Airport

74 Royal Waikoloan $$$ A smaller, more modest neighbor to the flamboyant Hyatt Regency Waikoloa, the Royal Waikoloan is for those who favor a more intimate Hawaiian ambience at a more reasonable price. The wide, generous **Anaehoomalu Bay,** essentially in the front yard, is a key attraction,

along with the **Royal Cabana Club** (an 18-room, two-story structure on the lagoon), Sunday luaus, a fitness center, six tennis courts, and two nearby championship golf courses are among the many amenities at this first-rate establishment. ♦ Off Queen Kaahumanu Hwy, Kohala Coast. 885.6789, 800/733.7777; fax 885.7852

Within the Royal Waikoloan:

Tiare Room $$$$ Continental cuisine is served in a setting of rich woods, etched glass, and crystal. The seasonal menu may include rack of lamb, roast duckling, or a platter of lobster medaillons, filet mignon, sautéed fresh fish, and baked stuffed shrimp. ♦ 926.0679

Hawaii from Top to Bottom

The eight major Hawaiian islands illustrated below are actually tips of enormous volcanoes. Centuries ago, these submerged volcanoes erupted over and over, building up lava until they finally emerged above the ocean surface some 2,400 miles off the coast of North America. Today they cover about 400 miles of the Pacific Ocean.

Nearly all of Hawaii's population lives on most of these islands, although there are another 124 islands and atolls northwest of Niihau that complete Hawaii's archipelago. The summits of the major islands pictured here, which are the youngest in the chain, range from 13,796 feet on the Big Island to 1,477 feet on Kahoolawe.

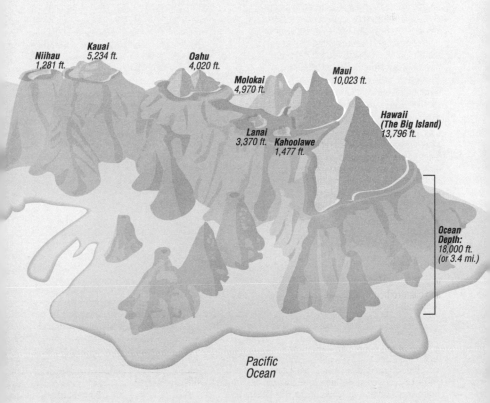

Niihau 1,281 ft.
Kauai 5,234 ft.
Oahu 4,020 ft.
Molokai 4,970 ft.
Maui 10,023 ft.
Lanai 3,370 ft.
Kahoolawe 1,477 ft.
Hawaii (The Big Island) 13,796 ft.
Ocean Depth: 18,000 ft. (or 3.4 mi.)
Pacific Ocean

Kona Village Resort Hut

75 Kona Village Resort $$$$ This is the ultimate "get away from it all" resort, once so remote guests had to be flown in. What sets this resort (pictured below) apart from the rest is what it *doesn't* have— phones, TVs, radios, suits and ties, or neighbors. The themes here are luxury, simplicity, and peace and quiet. Aside from the tennis courts, nothing here even vaguely resembles the standard hotel experience. The 125 individual thatched bungalows (see the illustration above), sprawling over 82 acres, are replicas of New Zealand, Samoan, Tahitian, Hawaiian, and other Polynesian structures. Guests are greeted with a flower lei and a mai tai, then set free to play with the toys, including canoes, sailboats, and snorkeling gear, ride in a glass-bottom boat, and attend cocktail parties, luaus, guided petroglyph tours, lei-making classes, and scuba dives. Readers of *Condé Nast Traveler* magazine voted Kona Village Resort the "Best Tropical Resort in the World." ♦ Off Queen Kaahumanu Hwy, 6 miles north of Keahole Airport, Kona. 325.5555, 800/367.5290; fax 325.5124

Within the Kona Village Resort:

Hale Moana ★★$$$ Chef **Glenn Alos** has made this restaurant his own creative playground. The luncheon buffet, with elegant samplings of Big Island favorites, is a memorable seaside repast. Dinner selections include fresh *opakapaka* broiled with saffron and orange butter, *ono* sautéed with lime and macadamia nut beurre blanc, and boneless quail in Cajun spices. Five panels displayed in this high-ceilinged Polynesian *hale* (house) pictorially describe Captain Cook's voyages to Hawaii. The panels, entitled *Les Sauvages de la Mer Pacifique*, are made of perfectly preserved 18th-century French wallpaper. They were rolled up and stored in a Paris attic for more than a hundred years before an American collector discovered them. ♦ Reservations required for nonguests. 325.5555

Kona Village Luau ★★★★$$$ The best luau in Hawaii begins with a tour of the luau grounds, where you will witness the unveiling of the *imu* (an earthen oven where the pig and sweet potatoes are roasted). With the ohia-log table, the *malo*-clad men chipping away at the *imu,* and the steam rising from the pit, this is a dramatic event. The feast is as authentic as a commercial luau gets, with *opihi* (limpets, a Hawaiian delicacy), banana pudding, sushi, *laulau* (steamed pork with taro leaves), *poki* (raw fish), and a show of delicacies from Hawaii and the South Pacific. The program, held across a lagoon from the thatched luau pavilion, is fiery and beautifully lit, with chants

Kona Village Resort

Hale Samoa

of Pele, Hawaii's volcano goddess, and ancient and modern dances. Look for Hawaiian artist **Herb Kane's** brilliant paintings on the back wall. ◆ F 6:30PM; tour at 5:30PM. Reservations required. 325.5555

Hale Samoa ★★$$$$ The fanciest of the two dining rooms at the Kona Village is highly recommended whether you're a guest or not (guests pay a surcharge to dine; nonguests must make reservations). The menu includes blackened sashimi, entrecote of Kona yearling beef, loin of lamb with lobster medaillons, and a sprinkling of Asian specialties served in a romantic room. The entrance is illustrated above. Closed Monday and Wednesday. ◆ 325.5555

76 Kona Coast State Park After a bumpy 1.5-mile drive through an eerie lava field (worth the trip in itself), you arrive at **Kaelehuluhulu Beach,** which has picnic tables, great snorkeling, and some interesting ruins in the lava fields behind the 6.5-acre coarse coral beach. ◆ Daily 9AM-8PM. Off Hwy 19, about 4 miles north of Keahole Airport, North Kona

77 Natural Energy Lab (NEL) Taking advantage of Keahole's unique geographical location, which receives more sunshine than any other U.S. coastal location and has deep water relatively close to shore, the NEL pumps up to 28,400 gallons of seawater per minute from depths of 50 feet and 2,000 feet. The engineers then use the temperature difference (40 degrees Fahrenheit) to operate heat exchangers, which in turn produce energy (something like a reverse refrigerator, making electricity instead of using it). As a by-product, the almost bacteria-free seawater is being used for all sorts of clever aquacultural

ideas, including controlled growing of "white-linen" food products such as Maine lobster and *hirame* (a flounder prized by the Japanese for sashimi), as well as a Tahitian black pearl lab and a salmon farm. Aside from an entertaining lecture on Thursdays at 2PM (call 329.7341 to make reservations), the lab is closed to the public. ◆ Off Hwy 19, 1 mile south of Keahole Airport Rd, Kona

77 Wawaloli Beach Park A long stretch of golden-sand beach with bathroom and shower facilities. Statistically, Wawaloli is the sunniest beach in the U.S. ◆ Daily 8AM-6PM. Natural Energy Rd, at Keahole Point, Kona

78 Kona to Hawi Drive Don't miss this scenic drive through cattle country, lava fields, and a vast mountain range. Done right, it's an all-day trip. From **Kona,** take Highway 190 (Mamalahoa Highway) north to **Waimea.** Turn left, and continue northwest on Highway 250 (Kohala Mountain Road) to **Hawi.** Turn left again and take the coastal road (Highway 270/19) back to Kona.

The process of burning sugarcane fields has an uncertain history. Laborers sometimes take credit for torching the first fields, claiming they did so as a form of protest. But sugar growers contend that the cane was burned deliberately as a means of pest control, and that it was discovered only inadvertently that it saves on labor costs, too; fire consumes the outer plant material, which needs to be removed anyway, but not the sugar-producing stalk. Now up to 70,000 acres of sugarcane go up in flames annually in Hawaii, beginning in late March and ending in November.

79 Holualoa Drive If you're staying in **Kona**, schedule an afternoon for this panoramic drive, easily the best in the area. Start from Palani Road (Highway 190) in Kona and head north toward **Honokohau** (the town, not the harbor). After four miles, look for a nursery on the right and turn right onto North Kona Belt Road/Mamalahoa Highway (Highway 180). Take a slow cruise south on Highway 180, stopping in quaint **Holualoa** to browse among the galleries and shops until sunset, then drive a half mile down the road to the Hualalai Road turnoff (Highway 182). Descending this road at sunset into Kona is what Hawaii is all about.

Win One for the Gaffer

Unlike many deep-sea fishing excursions that take hours to reach prime fishing spots, the fishing off the coast of **Kailua-Kona** begins minutes after your boat departs the dock, since some of the best fishing in Hawaii occurs within a mile or two off the Kona coast. On charter trips, no previous experience is necessary, since the captain provides all the equipment, plus expert advice and cheerful assistance for even the most inept of anglers. All you need to bring are food, drink, and sunscreen (fishing licenses aren't necessary). And leave the fish-bag at home (the captain has first choice of the catch, and he usually sells it at the market. Besides, what would you do with a one-hundred-pound tuna?). Half-day charters leave just after sunrise and return by noon, whereas the all-day trips are back in time for cocktails. Parties of up to six people can hire charters (with a captain and first-mate) for exclusive use, or you can share them by paying on a per-person basis.

One excellent service (and the oldest) is the **Kona Charter Skippers Association** (329.3600, 800/367.8047), which books 26-foot to 54-foot boats. Other reliable charter-boat companies include the **Kona Coast Activities Center** (329.2971), **Phil Parker's Kona Activities Center** (329.3171), and **Charter Locker** (326.2553).

Restaurants/Clubs: Red
Shops/ 🌳 Outdoors: Green

Hotels: Blue
Sights/Culture: Black

80 The Kona Hotel $ The large, ramshackle pink building, a **Holualoa** landmark for nearly 65 years, attracts a steady stream of artists, hikers, sportfishers, students, and adventurers from all over the world. Methodically disorganized, this charming hotel includes the world's most scenic outhouse, 11 sparse rooms without phones, very inexpensive rates, and permanent local fixtures dozing on the front porch. Even if you're just passing through, stop by for a "how's it going?" and a tinkle. ♦ 76-5908 Mamalahoa Hwy, Holualoa. 324.1155

81 Studio 7 Owned by artist **Hiroki Morinoue**, this gallery is small and serene, with a quality much like a Zen garden or a tasteful, unpretentious Japanese inn. Morinoue's own paintings and prints share space with the Big Island's best in all media. ♦ Closed Monday and Sunday. Mamalahoa Hwy, Holualoa. 324.1335

81 Holualoa Inn $$ One of the finest B&Bs on the Big Island, the Holualoa has a spectacular view of the Kona Coast from the immaculate, open-beamed living room. Polynesian and Asian themes characterize the suite and the three rooms, with careful attention to detail and artwork; a tiled pool and deck beckon from outside. Its location in the quiet, charming town of **Holualoa** is another major plus. ♦ Off Mamalahoa Hwy (take the gravel driveway just left of Paul's Place country store), Holualoa. 324.1121, 800/392.1812

82 Kimura Lauhala Shop Tsuruyo Kimura has been making and selling *lauhalas* (woven pandanus) since the days when *hala* trees were abundant in Kona and the Kimuras traveled around the island bartering. The 78-year-old shop is awash in the warm browns of woven fiber goods from Hawaii and the South Pacific—hats, mats, kitchen goods, purses, and wall hangings. Ask for the Kona *lauhala;* it's the best. ♦ Closed Sunday. Hualalai Rd and Mamalahoa Hwy (Hwy 190). 324.0053

Many Hawaiians—especially those of Japanese ancestry—believe the bird of paradise is a sign of good luck. They often plant this exotic flower in their front yards in hopes of bringing good fortune to the household. The bird of paradise with orange blossoms grows up to five feet tall, while those with white blossoms can reach heights of 20 feet.

83 Kailua Candy Company Considered by many to make the best chocolate in Hawaii, this small but prolific candy factory uses only fresh ingredients. Grab a handful of free samples and watch the "oompa-loompas" do their thing behind the glass windows of the factory, then send 30 pounds of sweets to your dietetic enemies all over the world. ◆ M-Sa 8AM-6PM; Su 10AM-6PM. 74-5563 Kaiwi St, Kona. 329.2522, 800/622.2462

84 Buns In The Sun ★$ Start your day munching on sinful pastries and sipping brewed coffee out on the sunny patio. Order a sandwich to go for lunch and you're set. ◆ 75-5595 Palani Rd, on the northeast end of Lanihau Shopping Center, Kona. 326.2774

85 Kona Ranch House ★$$ The patio bar and homey atmosphere of this plantation-style restaurant is popular with local families, who have made this a Kona favorite. There are two dining rooms: the **Paniolo Room,** offering family dining, and the **Plantation Lanai,** filled with elegant turn-of-the-century wicker furnishings. The emphasis is on Big Island beef (try the ribs), fresh fish, and local specialties. ◆ 75-5653 Ololi St, off Kuakini Hwy just south of the traffic light at Palani Rd and Kuakini Hwy. 329.7061

86 Kona Seaside Hotel $$ The best choice in town for the budget traveler, Kona Seaside Hotel features two swimming pools and 155 recently renovated rooms with big beds, A/C, cable TV, refrigerators, and private lanais. While the location is ideal for shopaholics, it's not recommended for anyone trying to get away from it all. ◆ 75-5646 Palani Rd, Kona. 329.2455, 800/367.7000

87 Quinn's ★$$ This little local hideaway, around the corner from Alii Drive, serves reasonably priced salads and sandwiches, vegetarian specialties, fresh fish, and beef in a small patio setting. Quinn's just celebrated its 14th anniversary, so you know it's a solid Kona oasis. ◆ 75-5655 Palani Rd, across from the Hotel King Kamehameha. 329.3822

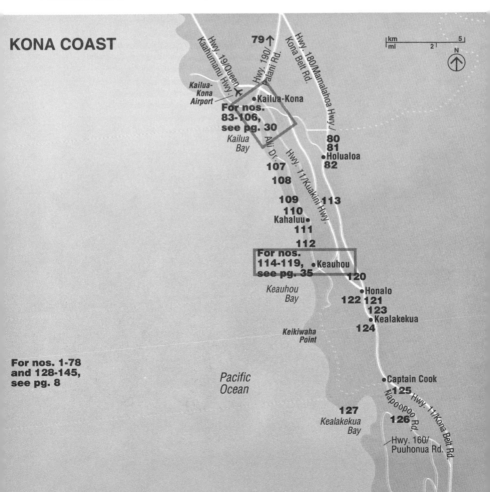

KONA COAST

Hwy. 19/Queen Kaahumanu Hwy.

Hwy. 190/Palani Rd

Hwy. 180/Mamalahoa Hwy.

79 ↑

Kona Belt Rd.

km 5
mi 2
N ↑

Kailua-Kona Airport

• Kailua-Kona

For nos. 83-106, see pg. 30

Kailua Bay

Ali Dr.

Hwy. 11/Kuakini Hwy

80
81
• Holualoa
82

107
108

109
110
Kahaluu •
111

113

112

For nos. 114-119, see pg. 35

• Keauhou

120

Keauhou Bay

• Honalo

122 121
123
• Kealakekua
124

Keikiwaha Point

For nos. 1-78 and 128-145, see pg. 8

Pacific Ocean

• Captain Cook

125

Napoopoo Rd.

Hwy. 11/Kona Belt Rd.

127
Kealakekua Bay

126

Hwy. 160/Puuhonua Rd.

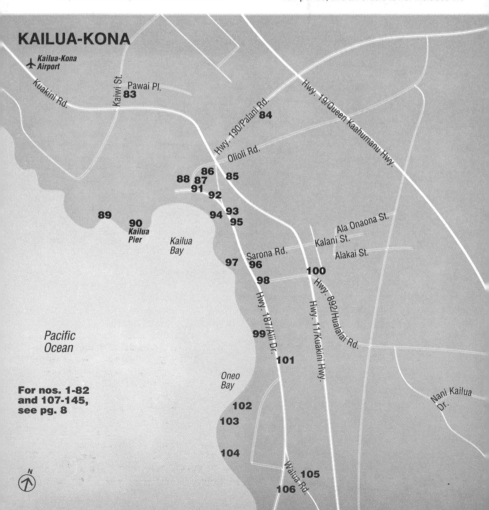

88 Hotel King Kamehameha $$$ If shopping and sightseeing are more important to you than secluded white sand beaches, look no further. The "King Kam" is located at the head of Kailua Village's main street, **Alii Drive**, within easy walking distance of **Kailua Pier** and the town's myriad shops, restaurants, and historic sites. The hotel's twin buildings have 460 rooms with lanais, TVs, A/C, phones, and refrigerators. Adjoining the lobby is Kona's only fully air-conditioned mall, containing 28 shops and a small museum of Hawaiian artifacts. The hotel offers guests—and nonguests, too—free tours of the grounds. Ask about the outstanding **Hula Experience**, which traces the history of the ancient hula. Pool, tennis courts, and a strand of beach along **Kamakahonu Bay.** ♦ Off Alii Dr, Kona. 329.2911, 800/367.6060; fax 922.8061

Within the Hotel King Kamehameha:

Kona Beach Restaurant ★$$ The meal deals here are the sunset dinner specials (served from 5:30PM to 7PM) and the prime rib and seafood buffet (offered Friday through Sunday from 5PM to 9PM). The daily breakfast buffet is also commendable. ♦ 329.2911

Hotel King Kamehameha Luau ★$$$ The beauty of the historical grounds gives this hotel luau added appeal and atmosphere. ♦ Tu-Th, Su 5:30PM. Reservations required. 329.2911

89 Ahuena Heiau In his final years, **Kamehameha the Great** ruled the newly united Hawaiian kingdom from this cove, known as **Kamakahonu** ("Eye of the Turtle"). Kamehameha died here in 1819, and his remains were taken to a secret resting place. The compound of thatched huts, plants, fish ponds, and an oracle tower includes the

KAILUA-KONA

Kailua-Kona Airport

Kuakini Rd.

Kaiwi St.

Pawai Pl.
83

Hwy. 190/Palani Rd.

Hwy. 19/Queen Kaahumanu Hwy.

84

Olioli Rd.

88 87 86
91
85
92

89
90
Kailua Pier

Kailua Bay

94 93
95

Ala Onaona St.

Kalani St.

Alakai St.

Sarona Rd.
97 96
98
100

Hwy. 892/Hualalai Rd.

Pacific Ocean

Hwy. 187/Alii Dr.

Hwy. 11/Kuakini Hwy.

99
101

For nos. 1-82 and 107-145, see pg. 8

Oneo Bay

102
103
104

Nani Kailua Dr.

Wailua Rd.
105
106

N

historic Ahuena Heiau, a refuge for the king in his final days. Dedicated to **Lono,** the Hawaiian god of fertility, this was an area of peace and prosperity. After Kamehameha's death, the entire old order was toppled when the queen regent **Kaahumanu** and her foster son **Liholiho** sat down and ate together, thereby breaking an ancient taboo. This picturesque historic site was restored by the **Hotel King Kamehameha** under the direction of the **Bishop Museum** of Honolulu. ♦ Free. Behind the Hotel King Kamehameha

90 Kailua Pier Everything that involves water activities in downtown Kona, including sportfishing, **Atlantis** and **Nautilus** rides, parasailing, dinner cruises, day cruises, diving trips, and late-afternoon outrigger **Canoe Club** practices, starts and finishes here. ♦ Off Alii Dr, across from the Hotel King Kamehameha

Activities on Kailua Pier:

Atlantis Submarine The 1.5-hour excursion, from launch craft to sub and back again, is a class act, starting with the bilingual (English and Japanese) introduction and photo-shoot and finishing with an official certificate of completion (a little hokey but cute). The 46-passenger air-conditioned craft is impressive—65 feet long and weighing in at 80 tons, with a silent cruising speed of 1.5 knots. The dives range from 100 feet to as deep as 150 feet, depending on the location, and all trips include divers swimming outside the sub (surrounded by hordes of seemingly ravenous tropical fish) and an on-board commentator. What you'll see outside the 21-inch view-ports depends on where you are and when (day or night); a few lucky passengers may see sharks, manta rays, dolphins, moray eels, and possibly whales. Atlantis is currently operating in **Kona** on the Big Island (329.6626); in **Lahaina** on Maui (667.2224); and in **Waikiki** on Oahu (973.9811). Yes, it's expensive, but considering it will probably be the most memorable part of your vacation, it's worth it.

Nautilus Semi-Submersible Not to be confused with Atlantis, which completely submerges underwater, the Nautilus Semi-Submersible never submerges. Instead, you do. Sitting five feet below the water line in a comfortable setting, complete with air-conditioning, padded seats, stereo music, and a video monitor, you get an up-close view of Hawaii's coral gardens and its denizens. Divers, swimming along with you, bring up creatures from the bottom, while a knowledgeable marine commentator answers questions. Ideal for those of you who hate

getting wet, Nautilus gives anyone at any age a chance to see Hawaii at its finest. The best times to go are before or around noon, when the sunlight penetrates the water and visibility is clearer. Nautilus is currently operating in **Lahaina** on Maui (667.2133) and in **Kona** on the Big Island (326.2003, 800/821.2210).

Captain Cook VI This 79-foot motor yacht offers morning and afternoon trips to **Kealakekua Bay,** where you can swim, snorkel, and dive, or just lounge around sipping mai tais. The exceptionally friendly crew makes this cruise work. ♦ 329.6411

Captain Beans' Dinner Cruise This is basically a floating luau on a crimson double-hulled barge. Despite the mediocre food and touristy entertainment, people always seem to be enjoying themselves. ♦ 329.2955

Body Glove The pseudo-sailboat takes the booby prize for homeliness, but it's the best dive boat off of Kona for beginners. ♦ 326.7122

The Ironman: A Triathlon Tradition

The western side of the Big Island is renowned for sportfishing, resorts, gourmet coffee, and potent marijuana (called *pakalolo* in these parts). But in recent years the town of **Kona** has garnered attention as the site of the world's most prestigious triathlon, the **Ironman Triathlon World Championship.** Launched in 1978 by long-distance runner and swimmer **John Collins,** this highly competitive race consists of three major endurance events: a 2.4-mile rough-water ocean swim, a 112-mile bicycle ride, and a 26.2-mile run. Every October, more than a thousand competitors from around the world begin en masse in Kailua Bay, then ride bicycles from Kona to Hawi and back again, stopping at Keauhou to dismount their bikes and run back to Kailua Pier. This grueling test of physical strength and endurance is a major event on the Big Island, with year-round preparation, major sponsors, and coverage by NBC Sports. For more information, contact Ironman Triathlon, 75-170 Hualalai Road, Suite D-214, Kailua-Kona, Hawaii 96740; 329.0063.

In 1916 Hawaii's first elephant, Daisy, arrived after a 20,000-mile sea voyage from Rhodesia. Although a sensation at the time, Daisy became increasingly more difficult to handle, and had to be chained to trees for weeks at a time. By 1933 Daisy's keepers were too afraid of her malicious temper to care for her, and only by public protest was a plan to execute the irritable elephant stayed. Her original keeper volunteered to care for her, but three days later Daisy picked him up with her trunk and gored him with her tusks. Police were then forced to shoot and kill her.

91 Ocean View Inn ★$ If Kona had a truck stop, this would be it. Sure there's a view of the ocean (if you look *really* hard through the louvered windows), but since 1935, when dinner cost 50 cents, the big attraction at this landmark hotel has been home cooking at nontourist prices. The menu is epic, with an eclectic mix of Hawaiian, American, Japanese, and Chinese standards that have attracted the likes of **Lucille Ball, Jimmy Stewart,** and **Lloyd Bridges.** There's even an old soda fountain that looks like it was shipped intact from the "Happy Days" set. Closed Monday. ◆ Alii Dr, across from Kailua Pier, Kona. 329.9998

92 Kona Art & Craft Gallery An oasis of originality among the throng of tourist traps. Eight charming women run what they consider "the only pure Hawaiiana shop in Kona," with every item handcrafted by local artists and sculptors. Some of the merchandise that you may not see anywhere else includes banana-bark art, petroglyph pottery, and handmade *makaleka* dolls. Also on display are native koa and milo woodcarvings, scrimshaw, Hawaiian musical instruments, and black coral jewelry. This is local talent at its finest. ◆ 75-5699 Alii Dr, across from the seawall. 329.5590

92 Cafe Sibu ★★$ Affordable and well-prepared Indonesian cuisine, served both indoors and outdoors, makes this small cafe an excellent lunch spot. It's casual and pleasant, with a variety of piquant curries, *satay* dishes in spicy peanut sauces, and barbecued meats and vegetables. The classic *gado gado* salad with peanut and lime dressing has a big following, as do the vegetarian stir-frys. Balinese masks, batiks, and artifacts give great ambience to the tiny place. Highly recommended. ◆ Kona Banyan Ct, 75-5695 Alii Dr, Kona. 329.1112

Harry Truman wore them. So did Bing Crosby, Frank Sinatra, Burt Lancaster, and Montgomery Clift (though they were paid to do so in the movie *From Here to Eternity*). Olympic surfer Duke Kahanamoku was an avid collector, as is Tom Selleck. All of these celebrities have sported classic Hawaiian shirts—those loud, blinding bursts of flowers, birds, palm trees, and pineapples—so tacky they're considered chic.

The history of the Hawaiian shirt dates back to the 19th century, when missionaries gave the natives plain shirts to cover their bare chests. The natives, in turn, painted the shirts by hand with colorful Hawaiian motifs, a design that's been copied ever since.

Hawaii depends on imported petroleum, primarily crude oil from Alaska, for 90 percent of its energy.

93 Noa Noa Stop to admire the hand-painted one-of-a-kind clothing and handbags. ◆ Off Alii Dr, next to Mokuaikaua Church, Kona. 329.8187

94 Hulihee Palace Hawaiian *alii* (royalty) spent their summer vacations at this Victorian-style structure made of coral and lava in 1838 by Big Island governor **John Adams Kuakini,** brother-in-law of **King Kamehameha. King Kalakaua** also favored the palace as a summer retreat. Operated as a museum by the **Daughters of Hawaii,** it is simple but impressive, with a massive koa dining table, **Queen Kapiolani's** four-poster bed, and fabulous 19th-century cabinetry and mementos. ◆ Admission. Daily 9AM-4PM. 75-5718 Alii Dr, Kona. 329.1877

95 Mokuaikaua Church Built in 1836 by the first missionaries, this is the oldest church of Christian worship in Hawaii. Its 112-foot steeple is still the tallest structure in town. The lava rock walls were mortared with a mixture of crushed, burnt coral and *kukui* nut oil. ◆ Daily 6AM-6PM. Off Alii Dr, opposite Hulihee Palace, Kona

96 Marty's Steak and Seafood Restaurant ★$$$ This used to be **Buzz's,** part of the reliable Honolulu chain. The menu is the same: steaks, fish, and Korean-style ribs, plus a good salad bar with hot bread. The open-air dining room above Alii Drive offers a great view of the bay. ◆ Alii Dr, opposite Hulihee Palace, Kona. 329.1571

96 Middle Earth Bookshoppe Who would expect a haven for the literati among the inert tourist shops of Kona? This is a bookstore for browsers, packed with a cornucopia of travel guides, children's books, Hawaiiana, maps, calendars, and art magazines, as well as the standard fiction and nonfiction. Book lovers, give yourself at least an hour for this one: ◆ 75-5719 Alii Dr, in the Kona Plaza Shopping Arcade, Kona. 329.2123

97 Hula Heaven Kitschy collectibles from Hawaii's halcyon days—the 1920s to the 1950s—an era that produced raffia-skirted hula dolls, hand-painted neckties, and the coveted Mundorff prints and Matson cruise-liner menus. The hula girl lamps, silk aloha shirts, and muumuus sold here can cost hundreds of dollars, but the charm bracelets and salt-and-pepper shakers go for much less. Great for browsing. ◆ 75-5744 Alii Dr, Kona Inn Shopping Village, Kona. 329.7885

Restaurants/Clubs: Red   **Hotels:** Blue
Shops/ 🌿 **Outdoors:** Green   **Sights/Culture:** Black

97 Kona Inn Restaurant $$$ The building is fondly remembered as the site of the wonderful old Kona Inn, which, unfortunately, was torn down in favor of yet another touristy shopping center. The Kona Inn Restaurant got the best of the deal—overlooking the manicured lawns with a million-dollar ocean view. The proprietors did the site justice by building a beautiful bar, patio area (great for sunset cocktails), and open-air dining room with lots of rich koa wood. Less imagination went into the menu, which relies on the unfailingly repetitive relics of the day (expensive here), a few other seafood dishes, plus steaks and prime rib. ♦ 75-5744 Alii Dr, Kona Inn Shopping Village, Kona. 329.4455

97 Fisherman's Landing ★$$$ The best thing about this gargantuan restaurant is its location right on the bay. There are indoor and outdoor dining rooms, with a lengthy menu heavy on the local ethnic favorites. *Poki* (raw fish), seafood, and steak dishes are some of the offerings. The view, however, far outshines the food. Stop here for a mai tai. ♦ 75-7544 Alii Dr, Kona Inn Shopping Village, Kona. 326.2555

97 Flamingo's T-shirts, silk sportswear, evening dresses, and a few choice items of antique clothing can be found here. ♦ 75-5744 Alii Dr, Kona Inn Shopping Village, Kona. 329.4122

Tongue-Tied

Keep your ears open for islanders speaking among themselves in pidgin, a fun but sloppy dialect that combines Hawaiian with English, Polynesian, Samoan, Filipino, Japanese, and other languages originally brought to the islands by traders and plantation workers. In fact, pidgin originally developed as a device to help traders communicate. Although the dialects of pidgin Hawaiian differ from island to island, the nuances are minuscule and only a pidgin-speaking local would notice the difference. Islanders are very possessive of their pidgin, so you probably shouldn't try to speak it until you've spent some time on the islands, and even then reactions may be somewhat negative unless you're fluent. But if you'd like to try, here's a tourist's guide to island slang.

Pidgin	English
An'den	And then?; So what, I'm bored
Any kine	Anything
Ass why hard	Life's tough, isn't it?
Bag	To leave
Brah	Brother; Pal
Buggah	Pal; Pest
Da	The
Da Kine	That whatchamacallit!
FOB	Fresh off the boat; Newcomer
Fo' days	Lots of; Long
Fo' real	Really?; You can say that again!; I mean it!
Fo' what	Why?
Garans	Guaranteed
Geev'em	Go for it; Give it all you've got
Grinds	Food
Haole	Foreigner; Caucasian
Hawaiian time	Late
Hele on	Take off; Get going
Innahs	Great!; Cool!; The "in" thing
Kay den	Okay then!; Alright already!
Laydahs	Later; Good-bye
Lesgo	Let's go
Like?	Would you like to?
Lolo	Crazy
Max	To do something all the way (variations: max out, to the max, da max)

Pidgin	English
Momona	Fat
No ack	Be cool; Quit acting up
No can	Cannot
No ka oi	The best
No shame	Don't be shy; You have no class!
O'wot?	Or what? (commonly added to the end of sentences)
Radical	To the extreme
Spahk	Look at; Check it out; See
Wahine	Woman; Girl

Boyz 'n the Hood: A Typical Pidgin-Hawaiian Conversation

Charlie: Eh, why you bag it, man? Dis party no ovah.

Bob: An'den? Dat Clyde one lolo buggah man. Hees mouth go on fo' days. Laydahs fo' me!

Charlie: Fo' real, brah. Main ting cool head. Time we hele on. Catch some grinds. Lesgo.

Bob: I can dig some grinds, too, man, but dis Hawaiian time, no mo' nahtin' open dis late.

Charlie: We go Maui side, all dem joints got some plenty eats.

Bob: Innahs, man! Dem wahines are da max, garans.

Charlie: No ack, man. You fo' real like them FOB chicks o'wot?

Bob: Brah, fo' me—any kine wahine.

Charlie: Fo' real, man, fo' real.

97 Don Drysdale's Club 53 ★$$ The late Los Angeles Dodger pitching great opened this nightclub, which is a local favorite known for its relaxed atmosphere with indoor and outdoor tables, an ocean view, cheap drinks, great bartenders, good service, and some say Kona's best cheeseburger—the Big G.D. This is a lively, comfortable spot where sports fans can nosh on soups, nachos, and buffalo burgers while watching their favorite sports events on TV. ♦ 75-5744 Alii Dr, Kona Inn Shopping Village, Kona. 329.6651. Also at: 78-6831 Alii Dr, Keauhou Shopping Village, Kona. 322.0070

98 Uncle Billy's Kona Bay Hotel $$ This one-time annex to the old Kona Inn was converted into a 125-room hotel run by bargain-minded **Uncle Billy Kimi** (who has 11 kids). **Kailua Village's** shopping and historic attractions are right outside the front door, and the **Banana Bay Buffet** offers unspectacular but reasonably priced food. ♦ 75-5739 Alii Dr, Kona. 329.1393, 800/367.5102 (mainland U.S.); fax 935.7903

99 Waterfront Row Food Arcade The **Charthouse** (★$$, 941.6669), **Jolly Roger Kona Restaurant** (★$$, 329.1344), and **Phillip Paolo's** (★★$$$, 329.4436) surround a half-dozen take-out joints selling everything from hot dogs to chicken, sushi, and coffee. The lanai dining area on the first floor is a major plus. ♦ 75-5770 Alii Dr, Kona

100 Eclipse ★$$ Kona's disco hot spot also doubles as a pseudo-upscale Continental restaurant. Specialties include blackened fresh catch, crepes Tajmahal, and veal Parmesan. ♦ 75-5711 Kuakini Hwy, Kona. 329.4686

101 Palm Cafe ★★★$$$ Opened in 1991 by chef **Daniel Thiebaut** of the **Mauna Kea Beach Hotel,** this open-air restaurant is a must-do. Large rattan chairs, green and white decor, and a spectacular view of **Kailua Bay** combine well with the consistently impressive French-Asian cuisine. Try the oven-baked *ono* in an almond sesame crust with ginger lime sauce and papaya and Kona tomato relish. There is also a commendable vegetarian menu. ♦ 75-5819 Alii Dr, Kona. 329.7765

102 Huggo's ★$$$ Yet another oceanside restaurant where the setting surpasses the food. Fortunately, if you don't like your entrée, you can feed it to the manta rays that play in the floodlights right outside. The lunch fare centers around sandwiches and such, with prime rib, steaks, and seafood (including, when available, fresh lobster and prawns) for dinner. Or, if you already have dinner plans, Huggo's is great for sunset cocktails. ♦ 75-5828 Kahakai Rd, just north of the Kona Hilton Beach and Tennis Resort, Kona. 329.1493

103 Kona Hilton Beach and Tennis Resort $$$ It's hard not to like the Kona Hilton, with its landmark saltwater lagoon and lava peninsula; it manages to be romantic, even for a somewhat large hotel. There are hammocks under coconut trees and an open-air dining room with a sweeping view of the Kailua coastline. The 445 rooms are in two towers at the south end of **Kona,** with private lanais landscaped with bougainvillea looking out at the ocean, mountains, or village. The Hilton's close proximity to **Kailua Village** is another plus. Amenities include four lighted tennis courts, a pool, and a small beach nearby. The hotel's luau is held oceanside on Mondays, Wednesdays, and Fridays from 6PM to 9PM, and the **Lanai Restaurant** (★$$$) is open daily. ♦ Off Alii Dr, Kona. 329.3111, 800/445.8667; fax 329.7230

104 Kona Reef $$$ The advantage of this condominium resort is its location; within easy walking distance of the shops and restaurants, it solves the problem of having to find a parking place. The package is loaded with all the comforts of home (fully equipped kitchen, washer/dryer, A/C, cable TV, telephone), even daily maid service. ♦ 75-5888 Alii Dr, next to the Kona Hilton Beach and Tennis Resort, Kona. 329.4780, 800/367.7040

105 Kanazawa-tei ★★$$$ Complete with sushi bar, black lacquer booths, and traditionally adorned waitresses, Kanazawa-tei is Kona's authentic Japanese restaurant. For a well-rounded meal, try the Kanazawa-tei *bento,* which includes sashimi, tempura, lobster, eel, and other tasty items. Dinner only; closed Sunday. ♦ 75-5845 Alii Dr, across from the Kona Hilton Beach and Tennis Resort, Kona. 326.1881

106 Tom Bombadil's Food & Drink ★$$ Named after a character in J.R.R. Tolkien's popular *Hobbit* trilogy, this watering hole is a favorite hangout for local fishers and triathletes. The fishers are partial to the strong mai tais, and the triathletes who converge in Kona each October for the **Ironman Triathlon** come here for low-priced carbo-loading, with pasta, pizza, beer, and the usual fish, chicken, and meat specials. Bombadil's roasted chicken is legendary. ♦ 75-5864 Walua Rd, at Alii Dr, Kona. 329.1292

107 Aston Royal Sea Cliff Resort $$$ Families who prefer to be self-sufficient will absolutely love these large, attractive condominiums. The stark, angular white structure stands out along the lava coastline and includes studios and one- and two-bedroom suites with lanais, washer/dryers, cable TV, daily maid service, full kitchens with dishwasher and microwave, two pools, and tennis courts. ♦ 75-6040 Alii Dr, Kona. 329.8021, 800/922.7866

108 Aston Kona by the Sea $$$ There's no real beach nearby, but the view is spectacular from the one- and two-bedroom suites. The accommodations in this four-story resort come with double baths, complete kitchens, and daily maid service; there's also a pool, Jacuzzi, and the **Beach Club** (★★$$$). ♦ 75-6106 Alii Dr, Kona. 329.0200, 800/922.7866

109 Jameson's by the Sea ★★$$$ One of the few oceanside restaurants that relies on its food instead of its view, which is equally impressive, Jameson's is also one of the only places in town that serves oysters on the half shell. Fresh *opakapaka,* mahimahi, and *ono,* along with scallops, pasta, and an especially delicious scampi, highlight the menu. ♦ 77-6452 Alii Dr, White Sands Beach, Kona. 329.3195

109 White Sands Beach Around March and April, White Sands Beach does a disappearing act, leaving a rocky shoreline (hence its nicknames, **"Disappearing Sands Beach"** and **"Magic Sands Beach"**). It's great for swimming, bodysurfing, and whale sighting (during winter months). ♦ Off Alii Dr, south of Pahoehoe Beach Park

110 Little Blue Church Built in 1889 and officially named **St. Peter's Catholic Church,** this tiny tabernacle is nicknamed for its blue tin roof. ♦ Off Alii Dr, north of Kahaluu Beach Park

111 Kahaluu Beach Park Local fishing enthusiasts have found this to be a worthwhile spot, and the beach is great for families and amateur snorkelers. But stay well within the protective bay; more rescues are made here than on any other beach in Kona. ♦ Off Alii Dr, next to the Keauhou Beach Hotel

112 Keauhou Beach Hotel $$ The most historic and genuinely Hawaiian of the Kona hotels is located in an area that used to be a playground of Hawaii's monarchs. The beauty of the setting hasn't changed much since then. The seven-story, 318-room hotel, adorned with cascading bougainvillea, is set amidst a coconut grove, with stone idols and a pond that **King Kalakaua** once used to stock fish on the grounds. Tall, stately monkeypods, lush plantings, petroglyphs, and the king's former home are among the attractions. Be sure to ask for a room in the renovated wing (garden rooms are all unrenovated), and check out the affordable seafood and Chinese buffets served

in the ground-floor restaurant—popular among the local folk. ♦ 78-6740 Alii Dr, Kona. 322.3441, 800/367.6025; fax 322.6586

113 La Bourgogne ★★★$$$ A few years ago, duck à l'orange, goose-liver pâté, and pheasant would have been wishful thinking in this seafood-oriented town. But thanks to owner/chef **Guy Chatelard,** the Gallic pleasures of sweetbreads, steak tartare, and classically prepared game are available in an intimate atmosphere of hushed tones and velvet banquettes. La Bourgogne is very small, with only 10 tables, so make reservations. Dinner only is served; closed Sunday. ♦ 77-6400 Nalani St, Kuakini Plaza South (off Hwy 11). 329.6711

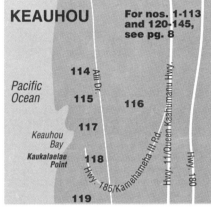

114 Kona Country Club Golfers staying in the Kona and Keauhou Bay areas will find this a convenient course, plus it's uniquely cut out of black lava rock. Magnificent ocean views and some of Hawaii's most consistently sunny weather make this recently expanded 36-hole course a sure bet. Par 72, 6,165 yards. ♦ Expensive green fees; preferred starting times and rates for Kona Surf Resort and Keauhou Beach Hotel guests. Pro shop 322.2595

115 Kanaloa at Kona $$$ These low-rise villas, with full kitchens, private lanais, and private Jacuzzis (in the ocean units only), rank among the most spacious accommodations in Kona, ideal for self-sufficient families. The resort, slightly off the beaten track, is extremely quiet, comfortable, and well-managed, with 37 villas sprawled over 17 acres in a cul-de-sac near Keauhou Bay. Some of the split-level units have great views of the ocean, golf course, or mountains. Ceiling fans compensate for the lack of air-conditioning, and the bathrooms all have double vanities and separate showers with double heads. Tennis courts, three pools, and a commendable terrace restaurant overlooking Heeia Bay make this a great value for couples or families who share a unit. ♦ 78-261 Manukai St, Kona. 322.2272, 800/777.1700; fax 322.3818

Kona Surf Resort

116 Alapaki's The shining gem in an otherwise dull shopping mall, this charming store won the 1990 Kahili award for "perpetuating the essence of Hawaii." Many items sold here, including koa wood jewelry and bowls, *kukui* nut and coral jewelry, fine original art, wooden *konane* board games (similar to checkers), and Hawaiian hula instruments, are handmade by local artists and craftspeople. ♦ 78-6831 Alii Dr, Keauhou Shopping Village, Kona. 322.2007

117 Mauna Loa Village $$$ When completed, Kona's newest condominium project will cover 40 acres with 469 condos and 27 swimming pools. It already has 14 tennis courts, a tennis stadium, **Players** restaurant and lounge, a **Golf Learning Center,** and a pro shop. ♦ 78-7190 Kaleopapa Rd, off Alii Dr, across from the Keauhou Shopping Center, Keauhou. 324.0620

118 Kona Coast Resort $$$ A top-of-the-line resort complete with fully stocked gourmet kitchens, washers and dryers, private lanais, expansive ocean and golf course views, and a plethora of grown-up toys, including Jacuzzis and tennis courts. It's expensive but worth it. ♦ 78-6842 Alii Dr, Kona. 324.1721, 800/359.2566; fax 322.2717

119 Kona Surf Resort $$$ A striking example of hotel architecture, the Kona Surf Resort (pictured above) is all the more impressive because its five four- and seven-story wings were erected on rugged lava fields formed centuries ago at the ocean's edge. Unfortunately, the resort looks a little rough around the edges, as it's in dire need of renovations (some of which are in process). The 535 rooms are large, though, and the lack of a sandy beach is eased by the exquisite ocean view and the manta rays that gather nightly at the point. Amenities include two swimming pools (one of which is saltwater), a massage room, the **Kona Golf Course,** tennis courts, and several shops. ♦ 78-128 Ehukai St, Kona. 322.3411, 800/367.8011; fax 322.3245

Within the Kona Surf Resort:

S.S. James Makee ★★$$$ Roast rack of lamb, chicken, pasta, and fresh seafood are served in a room with a nautical motif. A limited menu but pleasant enough for a dressy evening. Dinner only; closed Sunday. ♦ Reservations required. 322.3411

Mauna Kea on the Big Island is the only place in the tropical Pacific that was at one time a glacier—the entire summit was once buried beneath 500 feet of ice.

Restaurants/Clubs: Red	**Hotels:** Blue
Shops/ ♥ Outdoors: Green	**Sights/Culture:** Black

120 Fuku-Bonsai Center If you're even remotely into bonsai plants, take the self-guided tour of the nine theme gardens in this former quarry. Hundreds of plants are displayed. Learn a few "bonsai-growing secrets" and have them send a plant home. ◆ Admission. 78-6767 Mamalahoa Hwy (off Hwy 11, between the 115- and 116-mile markers, Haawina St, then left onto Mamalahoa Hwy), Holualoa. 322.9222

121 Teshima's ★★$ Order a classic *bento* (a Japanese box-lunch to go) and check out Hawaii's only combination dive bar/art gallery next door. Hit the road again and, chopsticks in hand, munch on fine Japanese-Hawaiian cuisine. ◆ At the junction of Hwys 11 and 180, Honalo. 322.9140

122 Aloha Theater Cafe ★★$$ This is the kind of cafe you wish would open in your own neighborhood. Big, home-baked breakfasts of French toast and omelets with corn bread and muffins are followed by huge, healthy sandwiches crammed with bean sprouts and such for lunch and grilled fish for dinner. The menu is pseudo-vegetarian, with an emphasis on homegrown freshness. It's definitely worth the drive from Kona. ◆ Off Hwy 11, Kainaliu. 322.3383

123 Kona Coffee Roasters You'll know by the blue awning and aroma of fresh-brewed coffee that you're in the right place. Kona's best coffee—espresso, cappuccino, and other variations—is roasted and ground on the premises and sold with gourmet teas and gifts. Drop in for a free sample. ◆ Off Hwy 11, Kainaliu. 322.9196, 800/338.7139

124 Canaan Deli ★$ Ever hear a New Yorker speak fluent pidgin? It's something worth witnessing as you order from the comprehensive (and low-priced) New York deli menu. Breakfast, pizza, and ice cream floats are also served. ◆ Off Hwy 11, Kealakekua. 323.2577

125 Manago Hotel $ A clean, modest hotel with character, a great view, and a restaurant that boasts an island-wide following, the Manago is 76 years old and still going strong, with second and third generation Managos now running the show. Cheap and quiet, the rooms come with private or shared baths and a pleasant view of the picturesque garden below. ◆ Off Hwy 11, Captain Cook. 323.2642

Within the Manago Hotel:

Manago Hotel Dining Room ★$ Locals come from up and down the coast for **Mrs. Manago's** fresh fish and pork chops. Budget prices, a luxury view, and Japanese-style home cooking distinguish this as one of West Hawaii's landmarks. Closed Monday. ◆ 323.2642

126 Royal Kona Coffee Mill and Museum Taste the brew that made Kona famous and observe the mill in seasonal operation (call for specific months). Old roasting equipment and photographs of past harvests are on display. ◆ Daily 9AM-5PM. Napoopoo Rd, between Captain Cook and Napoopoo. 328.2511

127 Captain Cook Monument Ancient Hawaiians' first contact with Europeans occurred on 17 January 1779, when the *Resolution* and *Discovery* laid anchor in this bay. Initially given a royal welcome by the awestruck Hawaiians, **Captain James Cook** and his crew would later suffer tragic consequences over the supposed theft of the *Discovery's* rowboat. Cook, who unwisely took the local chief hostage, was beaten to death, along with four members of his crew, at the water's edge (the poor captain couldn't swim), then burned and dismembered, as was the religious custom. The site of the historic misunderstanding is marked by a 27-foot-high white pillar, accessible only by boat but visible from the south shore of **Kealakekua Bay,** a marine preserve popular with snorkelers and scuba divers. ◆ Take the Napoopoo Rd exit (just north of Captain Cook) from Mamalahoa Hwy

128 The Painted Church Officially christened **St. Benedict's Church,** this petite place of worship is better known as the Painted Church because of the biblical scenes painted on the walls and ceiling circa 1900. For Hawaiians who couldn't read or write, **Father John Berchman Velghe** of Belgium illustrated Christianity with impressions not unlike those in the Spanish cathedral of Burgos. Open to the public. ◆ Off Hwy 160, 6 miles from Hwy 11

For an up-to-date report on Kilauea's lava flow, call the Big Island Park Service's information line at 967.7977.

129 Puuhonua o Honaunau When ancient Hawaiians broke *kapu* (a sacred law) or were being chased by the enemy in times of war, their only escape was to run and/or swim to the nearest *puuhonua* (place of refuge), where they were exonerated by a *kahuna pule* (priest). Because breaking kapu was believed to anger the gods and cause mass death and destruction (lava flows, tsunamis, floods, famine, etc.), offenders were often literally running for their lives, hiding out until things calmed down a bit. This puuhonua was the largest in Hawaii, resting on a 20-acre peninsula of lava, and is now part of a 180-acre National Historical Park. Dominating the sight is the **Great Wall,** a massive, mortarless barrier of lava rock—1,000 feet long, 10 feet high, and 17 feet wide—constructed around 1,550 *heiaus* (temples). Also on display are thatched huts, wooden idols, petroglyphs, and palace grounds. ♦ Admission. Daily 7:30AM-5:30PM. Off Hwy 160, south of Kona. 328.2326

Slip-Slidin' Away

There's no need to panic just yet, but geologists and seismologists recently have determined through satellite measurements that a well-populated southern flank of the **Big Island,** which includes the entire southern half of **Hawaii Volcanoes National Park,** is rapidly sliding into the ocean. **Kilauea,** the most active volcano on earth, now has been proclaimed the fastest sinking volcano in the world, disappearing at a rate of several inches per year. More ominously, scientists predict that any time in the next 100,000 years the volcanic rift zone (illustrated below) could suddenly break off and tumble into the Pacific, resulting in one of the greatest natural catastrophes of all time.

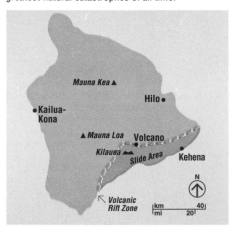

Kilauea (which loosely translates as "The Spewing") on the Big Island is the world's most active volcano, erupting, on average, every 11 months.

130 Hookena Beach Park Although it's hard to believe when you see it, Hookena was once the main port in South Kona. Now it's a modest, backward community adjacent to a salt-and-pepper beach favored by local families. Although the swimming and bodysurfing here are excellent, the road to the shore is narrow and steep, a trial for those prone to car sickness. Camping by permit. ♦ Turn off Hwy 11 to Hookena

131 South Point (Ka Lae) It's only 11 miles from Mamalahoa Highway to South Point, but at one point it feels like you're driving to the end of the earth. The road, once barely passable, was paved recently, making the trip thoroughly enjoyable. Besides being the southernmost point in the U.S., Ka Lae is believed to be where the first Polynesian discoverers of Hawaii landed circa AD 150. Be sure to stop at the **Kamaoa Wind Farm** and listen to the eerie symphony of 37 Mitsubishi wind turbine generators playing before a captive bovine audience. ♦ Turn off Hwy 11 near Waiohinu

132 Green Sand Beach Volcanic olivine crystals created the color and inspired the name of this secluded beach on **Mahana Bay.** Accessible only by four-wheel drive or by hiking, it's definitely a jaunt for the adventurous at heart. Once you get there, swim only if the water is exceptionally calm—currents can be treacherous and the next stop is Antarctica, 7,500 miles away. ♦ Three miles east of South Point, Kau

133 Naalehu There's not a lot to do here except check out the locals at the general store (and *be* checked out), but you can tell your friends back home you've been to the southernmost community in the United States. ♦ Off Hwy 11, South Point

134 SeaMountain Resort & Golf Course $$ The key word at this condominium resort is seclusion. Located halfway between Hilo and Kona, SeaMountain is so remote that most of the year it appears vacant, especially on the championship golf course (par 72). The one- and two-bedroom units have full kitchens, washer and dryer, and access to a pool, Jacuzzi, and tennis courts. It's not the fanciest of resorts, but for the price, seclusion, and amenities, it's a deal. ♦ Off Hwy 11, Punaluu. 928.6200, 800/344.7675; fax 928.8075

134 Punaluu Black Sand Beach Park One of the Big Island's best-known black sand beaches, offering picnic and camping facilities and a broad bay with concrete foundations, vestiges of its former days as a significant shipping point for Kau. Palm trees and spring-fed lagoons add to the beauty here, but the rocky bay is not recommended for swimming. ♦ Off Hwy 11, just past the SeaMountain Resort & Golf Course exit, Punaluu

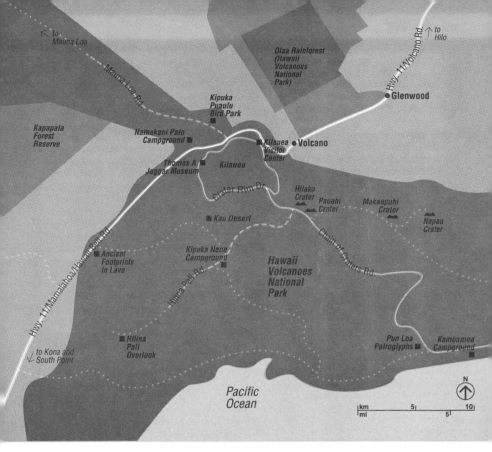

135 Hawaii Volcanoes National Park

Established in 1916, the 377-square-mile park begins at **Mauna Loa** near the island's center, narrows eastward, then fans south around **Kilauea** to the coast near what used to be the town of **Kalapana.** Although Mauna Loa is the most obvious landmark, almost all the tourist attractions revolve around Kilauea, the celebrity volcano that just won't quit. Kilauea's record-breaking eruptive phase has destroyed 178 homes since January 1983 (more than half in 1990 alone) and numerous prominent landmarks. A 1977 eruption sent lava less than half a mile from the now devastated Kalapana, while in 1960 the town of **Kapoho** was destroyed. That eruption added some 200 acres to the island, and Kapoho's lavascape served as a training ground for American astronauts to walk on the moon. Only one person has been killed by an eruption in modern times (an amateur photographer who got too close to a steam explosion in 1924). At the time of this book's publication, Kilauea was still putting on a spectacular show, but it's a daily hit-or-miss production.

Done right, a trip to the park should take all day and part of the night (when the lava glows, an unforgettable sight). Be sure to bring binoculars, a camera, a jacket, sturdy shoes or boots, and a picnic basket. Start your day at the **Kilauea Visitors Center,** taking the half-hour self-guided tour to familiarize yourself with the area, then grab a free guide and ask the ranger to point out where the lava flows are (if any). Map in hand, continue counterclockwise on the 11-mile Crater Rim Road, with a stop at the **Thomas A. Jaggar Museum.**

Once you've circumnavigated Kilauea, the park's network of roads allows you the option of driving to dozens of specific sights that can then be explored on foot. **Kipuka Puaulu Bird Park** is an easy 1.2-mile unpaved path through forest and meadows filled with birds and some of the last remaining indigenous fauna and flora in Hawaii. The **Halemaumau Trail** into the Kilauea caldera, leading across fresh lava flows, is for the hardier hiker. The self-guided 6.4-mile hike takes five hours round-trip, or you can meet a friend with a car at the Halemaumau parking area to avoid the hike back. A shorter trek is **Mauna Iki**—a 3.6-mile, two-hour round-trip (take **Footprints Trail,** between the 37- and 38-mile markers on Highway 11). The paved path crosses the **Kau Desert** and leads to ominous footprints made by warriors who unsuccessfully attempted to flee Kilauea's eruption of 1790. Chain of Craters Road, which used to continue into Puna, leads to the famous lava flows that have been oozing from **Puu 'O'o** since 1983, and ends abruptly 25 miles from Crater Rim

Drive, slightly east of the **Kamoamoa Campground.** You can't hike to the active vent because it's on state land (plus it's dangerous), but you can view it from the air by helicopter. Worthy stops on the return trip include the **Puu Loa Petroglyphs** and the **Hilina Pali Overlook** (off Hilina Pali Road, 18 miles round-trip). Warning: **Pele,** the volcano goddess, doesn't like visitors taking lava rocks home as souvenirs. The park annually receives rocks in the mail from travelers besieged with bad luck. Stay on the trails, heed warning signs, and leave the rocks alone! ♦ Admission. Visitors Center daily 7:30AM-5PM. Off Hwy 11 from Hilo. Volcano eruption information 967.7977

Within the Hawaii Volcanoes National Park:

Mauna Loa Sixty miles by 30 miles, **"Long Mountain"** is taller than Mount Everest and heavier than the entire Sierra Nevada mountain range. Measured from the seafloor, it is the most immense mountain on earth (although 117 feet shorter than neighboring **Mauna Kea**). Devoting two million years of its three-million-year existence to reaching the ocean surface, Mauna Loa sleeps for long spells between eruptions, the last of which was in 1984. Fortunately, the chances of being caught and incinerated in a surprise lava flow are slim to none, since the **Volcano Observatory** keeps a constant watch on the area; metal barricades on **Crater Rim Road** can be erected to stop motorists within minutes of an alert. Although reaching the summit of Mauna Loa is possible by four-wheel drive and a lengthy hike (take Mauna Loa Road), the trip exceeds the boundaries of recreational tourism.

Thurston Lava Tube Tubes form when a crust of lava hardens and a river of lava continues to flow beneath the surface. A 1975 earthquake temporarily closed this lava tube when a wayward boulder blocked the entrance. It is named for **Lorrin A. Thurston,** the Hawaii publisher who pushed for a Volcanoes National Park and was on the expedition that discovered this tube. ♦ Off Crater Rim Rd

Devastation Trail This eerie landscape looks like a science-fiction film locale. Dead ohia trees, burned clean of their leaves by cinders from a 1959 Kilauea eruption, stand like skeletons in a bed of black pumice. A half-mile wooden boardwalk crosses the region, ending at the Devastation parking area. ♦ Trailhead on Crater Rim Rd at the Puu Puai Overlook

Volcano Golf and Country Club An unusual location for a golf course, with the hottest bunker on earth. This high-altitude course is laid out along the rim of an active volcano—great for golfers seeking novel experiences. Par 72, 6,119 yards. Moderate green fees. ♦ Off Hwy 11, 1/2 mile east of Mauna Loa Rd. 967.7331

Volcano House $$ There has been a succession of Volcano Houses since 1846, ranging from grass shacks to timber structures, and all have offered something no other inn in the world can match: the opportunity to eat, drink, and sleep on the rim of an active volcano. **Mark Twain** and **Franklin Roosevelt** were among the early Volcano House guests. **Kilauea** is the hotel's backyard, best seen with a cocktail in hand at **Uncle George's Lounge** (named for **George Lycurgus,** a Greek who wound up in Hawaii because of a poker game and owned and operated Volcano House from 1895 to 1960). The present 42-room establishment was built in 1941, replacing an 1877 structure that became the **Volcano Art**

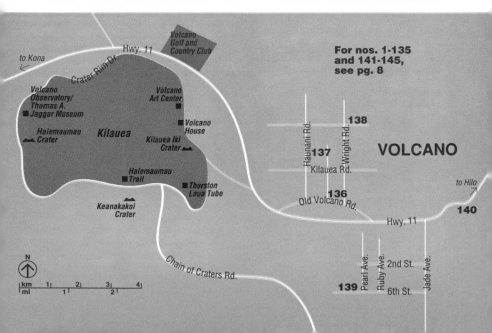

For nos. 1-135 and 141-145, see pg. 8

to Kona

Hwy. 11

Volcano Golf and Country Club

Crater Rim Dr.

Volcano Observatory/ Thomas A. Jaggar Museum

Halemaumau Crater

Kilauea

Volcano Art Center

Volcano House

Kilauea Iki Crater

Halemaumau Trail

Thurston Lava Tube

Keanakakoi Crater

Chain of Craters Rd.

N

km 1 2 3 4
mi   1   2

Haunani Rd.

Wright Rd.

138

137

Kilauea Rd.

VOLCANO

136

Old Volcano Rd.

Hwy. 11

to Hilo

140

Pearl Ave.

Ruby Ave.

2nd St.

Jade Ave.

139

6th St.

Center, a gallery of paintings, sculptures, and photographs.

The service here has declined, something several changes in management have not been able to remedy, and accommodations and the restaurant (regularly besieged by tour buses) are eclipsed by the new lodges and B&Bs in the area. The main structure has the feel of a hunting lodge, with a floor-to-ceiling lava rock fireplace whose fire has burned continuously since the 1870s, kept alive by glowing embers moved from one fireplace to another. ♦ Off Crater Rim Rd. 967.7321; fax 967.8429

Within the Volcano House:

Ka Ohelo Dining Room $$$ The best thing about this restaurant is the view of Halemaumau Crater, which far outshines the food served daily to mobs of tourists brought in on charter buses. Try breakfast or early dinner to avoid the rush, but don't expect gourmet fare. ♦ 967.7321

136 Kilauea Lodge $$ Built in 1938 as a camp lodge for the YMCA, this charming estate is, for quality and price, the best deal on the island. All 12 uniquely decorated units, including a cottage (ideal for families) and a suite, have private bathrooms, and most come with a fireplace and queen-size bed (be sure to ask). Gravel walkways lead through lush, impeccable landscaping to the best restaurant in the area, the **Kilauea Lodge Restaurant,** which overlooks a large manorial front yard teeming with blue hydrangeas. Considering the location, accommodations, and dining, this lodge is simply an unbeatable value. Complimentary full American breakfast. ♦ Off Old Volcano Rd, Volcano. 967.7366; fax 967.7367

Kilauea Lodge Restaurant ★★★$$$ The beef, chicken, and seafood specialties (and wonderful soups) concocted by owner/chef **Albert Jeyte** attract diners from all over East Hawaii. The large, high-ceilinged dining room was the gathering place of the YMCA, which left its mark in a fireplace built with rocks, coins, and memorabilia from civic and youth groups around the world. But the real highlights of this gourmet Continental restaurant (easily the best in town) are the cuisine, ambience, and service—all at a reasonable price. If you're anywhere near Volcano (which includes Hilo), make a reservation. Dinner only is served. ♦ 967.7366

137 Hale Kilauea $$ The nine rooms here are named after the siblings of owner **Morris Thomas,** who built this two-story walk-up (see the illustration above) on three acres. All of the spacious accommodations face the fern and ohia forests, but the corner room (named Heidi) has a balcony and the best view. It's not the nicest B&B in the area, but what it lacks in character is made up for in price and friendly service. ♦ Off Kilauea Rd, second left off Wright Rd, Volcano. 967.7591

138 Chalet Kilauea $$ One of the nicest B&Bs on the island, this two-story cedar-shingle home in the misty Volcano forest is run by **Brian** and **Lisha Crawford,** an engaging young couple with exquisite taste in interior decorating. The fantastical accommodations include the Out of Africa Room, the Oriental Jade Room, the Continental Lace Room, and the Treehouse Suite. High tea is served in the large communal living room (stocked with hundreds of CDs), which is surrounded outside by ohia trees, *hapuu* ferns, and brilliant hydrangeas. Gourmet breakfasts are served on fine china and linen in a cheerful Art Deco breakfast room, just down the hall from the Jacuzzi and the only communal bathroom you may ever regret leaving. If absolute privacy is your thing, the Crawfords also have three vacation homes, all with full kitchens, tasteful furnishings, gourmet breakfast foods (supplied daily), and unique settings. Either choice is highly recommended ♦ Off Wright Rd (at Laukapu Rd), Volcano. 967.7786, 800/937.7786

139 Carsons' Volcano Cottage $$ A short path winds through the foliage to an English cottage and three connected studios, each with its own unique setting. Dark cushions, old Hawaiian photographs, a Victorian interior, fresh flowers, a veranda, and large windows looking out to the pine and plum trees enhance the experience. **Tom** and **Brenda Carson** have given a personal, homey touch to each rental—provisions include coffeemakers, small refrigerators, heaters, and electric blankets (yes, even in Hawaii). ♦ Off Hwy 11 (take Jade Ave to Sixth St and turn right), Volcano. 967.7683

Restaurants/Clubs: Red   Hotels: Blue
Shops/ 🌳 Outdoors: Green   **Sights/Culture:** Black

140 Akatsuka Orchid Gardens A touristy display of orchids of all sizes, varieties, colors, and prices. Pre-certified plants and cut flowers can be shipped home immediately. Stop by to use the clean restroom and receive a free orchid. ♦ Free. 22½ miles south of Hilo. 967.8234

141 Puna Coast Drive Depending on the time of the year, the weather, and just plain luck, this can be one of the most interesting drives on the Big Island. Start at the old mill town of **Pahoa,** just off Highway 130, staying just long enough to buy some fresh fruit for the trip. Then head down Highway 132 through the stunning gauntlet of trees in **Nanawale Forest Reserve,** with a side trip to **Lava Tree State Park.** Continue on to **Cape Kumukahi** and see the world's luckiest lighthouse, supposedly spared from the volcanic explosion because its kindly keeper was the only one in town to share his food with an old beggar woman (**Madame Pele** in her favorite disguise). Head southwest on Highway 137 along the *pandani* and palm-lined Puna Coast, keeping an eye out for whales and dolphins and timing your trip to end up at Pele's latest showcase: lava flow from **Kupaianaha Vent** (best seen at night). Assuming the turnoff is still there, head back up Highway 130 to complete the drive.

142 Lava Tree State Park Fast-flowing lava from the 1790 eruption smothered this ohia forest, and while moisture from the trees cooled the lava and formed a hard outer shell, huge fissures in the earth were busy reclaiming the surrounding lava. The result is this captivating gaggle of ghoulish tree moulds. ♦ Open daily 24 hours. Off Hwy 132, near Pahoa

143 Mauna Loa Macadamia Nut Corporation Owned by **C. Brewer & Company** of Honolulu, this is the world's largest producer and marketer of the macadamia nut. The visitors center offers a slide show, viewing stations of the mill's processing and packing machines, and a few free samples. But don't make the mistake of thinking you can save money by buying macadamias from the source; you can usually get the nuts cheaper at a convenience store. ♦ M-F 8:30AM-5PM. Off Hwy 11, about 6 miles south of Hilo. 966.9301

144 Nani Mau Gardens

If Walt Disney was a botanist, this would be his amusement park. More than 2,000 varieties of flowers, shrubs, and trees line the 53 acres of theme gardens. Take the narrated tram tour, drive around in a golf cart, or stroll at your own pace along the paved walkways. Yes, it's touristy as all heck, but an orchid is an orchid. ♦ Admission. Daily 8AM-5PM. 421 Makalika St, Hilo. 959.3541

145 Panaewa Rainforest Zoo Even if you're not much of a zoo-goer, you'll like this one. Set deep within the lush rain forest, almost every bird, plant, and animal is indigenous to equatorial climates, living in a pseudo-natural environment (which eases the inevitable "poor fella" syndrome). In fact, after viewing the tiger playground, you start to wonder who's being fenced in. Come on a weekday and you'll have the zoo to yourself, sharing some private time with the squirrel monkeys, tapirs, giant anteaters (truly bizarre animals), and the zoobiquitous peacock. ♦ Free. Daily 9AM-4PM. Mamaki St (Stainback Hwy off Hwy 11), 4 miles south of Hilo. 959.7224

The Big Island's Mauna Loa volcano, at 10,000 cubic miles in mass, is the largest such feature in the solar system anywhere between the sun and the planet Mars.

"No alien land in all the world has any deep, strong charm for me but [Hawaii]; no other land could so longingly and so beseechingly haunt me sleeping and waking, through half a lifetime, as that one has done. Other things leave me, but it abides; others change, but it remains the same. For me its balmy airs are always blowing, its summer seas flashing in the sun, the pulsing of its surf-beat is in my ear; I can see its sugarlanded crags, its leaping cascades, its plumy palms drowsing by the shore, its remote summits floating like islands above the cloud rack; I can feel the spirit of its woodland solitudes, I can hear the splash of its brooks; in my nostrils still lives the breath of flowers that perished 20 years ago."

—Mark Twain, 1889

Bests

Noelani Whittington
Executive Director, Kohala Coast Resort Association, the Big Island

On the Big Island:

Volcano Village, a quaint setting just outside **Hawaii Volcanoes National Park,** must be about 3,000 feet above sea level. Nights are great for curling up with a good book or enjoying lively conversations around a fire; days give way to picking *ohelo* berries in the native forests, bicycling, and spending money on local art.

Four-wheel-drive treks with members of the **Kona Historical Society** into very inaccessible areas. Their historian's narration is superb—I always come away with a deeper appreciation of the Big Island.

Horseback riding in the **North Kohala mountains,** beautiful Big Island country.

Spending time in **Waipio Valley,** at the end of the Hamakua Coast, walking along unpaved roads and watching wild horses roam in streams or frolic on the beach.

Peter Merriman
Chef, Merriman's Restaurant, the Big Island

On the Big Island:

Moonlight strolls on **Hapuna Beach,** south of the Westin Mauna Kea.

A breakfast of granola and fresh Hayden mangoes.

Mai tais in the afternoon at the **Mauna Lani Beach Club.**

Kalua pig at the **Ocean View Inn** in Kailua-Kona.

A **Waipio Valley Wagon Ride.**

Brian and Lisha Crawford
Owners, Chalet Kilauea, the Big Island

On the Big Island:

Watching lava flow into the ocean at sunset at **Kilauea** and hiking the Mauna Iki Trail in **Hawaii Volcanoes National Park.**

Swimming in the thermal tide pools at **Kapoho.**

A full-moon picnic at **Kamoamoa Black Sand Beach** on the southeast coast.

Visiting the observatories atop **Mauna Kea.**

Pardee Erdman
Rancher/Owner, Tedeschi Winery, Maui

Lanai's **Lodge at Koele** for a weekend getaway.

Prince Court Restaurant on Maui.

Mauna Lani Bay Hotel and Bungalows on the Big Island.

Roy's Restaurant and the **Kahala Hilton Hotel** in Honolulu, Oahu.

Kaui Goring
Public Relations, Hawaii Prince Hotel, Honolulu

Ulupalakua Ranch on Maui. A nontouristy historic ranch with a sense of the true Hawaiian past. Beautiful views from the slopes of **Haleakala.**

Old plantation towns such as **Koloa** and **Hanapepe** on Kauai, **Makawao** on Maui, and **Holualoa** and **Waimea** on the Big Island.

Favorite activities: **Adventures on Horseback** on Maui; hiking or taking a helicopter ride through **Haleakala Crater** on Maui; a helicopter ride over the **Na Pali Coast** on Kauai; and snorkeling at **Molokini Island,** off Maui.

On Oahu—Honolulu Academy of Arts, an oasis of serenity in the city.

The Willows in Honolulu is the best Hawaiian restaurant.

The **Contemporary Museum** in Honolulu.

Windward Oahu (from **Waimanalo** to **Punaluu**), for gorgeous scenery and a leisurely Hawaiian lifestyle. The **Koolau mountains** are spectacular.

Barbara Campbell
President, Hawaii's Best Bed & Breakfasts, the Big Island

On the Big Island:

Bird Park in the town of Volcano. Beautiful, quiet, peaceful . . . a great way to spend an hour or so.

The **Bread Depot** in Kamuela for fresh muffins and cinnamon rolls in the morning.

Hulihee Palace in Kona.

Author's Bests

Sights:
Akaka Falls
Hawaii Tropical Botanical Gardens
Hawaii Volcanoes National Park
Lava Tree State Park

Restaurants:
Aloha Theater Cafe ★★$$
Cafe Pesto ★★★$$
The Canoe House ★★★★$$$
Dick's Coffee House ★$
Ocean View Inn ★$
Roussels ★★★$$$

Hotels:
Dolphin Bay Hotel $
Kilauea Lodge $$
Kona Village Resort $$$$
Waimea Gardens Cottage $$$

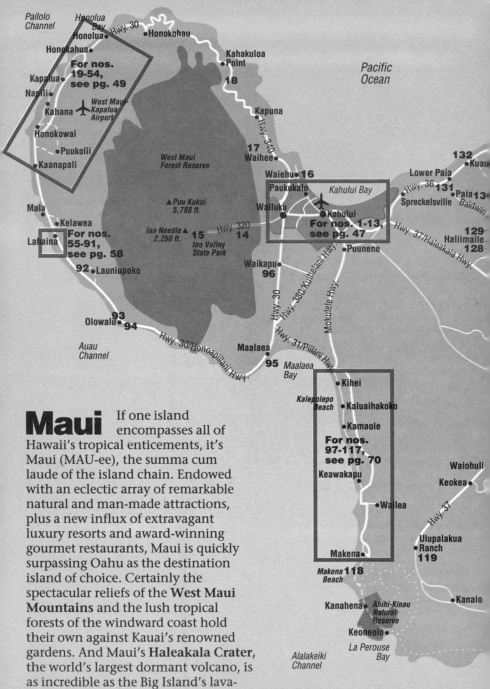

Pailolo Channel

Honolua Bay
Honolua
Honokahua
Hwy. 30
Honokohau
Kahakuloa Point

For nos. 19-54, see pg. 49

Kapalua
Napili
Kahana
West Maui-Kapalua Airport
Honokowai
Puukolii
Kaanapali

Pacific Ocean

18

Kapuna
Hwy. 340

17 Waihee
Waiehu 16
Waiehu

West Maui Forest Reserve

▲ Puu Kukui 5,788 ft.

Mala
Kelawea
Lahaina

For nos. 55-91, see pg. 58

92 Launiupoko

93
Olowalu 94

Auau Channel

Iao Needle ▲ 2,250 ft.

15 Hwy. 320 14
Iao Valley State Park

Waikapu
96

Hwy. 30/Honoapiilani Hwy.

Maalaea
95 Maalaea Bay

Paukukalo
Kahului Bay

Wailuku
Kahului

For nos. 1-13, see pg. 47

Lower Paia 132
Hwy. 36 131 Kuau
Spreckelsville Paia 13
Baldwin

Puunene

Hwy. 37/Haleakala Hwy.

129 Haliimaile
128

Hwy. 380/Kuihelani Hwy.
Hwy. 30
Hwy. 380/Kuihelani Hwy.
Hwy. 31/Piilani Hwy.
Mokulele Hwy.

Kihei

Kalepolepo Beach
Kaluaihakoko

Kamaole

For nos. 97-117, see pg. 70

Keawakapu

Wailea

Waiohuli
Keokea

Hwy. 37

Ulupalakua Ranch
119

Makena

Makena Beach 118

Kanahena
Ahihi-Kinau Natural Reserve

Keoneoio
La Perouse Bay

Kanaio

Alalakeiki Channel

Maui

If one island encompasses all of Hawaii's tropical enticements, it's Maui (MAU-ee), the summa cum laude of the island chain. Endowed with an eclectic array of remarkable natural and man-made attractions, plus a new influx of extravagant luxury resorts and award-winning gourmet restaurants, Maui is quickly surpassing Oahu as the destination island of choice. Certainly the spectacular reliefs of the **West Maui Mountains** and the lush tropical forests of the windward coast hold their own against Kauai's renowned gardens. And Maui's **Haleakala Crater**, the world's largest dormant volcano, is as incredible as the Big Island's lava-filled volcanic parks. Combine all this with exquisite beaches, sun-kissed bodies, and an easy-going Jimmy Buffett style of life, and you have Maui.

Hawaii's second-largest island can be divided into five general regions: **West Maui**, containing the bustling old whaling port of **Lahaina**, the glamorous beach resort area called **Kaanapali**, and the highest concentration of tourists; **Southwest Maui**, anchored by the Kihei strip of condominiums and the posh, 1,500-acre **Wailea** luxury resort; **Central Maui**, the center of commerce and government, which encompasses the industrial towns of Kahului and Wailuku and the main airport; **up-country Maui**, a rustic farming and ranching community on the grassy slopes of Haleakala and home of Maui's

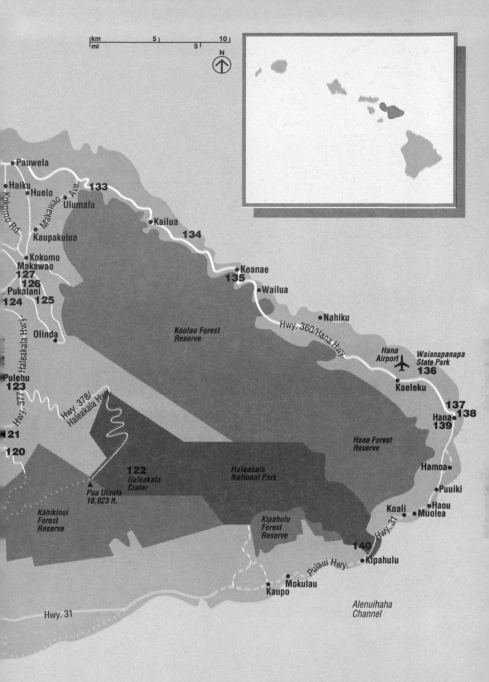

exclusive Mula onions as well as Hawaii's only winery; and the verdant **Hana Coast**, located on Maui's rugged, stunning eastern shores and accessed by the most scenic drive in all of Hawaii, the **Hana Highway**. While the majority of resorts line the sunny leeward coasts of West and Southwest Maui, the most spectacular attractions—the Hana Highway, Haleakala Crater, and the up-country—are spread across the island, so schedule a few days to explore all of them by car and on foot.

After landing at the newly remodeled **Kahului Airport**, most of Maui's two million annual visitors are shuffled off toward the western shoreline, where the weather is considerably better and the beaches are more accessible. While

Kaanapali—a self-contained mega-resort with a profusion of hotels and condominiums ranging from basic to super-luxurious—accommodates a larger percentage of tourists, the more affluent travelers tend to reside at the exclusive Kapalua and Wailea resorts. Often viewed as a playground for the rich, Maui has more millionaires per capita than the French Riviera or Palm Springs, but even starving college students enjoy the stellar beaches, stunning rain forests, and picture-perfect sunsets. Combine all this with the annual humpback whale migration to Maui's coastal waters, an awe-inspiring event that takes place from late November to early June, and it's easy to see why tourists and residents alike consider Maui *no ka oi* . . . simply the best.

Of course, Maui is not without its faults. Because of the island's popularity, traffic is quickly becoming a nightmarish problem, as are increasing incidents of vandalism, theft, and "time-share victims." Unbridled resort development (Maui's white-collar crime spree) has turned Kihei into a Condos-R-Us complex and Lahaina into a tropical Knott's Berry Farm, while property values have skyrocketed so high that local residents (particularly indigenous Hawaiians) can't afford to own homes. Yet despite these shortcomings, Maui continues to reign as Hawaii's top all-around destination, with more attractions and tourist activities, from championship golf courses to historic steam-engine train rides and exciting whale-watching excursions, than any other Hawaiian island. No wonder a significant number of Maui residents are tourists who decided to come back for good.

▶▶▶ ▶▶▶▶▶▶ ▶▶▶▶▶▶▶▶▶▶ ▶▶▶▶▶▶▶▶▶▶ ▶▶▶▶▶▶

1 **Alexander & Baldwin Sugar Museum**
Located in a restored plantation manager's house next to a still-operating sugar mill, this small museum documents the history of sugarcane in Hawaii, from its introduction as a crop to its key role in expanding the islands' ethnic diversity with the arrival of workers from Japan, the Philippines, and elsewhere. Photo murals, century-old artifacts, and a working-scale model of sugar-factory machinery make this one museum worth checking out. ♦ Admission. M-Sa 9:30AM-4:30PM. 3957 Hansen Rd, Puunene (head for the billowing trio of smokestacks on Hwy 311/350). 871.8058

2 **Best of Maui Cassette Tours** If you really want to do Hana Road or Haleakala right, stop at this yellow shack with the flashing light (located just before the Hana Highway turnoff in Kahului) and pick up a tour tape. A worthwhile investment for anyone making either trip, this high-quality, well-researched package of audiocassette tours includes a tape, a cassette player, a Hana Highway guidebook, bird and flower field guides, a detailed map, and a video of the trip—all for $25. The narrator has timed her information perfectly (presented with flawless Hawaiian pronunciation) to describe the various landmarks as you pass them. Highlights include atmospheric music, professional sound quality, pertinent historical background, and tips on where to

stop for a snack or picnic. ♦ 333 Dairy Rd (Hwy 380, just before the Union 76 station on the way to the airport), Kahului. 871.1555

3 **Maui Swap Meet** Haggle over new and used handicrafts, clothes, fresh fruits, baked goods, and assorted odds and ends at this down-to-earth flea market. ♦ Admission. Sa 7AM-noon. 142 Puunene Ave (across from the Texaco station), Kahului. 877.3100

4 **Ming Yuen** ★★$$ The talk of the island when it opened in 1981, this became Maui's top-rated Chinese restaurant virtually overnight. It boasts an enormous menu of Cantonese and Northern Chinese dishes; don't miss the lemon chicken, *moo shu* pork, and chilled lychee dessert. Despite the huge dining room, there's a long wait on weekends and sometimes a two-day backup on reservations, so book early; also call ahead to request the Peking or stuffed duck (both require 24-hour notice). ♦ 162 Alamaha St, Kahului. 871.7787

5 **Sir Wilfred's Espresso Cafe** ★★$ A mecca for java lovers, this informal coffeehouse offers croissants and pastries, a salad bar, sandwiches, and other deli items, plus a wide selection of gourmet coffees ready to be shipped. ♦ Maui Mall, Kahului. 877.3711. Also at: The Cannery, Lahaina. 667.1941

6 Chart House ★$$ The view could use a little work, but you'll find better prices here on steaks and fresh fish than at many other fish houses on the island. This Chart House was launched by the same people who used to own up-country Maui's best surf 'n' turf restaurant, the **Makawao Steak House;** the Lahaina Chart House has a much nicer view. ♦ 500 N. Puunene Ave, Kahului. 877.2476. Also at: 1450 Front St, Lahaina. 661.0937

7 Maui Seaside Hotel $$ Businesspeople from other islands frequent this hotel because of its proximity to Kahului Airport and to the business hubs of Kahului and Wailuku (plus it's cheap). It features sparse but pleasant accommodations, with a central pool and a small beach. If you're traveling on a tight budget, this is the place to stay. Two stories, 154 air-conditioned rooms. Free airport shuttle. ♦ 170 Kaahumanu Ave, Kahului. 877.3311, 800/367.7000; fax 922.0052

7 Maui Palms Hotel $$ If there was an award for the ugliest hotel in Maui, the Maui Palms Hotel would win it. Stay here only as a last resort, literally; the Maui Beach Hotel next door is much, much nicer. Two stories, with a large dining room serving Japanese food. ♦ 150 Kaahumanu Ave, Kahului. 877.0071, 800/367.5004; fax 871.5797

8 Maui's Best Stop in for a wide selection of Maui-made mementos and gifts, including candy, books, quilted pillows, handcrafted jewelry and clothing, and island plants (inspected and approved for travel). ♦ M-W, Sa 9AM-5:30PM; Th-F 9AM-9PM; Su 10AM-3PM. Kaahumanu Shopping Center, Kahului. 877.2665

9 Chums ★$ A diner atmosphere, upgraded local fare, and popular dishes such as saimin, Portuguese bean soup, oxtail soup, cheeseburgers, and hot turkey sandwiches make Chums a Wailuku institution. Early risers will like the hours (it opens between 6:30AM and 7AM) and budget-watchers the prices, lowered when new owners took over in 1989. Hotcakes, omelets, and French toast round out the breakfast menu; specials such as broiled *ono* and teriyaki chicken are offered the rest of the day. The poached mahimahi in white wine sauce for less than $7 is a real find. ♦ 1900 Main St, Wailuku. 244.1000. Also at: 2439 S. Kihei Rd, Suite 201-A, Kihei. 874.9000

10 Siam Thai ★★$$ Nothing fancy at this restaurant, just great spicy Thai food and friendly service. The vegetarian dishes stand out—as does the shoddy decor; still, owner **Mike Kachornsrichol's** cooking has kept people coming here for years. ♦ 123 N. Market St, Old Wailuku Town. 244.3817

11 Northshore Inn $ Hotelier **Katie Moore** transformed this shabby corner of Wailuku into a clean, cordial, hostel-like inn ideal for backpackers, windsurfers, and international budget travelers. The 19 rooms (single, double, and bunk) feature window boxes with bougainvillea, plus there's a small TV lounge, clean shared bathrooms, and a genial atmosphere. The host often takes her guests hiking, windsurfing, or to the beach for volleyball and barbecues. "Come as guests, leave as friends." ♦ 2080 Vineyard St, Wailuku. 242.8999

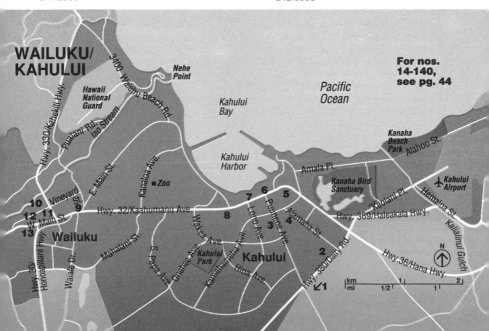

12 Saeng's Thai Cuisine ★★$$ Why the only two Thai restaurants in town chose to open a block away from each other remains a mystery, but Saeng's offers a slightly more pleasant ambience than Siam Thai, plus indoor and garden seating. Along with a spate of fiery green, red, and yellow curries, popular dishes are basil chicken and Masaman chicken cooked with potatoes, peanuts, and coconut milk. ♦ 2119 Vineyard St, Wailuku. 244.1567

13 The Bailey House Missionaries **Edward** and **Caroline Bailey** came to Maui in 1840 to teach at the **Wailuku Female Seminary,** founded in 1833 by **Reverend Jonathan Green.** Closed in 1858 due to lack of funding, it became home to the Baileys and their five sons for more than 40 years. Upon moving to California in 1885, the family dedicated the building to the display of Hawaiian artifacts, which now include quilts, tapa cloth, and the island's largest collection of relics from the days before Captain Cook: stone and shell implements, an outrigger canoe, and more (don't miss **Duke Kahanamoku's** redwood surfboard). The **Maui Historical Society** operates this gallery and museum, a noteworthy stop. ♦ Admission. Daily 10AM-4:30PM. 2375-A Main St, Wailuku. 244.3326

14 Kepaniwai Park and Heritage Gardens When the sun's out, you can't beat the drive into this valley setting. The elevated park pays tribute to Maui's various ethnic groups with exhibition pavilions and gardens reflecting the cultures of the Hawaiians, Japanese, Chinese, Filipinos, and Portuguese. Kids love the children's swimming pool and the picnic pavilions. ♦ Off Iao Valley Rd, west of Wailuku. 243.7408

15 Iao Valley State Park A 2,250-foot-high pillar of stone called the **Iao Needle** marks the spot where, in 1790, **King Kamehameha the Great** conquered the island of Maui during one of the bloodiest battles in Hawaiian history. The dead, legend has it, filled nearby Iao Stream until the water ran red. The Iao Needle is flanked by the walls of Puu Kukui and overlooks lush, verdant Iao Valley, where the ancients buried their *alii* (royalty) in caves to protect the bones—believed to contain spiritual powers—from damage or misuse. Iao's beauty is as stunning as its history is haunting; there's a hiking trail along with many secluded spots for picnicking. ♦ Daily 7AM-6:45PM Jan-Apr, Oct-Dec; daily 7AM-7:45PM May-Sept. End of Iao Valley Rd

---

The lowest temperature ever recorded in Hawaii was in January 1961—11°F at the summit of Haleakala Crater on Maui.

16 Waiehu Municipal Golf Course It's hard to reserve a tee time on this course because it's so reasonably priced—$25 for up to 18 holes. Local golfers and those seeking an alternative to the expensive resorts, where green fees reach $100 or more, keep the place busy. Call at least two days in advance for reservations. Par 72, 6,330 yards. ♦ Pro shop 243.7400

17 Swinging Bridges One of the best and least-known day hikes on Maui is on the windward side of the West Maui Mountains, just beyond the town of **Waihee.** Here you'll find a moderate trail winding through guava, mango, and passion-fruit trees; past bamboo forests, streams, and aqueducts; and across two seemingly perilous (but quite sturdy) swinging bridges. The reward for the 40-minute hike: a first-rate swimming hole fed by a man-made waterfall. Launch off from the rope swing and take a dip behind the fall (yes, the water is cold) for a once-in-a-lifetime experience. Warning: Don't attempt this hike if it's raining—flash floods are frequent and sometimes deadly in the area. ♦ From Wailuku, take North Market (Hwy 330) to Waihee (Hwy 340) and turn left about a mile past town on Waihee Valley Rd. Park at the end of the paved road and, on foot, turn right at the sign "Private Road, No Parking"; stay on the main trail

18 Highway 340 Although the highway is technically for residents only, dozens of adventurous tourists tackle this severely eroded pass every day in all sorts of cars. The windward side of West Maui, unquestionably stunning, is one of the few areas left undeveloped, but be prepared for a bone-jarring ride. Four-wheel drive isn't mandatory, but it's strongly suggested. ♦ From Wailuku to Honokohau, about a 2-hour drive

19 Honolua and Mokuleia Bays Located side by side, Mokuleia Bay (also known as **Slaughterhouse**) and Honolua Bay both make up a **Marine Life Conservation District,** a legally protected underwater preserve where the fish are fearless. Slaughterhouse has a gorgeous white sand beach that's relatively uncrowded, while Honolua Bay attracts snorkelers (when the surf's calm). ♦ Honolua: Off Hwy 30, near the 33-mile marker (look for the bullet-riddled "Marine Life Conservation District" sign and the gaggle of parked rental cars). Mokuleia: Just before Honolua Bay coming from Lahaina (look for the first group of parked cars off Hwy 30 about a mile past Kapalua)

20 Plantation House Restaurant ★★★$$$ With its elevated setting, open-air lanai seating, and stunning vistas of Molokai, Lanai, and the West Maui Mountains, this award-winning newcomer to Maui's gourmet dining scene is rapidly gaining a devoted following, owing in part to chef **Alex Stanislaw's** advocation of Hawaii regional cuisine. A blending of island flavors with Euro-Asian and Mediterranean influences, his repertoire includes such entrées as honey guava scallops and Cajun-seared sashimi, along with more traditional New York steak and poultry dishes. Breakfast, besides being surprisingly affordable, is simply unbeatable, especially when you're seated on the lanai and feasting on fresh pineapple dipped in a light cinnamon-sour cream sauce. ♦ 2000 Plantation Club Dr, within the Plantation Course Clubhouse, Kapalua (turn right just past the 31-mile marker). 669.6299

20 Kapalua Golf Club Until 1991 there were only two magnificent courses here, the **Village Course** and the **Bay Course,** both receiving numerous awards—including one from *Golf* magazine, which designated this golf resort among the 12 best in America. Now you can golf on a third course at Kapalua—the **Plantation Course**, designed by **Ben Crenshaw.** The massive 240-acre course includes such natural features as gradual slopes, deep valleys, native grasses, and long, generous fairways, and is already reaping various accolades (it's also home of the **Lincoln-Mercury Kapalua International**).

Meanwhile, the **Arnold Palmer**-designed Village Course and Bay Course, both cut into the base of a 23,000-acre pineapple plantation, are still stellar, with an ocean view from almost every fairway. The Village Course presents the greater test; its valleys, ridges, lake, and ironwood and eucalyptus trees make it a spectacularly scenic challenge. The older, flatter, more open Bay Course is the longtime home of the **Isuzu Kapalua International.** One general drawback: Kapalua Golf Club is often windy, and there's a greater chance of mist and rain than at Kaanapali or Wailea courses. Bay Course: par 72, 6,151 yards; Village Course: par 71, 6,001 yards; Plantation Course: par 73, 7,100 yards. ♦ Expensive green fees. Preferred starting times and fees extended to Kapalua Bay Hotel and Villas guests. 300 Kapalua Dr, Kapalua. Pro shop 669.8044

21 Fleming Beach Park This popular surfing, bodysurfing, swimming, and snorkeling beach extends from Kapalua Golf Club's 16th hole to the low cliffs beyond. Use caution when swimming here; the steep shoreline is subject to strong riptides. Picnic and public facilities. ♦ Take the Lower Honoapiilani Rd exit at the 31-mile marker on Hwy 30, Kapalua

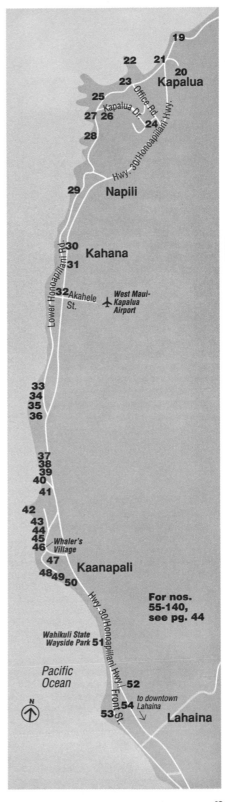

Restaurants/Clubs: Red   **Hotels:** Blue
Shops/ 🌳 Outdoors: Green   **Sights/Culture:** Black

22 The Ritz-Carlton, Kapalua $$$$ To build a major resort alongside the venerable Kapalua Bay Hotel and expect to succeed, you'd better be extraordinary. Fortunately, the new Ritz-Carlton, known for maintaining a high level of luxurious elegance, is just that; the hotel has been bustling since the day it opened. Set on 37 acres of gently sloping beachfront, it was designed to allow maximum coastal views with minimal disturbance to the contour of the land. The 550 garden- and ocean-view rooms and suites all feature spacious lanais, twice-daily maid service, and 24-hour room service. Other amenities include a white sand beach, three championship golf courses, a tennis complex, shopping boutiques, a pool and whirlpool, and a host of noteworthy restaurants. Like its sister resort in Mauna Lani on the Big Island, this stunningly appointed facility has raised the competition among the island's luxury-class accommodations to a new level. ◆ One Ritz Dr, Kapalua (take Office Rd off Hwy 30). 669.6200, 800/241.3333; fax 669.3908

23 Kapalua Resort In the mid-1970s **Colin C. Cameron,** a descendant of missionaries who presides over his family's **Maui Land & Pineapple Company,** took a sizable portion of his pineapple empire and commissioned a team of resort specialists to build the consummate luxury destination. He wasn't disappointed. The 1,500-acre property, sited near West Maui's most extraordinary bays against a spectacular backdrop of West Maui hills, boasts three first-rate golf courses. The 194-room **Kapalua Bay Hotel,** jointly owned by **Tokai Kanko** and Maui Land & Pineapple Company, remains the centerpiece; it also manages and rents 130 privately owned villas—actually multimillion-dollar homes—primarily on a short-term basis. Luxurious and self-sufficient but with fewer amenities than the hotel, the villas appeal to families, celebrities seeking privacy, and people who prefer full kitchens, a lot of space, and all the features of home. Access has been much easier since the West Maui-Kapalua Airport opened off Highway 30. ◆ 500 Bay Dr, Kapalua. 669.7110, 800/527.2582

24 Pineapple Hill ★$$$ Residents are quick to dismiss this as a touristy restaurant, which it is. Located in former plantation manager **D.T. Fleming's** home high above Kapalua's golf courses and pineapple fields, it's popular chiefly because of the panoramic view and the undeniable flavor of Hawaii's rich plantation history. Predictably, this is a restaurant where the scenery is more remarkable than the food, which leans toward standard beef, chicken, and seafood courses with mild attempts at Polynesian influences. For far superior cuisine and comparable views, reserve at the nearby **Plantation House Inn** instead. ◆ Take Office Rd off Hwy 30 in Kapalua and make the first left. 669.6129

Kapalua Bay Hotel and Villas

GEORGE MOU

25 Kapalua Bay Hotel and Villas $$$$ One reason the Kapalua Resort has become the venue for several world-renowned events is its reputation as the quietest, most distinctive facility on the island. The hotel has a spectacular natural setting (see opposite page) amid 19th-century pine trees and pineapple fields, dominated by ocean vistas on three sides (the fourth looks toward a woodsy golf course behind the hotel) and the West Maui Mountains. The 194 rooms feature private lanais and marble bathrooms with separate shower and tub, double marble vanities, and a telephone. The hotel is a haven for guests who prefer cocktail service around the pool to wandering in the wilderness. The resort regularly hosts such international gatherings as the **Kapalua Music Festival** and the **Kapalua Wine Symposium,** a noteworthy food-and-wine event. Also on the grounds is the Tennis Garden (with 10 Plexi-pave courts), one of the United States' best beaches, and an excellent scuba program. Although the local competition has certainly stiffened with the completion of the nearby Ritz-Carlton, this stately resort still holds its own as one of the most prestigious hotels in Hawaii. ♦ One Bay Dr, Kapalua. 669.5656, 800/367.8000; fax 669.4694

Within Kapalua Bay Hotel and Villas:

The Bay Club ★★★$$$ The brief shuttle ride or walk to this restaurant from the Kapalua Bay Hotel is especially enjoyable at sunset or on a clear, starry night. Set on a promontory over the ocean, The Bay Club has a sophisticated ambience that blends superbly with soft Maui evenings. The sunset view, recently cited by a Honolulu newspaper as the best on Maui, is enveloping, with palm trees beyond the veranda and the island of Lanai on the horizon. Fresh mahimahi, *opakapaka,* and *ahi* come in half a dozen preparations, and the bouillabaisse is excellent. There's also a piano bar. ♦ Jackets optional. 669.5656

Kapalua Beach Along with Napili Bay, this is the safest swimming beach on West Maui and a longtime local favorite. Rated No. 1 in the country by University of Maryland's Coastal Research Lab, this place has it all—perfect sand, incredible views, great snorkeling, and its own first-rate scuba program (including rentals, introductory dives, and lessons). The beach shack rents snorkel gear and sells assorted sundries, plus arranges sailing trips aboard the beautiful *Kapalua Kai.* An adjacent grassy area lined with palm trees is perfect for picnicking. Showers and restrooms; a bar and cafe nearby at the Kapalua Bay Hotel. ♦ Parking and public access located at the south end of Kapalua Resort (take the first left immediately after the Napili Kai Beach Club main entrance, park, then walk toward the restrooms), Kapalua

26 The Grill & Bar ★★$$$ Popular with residents, this handsome bar and dining room more than deserves its long-standing high reputation. Owned by **TS Enterprises,** the same operators of the reliable **Kimo's** in Lahaina and **Leilani's** in Kaanapali, it overlooks the Kapalua Golf Club and parts of Napili Bay; the sophisticated menu includes fresh island fish, pasta, steak, rack of lamb, and chef **Hole Lakes'** nightly specials. From 5PM to 6PM, diners receive a healthy discount. ♦ 200 Kapalua Dr (between the Tennis Garden and the golf club at Kapalua Resort), Kapalua. 669.5653

27 Napili Kai Beach Club $$$ This is the kind of seasoned, classic Hawaiian-style resort that is increasingly rare—yet often imitated—on the islands, so it's no wonder that up to 40 percent of its clientele are repeat guests. The tastefully landscaped grounds, bordered by a stone pathway fringed with hibiscus and *naupaka* bushes, adjoin one of the finest bays in Hawaii. Decks, barbecue areas, outdoor bars, and complimentary mai tai and coffee parties make this a convivial vacation spot where guests become friends, returning to savor the fabulous sunsets together again. All 180 units are oceanfront and spread out unobtrusively over 10 acres, and nearly all of them have full kitchens; the Lahaina Wing is closest to the beach. Ask the friendly staff about the **Napili Foundation,** a program in which the children of West Maui regularly practice hula and other Hawaiian arts, and then perform here on Friday night. Other amenities: five pools, a huge Jacuzzi, public access to Napili and Kapalua bays, excellent snorkeling, tennis, putting greens, and a restaurant. No credit cards accepted for the hotel. ♦ 5900 Honoapiilani Rd, Napili. 669.6271, 800/367.5030; fax 669.5740

One of Maui's most popular attractions is the annual migration of humpback whales from their northern feeding grounds off the coast of Alaska to Maui's warm, shallow, offshore waters. From late November until early June hundreds of these mammals come to mate, give birth, and nurse their young to the delight of thousands of whale-watchers.

27 Napili Bay Lined with low-rise hotels and condos and featuring a long, sandy beach between two rocky points, Napili Bay offers excellent swimming and snorkeling, and occasional winter surfing and bodysurfing (watch out for the coral, though). ♦ Public access off Lower Honoapiilani Hwy (turn left at the Napili Shores sign and park anywhere), Napili

28 Napili Shores Resort $$$ Choose from roomy, pleasant low-rise studios and one-bedroom condominiums with lanais and kitchens in this garden setting on the Napili Bay beachfront. An excellent choice if you're looking for a quiet, relaxing vacation. Two pools and two restaurants. ♦ 5315 Honoapiilani Hwy, Napili. 669.8061, 800/777.1700; fax 669.5407

Within Napili Shores Resort:

Orient Express ★$$$ Chinese food on Maui is rare, and good Chinese food is *very* rare, so the Express can get away with its high-priced menu featuring a blend of Chinese and Thai cuisine. The signature dishes include coconut chicken soup, spinach duck, Mandarin fish clay pot, and a hot beef and seafood dish named after the restaurant. The stuffed chicken wings and Thai noodle soup are first-rate. ♦ 669.8077

29 Coastline between Kaanapali and Napili West Maui's most prominent eyesore is a mile or so of shoreline located on the Honoapiilani Highway (Highway 30) between Kaanapali and Napili. Overdeveloped with condominiums of garish color and design, this stretch of coast represents the antithesis of beauty and serenity. Not surprisingly, accommodations here come cheaper. Some of the older condominiums are comfortable, but the new high rises are less appealing (units flush against the highway get a lot of traffic noise). With very few exceptions, the beaches here range from poor to middling. Although some condominiums advertise their proximity to the water, their beaches may be unsuitable for swimming. In addition, the area is a good distance from some of the best restaurants (aside from **Roy's Kahana Bar & Grill**), so you'll have to drive to Kapalua, Kaanapali, or Lahaina to get decent food. ♦ Hwy 30

30 Roy's Kahana Bar & Grill ★★★$$$ The only reason to drive to Kahana is this restaurant. If you haven't already sampled the Euro-Asian cuisine at any of his other restaurants, you're in for a treat: celebrity chef **Roy Yamaguchi** has, to the delight of Maui's gastronomes, opened a carbon copy of his original restaurant in Hawaii Kai, Oahu. Although the shopping-center location lacks a view and the ambience borders on cacophony during the rush hours, the high-ceilinged restaurant is packed with diners who faithfully ooh and aah at the sight of the grilled Mongolian-style loin of lamb, the panfried oysters with wasabi aioli, and every other dish that comes from the signature stainless-steel-and-copper open kitchen. An immediate success when it first opened, Roy's Kahana easily ranks as one of Maui's finest restaurants, awkward location notwith-standing. ♦ Off Hwy 30 at the Kahana Gateway Plaza (look for the McDonald's), Kahana. 669.6999

31 Dollies $ If you're on a tight budget and/or having trouble finding a good imported beer, this place is the answer. With nearly 40 brands of brew and an entire Italian-style menu under $10, Dollies has long been the hangout spot for West Maui *kamaaina*, especially when drink specials are available. ♦ 4310 Lower Honoapiilani Hwy, Kahana. 669.0266

32 Erik's Seafood Grotto $$$ The rustic, woody dining room offers an enormous selection of fresh island and mainland fish, plus good ocean views. You can choose from 11 fish dishes, several kinds of shellfish, and an award-winning bouillabaisse. If it's available, try the fresh island lobster stuffed with seafood and flame broiled. ♦ 4242 Lower Honoapiilani Hwy, Kahana. 669.4806

If you want to experience "hog heaven" in Maui, call or stop by Island Riders in Lahaina (741 Wainee Street; 808/661.9966), where you can rent the Harley Davidson of your choice, from the 883 Sportster to the 1200cc Wideglide, for a day or half-day. If, instead, your fantasy is to play Motorcycle Momma for a day, hire a friendly Road Captain to chauffeur you around Maui's sunny coast—it's an experience you won't soon forget.

33 Papakea Resort $$ The Papakea won't win any accolades soon, but this 13-acre resort offers a perfectly enjoyable family vacation, with all the amenities of the big-name resorts at nearly half the price. Located right on the beach, it sports two pools and spas, two putting greens, three tennis courts, and a host of activities. All studios and one- and two-bedroom condo suites have complete kitchens, washer and dryer, phone, cable TV, and daily maid service. ♦ 3543 Lower Honoapiilani Hwy, Honokowai. 669.4848, 800/367.7052

34 Aston Kaanapali Shores $$$ This super deluxe beachfront condominium resort has the full range of amenities, from studios to two-bedroom, two-bath suites with luxurious kitchens, large lanais, and oceanfront views. Kids (and their hassled parents) will like Aston's **Camp Kaanapali,** which offers various educational activities. ♦ 3445 Honoapiilani Hwy, Honoapiilani. 667.2211, 800/922.7866

35 Embassy Suites Resort $$$ From the highway, you can't miss this pink monstrosity, an enormous all-suites hotel occupying 14 oceanfront acres at the northern edge of Kaanapali Beach. As if to offset the heinous color and design, the 413 one- and two-bedroom luxury suites abound with amenities: A typical one-bedroom suite occupies 820 square feet and includes queen-size sofa beds, 35-inch big-screen TV, full kitchen, oversize bath with two marble vanities, and lanais accessible from both living room and bedroom. And, as if you weren't pampered enough by all this plus the views of Lanai and Molokai, suite rates include free full breakfast, a complimentary cocktail hour, a video/audio entertainment center, kitchenettes with minibars, and a health club and two pools. ♦ 104 Kaanapali Shores Pl, Kaanapali. 661.2000, 800/462.6284; fax 667.5821

36 Mahana at Kaanapali Condominium $$$ Managed by **Aston Resorts,** this beachfront complex has two 12-story towers with 141 units and a good swimming beach a hundred yards away. All studios and one- and two-bedroom units face the ocean, with fully equipped kitchens, refrigerators, TVs with VCRs, and daily maid service. For families and groups of friends, it's a decent choice. Pool, tennis. ♦ 110 Kaanapali Shores Pl, Kaanapali. 661.8751, 800/922.7866; fax 661.5510

37 Kaanapali Beach Resort In the early 1950s **Amfac Corporation** of Honolulu began planning a complex that would give Waikiki a run for its money. Kaanapali Resort, the first master-planned destination resort in Hawaii, was created on a chunk of barren land too dry for sugar cultivation yet lined with three miles of white sand beaches too lucrative to ignore. After the resort's unveiling in 1962, Maui became the first neighbor island to attract a volume of business previously seen only by Oahu. The property encompasses six hotels and six condominiums, two 18-hole championship golf courses, 37 tennis courts, a whaling museum, and the **Whaler's Village** shopping complex. Each hotel has its own beach facilities and at least one pool, and a three-mile beach connects the opposite ends of the resort.

Kaanapali is Hawaii's largest resort, occupying some 1,200 acres, less than half of which are developed. A jitney will take you around the grounds, or you can travel to Lahaina, six miles away, aboard a rebuilt sugarcane train or by shuttle bus. The planners of Kaanapali, aware that tourism was headed toward Maui, designed the resort with the intention of secluding it from the rest of the island; instead of dispersing the visitors among randomly located hotels and condos, the aim was to encourage staying in a self-contained environment. This plan has worked fairly well, although Kaanapali's proximity to Lahaina has turned that once-sleepy town into a major tourist attraction. ♦ 2530 Kekaa Dr, Lahaina. 661.3271

38 Kakekili Park Brand, spanking new, this beach access is distinguished from all of Kaanapali's others by its ample free parking. The small, grassy expanse and sheltered tables are perfect for picnicking. Bathroom facilities. ♦ Off Hwy 30; take the Puukolii Rd exit at the north end of Kaanapali. Daily 6AM-6:30PM

39 Maui Kaanapali Villas $$$ In 1983 the east side of the Royal Lahaina hotel was converted into condos under the management of the **Hotel Corporation of the Pacific.** About 200 of the 253 huge studios and one- and two-bedroom units are now available for vacation rental, currently managed by **Aston Hawaiiana** and various independents. The AAA three-diamond resort takes up 11 acres of prime Kaanapali beachfront, with three swimming pools and nearby golf and tennis. ♦ 45 Kai Ala Dr (at the stoplight at the north end of Kaanapali), Kaanapali. 667.7791, 800/922.7866

In the 1820s, the Hawaiian kingdom's greatest source of revenue was the whaling industry.

Restaurants/Clubs: Red   **Hotels:** Blue
Shops/ 🌳 Outdoors: Green   **Sights/Culture:** Black

40 Royal Lahaina $$$ One of Maui's larger resorts offers 542 recently renovated rooms and cottages in a variety of shapes and sizes, from two-story seaside cottages to oceanfront suites in the 12-story Lahaina Kai tower. The mix of low- and high-rise buildings is enhanced by 27 acres of tropical landscaping, bordered by the ocean, a golf course, and meandering walkways. There is more of everything at the Royal Lahaina: four dining rooms and lounges, three swimming pools and a whirlpool spa, tennis courts at the hotel's tennis ranch (including a stadium court), and two championship golf courses. The Royal Lahaina luau (held nightly) is a pleasant outdoor dining affair, with a program bolstered by *kumu hula* **Frank Kawaikapuokalani Hewitt,** one of Hawaii's luminaries who commutes from Oahu to perform. All rooms have private lanais and refrigerators, while the cottages have full kitchen facilities. ♦ 2780 Kekaa Dr (take Kekaa exit off Hwy 30, turn right), Kaanapali. 661.3611, 800/733.7777; fax 661.6150

41 Maui Eldorado Condominium $$$ These attractive apartments sit between the highway and the beach, alongside a golf course. More than half of the 204 units are available for vacation rentals and, although not on the water, the resort has its own private beach club within walking distance. Three pools and golf courses. ♦ 2661 Kekaa Dr (take Kekaa exit off Hwy 30, turn left), Kaanapali. 661.0021, 800/535.0085; fax 667.7039

42 Sheraton Maui $$$ The 503-room Sheraton occupies the longest and broadest stretch of Kaanapali Beach. Accommodations include four-story guest units on the 80-foot-high promontory known as **Black Rock,** two six-story units hugging the cliff walls, and, for people who like to stay close to the ground, 26 Polynesian-style cottages scattered across the 23-acre site. Although an extensive renovation program added new color schemes in the guest rooms and generally upgraded the landscaping and dining facilities, this is still a Sheraton, with Sheraton-level tastes and standards. The best thing about this hotel is its beach. The cove below Black Rock is excellent for beginning snorkelers, but be prepared for an abrupt shoreline drop-off. Two pools, tennis, golf. ♦ 2605 Kaanapali Pkwy, Lahaina. 661.0031, 800/325.3535; fax 661.0458

Within the Sheraton Maui:

Discovery Room ★$$$ The Sheraton's showcase dining room is built atop Black Rock and, although the breakfast buffet is substantial, the view eclipses the food. The Discovery Room dinner show offers a mix of modern and ancient Hawaiian entertainment with Continental fare—fresh fish *en papillote,* sautéed mahimahi, and Hawaiian appetizers and desserts. At sunset, in a tradition maintained since the hotel's opening, a diver plunges into the ocean from a spot near the **Sundowner Bar.** ♦ 661.0031

43 Kaanapali Beach Sort of a mini-Waikiki, Kaanapali Beach is perfect for swimming, tanning, and people-watching along the beautiful, mostly uncrowded three-mile stretch of sand. Just about any water-related activity can be found here, from scuba and windsurfing lessons to Hobie Cat rentals, and some great bars are right on the beach. The ocean is generally calm, but hotels post red flags when swimming is too dangerous. Still, keep an eye on the kids; the sandy bottom drops off abruptly. Free parking is available, but it usually fills up before noon. ♦ Off Kaanapali Pkwy, directly in front of the hotels

44 Kaanapali Beach Hotel $$$ Built in the shape of a horseshoe, the hotel features 431 rooms, all facing a center courtyard that opens to the beach. The whale-shaped pool is only a few yards from the ocean, and the complex's immediate neighbor is **Whaler's Village,** where you'll find an excellent collection of restaurants and shops. Pool, golf, refrigerators, and private lanais. ♦ 2525 Kaanapali Pkwy, Lahaina. 661.0011, 800/657.7700; fax 667.5978

Within Kaanapali Beach Hotel:

Tiki Terrace $$ It's still known for its Sunday champagne brunch, complete with a 24-foot-long pastry table and an omelet station, but the seafood and Polynesian cuisine are unspectacular. The dinner specialty is *kiawe*-roasted prime rib. Entrées include fresh fish, teriyaki chicken, and standard American fare, all served with soup and salad bar. ♦ 661.0011

45 Whaler Condominium $$$ These twin high-rise towers, 360 units total, sit on an excellent stretch of beach adjacent to **Whaler's Village.** It's a simple yet comfortable complex, with daily maid service and spacious studios. Pool, sauna, exercise room, and tennis. Minimum stay of two nights required. ♦ 2481 Kaanapali Pkwy, Lahaina. 661.4861, 800/367.7052; fax 661.8315

46 Leilani's on the Beach ★★$$$ When the locals want to check out the Kaanapali beach scene and "talk story" with friends, they come to Leilani's. There's something about a **TS Restaurant** atmosphere (they also run **Kimo's,** the **Grill & Bar, Chico's Cantina,** and a host of other popular restaurants in Hawaii and California) that appeals to everyone, making it *the* place to hang out. The food is always very good, and the ambience friendly and relaxing—everyone spends more time here than they should. The regular menu runs long on fresh Hawaiian fish, broiled steaks, and smoked ribs and chicken; for lighter appetites, Leilani's has added a seafood bar called the **Beachside Grill,** next to the cocktail lounge. ♦ Whaler's Village, Kaanapali Beach Resort, Lahaina. 661.4495

46 El Crab Catcher
★$$$ Although the Crab Catcher can't compete with its immediate neighbor, Leilani's, it usually draws a more genteel crowd. Open to the sea, this well-established spot offers the consummate West Maui scenario of poolside tables and informal alfresco dining. The straightforward menu features a variety of crab dishes, including crab bisque. Try the house specialty, crab-stuffed mushrooms with Maui onions, but leave room for the *onolicious* hula pie (made with ice cream). ♦ Whaler's Village, Kaanapali Beach Resort, Lahaina. 661.4423

46 Chico's Cantina ★$$ The colorful, Mexican-tile, open-air dining area is probably where you'll find yourself eating chips and salsa and drinking tropical concoctions and beer for the better part of the evening. The menu is good, standard fare: tacos, burritos, enchiladas, and chimichangas with rice and beans. There are also gringo selections such as burgers, sandwiches, etc. If it's the fifth of the month and you're in the fiesta mood, don't miss El Cinco de Chico night: *muchas personas y mucha tequila.* ♦ Whaler's Village, Kaanapali Beach Resort, Lahaina. 667.2777

About 30 percent of the people on Maui are tourists.

Restaurants/Clubs: Red   **Hotels:** Blue
Shops/ 🌴 Outdoors: Green   **Sights/Culture:** Black

46 Rusty Harpoon $$ This should be your last choice of the four main restaurants in Whaler's Village, unless you're seriously into fresh fruit daiquiris—Rusty's refers to itself as the "daiquiri capital of the world." The menu is your basic seafood, pasta, beef, and chicken fare without the sunset view. ♦ Whaler's Village, Kaanapali Beach Resort, Lahaina. 661.3123

47 Royal Kaanapali Golf Course Designed in the '60s by **Robert Trent Jones, Jr.,** the **North Course** offers spectacular views of the West Maui Mountains, the ocean, and the islands of Molokai and Lanai across the channel. It's a good golf test, with numerous water risks. The **South Course,** a former executive course extended to championship class, also has ocean views but is less exciting. Kaanapali can be windy, especially in the late afternoon, which is why the pro shop lowers the green fees after 2:30PM. North Course: par 71, 6,136 yards. South Course: par 72, 6,250 yards. ♦ Preferred starting times for guests at Kaanapali Beach Resort hotels. Kaanapali Pkwy, just north of the Westin Maui hotel. Pro shop 661.3691

48 Westin Maui $$$$ After selling the Hyatt Regency Maui, developer **Chris Hemmeter** turned right around and went into direct competition, taking over the Maui Surf a few doors away and turning it into the Westin Maui. The unveiling of his $155 million resort showed it was full of Hemmeter trademarks: a fantasy water complex consisting of five free-form, multilevel swimming pools, waterfalls, water slides, and meandering streams; a $2.5 million collection of Pacific and Asian art; exotic wildlife, including a yellow-crested Triton cockatoo from New Zealand; and eight restaurants and lounges. The 12-acre resort has two 11-story towers containing 761 rooms and suites, the top two floors of the Beach Tower are reserved for the **Royal Beach Club**—37 extra-elegant rooms with a private elevator, breakfast buffet, and reserved poolside seating. ♦ 2365 Kaanapali Pkwy, Lahaina. 667.2525, 800/228.3000; fax 661.5764

Within the Westin Maui:

Sound of the Falls ★★★$$$ The high-ceilinged, open-air dining room features distant views of Lanai and Molokai in an elegant setting highlighted by exotic birds swimming in the facing lagoon. Ranked one of the top 10 restaurants on Maui, the Falls has a Continental menu marked by French and Oriental influences, from poached *opakapaka* to free-range veal medallions. Come for the Sunday champagne brunch, with its mounds of fresh fruit. At night, dance under the stars to sentimental favorites in the **Supper Club.** ♦ 667.2525

Villa Restaurant ★★$$$ The hotel's sprawling lagoons, gardens, and waterfalls highlight the casual setting. The nightly seafood buffet is only $23 (a bargain in Kaanapali). ♦ 667.2525

Cook's at the Beach ★$$ This poolside dining spot is two cuts above the typical hotel coffee shop, serving island specialties, children's fare, health-conscious entrées, and an unhealthy-unconscious nightly prime rib buffet for about $20. Sunday champagne brunch from 9AM to 2PM. ♦ 667.2525

49 Maui Marriott $$$ In 1981 Marriott opened its first resort hotel in Hawaii, with 720 rooms and suites in two nine-story buildings. The design, with beautiful landscaping, cascading waterfalls, running streams, a coconut grove, and a trade-wind-touched lobby, reflects the hotel chain's attempt to upgrade its image, but critics say the architecture of the 15-acre site is too much like that of the Marriotts typically found near airports. Nevertheless, the hotel's swimming pool fronts Kaanapali Beach, and each room has a private lanai, almost all of which face the ocean. **Azuba USA Corporation,** a Japanese firm, recently bought the hotel and revamped the rooms to the tune of $9 million. Amenities include five tennis courts and a resident pro, a children's pool, a championship golf course, Hobie Cats, an exercise room, and a whole lot more. ♦ 100 Nohea Kai Dr, Lahaina. 667.1200, 800/228.9290; fax 667.0692

Within the Maui Marriott:

Moana Terrace ★$$$ The resort's main dining room opens onto gardens and is terraced to provide maximum ocean views. Lunch either from the 25-foot-long buffet or from the menu of burgers, sandwiches, pasta, and fish specials. ♦ 667.1200

Restaurants/Clubs: Red   Hotels: Blue
Shops/ 🌳 Outdoors: Green   Sights/Culture: Black

Nikko Steak House ★★$$$ Marriott's smartest move in Hawaii, the Japanese *teppanyaki* steak house has been a success since the day it opened, filling a void in West Maui, where exceptional ethnic restaurants are still rare. After Nikko's house soup, be adventurous with the teppanyaki selection and the savory sauces, but save room for the fried ice cream (sponge cake filled with ice cream and then deep-fried). ♦ 667.1200

Lokelani Room ★$$$ The decor in this restaurant (named after Maui's official flower) is Lahaina seafaring, and the menu is a mix of American, Continental, and Polynesian, with an emphasis on fresh seafood. Choose from five fish selections, as well as lobster specials, beef dishes, and chowders. ♦ 667.1200

Makai Bar ★★$ Known for its *pupus* (appetizers), the open-air Makai Bar is located at the southern end of the lobby, where it overlooks the beach from its elevated vantage point. The serious eating begins after 10:30PM, when the pupus are half-price. ♦ 667.1200

50 Hyatt Regency Maui $$$$ Developer **Chris Hemmeter** built this five-star "Disneyland for adults" in 1980 for $80 million, and seven years later, **Kokusai Jidosha,** a Japanese company, bought it for a cool $319 million (approximately $391,000 per room), throwing in another $12 million for renovations in 1990. The hotel consists of three 19-story connecting buildings on 18.5 oceanside acres, with 815 rooms and suites, plus meetings facilities. The renovations included custom-designed wall coverings, upholstery, and furniture, as well as Italian marble countertops and terracotta tile floors in every guest room. Hemmeter, however, should still be credited for the Hyatt's lavish collection of Asian and Pacific art, including **John Young** paintings, Hawaiian quilts, seven-foot cloisonné vases, Cambodian buddhas, Ming Dynasty wine pots, and battle shields from Papua New Guinea. Outside, a 154-foot enclosed water slide empties into the half-acre swimming pool. Artists in Mexico designed the 14-karat-gold tiles that embellish the sprawling pool's mosaic, painstakingly installed by numerical placement. Those who prefer things on the wet side will particularly like the swinging rope bridge and the swim-up **Grotto Bar,** set in a lava cavern between two waterfalls. Flamingos, swans, penguins, peacocks, and ducks add to the hotel's flamboyantly exotic flavor. The **Regency Club,** which occupies the top three floors of the Atrium Tower, is accessible only with a special elevator key; club members have access to a concierge on each floor, breakfast service, and sunset cocktails and appetizers. ◆ 200 Nohea Kai Dr, Lahaina. 661.1234, 800/233.1234; fax 667.4498

Within the Hyatt Regency Maui:

Lahaina Provision Company ★★$$$ The service and the food here haven't been up to par lately. Seafood, steaks, pasta, and salads are served in a garden setting with nautical touches, decent but hardly memorable. The lavish **Chocoholic Bar,** featured nightly, still has its fans. ◆ 661.1234

Swan Court ★★★$$$$ The large, elegantly appointed dining room of this award-winning restaurant overlooks its own lagoon with a flotilla of gliding swans. Soft piano music from the nearby lounge enhances the stunning view of the waterfalls and the sun setting between Lanai and Molokai. The fresh fish and roast duckling are excellent dinner choices, or try the roast rack of lamb, chateaubriand, salmon, or lobster in puff pastry. The wine list is long—and expensive. Swan Court also presents a lovely breakfast buffet with pancakes, French toast, and crêpes. ◆ Reservations required. 661.1234

Spats ★$$$ In its present incarnation (it keeps changing gears), Spats is an Italian restaurant/nightclub offering a decent selection of saucy seafood, fowl, meat, and pasta dishes. Its days as the dancing hot-spot in West Maui seem to be over. ◆ 661.1234

Drums of the Pacific $$$ An extravagant South Seas show, throbbing with Pacific sounds and colors, accompanies a lavish all-you-can-eat buffet. Main dishes include *kalua* pork, *shoyu* chicken, and coconut beef. ◆ 661.1234

51 **Wahikuli State Wayside Park** This popular swimming site has picnic pavilions, public facilities, and nearby tennis courts. There's also a beach, but it's very small, usually damp, and covered with debris. ◆ Rte 30 (between Lahaina and Kaanapali)

52 **Chart House** ★★$$$ The idea behind its high perch at the northern end of Lahaina was to give diners a great sunset and ocean view, which it successfully does. The Chart House's long-standing reputation for good steak and fish holds firm here, but if you're short on cash, the Caesar salad makes a fine meal. ◆ 1450 Front St (at Hwy 30), Lahaina. 661.0937

53 **Jodo Mission** Lahaina's Buddhist Temple, which consists of the Great Buddha, temple bell, main temple, and pagoda, was completed in 1970 to commemorate the centennial of the first Japanese immigrants to Hawaii, as well as loved ones who passed away in the last one hundred years. The Amida Buddha, at 12 feet and 3½ tons, is the largest of its kind outside of Japan. ◆ 12 Ala Moana St (next to Mala Wharf), Lahaina

54 **Lahaina Cannery Center** Whatever you need, from beach chairs to birth control pills, chances are you'll find it here for less. The center, a pineapple cannery from 1918 to 1963, opened in 1987 with two anchor stores (Long's and Safeway), 54 shops and food stands, and an adorable *keiki* (kids') hula show every Sunday at 1PM. **Compadres** (★$$), part of the popular Mexican restaurant chain, serves decent south-of-the-border dishes and stiff margaritas. It's an unusual mall in an unusual location (too far to walk from Front Street and too close to justify losing your parking space), but it's all blissfully air-conditioned, and there's a free shuttle from Lahaina Harbor that runs all day. ◆ Daily 9AM-9:30PM. 1221 Honoapiilani Hwy, Lahaina

55 **Seamen's Hospital** In Lahaina's wild whaling days (during **Kamehameha III's** reign), thousands of sailors were left behind on Maui by American and British whaling ships seeking to lighten their loads before embarking on trading trips to Canton; one of the hapless included a shipmate of **Herman Melville's.** Many of them died of a "disreputable disease" at this two-story hospital; in fact, the care of sick sailors in Lahaina and Honolulu used up half the budget appropriated by Congress for the care of all U.S. seamen. Ironically, the place was sold to a group of nuns in 1865 and served as a Catholic school for some 20 years and then an Episcopalian minister's vicarage for 30 years; the building was abandoned in 1908. In 1982, through a unique arrangement between the **Lahaina Restoration Foundation** and architect **Uwe Schultz,** the deteriorating eyesore was completely rebuilt to historical accuracy. ◆ Closed to the public. Front and Baker Sts, Lahaina

56 **Scaroles**
★★★$$$ **Jane Donovan** and her partner/chef **Ronald Lynch** offer Northern Italian cuisine in a tiny, stylish setting. From the fresh-baked onion rolls to the seafood pasta and veal Scaroles (with eggplant and prosciutto), the food is unequivocally superb, with nightly specials, a famous tiramisù, and Maui's only collection of Italian opera music. Located next to Kaiser hospital, Scaroles shouldn't be missed. Note: There's no liquor license, so bring your own wine. ◆ 930 Wainee St, Lahaina. 661.4466

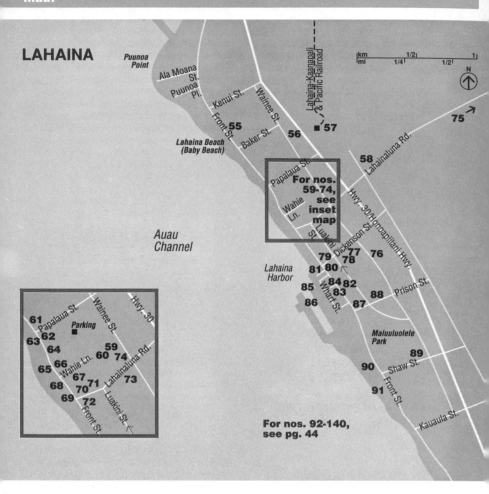

LAHAINA

57 Lahaina-Kaanapali & Pacific Railroad (Sugarcane Train) Children, train buffs, and people who like touristy attractions will enjoy a ride on the Sugarcane Train: a rebuilt, smoke-billowing, little-train-that-could that chugs along six miles of narrow-gauge tracks between Lahaina and the Kaanapali Beach Resort. Puffing beside much of the original track used by the **Pioneer Sugar Mill** since 1890, this steam locomotive (pictured on the opposite page) with whistle and open-air passenger cars recalls a bygone era, a real treat for kids who think all trains look like Amtrak. Buy one-way (about a 25-minute trip) or round-trip tickets, or take your choice of combination tours that include the **Omni Theater** movie or a museum tour. There's free bus transportation between the Lahaina depot and town, and a jitney links the Kaanapali station with hotels. If you're staying at the Kaanapali resort, there's also a boarding platform across the footbridge at the north end of the grounds. The narrated ride, which takes you past cane fields, mountains, and the seashore for a round-trip total of 12 miles, includes a singing conductor. ♦ Fee. Six round-trips daily 8:30AM-5PM. Three stations: Puukoli Station (Puukoli Rd off Hwy 30 at the north end of Kaanapali); Kaanapali Station (off Hwy 30 across from the Kekaa Dr exit, mid-Kaanapali); Lahaina Station (Hinau St off Hwy 30, just north of the sugar mill). 661.0089

58 Pioneer Sugar Mill Built by sugar magnate **James Campbell,** the **Pioneer Mill Company** thrived as others folded, and went on to become a kingpin of Maui sugar production, providing generations of Mauians with employment. The mill's smokestack is as familiar a part of the Lahaina landscape as the cane fields and boat harbors. ♦ Closed to the public. Lahainaluna Rd and Hwy 30

Lahaina, a town on Maui with some of the most beautiful sunsets in the world, means "merciless sun" in Hawaiian.

59 House of Saimin ★$ If you haven't experienced a bowl of saimin yet, do so. Basically a fancier version of Top Ramen with a few extras (such as fish cake and won tons), it's served in a huge bowl with chopsticks and a soup spoon. More than a cheap, healthy lunch, saimin is a cultural experience. The best side-order on this restaurant's succinct menu is the chicken sticks, which are so good you'll probably make a second order. ♦ Southeast corner of the Lahaina Shopping Center (next to the Nagasako Variety Market), Lahaina. 667.7572

60 Golden Palace $$ Chinese restaurants are about as plentiful on Maui as ski resorts, and the few that exist are usually hard to find. The Golden Palace—a misnomer of staggering proportions—is no exception; fortunately, it's really not worth finding unless you're seriously in the mood for greasy Chinese food. Takeout is available, too. ♦ Papalaua and Front Sts (in the Lahaina Shopping Center), Lahaina. 661.3126

61 Lahaina Center
This shopping center has the personality and charm of a refrigerator and the appeal of a time-share salesman, but it continues to receive busloads of tourists, and parking is no longer free, so the stores here must be prospering. The major outlets include **Liberty House, Hilo Hattie,** and **Woolworth.** ♦ 900 Front St (at Papalaua), Lahaina. 667.9216

Within the Lahaina Center:

Hard Rock Cafe ★★$$ Familiarity may breed contempt, but for the Hard Rock chain, all it breeds is success. As follows custom, the rock music is loud, the walls are adorned with rock and surf memorabilia, and there's always a line to buy T-shirts. The food, if unexceptional, is good enough to draw even the locals, who (after payday) come for the chicken-breast sandwiches and Texas-style ribs. Yes, it's predictable and very touristy, but you'd be hard-pressed to have a bad time at the Hard Rock. ♦ 900 Front St, Lahaina. 667.7400

Chili's Grill & Bar ★$$ The food at Chili's, part of an ever-expanding chain of pseudo-Mexican restaurants, is basically the same as Hard Rock's but with a slight Latin twist. If you can't stand the loud music at Hard Rock, come here. If you can, don't; the Hard Rock Cafe is much more entertaining for the same quality and price. ♦ 900 Front St, Lahaina. 661.3665

Blue Tropix The newest, hippest (well, for Lahaina at least) discotheque in town has put the pressure on its competition—Studio 505. The venue is basically the same: pricey drinks, flashing lights, loud music, and pompous staffers. The only significant difference is the size (it's bigger) and the location (Studio 505 is located on the opposite side of town). ♦ 900 Front St, Lahaina. 667.5309

Lahaina-Kaanapali & Pacific Railroad

R.M. SHERMAN

Seashells by the Seashore

Hawaii is a mecca for serious shell collectors and the island of Maui is their motherlode, for its shores hide some of the world's rarest and most valuable shells, including the prized checkered cowrie, which is illustrated on the opposite page. Some shellseekers are ingenious and dedicated treasure hunters who check the daily tide charts in their local newspaper, then scavenge tide pools to study the shells' habitats and camouflages. Many also snorkel or skin-dive for the precious shells.

The amateur sheller, however, should bear in mind that much more is involved here than meets the eye. For starters, reefs prevent most shells from reaching the shore wholly intact, making it necessary to search in deeper water, where inexperienced snorkelers may find themselves on the "Tahitian Current Express." To compound the danger, many shelled animals, namely those found in cone shells, have powerful bites or stings that can cause serious illness. What usually happens is an unwary victim pockets a live cone shell and finds out the hard way about the perils of shell-collecting.

While you're searching for sandy treasures, remember that a shell is not just another pretty rock, it's the home of a living sea animal better suited to its own ecological circle than to your living-room bookshelf. To avoid depleting the waters of the special specimens, leave the shells where you found them—unless, of course, the resident has already abandoned its home.

Triton's Trumpet (*Charonia tritonis*) These rare shells, which grow up to 18 inches in length, fasten themselves to coral in deep water.

Marlin Spike Auger (*Terebra maculata*) Found in depths of more than 10 feet, these grow up to 10 inches long and are the largest augers on earth.

Crenulated Auger (*Terebra crenulata*) Spiny pink or blue shells commonly found in shallow water. They are carnivores, usually about 5 inches long, with spiral rings distinguishing them from other island augers.

Knobby Spindle (*Latirus nodus*) This common pink shell houses a bright red sea creature.

Tile Miter (*Mitra incompta*) Miters are not generally prized by collectors, since the 4-inch-long, rough-textured shells are fairly common. They live among coral beds 30 to 80 feet deep.

Horned Helmet (*Cassis cornuta*) The largest of the Hawaiian shells, which may grow as long as 1 foot.

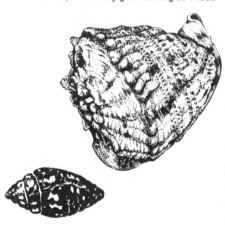

Lettered Miter (*Mitra litterata*) These tiny carnivores have a poisonous sting they use to capture worms for dinner. Only 1 inch long, they hide under loose coral at the water's surface.

Green-Mouthed Spindle (*Peristernia chlorostome*) More yellow than green, this common $1/2$- to $3/4$-inch shell lives in coral along the shore.

Fringed Cowrie (*Cypraea fimbriata*) This orange cowrie chooses orange coral as camouflage in depths of 2 to 60 feet.

Blood-Spotted Triton
(*Bursa cruentata*) A lovely, common triton with an inner rim ranging from white to pale violet.

Pimpled Basket
(*Nassarius papillosus*) A scavenger that hops along on a single muscle (or "foot"). Its shell grows 1 inch to 2¼ inches long.

Hawaiian Limpet
(*Petella sandwichensis*) This exclusively Hawaiian animal is an important local delicacy. It grows up to 2 inches long and is found in shallow water or on rocks exposed to waves.

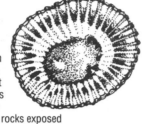

Golden Yellow Cone
(*Conus flavidus*) These 2½-inch-long shells range from white to greenish yellow. Like other cones, they often have an outer layer of thick *periostracum,* a substance that obscures the shells' fine colors until removed.

Brilliant Drupe (*Drupa rubusidaeus*) Long spines and a pinkish mouth distinguish this 1½-inch-long shell.

Snakehead Cowrie
(*Cypraea caputserpentis*) Hawaii's most common cowrie is a herbivorous night feeder that grows up to 1½ inches in length.

Checkered Cowrie
(*Cypraea tessellata*) This rare and beautiful prize is a native only to Hawaii. The tiny ¾- to 1½-inch-long shell hides in about 50 feet of water.

Knobbed Drupe
(*Drupa nodus*) A common shell found in shallow water. Look for its black spikes on a white background, and a lavender mouth.

Rough Periwinkle
(*Littorina scabra*) An edible animal that lives in shoreline coral.

Murex Pele (*Murex pele*)
Rough, craggy carnivores that use their spiky surfaces as spears to capture other mollusks. Found only in Hawaii, they hide in coral at depths of 40 feet.

Penniform Cone
(*Conus pennaceua*) Habitants of these cones fire darts to stun their prey; some species are even dangerous to humans. But the common 3-inch-long cones are safe as well as beautiful, with an intricate and varied design. They live buried in sand on the ocean floor.

Reticulated Cowrie (*Cypaea maculifera*) This
cowrie shell is prized by world collectors. Hawaiians use the shells as jewelry and decoration. The smooth, colorful specimen is found under rocks or on coral near the shore.

Longhi's

62 Longhi's ★$$$ When this restaurant was expanded several years ago to triple its previous size, the service predictably declined—a particularly big problem for a restaurant where the servers are known for reciting the menus. None but the most seasoned waiters can remember the extensive and rather complicated choices and still provide service that isn't spotty or hurried. Don't be afraid to ask the waiter to slow down, and, by all means, be sure to ask the prices. Portions are rather large, so be careful about over-ordering, especially if you plan on trying one of Longhi's trademark homemade desserts. The cuisine has an Italian flair, featuring pasta, seafood, and enormous sandwiches. Further eclipsed by new restaurants down the street, Longhi's is no longer *the* Lahaina dining spot, but it remains a local landmark and a breakfast favorite, and it occasionally books some spectacular bands. ◆ 888 Front St, Lahaina. 667.2288

63 Lahaina Broiler $$$ The proprietors say this is the biggest restaurant in Lahaina, but its real claim to fame is the 100-year-old monkeypod tree growing out of the roof. Portuguese bean soup, seafood chowder, and a host of steak, prime rib, seafood, and combination dishes are served in a superb setting over the water. In fact, the food, standard American fare, is not nearly as memorable as the view of Molokai and Lanai. ◆ Front St, Lahaina. 661.3111

64 Wo Hing Temple In 1909 throngs of Chinese laborers brought in to work in West Maui's sugarcane fields formed the **Wo Hing Society,** a mid-Pacific chapter of a 17th-century Chinese fraternal society. Three years later the group built a fraternal hall in downtown Lahaina equipped with a separate cook house, Chinese utensils, fire pits fueled with *kiawe* wood for the oversize woks, and implements reflecting the Chinese culture. In 1983 the **Lahaina Restoration Foundation** turned the building into a museum, a historical remnant of one of Hawaii's significant ethnic groups. You can also see films of turn-of-the-century Hawaii made by **Thomas Edison** here. ◆ Free. M-Sa 9AM-4:30PM; Su 11AM-4:30PM. Front St (across from Kimo's), Lahaina

65 Kimo's ★★$$$ Two young men who made a fortune with the **Rusty Scupper** chain on the mainland went on to build this popular oceanfront restaurant and bar (pictured below) on Front Street, overlooking Molokai and Lanai from the outside deck. The food isn't anything to write home about, but it's still consistently good, including your basic fresh fish, a huge cut of prime rib, steaks, and island specials such as *Koloa* pork ribs and Polynesian chicken. On Friday afternoons local singer **Scotty Rotten** puts on a great show, but the best entertainment by far is the spectacular sunset. ◆ 845 Front St, Lahaina. 661.4811

66 Avalon ★★$$$ Once you recover from the sometimes stunningly rude service, you're apt to conclude that this trendy restaurant is overpriced and overrated—which is a shame, given that some of chef/owner **Mark Ellman's** Pacific Rim creations are exceptional. Unfortunately, even the best cuisine can't compensate for the cheeky, presumptuous attitude of the staff; what works in Los Angeles and New York doesn't fly in Maui. ◆ 844 Front St, Lahaina. Reservations recommended. 667.5559

Kimo's

66 Moose McGillycuddys ★$$ Part of the restaurant chain that extends from Oahu to California, the Moose lacks in originality but makes up for it (at least in Lahaina) by supplying a necessity—a pleasing variety of reasonably good food at low prices. Favorites include prime rib, fish, chicken, steak and lobster, Mexican food (especially the fish tacos), giant salads, and a kids' menu. The breakfasts are huge (all the cops start their day here), and the bar has nightly specials and live dance music. The cheapest dinners in town are the early-bird specials from 4:30-7:30PM (try the prime rib or steak and lobster). ◆ 844 Front St, Lahaina. 667.7758

67 Alex's Hole In the Wall ★★$$$ For three generations the Didios have been serving Italian food, much of it from family recipes, at their small restaurant. Recently, owners **Alex** and **Tom Didio** added a new dining room upstairs and installed air-conditioning, making this considerably less of a "hole-in-the-wall" than before. Although the cuisine is textbook Italian, it's still very good textbook Italian, which accounts for the longevity of operation (nearly 20 years). ◆ 834 Front St (on Wahie Ln, across from Moose McGillycuddys), Lahaina. 661.3197

68 Lahaina Fish Co. ★$$ If you're confused by the names and pronunciations for the fish served in restaurants all over Hawaii, the Lahaina Fish Co. will set you straight. Comprehensive menus translate the Hawaiian word for each fish, and there's also a wall-mounted guide to island game fish. Although the cuisine isn't particularly memorable, the setting is—an open-air lanai overlooking Lahaina Harbor, Lanai, and Molokai. Prices for the Cajun mahimahi, shrimp Salvador, and catch of the day are very reasonable, considering the million-dollar sunset vantage point. If you're not a seafood lover, there's always the popular *yakitori* (skewered and broiled chicken or beef with vegetables). ◆ 831 Front St, Lahaina. 661.3472

69 Cheeseburger In Paradise ★$ Yes, the name comes from the popular **Jimmy Buffett** tune (or perhaps vice-versa; no one seems sure), which is the standard genre of the continuous background music, live and taped, played at this open-air burger joint. It's cheap, it's pretty good, and it's always jumping. And no, Jimmy never eats here. ◆ 811 Front St, Lahaina. 661.4855

70 Metropolitan Art Gallery The gallery's vast displays include traditional and modern works, from 19th-century American West paintings to bronzes and contemporary pieces by master artists. Oil paintings by **Gil Bruvel,** designated among the top 10 living French artists by the French Ministry of Culture, and Maui visionary artist **Andrew Annenberg,** who depicts marine life and nature, are featured here. ◆ Daily 9AM-10PM. 802 Front St, Lahaina. 661.5033

71 Lahaina Hotel $$$ In the 1860s, when Lahaina was the whaling mecca of the world, this hotel housed the thousands of whalers that came to port. When the whaling era ended, the old Lahaina Hotel became a gathering place for genteel travelers and local power brokers (rumor has it that singer **Fanny Brice** and "Swedish Nightingale" **Jenny Lind** often entertained here). The building served as a general store, and then business offices (destroyed by fire in the mid-1960s). Today it's a two-story, 13-room inn refurbished to new standards of old-style grandeur by its current owner, entrepreneur, preservationist, and antiques collector **Rick Ralston.** After a three-year restoration, the place is replete with luxurious turn-of-the-century artifacts, including beautiful armoires, leaded-glass lamps, floral wall coverings, and lace curtains. No kids under 15 are allowed, there are no TVs, and smokers are encouraged to use the lanai. Continental breakfasts, air-conditioning, and telephones are provided. ◆ 127 Lahainaluna St, Lahaina. 661.0577, 800/669.3444; fax 667.9480

Within the Lahaina Hotel:

David Paul's Lahaina Grill ★★★$$$ Once a seedy barroom on the ground floor of the old Lahaina Hotel, this new star on the local culinary scene possesses the same stylish aura that the owners struggled to preserve in the hotel. The restaurant just underwent a major expansion, doubling its seating capacity and adding a baby grand piano. The cuisine, according to part-owner and celebrated chef **David Paul,** is a gathering of "techniques and flavors from around the world perfectly blended with local ingredients." A few examples: tequila shrimp with firecracker rice, Kona coffee-roasted lamb, and *ahi* carpaccio. The service can be off at times, seriously affecting the overall dining experience. ◆ 127 Lahainaluna Rd, Lahaina. 667.5117

Restaurants/Clubs: Red   **Hotels:** Blue

Shops/ 🌴 Outdoors: Green   **Sights/Culture:** Black

72 Lahaina Marketplace The impeccable landscaping distinguishes this shopping arcade. Head toward the back and admire the sentinel-like fan palms, towering hedges, brick patio, and a formidable foliage tiki. ♦ Front St and Lahainaluna Rd

73 Plantation Inn $$$ A group of private investors took over three residential lots in the center of Lahaina and came up with this luxurious, elegant, and surprisingly affordable hotel. The 17 rooms and suites all have French doors, brass four-poster beds, verandas, stained glass, floral wallpaper and wainscoting, antique furniture, and hardwood floors with area rugs to give the feeling of an intimate plantation-style inn. Modern amenities include A/C, TV, VCRs, a swimming pool, and a spa. Adjacent to the inn is **Gerard's,** the best French restaurant in Maui (if not Hawaii), and only a block away are the shops and galleries of Lahaina's bustling Front Street. Rooms range from standard to suites. ♦ 174 Lahainaluna Rd, Lahaina. 667.9225, 800/433.6815; fax 667.9293

Within the Plantation Inn:

Gerard's ★★★★$$$$ An apprentice chef in France at age 14, **Gerard Reversade** trained with four of the country's culinary masters, acquiring the expertise that now makes him one of Hawaii's top chefs. Moving to Hawaii in 1973, Gerard worked in the finest French restaurants in the state and in 1982 established his own restaurant in downtown Lahaina—a small, charmingly unpretentious adjunct to the stately Plantation Inn. The entrées, such as breast of pheasant with grapes and apples in Sauternes wine sauce, are consistently impeccable and creative. Reversade holds to a policy of using fresh local ingredients in a classic French fashion. Yes, it's expensive, but it's also the best (besides, what do you think your credit card's for?). Guests of the Plantation Inn receive a discount. ♦ 661.8939

74 Fun Rentals Rent mountain bikes, scooters, snorkel sets, boogie boards, surfboards, baby joggers, and kayaks. ♦ M-Sa 8:30AM-5PM; Su 8:30AM-3PM. 193 Lahainaluna Rd, Lahaina. 661.3035

75 Hale Pai This structure is the only original building still standing on the **Lahainaluna High School** campus—the first American school established west of the Rocky Mountains. Founded in 1831 by Protestant missionaries to spread the Christian gospel to a Hawaiian people who had no written language, the school used a secondhand press to print the first-ever local newspaper, *Ka Lama Hawaii* (the *Hawaiian Luminary*), in 1834. The press, which the missionaries had brought with them on their journey around Cape Horn, also turned out translations, history texts, and even Hawaiian currency. The "House of Printing" has been fully restored by the **Lahaina Restoration Foundation.** ♦ Free. M-F 10AM-4PM. End of Lahainaluna Rd. 667.7040

76 Maui Islander $$ Lush tropical plants and quiet surroundings distinguish the Maui Islander, an unobtrusive, 10-acre complex of two-story walk-ups. Banana trees, ancient palms, plumeria, papaya, and large torch gingers transform this otherwise plain facility into a cool, pleasant oasis in the middle of simmering Lahaina. Its 372 newly decorated rooms, clean but unspectacular, include all the usual comforts: TVs, telephones, air-conditioning, and lanais for the two- and three-bedroom suites. For the price, location (a short walk from everything), and casual ambience, it's a fairly good choice for lodgings in Lahaina. ♦ 660 Wainee St, Lahaina. 667.9766, 800/367.5226; fax 661.3733

77 Lahaina Coolers ★$$ Very few dining establishments make it onto the locals' favorite-hangout list, but Coolers' informal atmosphere and friendly staff make this open-air restaurant and bar *the* place in Lahaina to unwind with a Kahlua and cream cocktail and a curry chicken and pasta appetizer. Open for breakfast, lunch, and dinner, the restaurant offers a host of daily specials in addition to an eclectic menu; it's hard to go wrong with the frittered French toast. Free entertainment is usually provided by the resident gecko family, which performs nightly under the neon lights. ♦ 180 Dickenson St, Lahaina. 661.7082

Restaurants/Clubs: Red   **Hotels:** Blue
Shops/ 🌴 **Outdoors:** Green   **Sights/Culture:** Black

78 Kobe Steak House ★★$$$ Lahaina's best sushi bar is located here among the teppanyaki grills and human Veg-o-Matics, whose culinary skills are as good as the food. The service is always friendly, the sushi is always fresh, and the bill is always higher than you think it'll be. For something different and unbelievably good, try the *unagi* (freshwater eel) and *dynamite* (baked scallops), with a Purple Haze (fortified sake) to wash it all down. ◆ 136 Dickenson St, Lahaina. 667.5555

79 Take Home Maui ★★$ The irony of this produce and deli shop is that it's obviously geared toward tourists (with pineapples, coconuts, Maui onions, papayas, macadamia nuts, and other delicacies to send home to loved ones), but it's always filled with locals, who come for the coffee, smoothies, pastries, and deli items. Before you spend the day driving around Maui, stop here for a cup of mac-nut or chocolate-raspberry Kona coffee and get a Moon Box lunch to go. Yes, the resident bird talks ("ah*row*ha"), and no, it won't bite (well, not often). ◆ Daily 8:30AM-6:30PM. 121 Dickenson St, Lahaina. 661.8067

80 Village Galleries In a town where marine comic-art represents big business, **Lynn Shue's** gallery, established in 1970, offers a refreshing change of genre. Roughly 90 percent of the pieces are from Hawaii's finest artists, including **George Allan** and **Pamela Andelin**, with works in all media. ◆ Daily 9AM-9PM. 120 Dickenson St, Lahaina. 661.4402

80 Baldwin House The **Reverend Dwight Baldwin,** a medical missionary, relocated from the mainland to Lahaina in 1835 for the sake of his own health, then wound up attending to the medical needs of the Hawaiians who gathered daily on his doorstep. In 1853 he singlehandedly fought to save Maui, Molokai, and Lanai from a smallpox epidemic. Until he moved to Honolulu in 1868, the reverend lived with his family in this white two-story house, the oldest standing building in Lahaina, made of coral, stone, and hand-hewn timbers. He received both ship captains and royalty, providing for them a seamen's chapel and Christian reading room. The **Lahaina Restoration Foundation** operates the Baldwin House as a museum and also has its administrative offices here. ◆ Admission. M-Sa 9AM-4:30PM; Su 11AM-4:30PM. Front St (opposite the Pioneer Inn), Lahaina. 661.3262

Friday in Hawaii is called "Aloha Friday" and most people—even the stodgiest executives—wear colorful aloha shirts and muumuus in celebration of the end of the workweek.

81 Sunrise Cafe ★$ Recovering nicely from a new face-lift, the Sunrise Cafe is a popular hangout for philosophic locals who enjoy deliberating over cappuccino and a pastry. If you miss your cafe back home, this will do in a pinch, serving light baked goods for breakfast, and sandwiches, quiche, homemade soup, and daily specials for lunch. Open at 6AM, it's also a good wake-up stop to make before an early-morning drive or boat trip. Take note, though: service is refreshingly slow. ◆ 693-A Front St (behind Lappert's Ice Cream), Lahaina. 661.3326

Gecko Roamin'

Reptiles have never had much success in the highly competitive household-pet market. But in Maui, the wall-walking Pacific gecko (or *gekkonidae peropus mutilatus*) is the island's favorite pet, leaving felines and canines in a distant second place. Why? For starters, these four- to six-inch-long lizards are free (they set up shop in people's homes, whether they're wanted or not); they don't need any maintenance; superstition holds that they bring good luck to the household; they feast on bugs, especially cockroaches; they're fascinating to watch, particularly when feeding or mating; they're completely harmless and non-poisonous; the critters make cute clucking noises; they usually remain hidden until sunset, when they start scurrying along the walls; and geckos are just plain adorable.

Not indigenous to Hawaii, the first geckos (*mo'o* in Hawaiian) probably arrived by boat, although geckologists agree that their eggs could have been carried on organic flotsam, incubating during the journey. Without many natural predators (i.e., snakes), the gecko population quickly found its niche in the households of Hawaii, particularly in Maui, and easily surpassed the television for home-entertainment value (granted, the competition was weak). Quick to seize the opportunity to make a buck, souvenir-retailers jumped on the reptilian bandwagon and, by the mid-1980s, geckomania was in full swing with gecko T-shirts, toys, tattoos, towels, and even jewelry (gold gecko pins sell for more than $275) dominating the stock of many tourist shops. In just a few short years, modern marketing catapulted this shy, innocuous reptile into the elite ranks of Mickey Mouse and Bugs Bunny—heady stuff for a little lizard.

The best location for gecko-gawking is in Lahaina, Maui, at **Lahaina Coolers,** where the hungry (and horny) wall-walkers do their intimate thing at dusk under the neon sign just over the bar. For the price of a beer, it's some of the best entertainment in town.

Banyan Tree
GEORGE ALLAN

82 The Wharf Cinema Center The Cinema Center is touristy beyond belief, housing some of Lahaina's most mediocre shops and restaurants. But it does have the only movie theater in town (when it gets *really* hot in Lahaina, even Claude Van Damme flicks are worth suffering through for 90 minutes of air-conditioned comfort). ◆ Off Front St (across from the banyan tree), Lahaina

Within The Wharf Cinema Center:

Whaler's Book Shoppe An excellent collection of books on Hawaiiana and, for its size, a respectable assemblage of fiction, nonfiction, biographies, postcards, and more. This quiet oasis from the Front Street mayhem also serves fresh-brewed gourmet coffee on the adjacent readers' terrace. ◆ Daily 9AM-9PM. 667.9544

Benihana ★$$$ As with the rest of the Benihana chain, the specialty here is *teppanyaki,* the Japanese technique of grilling food at your table. Knife-wielding performance chefs slice meat and vegetables in seconds, then grill everything tableside and serve it with a flourish. If you're in the mood for really good Japanese food, though, you'll fare better at the Kobe Steak House around the corner. ◆ 667.2244

Restaurants/Clubs: Red   Hotels: Blue
Shops/ 🌳 Outdoors: Green   **Sights/Culture:** Black

83 Banyan Tree It's hard to believe that this huge banyan—nearly a block in size with roots and overhang—stood a mere eight feet when brought to Lahaina from India. Planted in 1873 by **Sheriff William Owen Smith** to commemorate the 50th anniversary of Lahaina's first Protestant Christian mission, the venerable tree (pictured above) is among the oldest and largest in the islands. It reaches up more than 50 feet and stretches outward over a 200-foot area, shading two-thirds of an acre in the town's landmark courthouse square. ◆ Corner and Front Sts, Lahaina

83 Lahaina Courthouse The courthouse and palace of **King Kamehameha III** once stood on the site of this semidilapidated structure, but they were leveled in 1858 by gale-force winds. In 1859 the stones from the destroyed building were used to build the present courthouse, which at one time was the governmental center of Maui County. Now it's the center for the **Lahaina Arts Society,** as well as the **Old Jail Gallery** and the **Banyan Tree Gallery.** ◆ 649 Wharf St (opposite the boat harbor), Lahaina. 661.0111

83 Waterfront Fort In 1831 a legal battle raged between the whalers who were accustomed to some immediate R&R with the natives when their ships pulled into harbor and the missionaries who regarded the whole affair with disgust. A law was passed prohibiting local women from swimming out to greet the incoming ships, which prompted the rowdy whalers to fire cannons at the missionary complex. At **Queen Keopuolani's** orders, a one-acre area was then walled off to protect the citizens, with huge coral blocks hacked from the reef fronting the Lahaina shores. The fort was torn down in 1854 and the stones used to build Lahaina's prison. When Lahaina became a historical landmark, a heap of coral blocks was put together to resemble a corner of the fort—and that's about what it looks like today. ♦ Lahaina Pl on Wharf St, Lahaina

84 Pioneer Inn $ Weathered and run-down, the Pioneer Inn (pictured below) shows just how far $35 will get you in Maui if you're willing to endure a few hardships. **George Freeland,** a member of the Royal Canadian Mounted Police who fell in love with Lahaina after following a criminal to the area, built the inn at the turn of the century. Today, whaling memorabilia and funky decor complement (or partially offset) the creaky steps and stained carpets. The rooms offer bare-bones shelter for those who don't mind the noise from the saloon downstairs, which stays open until 4AM (room rates vary according to distance from the bar). Located right next to the wharf, this is precisely the place *not* to go to get away from it all. ♦ 658 Wharf St, Lahaina. 661.3636, 800/457.5457; fax 667.5708

Within the Pioneer Inn:

Pioneer Inn Harpooners Lanai $ If you're going to spend your day in Lahaina, you might as well start it here with breakfast. Although the food is hardly memorable, the energy level reflects its prime location across from the wharf. After breakfast, it's usually too hot to eat or drink here until the late afternoon, when entertainer **Trevor Jones** sings the same salty numbers he's sung for nearly a decade (3:30PM to 7:30PM every day but Friday). And thanks to some archaic legal clause, the PI doesn't stop serving alcohol when everyplace else in town does, so by 4AM *everyone* is looking good. ♦ 661.3636

Pioneer Inn Snug Harbor $ Rest your parched, wearied bones for a spell and work on a cone of shave ice. On a typical ridiculously hot Lahaina day, you'll be glad you did. ♦ 661.3636

85 Carthaginian II The original *Carthaginian* left Lahaina for Honolulu in 1972 for dry dock but instead hit a reef and sank. This cathartic 93-foot replacement—*Carthaginian II,* the only authentically restored brig in the world—sailed here from Denmark and is operated by the **Lahaina Restoration Foundation.** Below deck you can visit a museum of whaling history and watch an informative program on humpback whales, which migrate to Maui waters every winter. ♦ Admission. Daily 9AM-4PM. On the wharf opposite the Pioneer Inn, Lahaina. 661.8527

Pioneer Inn

GEORGE ALLAN

86 Lahaina Harbor Nearly all Lahaina's water activities start and finish at Lahaina Harbor, located next to the banyan tree off Front Street. Even if you have no intention of setting foot on a boat, it's worth a stroll down the harbor to watch the hustle and bustle of what used to be one of the world's busiest whaling ports. Here's a list of available activities and recommended companies: **sailing** with *First Class* (667.7733) or *Scotch Mist* (661.0386); **fishing** with *Islander II* (667.6625); **scuba diving** with Hawaiian Reef Divers (667.7647); **dinner cruises** with *Manutea* (879.4485); **all-day sailing/snorkeling trips** with *Trilogy* (661.4743); **rafting** with Ocean Riders (Mala Wharf, 661.3586); **whale watching** (in season) with *Lahaina Princess* (661.8397); **submarine rides** with *Atlantis* (see pg 31; 667.2224); and **glass-bottom-boat rides** with *Nautilus* (see pg 31; 667.2133).

87 Cafe Maestro ★$$ The Maestro serves your basic Italian pasta and salads for lunch and a full Italian menu for dinner. The relatively new restaurant doesn't quite have its act together, but its location, across from the banyan tree on Front Street, is convenient for weary shoppers who want a quick, light lunch. After dinner, the Maestro performs to a mostly gay audience. ♦ 608 Front St, Lahaina. 661.8001

87 Dan's Greenhouse Although it's only a half-block off Front Street, this plant and animal emporium is easily bypassed—but shouldn't be. The specialty here is certified bonsais ready to ship home, along with orchids, Maui onion seeds, sprouted coconuts, and other packaged Hawaiian plants. The showstoppers, though, are the "super-tame tropical birds" that love to cuddle and croon. They're also for sale, but before you get too attached, check out the price tags—ol' Prince Ele, a quixotic and enigmatic black palm cockatoo from way far away, goes for $25,000. Not for sale are the frisky gold-handed tamarins caged in the parking lot around the entrance. Ask the friendly staff for a handful of Cheerios to feed them. ♦ Daily 9AM-5PM. 133 Prison St, Lahaina. 661.8412

88 Hale Paahao Built in 1852 by convicts, this structure was once Lahaina's prison (the name means "the stuck-in-irons house").

Most of the inmates were drunken sailors who failed to return to their ships at sundown, although some were confined for desertion, working on Sunday, or dangerous horseback riding. Ball-and-chain and wall shackles further restrained troublemakers. ♦ Prison and Wainee Sts, Lahaina.

89 Wainee Churchyard Both prominent and anonymous residents of early Lahaina are buried in this first Christian cemetery in Hawaii, built in 1823. Many of the graves are those of missionaries' children (infant mortality was high then); others belong to Hawaiian royalty, including **Queen Keopuolani**—wife of **King Kamehameha I**, mother of **Kamehameha II** and **Kamehameha III**, and the first Hawaiian convert to be baptized a Protestant and given a Christian burial; her daughter, **Nahienaena**; the last king of Kauai, **King Kaumualii**; high chief **Hoapili**, Keopuolani's second husband; and **Kekauonohi**, one of the five queens of Kamehameha II.

To the right of the churchyard is the latest rendition of **Wainee Church.** The original Wainee, the first stone church on Maui, was built by Hawaiians for the missionaries in 1832, seating up to 3,000 on the floor. Its history is one bad luck story after another: the church lost its roof in an 1858 whirlwind; was burned down in 1894 by Hawaiians opposed to the overthrow of their monarchy; was rebuilt in 1897, only to be partly destroyed by fire in 1947; and was toppled by another whirlwind in 1951. Again the church was rebuilt—this time with a changed name, in hopes of breaking the spell. ♦ 535 Wainee St, Lahaina. 661.4349

90 505 Front Street Designed to resemble a New England whaling village, this small jumble of boutiques, stores, restaurants, and a dance club actually offers more than most of the larger malls lining Front Street. And it's within easy walking distance of the banyan tree. ♦ Lahaina

Within 505 Front Street:

Old Lahaina Luau ★★$$$ As commercial luaus go, this is West Maui's finest—a smooth blend of exoticism, good food, and memorable entertainment. Torches and palm trees, traditionally clad young men and women, and an *imu* (earthen oven) roasting a 200-pound pig combine to make for an enjoyable evening. Far from the patronizing program that characterizes many "authentic" native shows, this one includes both ancient and modern renditions of the hula, along with impressive dramatic touches such as a torch-lit canoe offshore. The all-you-can-eat buffet of Hawaiian favorites likewise surpasses the norm. Open bar. ♦ Tu-Sa 5:30-8:30PM. Reservations recommended. 667.1998

Juicy's Tropical Juice Bar ★$ Like the name says, it's a juice bar that doubles as something else: in this case a health-food cafe serving garden burgers, veggie burritos, salads, smoothies, and monthly veggie specials. Winner of the "Da Kine Grinds" health-food contest, Juicy's is the only juice bar in Lahaina. Outside seating or take-out. ♦ 667.5727

J.J.'s Beach Grill ★$$$ J.J.'s selling point is its memorable outside dining area with a view of the island of Lanai and some of the most beautiful sunsets on the planet. The Continental cuisine, while no match for the setting, is still quite good, especially the rack of lamb, New York steak, and the seared sashimi appetizer (simply unbelievable, folks). The polished wood bar is perfect for an afternoon cocktail or seven, with a friendly staff and a laid-back ambience that attracts even the hard-to-please locals. ♦ 667.4341

Village Pizzeria ★$$ There's no view, no live music, and yet no question that Village Pizzeria serves the best pie in Lahaina: the halitosis house special, clam and garlic pizza. Bring your toothbrush. ♦ 661.8112

Studio 505 Until Blue Tropix came to town, Studio 505 was the only dance club around. Part-owned by **Stephen Stills**, it's unquestionably trendy, with the standard disco setup: flashing lights, action videos, elevated dance floor, overpriced drinks, monolithic bouncers, clueless bachelors, and a pounding dance beat. On weekends **Marty Dread** does a reggae act that's worth seeing once. If you like to dance or just stand around and look cool, you'll probably enjoy 505. ♦ Cover. Daily 9PM-2AM. 661.1505

91 Lahaina Shores $$$ What makes Lahaina Shores unique is that it's the only hotel in town that's right on the beach, with a comfortable pool and a grassy sunbathing area bordering the sand. Once a rambling, plantation-style mansion, the building has been converted into a 199-room hotel with studios, one-bedrooms, and penthouse suites, all with full kitchens, daily maid service, and reasonable rates. Considering the location, price, and spacious accommodations, the Shores won't disappoint even the pickiest of travelers. ♦ 75 Front St, Lahaina. 661.4835, 800/628.6699

92 Puamana Beach Park Small and unspectacular, Puamana is the closest beach park to Lahaina. The water is fairly shallow, with a rock and sand ocean floor. Fair swimming, summer surfing, and picnic facilities. ♦ Public access on Front St, 2 miles east of Lahaina

93 Olowalu Historians know this seaside village as the site of the 1790 Olowalu Massacre, when **Captain Simon Metcalfe**, seeking revenge for the loss of a sailor and a boat (presumably at the hands of local thieves), invited a group of Hawaiians to visit his American trading ship under the pretense of trading goods. Once the natives had gathered on the starboard side of the *Eleanora*, Metcalfe ordered the gunwales uncovered. He and his men fired down on the startled, defenseless islanders, killing more than one hundred and seriously wounding many more. An equally morbid story is the recent shark attack of an unfortunate Olowalu resident who swam directly into a feeding frenzy (she didn't survive). A nearby cliff face covered with petroglyphs indicates that the impervious West Maui Mountains were once traversable through an ancient trail connecting Olowalu to Iao Valley. ♦ Off Hwy 30, 4 miles south of Lahaina

93 Chez Paul ★★$$$$ A dining landmark in West Maui, Chez Paul dates back more than a decade, when Boston Irishman **Paul Kirk** and his French wife, **Fernie**, sold their highly successful Santa Barbara restaurant and opened a tiny French place in the middle of nowhere. Their unusual operation was in a shabby building that had a certain cachet, especially when juxtaposed against the ultra-chic Kaanapali establishments. Today's Chez Paul, run by **Lucien Charbonnier**, loses big points for its outdated, overpriced menu and tired ambience. Besides, for only a few dollars more and four miles away, connoisseurs of fine French cuisine can dine at **Gerard's** (*bon appétit!*). ♦ Off Hwy 30, Olowalu. 661.3843

93 Olowalu General Store Another classic Hawaiian phenomenon is the old-fashioned general store, which sells a little of everything you'll ever need on an island. If you're going to spend the day at Olowalu Beach, stop here first and pick up some *onolicious* homemade local grinds, all packaged and ready to go. But watch out for the treacherous turnoff—locals don't slow down. ♦ M-F 5:30AM-6:30PM; Sa 7AM-6:30PM; Su 8AM-6PM. 820 Olowalu Village, Olowalu. 661.3774

94 Olowalu Beach It remains a Maui mystery why so many tourists are smitten with this beach. Yes, the snorkeling is usually good, especially for beginners, but the stretch of gray sand just south of Olowalu is tiny, damp, and right off a busy highway. No facilities. ♦ Off Hwy 30 at the 14-mile marker

---

Restaurants/Clubs: Red   Hotels: Blue
Shops/ 🌿 Outdoors: Green   **Sights/Culture:** Black

69

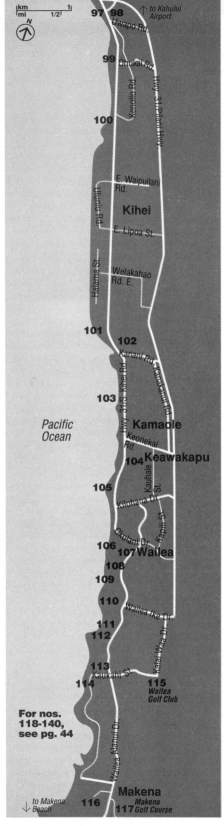

For nos. 118-140, see pg. 44

95 Maalaea Harbor Unless you're told by tour operators to come here, there's no real reason to stop unless you're craving a bowl of clam chowder at **Buzz's Wharf** ($$). ♦ Off Hwy 30, near the N. Kihei Rd turnoff

96 Maui Tropical Plantation Sugarcane, pineapples, bananas, papayas, coffee beans, macadamia nuts, exotic flowers, and other crops can be found in this 112-acre showcase for Hawaii agriculture. The park was developed by Australians **Bill** and **Lynn Taylor** on land owned by the **C. Brewer Corporation.** More than a dozen crops in the shape of a fan emanate from the restaurant and market area; 45-minute narrated tram tours take you through 50 acres of the plantation with stops for walking around to take a closer look. The *kapu* (Keep Out) signs posted in most agricultural areas in the islands are nowhere in sight here.

Orchids, hibiscus, and other greenhouse plants in the nursery can be shipped home, and a marketplace sells produce grown on the property, including a specially bred fruit that's been inspected and approved for shipment from the island. The **Tropical Restaurant** (★$$) serves fresh fruit creations (try the *lilikoi* and ginger parfaits); around noon there's a tropical luncheon buffet; and on Tuesday, Wednesday, and Friday (5PM to 7:30PM) the plantation puts on a Hawaiian country barbecue with *paniolo* (cowboy) entertainment and square dancing, featuring steaks, chili, a salad bar, and macadamia nut pie. All in all, it's touristy but enjoyable. Shuttle service is available from designated pick-up points. ♦ Daily 9AM-5PM. Hwy 30, Waikapu. 244.7643

97 Kihei The town of Kihei is a prime example of what happens when there's no central planning for urban development. Shamefully overbuilt and crowded, and utterly lacking any cohesive form or design, this stretch of coast has just one or two selling points apart from the consistently sunny weather: less-expensive accommodations than in Lahaina, and above-average beaches (unfortunately, though, most are hidden behind a ragtag assortment of hotels and condos, and they're also notoriously windy; by early afternoon, you'll give up trying to keep your beach towel in place). ♦ For information about condominium rentals in Kihei, call Condominium Rentals Hawaii at 879.2778, and be sure to specify if you want a room on the beach.

98 **Surfer Joe's** ★$ This casual indoor/outdoor tavern offers an array of local and American favorites but mainly focuses on Mexican food (burritos, enchiladas, etc.). It's a good place to stop and relax with a beer and a fried zucchini appetizer. ◆ 61 S. Kihei Rd, Kihei. 879.8855

99 **Mai Poina Oe Lau Beach Park** Although the wind picks up in the afternoon, this is a good swimming beach with a few rocks on the sandy ocean bottom. You can still see what's left of the old Kihei Landing at the shoreline. Picnic and public facilities. ◆ Off S. Kihei Rd, Kihei

100 **Kalepolepo Beach** Remains of a fish pond create a nice wading pool for children, but ocean swimming is trickier because of the rocky bottom. This area was once a Hawaiian village with taro patches, coconut groves, shoreline fish ponds, churches, and a small whaling station. Picnic and barbecue facilities. ◆ Off S. Kihei Rd, Kihei

101 **Kalama Beach Park** This 36-acre park is more for sports enthusiasts than beachgoers, the prime attractions being soccer and baseball fields, volleyball and basketball courts, tennis courts, and a children's playground. ◆ Across from the Kihei Town Center, Kihei

102 **Island Fish House** ★★$$$ The excellent fresh fish, usually a choice of *ono,* mahimahi, *opakapaka, ahi,* or *uku* (when available) is served either sautéed, charbroiled, baked, or deep fried, depending on your preference. Steak and chicken are also on the menu, but this is the best place in Kihei to feast on the catch of the day. ◆ 1945 S. Kihei Rd, Kihei. 879.7771

103 **Kamaole Beaches** All three beach parks (marked I, II, and III) run along the south end of Kihei and have great sand, good swimming, and picnic and public facilities (including lifeguards). Kamaole III has a playground, while the reef area between II and III is good for snorkeling. ◆ S. Kihei Rd (about 1 mile south of Kalama Beach Park), Kihei

104 **Aston Kamaole Sands** $$ One of the best deals on Maui, especially for families. The well-managed, roomy condos sit on 15 acres across the street from the Kamaole Beach parks, and many of the suites look out across the ocean to the islands of Molokini and Lanai. Fully equipped kitchens include a dishwasher, and there's also a washer/dryer and daily maid service. Amenities include a swimming and wading pool, two spas, a restaurant and barbecue area, and tennis courts. ◆ 2695 S. Kihei Rd, Kihei. 874.8700, 800/922.7866

105 **Mana Kai Ocean Terrace** ★$$$ The same folks who run the **Island Fish House** turned this restaurant into a pleasant spot for oceanside dining, with half the seating area open to the sea. The sunny ambience is perfect for casual meals: burgers, sandwiches, and salads for lunch; steaks, chicken, and fresh fish for dinner. Ask about the early-bird dinner specials from 5PM to 6PM. ◆ 2960 S. Kihei Rd (in the Mana Kai Maui Resort), Kihei. 879.2607

105 **Carrelli's** ★★$$$ One of the few highly commendable restaurants in Kihei is ideally situated right on the beach, serving gourmet Italian cuisine in an open-air setting. Menu selections include homemade pizzas, fresh seared *ahi sorrentine,* and the *specialità della casa*—Carrelli's *zuppa di mare cioppino,* a tempting assortment of clams, mussels, scallops, prawns, lobster, squid, and crab in a spicy tomato sauce. Factor in Maui's stunning sunsets, and it's hard not to enjoy an evening at Carrelli's. ◆ 2980 S. Kihei Rd, Kihei. 875.0001

106 **Keawakapu Beach** South Kihei Road dead-ends at the parking lot of this charming beach with excellent swimming (thanks to a sandy bottom) and fair snorkeling. ◆ End of S. Kihei Rd, Kihei

The Mighty Mongoose

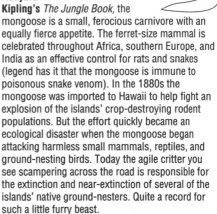

Made famous as Rikki-Tikki-Tavi in **Rudyard Kipling's** *The Jungle Book,* the mongoose is a small, ferocious carnivore with an equally fierce appetite. The ferret-size mammal is celebrated throughout Africa, southern Europe, and India as an effective control for rats and snakes (legend has it that the mongoose is immune to poisonous snake venom). In the 1880s the mongoose was imported to Hawaii to help fight an explosion of the islands' crop-destroying rodent populations. But the effort quickly became an ecological disaster when the mongoose began attacking harmless small mammals, reptiles, and ground-nesting birds. Today the agile critter you see scampering across the road is responsible for the extinction and near-extinction of several of the islands' native ground-nesters. Quite a record for such a little furry beast.

Most rental-car companies have banned the use of their vehicles on Maui's Crater Road because of repeated brake failure while descending Haleakala volcano. (Car manufacturers blamed brake failure on drivers who fail to shift into low gear, while local mechanics argue that the brakes are poorly designed.)

107 Wailea In 1973 it was hardly imaginable that this 1,500-acre stretch of coastline dotted with patches of scraggly *kiawe* and *wiliwili* trees would become the site of a deluxe resort area, but Wailea had two lucrative things going for it: great weather and white sand beaches. Located on the dry, leeward side of Haleakala, the area has an average yearly rainfall of 11 inches and an average temperature of 75.15° F. Not only is the volcano a beautiful backdrop, but it also acts as a natural buffer from rain and wind. Each of Wailea's five beaches has a smooth, sandy bottom protected by coral reefs, excellent for both swimming and snorkeling.

Built in 1976, the **Maui Inter-Continental** was the first Wailea resort hotel, followed two years later by the **Stouffer Wailea Beach Resort.** In 1990 the **Four Seasons Resort** opened, followed by the **Grand Hyatt** in 1991 and, soon afterward, the enigmatic **Kae Lani Hotel.** All of this portends well for Wailea, which is beginning to be considered a luxury resort on the level of the Big Island's Kohala Coast. Within the region you'll find 36 holes of golf, one of the largest tennis complexes on the islands, the Wailea Shopping Village, and a number of first-rate restaurants.
◆ S. Kihei Rd and Kilohana Dr

108 Stouffer Wailea Beach Resort $$$$ Newly renovated to the tune of $43 million, this AAA five-diamond hotel—the only one in Hawaii to receive that rating for 11 consecutive years—has never been better. It's a luxury hotel for the traveler who likes to get away from it all but not too far from room service or a world-class restaurant. The secluded setting is small (15.5 acres) and intimate, with dense, lush landscaping and an array of bridges and pathways that lend themselves to romance, lingering, and the occasional wedding. Many of the 350 rooms have ocean views, and all are the same size—small but very pleasant, with spacious lanais.

The **Mokapu Beach Club,** a separate wing with 26 cottagelike suites on the beach, offers VIP perks and services: a club host, Continental breakfast brought daily to the room, and other assorted luxuries. The beautiful, peaceful beach is ideal for swimming, sunning, snorkeling, or windsurfing. Stouffer Wailea is also the site of the **Maui Marine Art Expo,** a widely acclaimed, wildly successful event featuring hundreds of works. Pool, three new whirlpool spas in the garden, golf, and tennis. ◆ 3550 Wailea Alanui Dr, Wailea. 879.4900; 800/992.4532; fax 874.5370

Within the Stouffer Wailea Beach Resort:

Raffles ★★★$$$$ This spacious and beautiful dining establishment was named after **Sir Thomas Stamford Raffles,** founder of the city of Singapore, home to the legendary **Raffles Hotel.** Bronze chandeliers, teak floors, Oriental rugs, and Chinese ceramics complement chefs **Peter Genera** and **Richard Matsumoto's** Euro-Asian cuisine prepared with an island flair (about 75 percent of the herbs, produce, poultry, and fish are from local sources). Try the wok-seared mahimahi with green papaya relish and *lilikoi* shallot butter. The menu includes many fresh seafood specialties, rack of lamb, and a renowned dessert soufflé. Raffles' lavish Sunday brunch shouldn't be missed. Piano music nightly. ◆ 879.4900

109 Ulua Beach Located in front of the Stouffer Wailea, this well-maintained white sand stretch is the most popular of the Wailea beach quintet, and the best for bodysurfing. On calm days, snorkeling is excellent because of the exceptionally clear water. ◆ Use the Alanui Dr access road just after the Stouffer Wailea Beach Resort and take the walkway from the landscaped park to the beach on the left

110 Maui Inter-Continental Wailea $$$ In 1991 a lengthy $37 million renovation left this AAA four-diamond hotel with a dramatic design, including a new porte cochere, a Hawaiian roofline based on the architecture of **C.W. Dickey,** and lounges and restaurants that had been redecorated, renamed, and revived (unfortunately, the best restaurant, **La Perouse,** was somehow lost in the shuffle). Flanked by a white sand crescent beach on either side, it occupies 22 acres of oceanfront, with 550 rooms and suites in seven low-rise buildings, and a seven-story tower. Activities include privileges at the **Wailea Golf Club** and the 14 tennis courts (grass and hard). ◆ 3700 Wailea Alanui Dr, Wailea. 879.1922, 800/332.4246; fax 879.7658

111 Grand Hyatt Wailea $$$$ As usual, the designers from Hyatt have taken the concept of a mega-resort hotel to an entirely new level of opulence. Spearheaded by developer **Takeshi Sekiguchi,** this Disney-esque creation peaked at a final cost of a whopping $600 million, with 787 rooms and suites covering 40 acres of impeccably maintained landscape and attractions, including: a $15 million water playground (at Hyatt, there's no such thing as a "pool"); $30 million in museum-quality artwork from around the world, including Colombian sculptor **Fernando Botero's** nine buxom bronzes (a must-see) and various other works from Frenchmen **Jan Fisher, Fernand Leger,** and a dozen others; a 300,000-square-foot floor of stone composite quarried from around the world; 12 lounges and six restaurants—including the celebrated **Cafe Kula** (★★★$$); **Camp Hyatt Wailea,** a phenomenal kids' program; a 50,000-square-foot health spa; and various recreational activities, including golf, tennis, scuba diving, sailing, windsurfing, and deep-sea fishing.

With rates starting at $350 and topping out at $8,000 per night, the Hyatt obviously caters to an exclusive clientele, but nonguests are more than welcome to ogle and explore what unlimited funds and a prodigal imagination can accomplish. ◆ 3850 Wailea Alanui Dr, Wailea. 875.1234, 800/233.1234; fax 874.5143

112 Four Seasons Resort $$$$ Billing itself as an island of tranquility within an island, this eight-story, 380-room hotel offers comfortable rooms and super-deluxe, mansionlike suites on 15 acres at Wailea Beach. The specially commissioned works of art in the public areas are scaled to the architecture—understated, yet impressive. The rooms feature teak interior on the lanais, potted orchids, and thick-cushioned rattan furniture. The enormous bathrooms are all marble and mirrors, each with a deep bathtub, separate glass shower, and an eight-foot marble counter with double vanities. Most of the rooms have ocean views, and all have large lanais; TV and VCR; a fully stocked refrigerated bar; and twice-daily maid service.

The Four Seasons also prides itself on its personal services: Attendants on the large pool terrace will bring you towels and chilled Evian spritzers, gratis, and your shoes are shined while you sleep; general manager **Peter O'Colmain** trots out the sterling silver coffee urns and croissants at 5AM for jet-lagged international tourists. To keep up with changing demands, the Seasons has added an extensive aerobic facility and weight room, as well as a kids' program that focuses on Hawaiian culture and nature. ◆ 3900 Wailea Alanui Dr, Wailea. 874.8000, 800/334.6284; fax 874.6449

Within the Four Seasons Resort:

Seasons ★★★$$$$ The open-air dining room has a piano, a small dance floor, and an unforgettable menu. You can't help but notice the effort to use island ingredients in innovative ways. There's a spinach salad with local mountain apple, a Big Island pink-abalone ceviche, *lilikoi* (passion fruit) risotto, and, of course, fresh fish or chicken embellished with mango, watercress, seaweed, and papaya. The extraordinary dining experience is enhanced by the crisp,

cordial service. Be sure to try the desserts (ask about the chocolate *marjolaine*) and vintage port, then end the evening by dancing cheek-to-cheek. ◆ Jacket required. 874.8000

113 Kea Lani Hotel $$$$ If you can get past the garish Arabian architecture (a bombardment of whitewashed domes, arches, and tents), you'll find 450 of the largest suites in all of Hawaii. At a minimum of 840 square feet each, every unit of Hawaii's first all-suite luxury resort is literally twice the size of an average hotel room and impeccably furnished, with marble European bathrooms containing oversize "love-tubs"; entertainment centers including VCR, CD player, and wide-screen TV; a fully stocked bar; and a huge bedroom with a cozy king-size bed. Amenities include two restaurants, three pools, an excellent white sand beach for snorkeling and swimming, and complimentary transportation to the nearby championship golf courses and tennis courts. For honeymooners who don't plan on getting out much, this is the place. ◆ 4100 Wailea Alanui Dr, Wailea. 875.4100, 800/882.4100; fax 875.1200

114 Polo Beach Club $$$$ If the Grand Hyatt is exactly the type of resort you want to avoid, then perhaps you'd prefer this subdued condo resort. Hidden behind the Kea Lani Hotel, the well-appointed two-bedroom, two-bathroom ocean-view apartments are set on a white sand beach. The club includes a pool, spa, and sun deck, with easy access to Wailea's golf and tennis clubs. ◆ 20 Makena Rd, Wailea. 879.1595, 800/367.5246; fax 874.3554

114 Polo Beach Because of its somewhat remote location, Polo Beach used to be comparatively uncrowded until the Kea Lani Hotel was built directly behind it. There's still public access (by law), along with a parking lot in front of the Polo Beach Club. The sandy bottom and rock outcroppings make this a great swimming and snorkeling beach. Public facilities. ◆ Off Wailea Alanui Dr (turn right just past the Kea Lani Hotel), Wailea

115 Wailea Golf Club One of Wailea's main attractions is a pair of carefully manicured, bone-dry courses on the leeward slopes of Haleakala Crater. The **Blue Course** is visually pleasing but less exciting than the longer **Orange Course,** which has more hills and trees, and even ancient Hawaiian stone walls. Be prepared for strong afternoon winds. Orange Course: par 72, 6,810 yards. Blue Course: par 72, 6,700 yards. ◆ Expensive green fees; preferred starting times to Wailea Resort hotel guests. Pro shop 879.2966

73

116 Maui Prince Hotel $$$$ Somewhat controversial when it opened in 1986 owing to its spare, Japanese-influenced architecture and decor, the Maui Prince has matured into a beautiful resort that many former critics have grown to appreciate. The 310 rooms, each designed in an arrowhead shape, have wide, unobstructed ocean views encompassing the islands of Molokini and Kahoolawe. The central courtyard, with waterfalls, rock gardens, fish ponds, and footpaths, is a lush, pleasing centerpiece where musicians perform for passersby. On arrival, guests are greeted with hot, almond-scented towels (the traditional *oshibori* service) to freshen up after their journey to this rather isolated location at the western end of the island. Compared to the nearby resorts of Wailea, the Maui Prince leans toward the unpretentious, capitalizing on its secluded location to attract a clientele that prefers anonymity. The resort also contains the **Makena Golf Course,** an award-winning tennis facility, and two pools. ♦ 5400 Makena Alanui, Makena. 874.1111, 800/321.6284; fax 879.0082

Within the Maui Prince Hotel:

Hakone ★★★$$$ The Japanese wood interior, black slate floors, and clean, refined ambience are well-suited to the fine food and professional service. Multicourse *kaiseki* dinners consist of dainty samplings of soup, salad, appetizers, and fish—raw, boiled, grilled, or fried. The sushi is excellent, the *chawanmushi* (a light steamed custard) otherworldly, and ordinary dishes such as tempura and noodles are cooked to perfection. ♦ 874.1111

Prince Court ★★★★$$$$ Chef **Roger Dikon** catapulted this restaurant into Maui's culinary heights with his exuberant menu. Listed in the *Who's Who in American Restaurants,* it's a place where even the appetizers—notably Hawaiian slipper-lobster ravioli, stuffed sashimi, and sautéed crab cake (with grilled Maui onion guacamole)—become dining adventures. And the world-class Hawaiian regional cuisine, which includes exotic entrées such as *kiawe*-grilled shrimp in a lime-leaf marinade, catch of the day in avocado butter and macadamia-nut oil, and Hawaiian slipper-lobster in a curry sauce, perfectly complement the elegant setting and sunset views. The Sunday brunch, with free-flowing champagne and hundreds of international dishes, shouldn't be missed. ♦ 874.1111

117 Makena Golf Course Robert Trent Jones, Jr., designed this Makena Resort course, which has mountain and ocean views, tight fairways, huge greens, and enough sand to cover a generous portion of beach. Named one of the top 10 courses in Hawaii by *Golf Digest,* it was recently expanded by an additional 18 holes. The 15th and 16th holes skirt the ocean, and throughout you can spot glimpses of quail, *panini* plants, hibiscus, and the rolling hills of Ulupalakua. Par 72, 6,739 yards. ♦ 5415 Makena Alaniu, Makena. Pro shop 879.3344

118 Makena Beach More than 3,000 feet long and 100 feet wide, this is the beach of choice for Maui's *kamaaina* (locals), who have been coming here with their families and their coolers for generations. Makena (also called **Oneloa Beach**) is a glorious, golden stretch still fondly remembered as "Big Beach"; over a hill to the right is Little Beach. Both are excellent swimming spots but must be approached with caution because of occasional steep shore breaks and riptides. Though Makena is unofficially thought of as a nude beach, visitors who have been arrested have found out the hard way that nude sunbathing is prohibited by Hawaii state law. ♦ Off Makena Rd, 1.1 miles past the Maui Prince Hotel (look for the newly paved road and parking lot), Makena

119 Tedeschi Vineyards The rich volcanic soil of Ulupalakua has proved fertile ground for Hawaii's first and only commercial vineyard. Today the 22-acre enterprise produces a variety of wines, including a Pineapple Blanc, the Maui Brut Champagne Blanc de Noir, the Rose Ranch Cuvee, the Maui Blush, and the Maui Nouveau. It all began in 1974, when vintner **Emil Tedeschi** (te-DES-ki) and **Pardee Erdman,** owner of the surrounding 22,000-acre **Ulupalakua Ranch,** experimented with numerous varieties of grapes to determine which would best adapt to the 2,000-foot elevation. They eventually decided that the Carnelian grape, a cross developed at the University of California at Davis, had the best prospects. You can tour the winery (an old whitewashed structure that was once the jailhouse on the ranch), where Hawaiian royalty and visiting dignitaries used to gather for lavish parties. An interesting side trip for wine connoisseurs or anyone driving through Maui's beautiful up-country. ♦ Free guided tours daily 9:30AM-2:30PM; tasting room daily 9AM-5PM. Take Hwy 37 from Kahului toward Haleakala to the junction of Hwys 37 and 377, then continue 10 miles uphill on Hwy 37. 878.6058

According to the *New York Times,* the residents of Hawaii are America's leading consumers of Spam, a canned meat.

Restaurants/Clubs: Red   **Hotels:** Blue
Shops/ 🌳 **Outdoors:** Green   **Sights/Culture:** Black

120 Bloom Cottage $$ Situated high on the western slopes of Haleakala overlooking Maui's picturesque leeward coast, Bloom Cottage is perhaps the nicest B&B on the island. **Herb** and **Lynne Horner's** secluded inn is reminiscent of an English country cottage, with a four-poster bed, fireplace, handmade quilts, Victorian prints, and an aromatic display of fresh herbs picked from their garden. Also included in the surprisingly reasonable price is a fully stocked kitchen, an alcove with a single bed, and complete privacy. Located just off the Kula Highway, this bright, cheerful, and wonderfully decorated hostelry is highly recommended. ♦ 229 Kula Hwy (between the 15- and 16-mile marker at Maukanani Rd), Kula. 878.1425

120 Country Garden Cottage $$ Located next to Bloom Cottage, **Barbara** and **Robert Wimberley's** one-bedroom B&B is heavily ensconced by plants and trees from around the globe, brought back and planted by a sea captain who once lived here. Connected to the main house by a common porch, this relatively new establishment isn't quite up to its neighbor's standards (yet) but offers some unique services, including baby-sitting (Barbara's kids make great playmates) and personal room service that includes a nightly stocked fireplace. The cottage comes with a fully supplied kitchen, queen-size bed, double futon, comfy couch, and (upon request) complete privacy. ♦ 224 Kula Hwy (between the 15- and 16-mile marker at Maukanani Rd), Kula. 878.2858

121 Halemanu $$ The lack of hotels and resorts in Kula and its growing popularity have inspired some terrific bed-and-breakfast operations in the area. Because these retreats are small, few, and far between, they don't impede on the rural experience yet do offer a combination of first-class accommodations and exceptional, personal, friendly service. Halemanu, meaning "Perch" or "Birdhouse," is just that—an elevated, 3,600-foot aerie with a spectacular view, along with a hostess who has impeccable taste and loves to cook. Maui native and newspaper columnist **Carol Austin's** two-story B&B inn is filled with collectibles from all over the world, and complete attention to detail is evident right down to the design (e.g., the bathtub faces the ocean). The guest room has a queen-size bed, private bath, and a deck overlooking a spectacular vista. If you don't mind the 40-minute drive to the beach, this is an excellent choice for a memorable vacation. ♦ 221 Kawehi Pl, Kula. (Take Kula Hwy toward Kula. Just before the 14-mile marker, turn left onto Kekaulike Hwy and, after 3/10ths of a mile, turn right on Waipoli and right again on Kawehi Pl and look for the "Halemanu" sign.) 878.2729

Cruising the Up-Country

The cattle and farming land on the fertile slopes of **Haleakala** is Maui's "up-country," extending from the 10,000-foot summit to the island's isthmus and resting at the foot of the West Maui Mountains. A casual drive to these parts offers a chance to explore another side of Maui—where people, including residents, go to escape the crowded beach scene. The verdant rolling hills and cool, fresh air seem to miraculously erase tension and worry. In fact, it's quite common for smitten tourists to make the up-country their new home—it's that pleasant.

The best route to the up-country is along **Baldwin Avenue,** which begins in lower Paia just east of Kahului Airport. The gently ascending road is bordered by fragrant eucalyptus trees, cactus plants, brightly flowering jacarandas, and green hillsides where cattle graze among brilliant wildflowers. The air grows much cooler as you reach the top, so bring a jacket. And on your way, take the time to stop in **Paia,** once the hub of Maui's commercial scene (notice all of the closed gas stations) and now just a pleasant shopping and snacking stop on everyone's way to somewhere else; **Makawao,** an artsy little town with great shops and restaurants; and the area of **Kula,** where the scenery alone is worth the excursion.

122 Haleakala Crater Haleakala (which means "House of the Sun"), the world's largest dormant volcano, is the showpiece of the 27,284-acre **Haleakala National Park.** High above the ubiquitous cloud layer is the huge, moonlike crater—21 miles in circumference and 3,000 feet deep, with 30 miles of interior trails winding around nine cinder cones. Measuring 10,023 feet from the seafloor, it is definitely Maui's highest elevation—ideal for a gorgeous sunrise or spectacular vista.

Hawaiian legends flourish around this giant landmark, and modern-day spiritualists make a pilgrimage here for inner renewal (even U.S. Air Force research indicates Haleakala is the strongest natural power point in America). The drive takes about 90 minutes from Kahului to the summit (open 24 hours daily), and it's a good idea to bring something warm to wear or wrap up in. If you're going to see the sunrise, bring something *very* warm, because it's at least 30 degrees cooler here than down in the flatlands. A flashlight will also help you navigate from the parking lot up to the unattended observatory at the summit lookout. Be sure to call park information (572.7749) the night before for sunrise time and viewing conditions.

If the idea of rolling out of bed at 4AM doesn't appeal to you, there's still plenty to see and do here during the day; stop at the headquarters near the park entrance for maps, information, or camping and hiking permits. En route to the summit 11 miles from the entrance are two overlooks and a **Visitors Center,** where park rangers conduct scheduled tours. Although many car-rental companies don't want their vehicles on Haleakala Highway for fear of possible brake failure, you're only held liable if something goes wrong with the car (in other words, nobody's checking); drivers of any vehicles should make sure to use the lower gears when descending. For a truly unforgettable experience, see if you can score one of the very inexpensive Haleakala cabins. (Reserved by monthly lottery; cabin requests must be made 90 days in advance. Send requests with preferred and alternate days to Haleakala National Park, Box 369, Makawao, Hawaii 96768.) Like the Grand Canyon or Niagara Falls, Haleakala Crater is one of those things that has to be seen at least once in your life. ♦ Admission charge per car. Park Headquarters/Visitors Center open daily 7:30AM-4PM. Haleakala Visitors Center open daily sunrise-3PM. From Kahului Airport, follow the signs from Hwys 37 to 377 to 378 to Haleakala (37 miles). 572.9306

123 Kula Lodge $$$ When the residents of Maui need a mini-vacation or a weekend of romance, they come here. Located high upon the cool grassy slopes of Maui's up-country, the Kula Lodge is an extreme digression from the typical Hawaiian resort: there's no sand, no activities, no tropical ambience, and the temperature at 3,200 feet rarely rises above cool. The five individual chalets are small but cozy, with private lanais overlooking incredible vistas. Three of the chalets have fireplaces (a must for couples), and four have lofts for children. The adjoining **Kula Lodge Restaurant** (★$$$) has the best panorama in Maui, although the cuisine and service could stand a little improvement (fortunately,

excellent restaurants are only a short drive away). Spending the day at nearby **Makena Beach** (one of the best) and the evening by the fire at the lodge watching the sun set is as good as it gets on Maui. ♦ Off Hwy 377. Take Hwy 37 from Kahului to Hwy 377 (Haleakala Hwy), Kula. 878.1535, 800/233.1535; fax 878.2518

124 Bullocks of Hawaii ★$ Before touring Haleakala Crater, stop at this funky little diner, home of the "moonburger": two all-sirloin patties, special "moon" sauce, and the works on a buttered and grilled bun (and ask **Hazel Bullocks** to whip up a pure fruit-nectar shake). ♦ 3494 Haleakala Hwy, Pukalani. 572.7220

125 Olinda Drive If you continue on **Baldwin Avenue** (Highway 390) past Makawao, it turns into Olinda Road, a pleasant, nine-mile loop of scenic vistas, small forests, and enviable homesteads. The narrow, winding road eventually returns to the main highway just below Makawao. ♦ Hwy 390, about a 45-minute drive

Braking Away: Maui by Bike

Those of you willing to wake up at an ungodly hour and spend about $100 to bike down a 10,000-foot volcano, keep reading. A unique vacation experience awaits you in Maui: coasting for 38 miles down the slopes of **Haleakala Crater** on a specially designed bicycle. Before sunrise, a driver will pick you up at your hotel and, after coddling you with coffee and doughnuts, take you to the top of Haleakala, where you will be outfitted with a single-speed bike (equipped with megabrakes), a windbreaker, gloves, and a helmet. The chilly but pleasant ride takes about three-and-a-half hours, cruising through cattle ranches, protea farms, and sugarcane and pineapple fields, with a stop in the picturesque town of **Kula** for lunch. The entire trip ranges from memorable to miserable depending on the unpredictable weather, but one thing is certain: it's downhill all the way.

Bicycle tours from Haleakala are offered daily by **Cruiser Bob's Haleakala Downhill Bike Ride,** 579.8444 or 800/654.7717; **Maui Mountain Cruisers,** 871.6014; and **Maui Downhill,** 871.2155.

Hawaii, the southernmost state in the United States, is the only island state in the country, and it is larger than Rhode Island, Delaware, and Connecticut combined.

126 Makawao Rodeo If y'all plan on being in Maui around the Fourth of July, try to score tickets for the island's most anticipated event: the annual Makawao Rodeo. It's a real down-and-dirty experience, with the best *paniolos* (cowboys) from Hawaii roping and riding wild broncos and bulls while jubilant spectators revel in the beer, junk food, and country music. ♦ Oskie Rice Rodeo Arena, Olinda Rd, Makawao

127 Casanova Italian Restaurant & Deli

★★$$$ Recently voted "Best Italian Restaurant" by readers of *The Maui News*, what started as a chic deli that wholesaled squid-ink pasta to upscale hotels (before it was in vogue) has evolved into an extremely popular restaurant and nightclub. Pack a picnic of lasagna, ravioli, pasta salads, cheeses, and desserts from the petite but bountiful deli, or go next door and dine on classic Italian cuisine. Fresh fish, Big Island beef, wood-oven-fired pizzas, carpaccio, and linguine with fresh oysters and prawns are only a few of the items on the lengthy menu. There's also music and dancing six nights a week, including country-western on Tuesdays and an occasional appearance by part-time resident **Willie Nelson.** Watch the alcohol consumption; it's a long drive home. ♦ 1188 Makawao Ave, Makawao. 572.0220

127 Polli's Mexican Restaurant $$ It's a strange location for a Mexican restaurant, but then Makawao isn't your normal town. Polli's serves traditional Mexican food (try finishing their Haleakala-size chimichanga) with all the trimmings, plus live music Thursday through Saturday nights. Order takeout for an up-country picnic. ♦ 1202 Makawao Ave, Makawao. 572.7808

127 Komoda's This sparse yet charming Makawao landmark is half a century old—a combination old-fashioned general store and bakery that's famous throughout the islands for its monumental cream puffs. The *azuki* bean pie is popular, too. ♦ M-F 7AM-5PM; Sa 7AM-2PM. 3674 Baldwin Ave, Makawao. 572.7261

127 Makawao Steak House ★★★$$$ What makes **Dickie** and **Judy Furtado's** up-country establishment the best steak house on the island isn't its bare-bones menu, which lists the basic beef, lamb, poultry, fish, and salads; it's the consistently excellent dishes and top-notch service, all executed in a soothing environment of flickering fireplaces, dim lighting, and polished woodwork. If you like steak houses, you'll love this one. ♦ 3612 Baldwin Ave, Makawao. 572.8711

127 Viewpoints Gallery The island's only fine arts collective is a cooperative venture dreamed up, designed, and run by 30 Maui artists and represents a wide range of media, including oil paintings, sculpture, tapestry, pottery, watercolors, and even etchings printed on Hawaiian-fiber paper. ♦ Daily 11AM-9PM. 3620 Baldwin Ave, Makawao. 572.5979

Maui's Mane Attraction

Islanders were first introduced to horses in the early 1880s when *lio* (wild mustangs) were brought over from Mexico. These animals quickly adapted to the rough terrain, and today their docile descendants can carry you on a trek through Maui's beaches, valleys, pineapple fields, volcanoes, and waterfalls. Here are a few of the outfitters with horses for hire:

Adventures on Horseback offers a five-hour tour into a rain forest, through waterfall country, and across the verdant slopes of Haleakala Crater. Includes a guide, Continental breakfast, refreshments, and lunch. For additional information, write to Adventures on Horseback, Box 1419, Makawao, Hawaii 96768; or call 242.7445.

Pony Express Tours takes riders on a unique all-day or half-day horseback trip into Haleakala Crater with a guide who narrates the dormant volcano's geologic history and related legends. Lunch, jacket, and raincoat are provided. Other options include one- and two-hour rides on Haleakala Ranch lands. For additional information, write to Pony Express Tours, Box 535, Kula, Hawaii 96790; or call 667.2200.

Rainbow Ranch Stables operates out of cool, scenic Napili with one-hour to two-and-a-half-hour rides through pineapple fields and a two-hour sunset ride. Trips vary according to the experience of the riders. For additional information, write to Rainbow Ranch Stables, Box 10066, Lahaina, Hawaii 96761; or call 669.4702.

128 Haliimaile General Store ★★★★$$$
Bev and **Joe Gannon** converted an old plantation store in the middle of the pineapple fields into an oasis of fine dining. High ceilings, hardwood floors, two dining rooms, and works by noted Maui artists provide a great ambience, while the kitchen produces some of the best cuisine on Maui. Gastronomes from all over the island drive to the 1,200-foot elevation for the brie-and-grape quesadilla, Bev's *boboli* (a pizzalike crust) with crab dip, the blackened sashimi, and the Hunan-style rack of lamb (simply unbelievable). The wine list is outstanding, as is the chocolate-macadamia nut pie. The owners' show-biz background (Joe currently produces concerts for Julio Iglesias, Alice Cooper, and Ringo Starr; Bev was once the road manager for Liza Minnelli and Joey Heatherton) makes this a celebrity haunt, too. You never know who just might show up. ♦ 900 Haliimaile Rd, Haliimaile. 572.2666; fax 572.7128

129 Hui Noeau Visual Arts Center Noted architect **C.W. Dickey** designed this 1917 stucco mansion (pictured above), ensconced within a manorial five-acre setting. Vestiges of one of the island's first sugar mills mark the tree-lined entrance. Originally built for prominent Maui *kamaaina* **Harry** and **Ethel Baldwin**, the estate was turned into an arts center by their grandson, **Colin Cameron**, in the late 1970s. Today Hui Noeau offers ongoing exhibits, and regular classes in line drawing, printmaking, and other arts. The gift shop features earrings, paintings, ceramics, and handmade paper. ♦ Tu-Su 10AM-4PM. 2841 Baldwin Ave, Makawao. 572.6560

Miffed whalers brought the first mosquitoes to Hawaii, intentionally planting larvae in the freshwater ponds surrounding the home of Reverend Baldwin in Lahaina, Maui. The Reverend's unpopularity stemmed from his views on "philandering" with the native women.

130 The Vegan Restaurant ★★$$ This small restaurant is persuading more and more people around the island that pure vegetarian cuisine is not only wholesome but even delicious. Bovine-free dishes include *tofucci* (a lasagna without meat or dairy products), potato Wellington, and *banini* (a banana shake without milk or sugar). A favorite is the vegan burger, made of cleverly combined wheat gluten, tempeh, and grains. ♦ 115 Baldwin Ave, Paia. 579.9144

131 Picnics ★★$ If you're going to make the trip to Hana, stock up on edibles at Picnics, which is basically a take-out counter serving hot and cold sandwiches, salads, burgers (their spinach-nut burger has fans around the world), and complete box lunches ranging from spartan to exotic. Espresso and cappuccino are also available (a godsend for hungover Hana-bound drivers). The huge newsprint menu is reason enough to visit: on the flip side you'll find a guide to Hana, a map of Maui, a list of the state and county parks, and a time chart for distances on the road to Hana (it even lists Hana's 56 bridges). A tablecloth, ice chest, and ice are provided for a fee. ♦ Daily 7:30AM-7PM. 30 Baldwin Ave, a half block from Hana Hwy, Paia. 579.8021

132 Mama's Fish House
★★★$$$ Despite its remote location in a converted beach house on the northeast coast, Mama's has been Maui's best-known fish house for more than 20 years. Located just past Paia, it specializes in catches from the restaurant's own fishers cooked to each diner's preference. The quality of the fare varies, but the landscaped grounds, ocean view, and rustic Polynesian decor are memorable, as is the house specialty, stuffed fish Lani—a fresh fillet filled with herbs, bay shrimp, mushroom sauce, and honey wheat bread. For dessert, try the Hookipa sundae: ice cream, Frangelico, amaretto, cocoa, cream, and nuts. ♦ 799 Poho Pl, Hana Hwy, 1 mile past Paia. 579.8488

133 Hana Highway With its 53 miles of horseshoe turns, one-lane bridges, and narrow shoulders, Hana Highway offers one of Hawaii's most demanding yet popular drives. Since the route itself is the main attraction, it should be undertaken at a very leisurely pace; if you plan to make the entire trip in a day, try to start early (although driving back at night is actually faster and safer). Those prone to car sickness should take Dramamine first, and picnickers should bring insect repellent. Start with a full tank of gas, as there are no stations between Paia and Hana (and gas may not be available in Hana after dark); packing a lunch is also wise, even if you choose not to picnic among the waterfalls and jungle foliage; food service along Hana Highway can be limited to what's growing on the trees. But don't let all this intimidate you—the Hana Highway deserves to be ranked among the wonders of the world and shouldn't be missed under any circumstance.

The drive begins near the **Kahului Airport,** where you'll see the sign: "Hana 54 miles"—a gross understatement. The road seems much longer; it not only curves but twists and curls and pirouettes to the tune (some say) of 617 turns and 56 miniature bridges and is so narrow it's often impossible for two cars to pass unless one pulls over. The road took several years to build by pick and shovel and several more to pave, using convict labor. Before it was paved, the road often washed out; drivers blocked from passing by mud slides would swap cars and then continue on their respective ways, later meeting back at the same mud slide to switch cars again for the return trip. The **Keanae Chinese Store** provided free overnight beds for these stranded motorists.

Of course, the infamous road itself is only one reason why the drive to Hana takes so long. After all, it would be a crime not to make an occasional stop to explore the myriad waterfalls, gardens, multicolored beaches, freshwater caves, and the dozens of swimming holes. The roadside harbors a living catalog of Hawaiian plant life, with ferns and flowers vying for space among trees hung with breadfruit, mango, and guava. Picturesque rest stops include **Waikamoi Bamboo Forest Trail and Nature Walk** (leading to a forest perfect for picnicking), **Puohokamoa Falls** (where you can swim in a natural pool), **Keanae Lookout,** and the **Waianapanapa Black Sand Beach.** About 10 miles beyond Hana is **Oheo Gulch,** part of **Haleakala National Park.** Since it's impossible to see everything in one day, try to keep to some sort of schedule (but not too rigidly) and remember to save some energy for the trip back.

The **Piilani Highway,** which starts at Hana and continues around Haleakala toward Kihei, is supposedly off-limits to rental cars because of the somewhat rugged terrain, but tourists drive it all the time anyway. While much of the highway was paved years ago, it's still punctured with potholes further deepened by the tour buses that careen down it regularly. Although this way around is longer and much more energy-sapping, it's worth it just to witness the dichotomy of terrain within a matter of miles, from lush jungle growth to barren deserts of lava rock.

134 **Waikamoi Ridge Trail** Because it is unmarked and relatively unknown, the Waikamoi Ridge Trail makes an ideal setting for an all-day excursion to one of the most isolated and beautiful picnic areas in Hawaii. Starting at the sign "QUIET—TREES AT WORK," hike for about 15 minutes up the lush, canopied ridge to a small, sun-filled oasis with a manicured lawn and a picnic table with a barbecue grill. After lunch, continue to explore the significantly narrower trail that leads through bamboo forests and passes numerous pools and waterfalls. Bring mosquito repellent. ♦ Off Hana Hwy (look for a small dirt turnoff on the *mauka* side between the 9- and 10-mile markers with a metal gate and a green post marking the trailhead)

135 **Keanae Arboretum** Don't miss this spectacular collection of native and introduced plant life that includes trees from around the world, notably a stunning collection of towering eucalyptus trees. Past the taro patches irrigated by the meandering **Piinaau Stream** is a small trail that leads to a pleasant forest. ♦ Free. Off Hana Hwy at Keanae Peninsula

136 **Waianapanapa State Park** Try not to leave Hana before exploring the rugged volcanic shoreline of **Waianapanapa** (which means "glistening water" and refers to the cold, crystal-clear freshwater pool in a cave in the park). You can hike along an ancient three-mile trail to Hana, sunbathe at the black sand cove (although swimming there can be treacherous), and look for turtles and seabirds from the elevated trail over the lava rock outcroppings. Cabins, picnic facilities, and camping (by permit). ♦ Off Hana Hwy, 3 miles northwest of Hana

137 **Hotel Hana-Maui** $$$$ With its secluded location, soothing atmosphere, and cordial staff, Maui's top hotel has attracted celebrities, VIPs, and respite-seeking world travelers for more than 40 years (not surprisingly, it has a repeat-visitor rate of 80 percent). Just a few of its numerous awards: Most Romantic Resort in the World (*Romantic Hideaways*); Top 10 Resorts in the U.S. (*Harper's Hideaway Report*); Top 10 Tropical Resorts in the U.S. (*Condé Naste Traveler* magazine); and Best Small Hotel in Hawaii (*Aloha* magazine).

In 1984 the powerful **Rosewood Corporation** of Dallas announced its purchase of the hotel and the **Hana Ranch Inc.,** Hana's two largest employers. Under the direction of then general manager **Carl Lindquist** and Rosewood, the Hotel Hana-Maui kept its warmth and charm while attaining even higher levels of service and accommodations. But following the hotel's $24 million renovation, Rosewood sold the property to present owners **Keola Hana Maui Inc.,** a group of Hawaiian, Japanese, and British investors. **ITT Sheraton Corporation** took over management in 1990 (to the distress of some), but so far there's no visible evidence of decline.

The 66-acre site houses 96 rooms and suites in various one-story cottages and large, luxurious suites that are both spread out and private. The **Sea Ranch Cottages,** stained dark green like charming old plantation homes, skirt the shoreline with stone pillars, pitched corrugated-iron roofs, and borders of lava rock. The decor is elegant Hawaiian beach cottage, with bleached hardwood floors, quilts, tiled baths that open onto private gardens, and lots of rattan, bamboo, fresh orchids, and greenery. Another extra-nice touch: every room comes stocked with fresh Kona coffee beans and a coffeemaker. But the greatest luxuries are the four-poster bamboo beds and the huge decks with Jacuzzis and ocean views. The leisurely pace and various recreational activities—hiking, picnics, horseback riding—will give you ample opportunity to enjoy the natural surroundings.

The restored **Plantation House,** formerly the plantation manager's home, sits on a hill away from the beach—ideal for weddings, meetings, and groups of up to 20. The new **Hana Health and Fitness Retreat** offers ongoing programs in nature walks and hikes, aerobics, yoga, exercise, and diet. The hotel offers cookouts, bicycle riding, and planned outings to the historic **Piilanihale Heiau,** a nearby stone temple, and the adjacent **Kahanu Botanical Garden.** And don't miss the hotel's luau, put on every Tuesday by employees who are mostly longtime Hana residents; it's among the best in all of Hawaii. Although the drive to the hotel from Kahului Airport is pleasant, most guests choose to fly in via the nearby Hana Airport, which is serviced three or four times daily by Aloha IslandAir from Kahului and Honolulu. As you can imagine, the rates are astronomically high, with rooms starting at over $300, but that's the price you pay for perfection. ♦ Off Hana Hwy, Hana. 248.8211, 800/321.4262; fax 248.7202

Within Hotel Hana-Maui:

Hotel Hana-Maui Dining Room

★★★$$$$ If you want to do Hana in style, make reservations for the Dining Room, the finest restaurant in town. In an open-beamed room best described as Old Hawaii Elegant, with polished wood floors and views of the verdant courtyard, you can savor a blend of Pacific Island, American, and Oriental cuisine such as bamboo-steamed Pacific lobster tail with Hana garden vegetables or *kiawe*-grilled *ahi* with passion fruit beurre blanc. Although expensive, meals incorporate wonderful local touches, even on the breakfast menu, which offers taro hash browns and banana-macadamia nut waffles with guava, *lilikoi* (passion fruit), and coconut syrup. The kitchen also prepares fabulous picnic baskets. ♦ Reservations required of nonguests. 248.8211

Hana Coast Gallery All of the artists (about 42) whose work is displayed here live in Hawaii. The gallery serves as a showcase of original art and master crafts (no reproductions) reflecting the beauty and heritage of the islands and their people. Pieces range from bronzes of the volcano goddess Pele and rare paintings by **Herb Kane** to **Todd Campbell's** turned-wood bowls and the lush landscape paintings of **James Peter Cost**. The owners are **Gary Koeppel**, producer of the annual **Maui Marine Art Expo**, and **Carl Lindquist**, a longtime prominent Hana citizen and former manager of the Hotel Hana-Maui. ♦ Daily 9AM-5PM. 248.8636

 Hana Ranch Stables Although the stables are part of the Hotel Hana-Maui activities program, nonguests are welcome to participate in the hour-long horseback rides along the scenic Hana coast. Also offered is a two-hour luau ride that goes up into the hills and back down to **Hamoa Beach** (with an extra charge for the luau). Make arrangements through the Hotel Hana-Maui's activities desk. ♦ 248.8211

Hana Cultural Center Located on the grounds of the old courthouse and jail, the center houses a modest collection of Hawaiian artifacts. Also called **Hale Waiwai,** the center has more than 200 members who collect and display photographs, shells, quilts, and other objects and artifacts. The adjoining jail was in use from 1871 to 1978, and everyone in town knew when it held an inmate because, with grounds-keeping a required prison task, the lawn would suddenly be mowed. ♦ Daily 10AM-4PM. Uakea Rd at Keawa Pl, Hana. 248.8622

In 1974 Democrat George Ariyoshi became the first American of Japanese descent to govern an American state. After three terms, Ariyoshi passed the office to another Democrat, John Waihee, the first person of native Hawaiian ancestry to serve as governor of the islands.

Restaurants/Clubs: Red   **Hotels:** Blue
Shops/ ♣ **Outdoors:** Green   **Sights/Culture:** Black

Fresh Fruit that's Free to Boot

Tired of spending your hard-earned vacation dollars on food that's mediocre at best? Then keep your eyes open for the plethora of tropical fruit trees that thrive on Hawaii's isles. Chances are you've already overlooked numerous trees bearing ripe (and free) bananas, avocados, breadfruit, mangoes, papayas, guavas, coconuts, apples, and more. In general, it's okay to pick wild fruit for personal consumption (you can't take uncertified plants and fruit off the island anyway), although private property is off limits. So grab a pocketknife, take another look at the greenery around you, and discover for yourself what the locals have always known—that the best things Hawaii has to offer are usually free.

Coconuts

Cursed with a tough, hairy shell within a smooth, oblong outer husk, the coconut is the ugly stepsister of the fruit family. Yet however unattractive, its tough exterior protects the delicious creamy milk and sweet meat that was a coveted islander staple for centuries. The Polynesians brought the first coconut trees to Hawaii, planting them immediately upon arrival, since the trees were an integral part of their daily life. Every part of the coconut tree was used: trunks for building homes and *heiaus* (temples); husks for bowls, utensils, and jewelry; and husk fiber for *'aha* (the most saltwater-resistant natural rope ever made). For every newborn child, a coconut tree was planted to provide a lifelong source of fruit. Even sailors, explorers, and traders kept them on hand for sustenance. Today, fresh and packaged coconut are still important island staples, and make great gifts to mail home.

Papayas

In 1778, **Captain James Cook** offered a handful of seeds to the Hawaiian king, thus ensuring that papaya trees would prosper on the islands. The mellow fruit became a favorite among Hawaiian rulers, who exchanged papayas as gifts. The papaya's rosy, golden meat is reminiscent of the cantaloupe and peach, yet it has its own exotic flavor.

Also called "pawpaws," papayas grow in clusters on tall trees that look like a cross between breadfruit trees and palms. These trees are divided into three sexes—male, female, and hermaphrodite. The hermaphrodite fruit combines the juiciness of the female fruit with the leanness of the male fruit and has the best flavor. Papayas are also commercially important to Hawaii; millions are grown every year in sprawling groves and sold whole or puréed as a multiuse pulp that's low in calories and rich in vitamins. The enzyme papain, found in the juice of unripe papayas, is used to manufacture digestives and meat tenderizers.

Pineapples

No one knows when the first pineapple arrived in Hawaii, but a Spaniard wrote about the fruit (then called *halakahiki*) on his first visit to Hawaii in 1813. By the end of the 19th century, **James Dole** had seized on the pineapple's popularity and organized commercial production of the fruit by establishing the very successful **Hawaiian Pineapple Company.** In Dole's advertisement introducing the pineapple to mainland America, he said, "You eat it with a spoon like a peach."

The pineapple has since come a long way, although its presence in Hawaii is ebbing after a hundred years as one of the state's leading industries. Hawaii's pineapples now compete in the marketplace with those grown in the Philippines, Taiwan, Thailand, and other countries where labor costs are cheaper.

The plant itself grows about 2 to 4 feet tall, and takes about 18 to 20 months to produce a 4- to 5-pound fruit. The first harvest yields one pineapple per plant, and the second and third harvests yield one or two. After three seasons the plants no longer produce marketable pineapples and must be replaced.

Papaya Tree

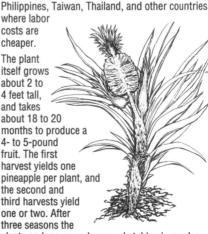

ERIC J.W. LEE

138 Hana Beach Park The safest swimming area in town, Hana Beach park is great for children. The bay has been a surfing spot for centuries, with the best breakers occurring in the middle of the bay. There's a pier to one side and an island, **Puu Kii,** beyond it. Picnic and public facilities. ◆ End of Uakea Rd, off Hana Hwy, Hana

138 Tutu's at Hana Bay $ This small take-out stand on Hana Bay is known for its Maui-made *haupia* (coconut pudding) ice cream. ◆ Daily 8:30AM-3:30PM. Hana Beach Park, Hana. 248.8224

139 Hasegawa General Store More than a general store, Hasegawa doubles as Hana's sole attraction, both a gathering place and a purveyor of everything from appliances to food and fishing supplies. A song has even been written about it. The Hasegawa family created an institution by piling their shop from floor to ceiling with a cornucopia of assorted goods no one can live without.

The recently added automatic teller has brought it into the modern era; plans are in the making to move the store down the street to a bigger location. In the meantime, chances are that if you need something, Hasegawa has it (you just have to figure out where they've hidden it). ◆ M-Sa 8AM-5:30PM; Su 9AM-3:30PM. 5165 Hana Hwy, Hana. 248.8231

139 Hana Ranch Restaurant ★$$ This down-home, ranch-style restaurant has been a runaway success since reopening after renovations in 1986. The take-out counter at one end serves eggs, ham, French toast, and bacon for breakfast, and burgers, hot dogs, and teriyaki sandwiches (a favorite) for lunch, while the dining room doesn't swing into operation until Thursday "pizza nights." ◆ Off Hana Hwy, just past the Hotel Hana-Maui. 248.8255

140 Kipahulu (The Pools) As a promotional scheme, an activities director at a Hana hotel nicknamed the pools at Kipahulu the "Seven Sacred Pools," which soon became a misnomer of staggering popularity (much to the dismay of Hawaiians, many of whom will sardonically respond "The seven what?" when asked about the pools). Although the pools are inspiring and beautiful, they are neither "sacred" nor seven (it's more like 24, but who's counting?). The long series of freshwater pools cascades down to the sea, creating a perfect setting for swimming, picnicking, and camping. A road bridge passes between the fourth and fifth pools; slightly farther ahead is the **Haleakala National Park** headquarters, where you can leave your car and either walk the trail down to the lower pools near the ocean or take the

pleasant 30-minute hike to the higher pools, which are much more entertaining.

If you choose to venture upward, you'll be rewarded by the **Makahiku** and **Waimoku** waterfalls, a bamboo forest, and a series of interconnecting pools. (Note: If trekking uphill, it's a good idea to ask the park ranger about the weather conditions first. Also, get out of the pools immediately if the water suddenly rises: On at least five occasions, ranger **Pu Bednorse** has risked his life to save people from drowning in the quickly rising streams—receiving a presidential citation for his heroism.) The national park provides free campground areas. ◆ Off Hwy 31, 10 miles south of Hana

Bests

Bonnie Friedman
Co-Owner, Grapevine Productions, Maui

A *dim sum* and *manapua* breakfast on Oahu in Honolulu's **Chinatown.**

A full-moon picnic at Maui's **Keawakapu Beach.**

Driving through up-country Maui's **Kula District** on a May morning when the jacaranda trees are in full bloom. The best place to end up is at **Grandma's Coffee House** in Keokea for a cup of java.

Sharing a pizza at **Casanova Italian Restaurant** in Makawao and a dessert and cappuccino at **Haliimaile General Store,** both on Maui.

Dinner at **Merriman's** on the Big Island.

Sunday brunch at the **Maui Prince Hotel.**

Renting a cabin at **Waianapanapa State Park** in Hana, on Maui, and walking the beach trail at sunrise.

Watching an **authentic hula.**

Flower leis—for me, the giving (and receiving) of leis is the most beautiful of Hawaiian traditions.

Sitting outside on a clear, starlit night watching for moonbows (a rare phenomenon, similar to a rainbow but at night), shooting stars, and *pueos* (Hawaiian owls that symbolize good luck).

Robert J. Longhi
Restaurateur, Longhi's, Maui

On Maui:

Watch a sunset from the **Kea Lani Hotel's** beach, then listen to jazz in the lounge.

Golf at **Kapalua Village Course** or at any of the other nine great courses on the island.

Check out the surfers at the **Shark Pit** in Lahaina.

Watch the whales do their annual dance from November through May.

Carol P. Takashima
Captain of a snorkel, whale-watch, and dinner-cruise catamaran; Ocean Activities Center, Maui

All the islands have different "flavors"—try to visit each one.

On Maui:

The **Plantation House Restaurant** and **The Grill & Bar** in Kapalua, **Erik's Seafood Grotto,** and the **Old Lahaina Luau.**

Ed Robinson's scuba-diving classes.

Drive up or bike down **Haleakala Crater.**

Don't miss the **Merry Monarch Festival** in April and the **Prince Lot Festival** in June, both on Oahu; or the **Sola Hula** competition and the **Kamehameha** celebration in June—a local fund-raiser—on Maui.

Whale-watching, especially in February and March.

Cruising Maui and stopping at the little mom-and-pop stores.

Carl Lindquist
Publisher/Writer, Maui

On Maui:

The **Hana Coast** at sunrise provides the mystical light and innate sense of power that accompanies the beginning of each Hana day.

Pi'ilanihale Heiau, the largest of the ancient stone temples left standing, is a place revered for its antiquity and its *mana* (spiritual power).

Ulupalakua at sunset. Sipping wine high on the slopes of **Haleakala Crater** (the world's largest dormant volcano) as the sun fades, then taking a leisurely drive through Kaupo to Hana. Haleakala has the kind of grandeur and silence that puts one's life back in perspective.

Blackie's Bar in Lahaina has good live jazz and the kind of meat-loaf sandwiches Mom never made.

John Pope
General Manager, Moose McGillycuddy's, Maui

Golf Courses:

On Maui, the **Plantation** and **Village** courses at Kapalua and the **Sandalwood** in Waikapu; **The Experience at Koele** on Lanai.

Activities on Maui:

Swimming at **Old Airport Beach** on the west side of the island.

Snorkeling in **Kapalua Bay.**

Windsurfing in **Hookipa** near Paia.

Sailing on the *Scotch Mist.*

Night Life:

Fine dining at **The Grill Restaurant** in the Ritz-Carlton Mauna Lani on the Big Island.

Dancing at **Moose McGillycuddy's** on Maui.

Favorite Pacific Rim dining—**Avalon** on Maui.

Jody Baldwin
Owner, Kilohana Bed & Breakfast, Maui

On Maui:

Driving to **Tedeschi Vineyards** at Ulupalakua and stopping for cappuccino at **Grandma's Coffee House** in Keokea.

A windy day at **Hookipa Beach** (outside of Paia), watching the pro windsurfers.

Gala art openings at the **Hui Noeau Visual Arts Center** in Makawao.

Moonlight concerts at the **Maui Prince Hotel's** outdoor theater in Makena.

Hiking **Haleakala Crater**—from Sliding Sands to Kaupo Gap—and spending the night at **Paliku Cabin.**

Ann Fielding
Marine Biologist/Tour Director, Snorkel Maui

Reef's End at Molokini Island. This shallow, coral-covered ridge rises hundreds of feet off the ocean floor to within only a few feet of the surface. The colors are vibrant, and the water very clear.

Mark Ellman
Chef/Owner, Avalon Restaurant & Bar, Maui

Whale-watching excursions . . . there are hundreds of beautiful humpbacks out there.

Breakfast at **Longhi's,** lunch at **Kimo's,** dinner at **Roy's** or **Avalon** (better make a reservation), and Sunday brunch at the **Ritz-Carlton,** all on Maui.

A Sunday drive in up-country Maui for a late lunch at the **Halimaile General Store.**

Lie on the beach. Lie on the beach. Lie on the beach.

Author's Bests

Sights:
Haleakala Crater
Hana Road Highway
Swinging Bridges
Up-country

Restaurants:
Gerard's ★★★★$$$$
Haliimaile General Store ★★★★$$$
Lahaina Coolers ★$$
Take Home Maui ★★$

Hotels:
Bloom Cottage $$
Hotel Hana-Maui $$$$
Kula Lodge $$$
Papakea Resort $$
Pioneer Inn $

Kahoolawe

Although barren, dry, and, aside from a few wild goats, uninhabited, Kahoolawe (kah-HO-oh-LAW-vay) is one of Hawaii's most controversial islands. Located about seven miles off the southeast coast of Maui and easily visible from both Maui and Lanai, for decades this brown and green mottled promontory has had the dubious honor of being the most heavily bombed island in the Pacific, used until 1990 as a practice range by the U.S. Navy (the island is still littered with unexploded ammunition). Now, four separate factions are contesting the property rights to this 73-square-mile bull's-eye: the federal government, the state, Maui County, and a Hawaiian activist group called **Protect Kahoolawe Ohana** (*ohana* means family in Hawaiian). The government refuses to foot the multimillion-dollar bill to clean up the island, yet, because of its "importance to national security," is reluctant to give it back to the state, which, along with Protect Kahoolawe Ohana, would like to see Kahoolawe turned into a cultural reserve. Currently the island is off-limits to the public and has no facilities other than an old military campsite.

But Kahoolawe, which is the smallest of Hawaii's eight major islands, wasn't always so deserted and lifeless. For centuries it was a sacred place inhabited by ancient Hawaiians, who left their mark with what are now scattered, bombed remains of ancient temples, fishing shrines, and villages. Possibly abandoned because of an unfavorable shift in climate, the island wasn't inhabited by people again until 1839, when it served unsuccessfully as an Alcatraz of sorts for convicted criminals. In 1858 the first of several attempts to turn the island into a large cattle ranch was made and, after a long period of trial and error, Kahoolawe managed to sustain horses, cattle, fowl, and an assortment of trees and grasses. But in 1939 the ranchers made the grave error of leasing the

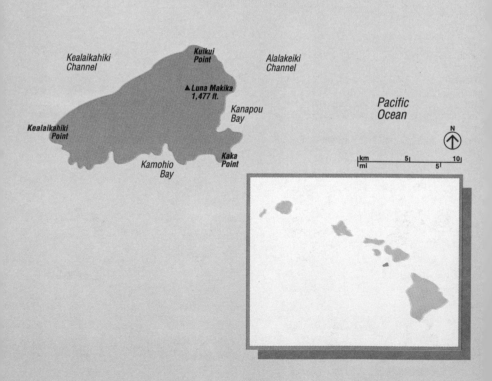

southern end of the island to the Navy for $1 a year for target practice. After the attack at Pearl Harbor in 1941, the Navy unceremoniously booted the ranchers and their stock off Kahoolawe and turned the entire island into a gunnery range, providing an occasional pyrotechnic display for the citizens of Maui as huge battleships proceeded to blast the extinct volcano with their 16-inch guns.

Although Maui County has voiced an interest in turning Kahoolawe back into an island fit for human habitation, and Hawaii **Governor John Waihe'e** has introduced a bill to make it a cultural reserve, the fate of Kahoolawe remains uncertain. But regardless of who wins the territorial tug-of-war, everyone agrees that the future of this battered yet potentially profitable ex-bombsite is certainly more optimistic than it was just a few years ago. After all, in Hawaii, even bomb-riddled real estate is worth fighting over.

Hula Kahiko: The Return of the Traditional Hawaiian Dance

If you are watching—or learning—a hula dance, think hands, not hips. While the body sways gracefully to the rhythm of the music, the hands and facial expressions tell a story. According to a popular Hawaiian legend, the first hula was performed by **Laka,** the goddess of dance, to entertain her fiery sister **Pele,** the volcano goddess. Pele reacted by lighting up the sky with delight, and *hula kahiko* (ancient hula) thus became a sacred part of Hawaiian religion, performed by men and women in honor of the gods. Hundreds of interpretive dances telling stories of Hawaiian history and life have since been passed on from generation to generation.

Nathaniel Emerson, author of *The Unwritten Literature of Hawaii,* called the hula "the door to the heart of the people." But when missionaries arrived in the 19th century, they were disgusted by the ritual dance. They found the costumes (men in loincloths and topless women in *kapa* skirts) and the thrusting *opu* (pelvic) movements sexually explicit and vulgar, and promptly banned the hula.

Hawaiians responded to the ban by dancing in secret until **King Kalakaua** came to power in 1883 and brought the ancient ceremony out of hiding, albeit with a few changes. Women were restricted to wearing long skirts under their ti-leaf skirts and long-sleeved, high-necked tops, though men remained dressed in loincloths.

In the 20th century, when the hula dance became a major tourist attraction, its traditional meaning was lost somewhere between the swaying grass skirts and the ukuleles. But in the last 15 years the inner spirit of the hula has returned in full force, and the ancient dance is once again performed for historical and cultural reasons. Spring dance celebrations such as the **Prince Lot Hula Festival** in July at the Moanalua Gardens on Oahu and the **Merrie Monarch** in April in Hilo on the Big Island are flourishing. The tradition is likewise being kept alive in public schools, where hula competitions are now almost as popular as football games. And for visiting hula enthusiasts, introductory classes are offered by many of the major hotels.

M. BLUM

Lanai

For nearly a century the entire island community of Lanai (lah-NIGH) worked under a single employer to harvest what was once the largest pineapple plantation in the world. But in October of 1993, **Castle & Cooke Properties**, a subsidiary of **Dole Foods**, shut down the pineapple operation because of high labor costs, shifting the bulk of its operations to Thailand and the Philippines. Faced not only with immediate unemployment but with an end to a way of life, Lanai's 2,500 residents were determined to retain their strong ties to the land and the community. Hands calloused from harvesting pineapples were retrained to drive shuttles and tend gardens as Lanai's major luxury resorts, the **Manele Bay Hotel** and **The Lodge at Koele**, opened the doors to tourism on an island that was uninhabited for hundreds of years in fear of the ghosts of *alii* (Hawaiian royalty) buried on the island.

When visiting Lanai, you will immediately sense an esprit de corps among the people who live here. The majority of residents live in Lanai's only town, **Lanai City**—a cool, sleepy mountain community elevated 1,700 feet above the sea. Lightly coated with a fine, ferrous-rich dust and lined with majestic Norfolk and Cook Island pines, Lanai City consists mainly of multicolored tin-roof plantation houses that reflect a bygone era when **James Dole** first laid out the town in 1924 after purchasing the entire island for $1.1 million. Residents often gather together to "talk story" (the Hawaiian expression for gossiping) while roasting local mouflon sheep or axis deer on someone's porch, perhaps sharing a case of Budweiser brought over from Maui. It's a close-knit community, proud of its hardworking lineage yet somewhat unaware of its narrow escape from extinction—for if tourism hadn't replaced the pineapple industry, Lanai inevitably would have been returned to the restless spirits.

There are only three main roads trisecting the 140-square-mile island, but dozens of unpaved roads lead to remote beaches, well-preserved *heiaus* and petroglyphs, misty mountaintops, and various other natural wonders, so renting a four-wheel-drive vehicle is mandatory if you want to truly explore Lanai. The island is also ideal for camping, hunting, hiking, and mountain-bike riding, and the exquisite beach at **Hulopoe Bay** (a popular playground for spinner dolphins) makes for a pleasant day trip from Maui aboard **Expeditions** (for reservations, call 661.3756. Lanai's only shuttle service leaves from Maui's **Lahaina Harbor** daily (whether arriving by plane or boat, make sure arrangements have been made with your hotel or Lanai City Service to pick you up, since there are no shuttle or taxi facilities at the Lanai harbor or airport). Tourists who can't foot the $300-plus per night room fees for either resort hotel will most likely be content staying the night at Lanai's only other inn, the **Hotel Lanai**—a cozy, unpretentious, and moderately priced ex-clubhouse of James Dole's in the heart of Lanai City. Either way, it's impossible to spend a few days on Lanai and not fall under the charm of this island and its people.

ERIC J. W. LEE

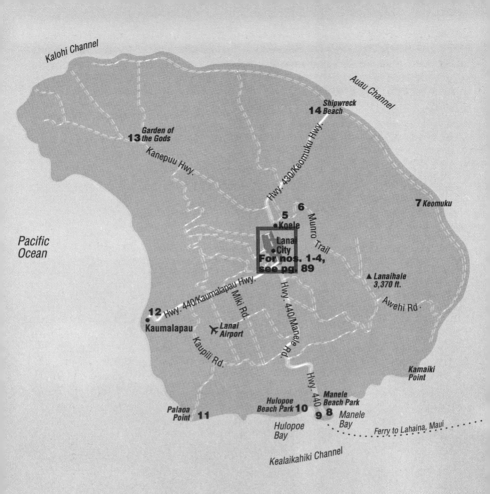

Kalohi Channel

Auau Channel

14 Shipwreck
Beach

13 Garden of
the Gods

Kanepuu Hwy.

Hwy. 430/Keomuku Hwy.

7 Keomuku

Pacific
Ocean

5 • Koele
6

Munro Trail

Lanai
City

For nos. 1-4,
see pg. 89

▲ Lanaihale
3,370 ft.

Awehi Rd.

12 Hwy. 440/Kaumalapau Hwy.

Miki Rd.

Hwy. 440/Manele Rd.

• Kaumalapau

✈ Lanai
Airport

Kaupili Rd.

Kamaiki
Point

Hulopoe
Beach Park **10**

Manele
Beach Park

9 **8** Manele
Bay

Palaoa
Point **11**

Hwy. 440

Hulopoe
Bay

Ferry to Lahaina, Maui

Kealaikahiki Channel

N

| km |
| ml | 2 | 5

Tropical Treasures

Chances are, your first introduction to the Hawaiian islands will include a memorable gift of flowers, since most guests are greeted with leis either at the airport or their hotel. Hawaiians take great pride in their flowers; here's a brief guide to some of their finest flora.

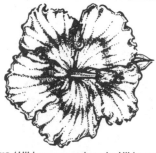

Hibiscus (*Hibiscus rosa-sinensis; Hibiscus koki'o*) Hibiscus shrubs grow easily on all the islands and come in several colors and shapes. They're rarely used in leis, because the large showy flowers are so fragile.

Bird of paradise
(*Strelitzia reginae*) An ostentatious flower that's easy to identify—just look for plumage (bright orange and blue petals) topping a long gray-green stalk. Each flower blooms in six stages, a new one every couple of days. This colorful showpiece (illustrated at right) hails from South Africa.

Night-blooming cereus
(*Hylocereus undatus*) A nocturnal beauty, this cactus blooms from June to October for about two weeks. The fragrant yellow blossoms open at dusk and close when the sun rises.

Anthurium (*Anthurium andraeanum*) This heart-shaped flower grows in many colors, including white, greenish white, pink, red, lavender, and pink-streaked. The surface of the bloom has a waxy shine that looks almost artificial. When anthuriums are cut and placed in a vase, they last for weeks.

Lobster-claw heliconia
(*Heliconia humilis*) A member of the same family as the bird of paradise, this plant has leaves the color and shape of cooked lobster claws. Cradled within these leaves are small green flowers.

Silversword
(*Argyroxiphium sandwicense*) This plant grows in Maui's Haleakala National Park and on the Big Island in rock or volcanic earth at altitudes of 6,000 to 12,000 feet. You'll recognize its silver spike leaves growing on a six-foot-tall stalk (such as the one shown here), which is capped in August by blooming tufts of flowers.

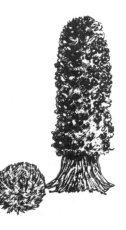

Plumeria (*Meli; Frangipani*) A favorite of lei-makers, the plumeria is a fragrant, durable flower. The name frangipani (French for thick milk) refers to its poisonous milky sap.

LANAI CITY

Cavendish Golf Course

Koa Dr.

Puulani Pl.

Dole Park

For nos. 5-14, see pg. 87

to Lanai Airport

km 1/2 1
mi 1/4 1/2

N

HÓTEL LANAI

3 Hotel Lanai $$$ If you don't mind staying miles from the nearest beach, the Hotel Lanai is an excellent choice. Built in 1923 to house guests and provide an entertainment center for **James Dole's** executives, it was for decades the only hotel on the island. Now dwarfed by two super-luxury resorts, the Hotel Lanai continues to fill a necessary niche in Lanai's tourist industry, providing reasonably priced rooms and affordable dining. The 11 rooms are all small and tastefully decorated, and the staff is friendly to a fault. There's a shaded veranda that doubles as a bar, a rustic dining room, and acres of cool green lawns shaded by Norfolk pines, plus two nearby golf courses. ◆ 828 Lanai Ave, Lanai City. 565.7211, 800/624.8849

Within the Hotel Lanai:

Hotel Lanai Dining Room ★★$$ The cozy fireplace, large wood tables, paintings and photographs by island artists, and the friendly staff create a pleasant ambience. Locals are often found here at breakfast ordering banana pancakes or specialty omelets. Soups and sandwiches are served for lunch, while the dinner menu consists of steaks, chicken, pasta, and fresh fish (if seafood marinara is one of the evening's specials, don't miss it). ◆ 565.7211

4 Lanai City Service Don't try shopping around for a better deal, because this is the only car-rental agency and gas station on the island. City Service also does a brisk business renting four-wheel-drive Geo Trackers, so make reservations as far in advance as possible; they also rent snorkel and dive gear. ◆ 1036 Lanai Ave, Lanai City. 565.7227

5 The Lodge at Koele $$$$ Once the site of Lanai's ranching operations (a big business before the pineapple industry took over), the

1 Lanai City The only town on the island is a 10-minute drive from the airport and a 25-minute drive from Manele Harbor. **The Lodge at Koele** and **Hotel Lanai** are both located here, as are a few interesting galleries, boutiques, stores, and cafes—all at the edges of **Dole Park.** ◆ Off Hwy 440

2 Blue Ginger Cafe ★$ This is the better of Lanai City's two choices (**S&T Properties** being the other) for low-priced local grinds. The cafe doubles as a bakery, serving croissant sandwiches along with omelets, hamburgers, and pizza. The Blue Ginger Cafe is also a great place to meet and chat with friendly locals. ◆ 409 Seventh St, Lanai City. 565.6363

2 S&T Properties $ Lanai City's version of a short-order diner, serving island-style breakfast and lunch at a counter with swivel stools. The shakes are the best choice, made at an old-fashioned soda fountain that ranks as one of Lanai's favorite attractions. ◆ 419 Seventh St, Lanai City. 565.6537

The first flight from the West Coast to Hawaii was made in 1925, although it wasn't exactly a nonstop flight. A two-engine PN-9 Navy seaplane left San Francisco on 25 August but ran out of gas 300 miles short of Maui. The pilots improvised sails and landed the seaplane on Kauai on 10 September. Two years later, an army Fokker C-2-3 Wright 220 Trimeter made the first successful nonstop flight from Oakland, California, to Wheeler Field on Oahu.

grounds here now combine the elegance of an English manor with the rustic comfort of old Hawaii. The riding stables, bowling lawn, croquet course, swimming pool, tennis courts, reflecting pool, and acres of meticulously maintained lawns impart the sense that you're entering an elegant English estate, which accounts for the high percentage of European clientele. The mood here is a welcome change from the sea-level tropicana that envelops most Hawaii visitors, and the chilly upland air is equally invigorating.

The aptly named **Great Hall,** with 35-foot-high ceilings and immense stone fireplaces, is an ideal place to linger with a book and a glass of port. The rooms and suites are decorated in an old plantation style, with hand-carved four-poster beds and oil paintings and artifacts from around the world. There's even a music room for listening to the classical selection of the day, as well as a library, tea room, game room, and the full range of activities, from horseback riding to tennis, boating, hiking, and croquet. The 18-hole championship golf course, designed by **Greg Norman** and **Ted Robinson,** opened in 1991. ♦ Off Keomuku Hwy, just north of Lanai City. 565.7300, 800/223.7637; fax 565.4561

Within The Lodge at Koele:

The Dining Room at the Lodge at Koele
★★★★$$$$ Inventive gourmet dishes are served in an elegant octagonal-shaped dining room looking out over the English gardens and pools. The cuisine is Pacific Rim, with entrées including guava-smoked scallops in *shoyu* sauce, roasted *uku,* smoked marlin, local axis deer, veal with shiitake mushrooms, and seafood caught that day and served steamed, poached, smoked, raw, or however you like. The vegetables and fruit are picked at an organic farm a few miles away. Although the competition is slim to none, this is unquestionably the best restaurant on the island, and one of the best in the state. ♦ Jacket required. 565.7300

6 Munro Trail This winding dirt road extends the length (about one and a half miles) of 3,370-foot **Lanaihale** mountain, to the southeast of Lanai City. New Zealander **George Munro,** Lanai's answer to Johnny Appleseed, scattered seeds and plants from his homeland along this ridge in the early 1900s. His Norfolk pine trees were so successful at trapping moisture on the mountain that more were planted in Lanai City, helping to keep it cooler. Take heed, though—it's not an easy trail for hiker, mountainbiker, or Geo Tracker, especially when wet. ♦ Trail begins 1.2 miles past The Lodge at Koele and ends on southeast section of Hwy 440

7 Keomuku An extreme example of what happens to a town when a nearby sugar plantation fails, Keomuku was abandoned at the turn of the century when a commercial sugar venture collapsed. All the buildings vanished except for the **Ka Lanakila o Ka Malamalama Church.** Built in 1903, it still stands as testament to the deserted village, once home to nearly 2,000 people. ♦ At the end of Hwy 430 (Shipwreck Beach), turn right and follow the dirt road along the coast

8 Manele Bay Along with Hulopoe Bay, this was once the site of an ancient Hawaiian village. Manele Bay, the only public harbor on the island, is now part of the **Marine Life Conservation District.** It's also a docking area for the **Expeditions** (661.3756) shuttle service. Swimming is unsafe here because of heavy boat traffic, so don't bring your flippers. ♦ Southeast end of Hwy 440

9 Hulopoe Bay Watch spinner dolphins play around while you sunbathe or snorkel in the usually calm water. The tide pools around the bay are great for exploring, especially at low tide. According to legend, **Puupehe,** the rock islet just off the southwest point of the bay, is the burial sight of **Pehe,** a wife so beautiful that her jealous husband, **Makakehau,** hid her in a sea cave, where she sadly drowned during a storm. With the help of the gods, Makakehau scaled the cliff with Pehe's body and buried her at the summit, now known as the **Hill of Pehe.** This is by far the nicest beach on the island. ♦ Southeast end of Hwy 440, at the base of Manele Bay Hotel

10 Manele Bay Hotel $$$$ In 1991 **Rockresorts** opened their second major luxury hotel in Lanai on the hills of beautiful Hulopoe Bay. In direct contrast to The Lodge at Koele, the Manele Bay Hotel operates on the basic tropical resort principle: an expansive white sand beach, a central pool with dozens of deck chairs, and numerous water activities (sailing, fishing, snorkeling, and swimming). The decor reflects Mediterranean and Asian influences and the grounds are lined with Hawaiian, Japanese, and Chinese gardens. There are 250 luxury villas and suites with private verandas and ocean views. The **Ihilani Terrace** (★★$$$$) is good but no match for The Koele's restaurant. And until the new golf course by **Jack Nicklaus** is completed in late 1993, the nearest course is at The Koele. ♦ Southeast end of Hwy 440. 565.7300, 800/223.7637; fax 565.4561

11 Kaunolu The fishing grounds of this well-preserved ancient Hawaiian village were **Kamehameha the Great's** favorite. Archaeologists have found 86 house sites, 35 stone shelters, and numerous grave markings here. The road leading to the site is difficult to find and even harder to negotiate (a four-wheel drive is a must), but the red sand beach—perfect for sunbathing—is worth it. ♦ Near Palaoa Point, 7 miles south of Lanai City. Take the lower road through the pineapple fields until you see a small wood sign marking the turnoff. Good luck.

12 Kaumalapau Harbor The harbor was completed in 1926 by the **Hawaiian Pineapple Company** (later the **Dole Company**) to ship pineapples from Lanai to a cannery in Honolulu. From 1968 to the mid-1970s, when pineapple operations were in high gear during the summer months, more than a million pineapples a day were transferred from trucks to barges for the journey. It's still the principal seaport for Lanai (tourist operations use Manele Harbor), with good shore fishing. ♦ West end of Hwy 440, Kaumalapau

13 Garden of the Gods The scattered assemblage of huge rocks and unusual lava formations gives every indication of having dropped in from outer space. During sunrise and sunset, the eerie moonlike shapes are in every shade of purple, pink, and sienna. The stacked rocks signify absolutely nothing (they're stacked by tourists only). The fenced-in area just before The Garden of the Gods is a project by **The Nature Conservancy of Hawaii** to maintain Lanai's native dryland forest, one of the fastest disappearing ecosystems in the world (the fence is to keep the axis deer out). Extremely rare species of plants, including a dryland gardenia tree, are able to survive here. ♦ Take the dirt road turnoff just before the tennis courts at The Lodge at Koele and head about 7 miles northwest on the most well-worn dirt road

14 Shipwreck Beach The hull of a World War II ship marks the spot where many vessels from West Maui end up when they break their mooring. Timber from other unlucky vessels was used to build nearby squatters' shacks. A spectacular collection of Hawaiian petroglyphs is located a few hundred feet inland from the end of the dirt road leading toward Molokai. The beach is good for wading and beachcombing. ♦ Turn left at the end of Hwy 430

Mokihana, a rare, fragrant fruit that grows only on Kauai, is used to make exotic leis; however, mokihana leis cannot be worn against bare skin because the berry-size fruit is so potent it can burn your flesh.

Shaka to Me, Baby!

First, make a fist. Next, stick out your pinkie finger. Then give the thumbs-up signal, wiggle your wrist a little, and say *shaka bra* (SHOCK-ah-brah). Congratulations, you've just made the unofficial Hawaiian hand signal: the shaka.

Chances are you've encountered the shaka sign before, even if you've never been to Hawaii. Seventy million TV viewers saw it as island girl **Carolyn Sapp** walked the Miss America victory stroll; **Johnny Carson** buffs may remember **Doc** greeting his boss the same way after returning from a Hawaiian vacation; and sports fans saw the shaka flashed at the camera every time Hawaii's **Russ Francis** or **Mosi Tatupu** scored an NFL touchdown.

The shaka sign's origin was first pegged to a 1906 photograph featuring newsboys poised in front of a printing plant. But the boy thought to be giving the shaka sign turned out, after closer examination, to be picking his nose with his pinkie. Now credit for popularizing the thumb-and-pinkie sign goes to car salesman **"Lippy" Espinda,** who used the expression and sign together for his 1960s TV commercials. He claims the word shaka originated from his childhood marble games, where any good marble shooter was called a *shaka kini* (kini refers to the marble). Hence, shaka evolved to mean anything nice or fine, like Lippy's used cars. While locals often have personalized shaka signs (with subtle but important variations in meanings that only the most astute shaka signers would detect), the basic shaka hand signal is used mainly as a standard greeting, which is now as familiar a part of Hawaiian pop culture as aloha shirts and plastic leis.

Author's Bests

Sights:

Garden of the Gods

Hulopoe Bay

Kaunolu

Munro Trail

Restaurants:

Blue Ginger Cafe ★$

The Dining Room at The Lodge at Koele ★★★★$$$$

Hotel Lanai Dining Room ★★$$

Hotels:

Hotel Lanai $$$

The Lodge at Koele $$$$

Restaurants/Clubs: Red	Hotels: Blue
Shops/ ♥ Outdoors: Green	**Sights/Culture:** Black

Molokai

Compared to its neighboring islands, Molokai (moh-loh-KAH-ee) is in a world of its own—and according to its 6,800 residents, it's going to remain that way. Molokai has a city but no stoplights. It has a major resort but no fast-food chains. It even has an exotic wildlife park but no movie theater. It is an island of enigmas with a checkered history and an uncertain future. For hundreds of years Molokai was home to powerful *kahuna* priests who were feared throughout the island chain, and the island was given a wide berth by warring chiefs who called it "**The Lonely Isle.**" When victims of leprosy were unceremoniously dumped on the island in the late 1800s, Molokai garnered international infamy and was dubbed "**The Forbidden Isle.**" Now, in an attempt to convalesce from a rather unjustified historical drubbing, the state's fifth-largest island has retitled itself "**The Friendly Isle,**" which, when treated with due respect, is unquestionably accurate.

Molokai, the only major Hawaiian island except for Niihau where most of the population is of native descent, is also one of the islands least dependent on tourism. Its two largest attractions are products of circumstance: **Kalaupapa**, the infamous exile colony for victims of Hansen's disease (a euphemistic term for leprosy), is now a National Historic Park and the subject of various tours; and the wildlife preserve run by **Molokai Ranch**, which imported animals from Africa about 30 years ago as an environmental project to control the mesquite brush encroaching on the ranch's grazing land, is now a 52,000-acre preserve with more than a thousand free-roaming animals, from antelope to zebra. Aside from those two man-made attractions, Molokai relies mostly on its natural wonders—the 300-foot waterfalls of **Halawa Valley** in the east, record-breaking sea cliffs on the north shore, and Hawaii's longest white sand beach in the west—to lure visitors from the more popular destination resorts on Maui and Oahu. But, unlike Lanai, Molokai will most likely never rely solely on tourism to sustain its economy. While many of Molokai's residents have to earn a living working in Maui, they want Molokai, with its blissfully antiquated lifestyle, to remain the same, immune to the trade winds of change.

You can get to Molokai via the *Maui Princess* (for schedules, call 553.5736), a 118-foot yacht that shuttles tourists and residents between Maui and Molokai twice a day. There is only one main road on the island, running from one extreme end to the other, and, unlike on Lanai, most of the sights worth seeing don't require a four-wheel-drive vehicle. Although there are various tour companies that will shuttle you around, Molokai is best traveled by car, allowing you to set your own pace (plus, it's impossible to get lost, even

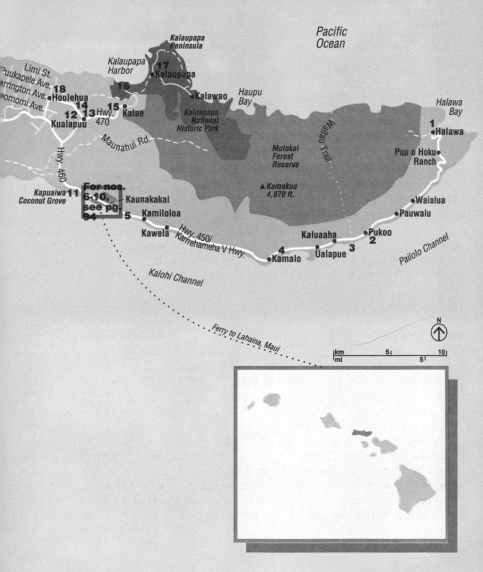

without a map). Don't expect any luxuries here aside from peace and quiet, for the shopping is poor, and the dining is even poorer (if you're staying for more than a few days, get a room with a kitchen). Aside from the **Colony's Kaluakoi Hotel and Golf Club**, the island's only destination resort, Molokai is geared mostly toward adventurous types who don't mind getting a little muddy or salty from hiking or swimming, and who appreciate the austerity that characterizes this unique isle.

1 Halawa Valley The major adventure on Molokai is driving to Halawa Valley and hiking through its lush, green-carpeted jungle, which is marked by a pair of beautiful waterfalls, a charming lagoon, and a beach. The valley begins at the northeastern tip of the island, where Highway 450 ends. Hundreds of families once occupied the valley, but a tidal wave in 1946 prompted their evacuation and only a few families returned. Remains of the once-thriving taro patches and old irrigation ditches can still be seen. The two-hour hike to the falls is well worth the time, but it is more than a minor outing. Come prepared with clothing that can get wet (you'll be wading across streams), a thick shield of insect repellent, and an adventurous spirit. Beware the giant *mo'o* (lizard), Hawaii's own version of the Loch Ness monster. Legend has it that it's only safe to swim in the pool at the bottom of the falls if a ti leaf thrown into the water floats. ♦ Take Hwy 450 around the east side of the island until you can't drive any farther, about 37 miles from the airport and 48 miles from the Kaluakoi Hotel

2 Molokai Horse & Wagon Ride If you can't find a luau on the island, this will suffice nicely. Jovial, guitar-playing **Larry Helm** will serenade you with Hawaiian songs as you depart from the beachside hut into a 50-acre mango patch and straight up the mountain to a turn-of-the-century stone temple. You'll cross a stream on this wagon ride, smell the wild guavas and flowers, and return to the beach, where you'll be greeted with a laid-back, Hawaiian-style barbecue. ♦ M-Sa 10:30AM. Off Hwy 450, just after the 15-mile marker. 567.6773

3 Our Lady of Sorrows Church **Father Damien** built this church in 1874. There is a statue of him in the pavilion. ♦ Off Hwy 450, after the 14-mile marker

4 St. Joseph Church A wood-frame church built in 1876 by **Father Damien**. ♦ Off Hwy 450, just past the 10-mile marker

KAUNAKAKAI

Makaena Rd.
Kaunakakai Gulch
Rock Wall
Hwy. 460/Maunaloa Hwy.
Manila Pl.
Home Olu
Ilio Rd.
Kikipua St.
Kokio St.
10
9 Ala Malama Ave.
Kamoi St.
Kolapa Pl.
8
Kaunakakai St.
Mohala Pl.
Ailoa St.
Kamiloloa Gulch
Beach Pl.
7
Oki St.
6
Hwy. 450/Kamehameha V Hwy.
Seaside Pl.
Kaunakakai Harbor

For nos. 1-5 and 11-24, see pg. 92

Kaunakakai Landing

Ferry to Lahaina, Maui

Kapaakea Loop

Kalohi Channel

N

km   1/2   1
mi   1/4   1/2

5 Hotel Molokai $$
Retreat to a narrow strip of beach on Molokai's south shore, where the Hotel Molokai offers 56 A-frame bungalows, equipped with swinging love seats and lanais. You won't find TVs, radios, or telephones in the rooms, but a few overlook the ocean. The larger rooms have lofts with twin-size beds. Like the island, this is a friendly place to stay, although the change in management of the hotel's restaurant, **Holo Holo Kai** (★$), has disappointed many regulars—it's simply not as good as it was. ◆ Off Hwy 450 (2 miles east of Kaunakakai), Kamiloloa. 553.5347, 800/423.6666; fax 531.4004

6 Kaunakakai This is the town that inspired the song "The Cock-Eyed Mayor of Kaunakakai," although, truth be told, Kaunakakai has no official mayor (Molokai is technically a part of Maui County and therefore falls under the jurisdiction of Maui's mayor). The town's two biggest attractions are its main street, **Ala Malama,** which looks like a Hollywood Western set in the 1920s, and the half-mile-long wharf, a popular spot for teens, who drive their cars on the wharf over the ocean. The pace is blissfully slow here. ◆ Off Hwy 460

7 Pau Hana Inn $$ A cottage-style inn on the fringe of Kaunakakai, the Pau Hana overlooks the ocean and has lots of down-home charm. The budget-priced accommodations include poolside studios with kitchenettes. Pau Hana means "after work," and, true-to-form, the bar here is often the gathering place for locals. The open-air **Pau Hana Inn Restaurant** (★$$) offers decent Continental cuisine, and the **Friendly Isle Band Rhythmic Experience (FIBRE)** plays on Friday and Saturday nights. Cool off in the pool after a night of dancing. ◆ Off Hwy 450, Kaunakakai. 553.5342, 800/423.6666

Molokai suffered its first bank robbery on 8 October 1992 at 10:45AM. The rifle-toting thief made his getaway with an undisclosed amount of money from Molokai Federal Credit Union in Kaunakakai; he was described as 5 feet 8 inches tall with dark brown hair.

Restaurants/Clubs: Red   Hotels: Blue
Shops/ 🌿 **Outdoors:** Green   **Sights/Culture:** Black

8 Molokai Drive Inn ★$ A Molokaian McDonald's of sorts, this take-out counter with fish-plate lunches is a rarity, even in Hawaii. If the fishing is good, try the fresh mahimahi or *opakapaka,* a perfect complement to the french fries. The hamburgers are also popular, as is the Japanese-style *bento* (box lunch). ◆ Off Hwy 450, Kaunakakai. 553.5655

9 Molokai Outpost Natural Food ★$ A great stop for a healthy take-out snack, hot or cold, the juice bar is known for its Mexican food, smoothies, and sandwiches. The organically grown produce is mostly fresh from Molokai. ◆ M-F, Su 9AM-6PM. Kaunakakai. 553.3377

10 Molokai Fish & Dive The island's only sporting goods store is also the home of the "original Molokai T-Shirts & Caps," two items you just can't be without. Fish & Dive also rents snorkeling gear, boogie boards, fishing poles, and golf clubs. Stop in and check it out (what else do you have to do?). ◆ Kaunakakai. 553.5926

10 Molokai Island Creations Swimwear, T-shirts, fragrances, soaps, Hawaiian note cards, original Molokai glassware and coral jewelry, and other Molokai miscellany are offered at this pleasant country boutique, right next door to Molokai Fish & Dive. ◆ Kaunakakai. 553.5926

10 Rabang's $ Filipino food and hamburgers are the main items on the menu. Rabang's has a take-out counter and only a few tables, which fill up quickly with local families. ◆ Ala Malama, Kaunakakai. 553.5841

On a clear day off the coast of Molokai, you may spot kamikaze environmentalist Steve Perlman dangling from the end of a knotted nylon line, two thousand feet above the base of a cliff, holding a paintbrush. If you look closely, you'll see that he's pollinating (or at least trying to) a rare Hawaiian plant called *Brighamia.*

Catch of the Bay

Whether you're peering through your diving mask or admiring the entrée on your dinner plate, you will encounter a mind-boggling variety of fish in Hawaii. To make things doubly confusing, each fish can have several names, including a Hawaiian name (for instance, broadbill swordfish are also called marlin and *a'u*). Here's a brief illustrated guide to the fish you'll find on many of Hawaii's menus (usually deep-water fish) as well as those cruising the local reefs.

Fish to Eat

A'u (broadbill swordfish or marlin) An expensive delicacy that, once caught on the hook, puts up a legendary fight. The meat is white, moist, and exceptionally good.

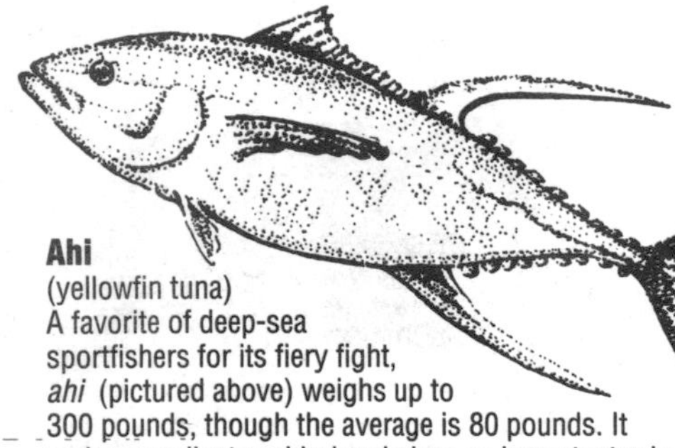

Ahi
(yellowfin tuna)
A favorite of deep-sea sportfishers for its fiery fight, *ahi* (pictured above) weighs up to 300 pounds, though the average is 80 pounds. It makes excellent sashimi and plays an important role in Hawaii's tuna industry.

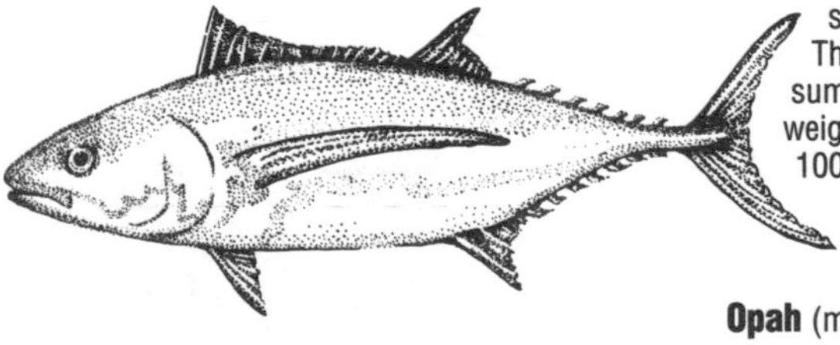

Ahipalaha/Tombo Ahi (albacore) The world's premium tuna (pictured above), usually destined for U.S. canneries, is a small predator that averages 40 to 80 pounds. It migrates extensively throughout the north Pacific, far away from Hawaii, and is occasionally substituted for *ahi* and *aku* (other types of tuna) in raw fish preparations.

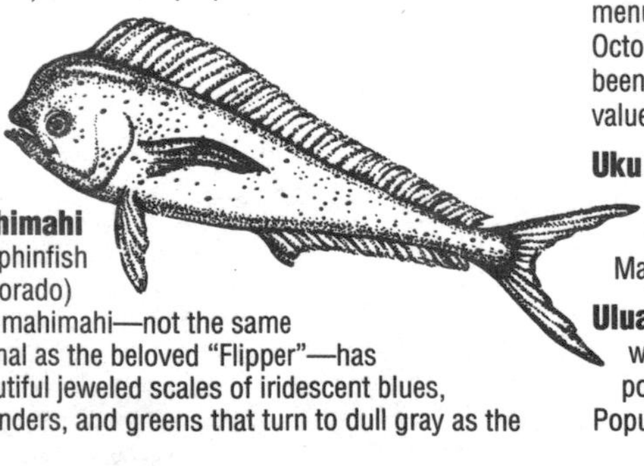

Mahimahi
(dolphinfish
or dorado)
The mahimahi—not the same animal as the beloved "Flipper"—has beautiful jeweled scales of iridescent blues, lavenders, and greens that turn to dull gray as the fish (pictured on the bottom left) dies. A playful swimmer weighing up to 25 pounds, it is commonly seen chasing flying fish through the waves. Mahimahi is a favorite local food that's sold most of the year, although availability peaks from March through May and September through November. Frozen fillets from Taiwan and Japan have made this fish available to budget-conscious diners, while fresh mahimahi can be a coveted item on pricey Continental menus.

Onaga (red snapper) A popular bottom fish served in upscale restaurants, *onaga* ranges from 1 to 18 pounds in Hawaiian waters. Availability peaks in December.

Ono (wahoo) *Ono* is Hawaiian for "good to eat"—an apt name for this fish. Its flaky white meat is served in everything from grilled sandwiches to sophisticated Continental preparations. The best time to look for *ono* is during the summer and fall months. In Hawaii it typically weighs 8 to 30 pounds, but it can grow up to 100 pounds.

Opah (moonfish) One of the most colorful commercial fish species in Hawaii, with crimson fins and large, gold-encircled eyes. Well-liked for their moist, extremely flaky texture, *opahs* range from 60 to 200 pounds.

Opakapaka (pink snapper) Hawaii's premium table snapper is usually caught in deep water. It's a versatile fish that appears abundantly on island menus year-round, although availability peaks from October through February. For nearly a century it's been Hawaii's most important bottom fish for its value and weight (18 pounds on average).

Uku (gray snapper) One of Hawaii's three most popular deep-water snappers, usually weighing 4 to 18 pounds. Most abundant from May through July.

Ulua (jackfish) A favorite sport fish among deep-water spearfishers. Ranges from 15 to 100 pounds and has white flesh with a meaty texture. Popular year-round.

Fish to Meet

Humuhumunukunukuapua'a (triggerfish) The fame of this fairly common fish, which was briefly Hawaii's state fish, comes from its long name. *Humuhumu* means "to fit pieces together," and *nukunukuapua'a* is Hawaiian for "nose like a pig." The triggerfish (illustrated above) is equipped with two protective devices: when frightened, it dives for its nest and locks itself in place with its dorsal fin, and its eyes can rotate independently, enabling it to see in two directions at once.

Oiliuwiuwi (fan-tailed filefish) Yellow with black dots, the fan-tailed filefish (pictured above) is named for the grunting and squealing noises it makes when removed from the water (*oiliuwiuwi* means "squealing oili"). Early Hawaiians used them as fuel to cook tastier fish since they were too scrawny to eat.

Kihikihi (moorish idol) The breathtaking beauty and fragility of the *kihikihi* (pictured above) places it in a class by itself. It's usually found in small schools using its long snout to probe for food in the crevices of reefs.

Uhu (parrot fish) A fascinating fish, often found in the waters of Hanauma Bay off Oahu, that scrapes algae off the coral with its jagged beak. By day, *uhus* (like the one above) flash their one- to four-foot-long gaudy bodies covered with blue-green, gray, and rust-colored scales. While sleeping at night, they cover themselves in a secretion that forms a protective bubble. Remarkably, uhus can change their sex; those born as males eventually turn into females. The omnivores also create sand: they eat coral, crustaceans, and mollusks, which are excreted as grains of sand.

Lauwiliwili (crochet or lemon butterfly fish) The *lauwiliwili* (shown above) is found in abundance throughout Hawaii but so far has been seen nowhere else. You can identify this fish, which grows up to 6 inches long, by the 11 vertical rows of spots on either side of its body.

Of the 680 types of fish found in Hawaiian waters, about 200 are found nowhere else in the world.

Octopus, commonly referred to as *tako* by locals, is often mistaken for Mexican food by tourists. Try the tako with *limu* (seaweed) if you're feeling adventurous—it's *onolicious*.

On a typical day in Hawaii, 171,000 people hang out at the beach, 25,000 go fishing, 22,000 ride the waves, 20,000 scuba dive, and 3,000 paddle canoes.

The tally for extinct species in Hawaii adds up to a sobering 100 plants, 88 invertebrates, and 24 birds; endangered species total 41 invertebrates, 29 birds, 19 plants, 8 marine mammals, 2 reptiles, and 1 land mammal.

10 Kanemitsu Bakery ★$ Open since 1925, Kanemitsu Bakery is a Molokai legend, with bread that appears on menus all over the island. When other islanders visit Molokai, they inevitably return home with some of the famous Molokai bread, a round white loaf that's simply delectable. You'll also find Molokai raisin-nut, onion-cheese, or wheat bread, along with doughnuts, pies, cakes, cinnamon crisps, and a first-rate *haupia* jelly-roll cake. Try to get here early, though, because everything tends to go fast. ♦ Kaunakakai. 553.5855

11 Kapuaiwa Coconut Grove Kamehame-ha V planted a thousand palm trees here in the 1860s when he was only a prince, and several hundred of them can still be seen in one of Hawaii's last surviving royal groves. There's a shoreside park nearby for picnicking. ♦ Hwy 460, near Kaunakakai

12 Kualapuu Reservoir The rubber-lined reservoir is the world's largest, containing 1.4 billion gallons of water. Molokai residents are very proud of it. ♦ Off Hwy 470, near Kualapuu

13 Kualapuu Cookhouse ★$ A tiny converted plantation house, Kualapuu Cookhouse feels like an old-fashioned diner, complete with Formica tables and enormous omelets. Chili, saimin, salads, nachos, teriyaki chicken sandwiches, and quarter-pound burgers appear on the menu, but the real specialties are the plate lunches and homemade pies. ♦ Hwy 470, Kualapuu. 567.6185

14 Purdy's All-Natural Macadamia Nut Farm With heavy emphasis on the "all natural" part, friendly and vivacious **Tuddie Purdy** will teach you everything you ever wanted to know about macadamia nuts. You'll learn how to crack the hard inner shell of the nut without breaking your nails, how long it takes for a nut to mature (nine months), how to open a coconut and then dip its flesh into honey, and how long macadamias have been in Hawaii (one hundred years). He'll also reassure you that macadamia nuts roasted without oil have very few calories and no saturated fats or cholesterol. Best of all, he'll tell you all this just because he thinks you should know, never putting on the pressure to buy his nuts (which you will anyway out of guilt). Purdy's nut farm is one of Molokai's top attractions. ♦ Daily 9AM-1PM. Off Hwy 470 (on Lihi Pali St behind the high school), Kualapuu. 567.6601 (days), 567.6495 (evenings)

Restaurants/Clubs: Red **Hotels:** Blue
Shops/ ♥ Outdoors: Green **Sights/Culture:** Black

15 Ironwood Hills Golf Course The 1,500-foot elevation and majestic eucalyptus and ironwood trees make this a distinctive course—not well-known, but scenic and enjoyable. Play the nine-hole championship course twice for an 18-hole round. For 18 holes: par 68, 6,176 yards. ♦ North on Kalae Hwy: turn left 8 miles after the 4-mile marker. 567.6000

16 Palaau State Park One of Molokai's few designated recreation areas, 234-acre Palaau forms part of the **Molokai Forest Reserve** on the north side of the island. Camping and picnic facilities are available in this forested mountain area. ♦ Off Hwy 470, north of Kualapuu

Within Palaau State Park:

Kalaupapa Lookout Considered one of the finest views in Hawaii, this 1,500-foot-high lookout offers an exquisite view of Kalaupapa. A series of displays tell the story behind the settlement below. ♦ At the end of Hwy 470

Phallic Rock If you think Mother Nature lacks a sense of humor, check out this large and rather provocative stone, which has given rise to various legends, including the tale that childless women who spend the night at the base of the stone will go home and soon become pregnant. Bring the camera for this one. ♦ Near Kalaupapa Lookout

Molokai Mule Ride The popular mule ride was forced to close operations in early 1993 because of high insurance costs. Visitors who still want to visit Kalaupapa can do so by plane. ♦ For information, contact **Rare Adventures** at 800/624.7771.

17 Kalaupapa This little town on the flat, isolated peninsula of Kalaupapa figures poignantly and tragically in the history of Molokai. In 1866 Hawaiian monarchy began banishing people with Hansen's disease (leprosy) to this area, separating them from families and loved ones. Lacking decent food and shelter, they lived here in great misery until their death. After arriving in 1873, a Belgian priest by the name of **Father Damien de Veuster** chose to live in isolation with these people, selflessly providing them with spiritual and physical aid for the rest of his life. Damien contracted the disease in 1884 and died five years later, shortly after the completion of his **St. Philomena's Church** in Kalawao.

After his death, Father Damien became known as the "martyr of Molokai" for his heroic dedication to the leprosy victims. When sulfone drugs brought the disease under control in the 1940s, the patients still

living here were cured and therefore free to go. However, since Kalaupapa had been their home since childhood, they chose to stay. Today, fewer than 90 still remain. A steep, zigzag foot trail leads down the 1,600-foot slopes overlooking the settlement, but it's reserved for invited guests and tours only.
♦ Air taxi service is available from the Molokai Airport through **Rare Adventures** (800/624.7771).

State Standouts

Nene Bird

State Bird The rare and fascinating nene (pronounced NAY-nay) is the state's largest bird, a species of goose that is able to survive in the rugged terrain of old lava beds. The nene has clawlike digits instead of webbed feet.

State Flower The Mallow Marvel, which belongs to the Malvaceae or Mallow family, is a large and showy hibiscus. This edible flower is sometimes used in salads.

State Mammal Humpback whales, which visit Hawaii's waters during their annual winter migration, were named the official state mammal in 1979.

State Motto *Ua mau ke ea o ka aina i ka pono* (Hawaiian for "The life of the land is perpetuated in righteousness") was written by King Kamehameha III in 1843, when Great Britain restored Hawaiian sovereignty. It became the official state motto in 1959.

State Song *Hawaii Pono'i,* which means "Great" or "Mighty Hawaii," was composed by King Kalakaua in 1874, with music by royal bandmaster Henri Berger. The song was written as a tribute to Kamehameha I, Hawaii's great ruler and warrior.

State Tree The *kukui* (or candlenut tree) produces a quarter-size nut filled with an oil that is used as a healing aid, for dyes, and to make candles.

Hawaii has the greatest number of threatened, endangered, and extinct indigenous species of flora in the nation.

18 Hoolehua Known for its cockfights, quilted patches of farmland, and budding taro industry, Hoolehua is an agricultural area in the northwest part of the island.
♦ Off Hwy 480

19 Maunaloa General Store It's the only store within miles of Maunaloa, an old plantation town, and its merchandise is appropriately diverse. You'll find everything from picnic supplies to fishing equipment.
♦ Maunaloa. 552.2868

19 Big Wind Kite Factory and Plantation Gallery It took a windy town like Maunaloa to spawn Hawaii's only kite factory. **Jonathan Socher** and his wife, **Daphne**, design and make kites with images of Diamond Head, tropical fish, milk cows, and other colorful Hawaiian motifs. Adjoining the kite shop is their gallery of local and Indonesian crafts—clothing, handbags, T-shirts, native wood bowls, Balinese carvings, and the like. ♦ M-Sa 8:30AM-5PM; Su 10AM-2PM. Maunaloa. 552.2364

19 Jojo's Cafe $ **Jojo Espaniola's** specialty is fresh fish, complemented by Portuguese bean soup, Korean short ribs, teriyaki steak, burgers, hot dogs, saimin, and chicken, all served in a homey atmosphere. Locals go for Jojo's fish and ribs in ethnic preparations (which is a good thing, considering it's the only place to eat in town). Open for lunch and dinner.
♦ Maunaloa. 552.2803

20 Molokai Ranch Wildlife Park Hailed as one of the finest natural-game preserves, this African safari-like wildlife preserve has hundreds of exotic animals, including antelope, greater kudu, oryx, Indian black buck, eland, giraffe, and Barbary sheep. They're all raised on one thousand acres of fenced-in pastureland, a venture of the cattle-raising and hay-growing Molokai Ranch. Groups of up to 14 can picnic in the park, an affair that inevitably attracts the gregarious giraffe, who may lean over the fence to say hello. The narrated tour of the wildlife preserve takes about two hours. Tours are booked daily at the activities desk of the **Colony's Kaluakoi Hotel and Golf Club.** ♦ Admission. 552.2555

21 Paniolo Hale Condominiums $$$ Of all the possible places to stay on Molokai, Paniolo Hale is probably the best. Some of the 36 rentals at this six-acre property on **Kepuhi Beach** feature private hot tubs on the lanais, and all of them have telephones, full kitchens, and washers and dryers. There's also a pool and golf at the nearby Kaluakoi course. Choose from studios and one- and two-bedroom suites. ♦ Off Kakaako Rd, Maunaloa. 552.2731, 800/367.2984; fax 552.2289

22 Kaluakoi Villas $$$ Each of the hundred units features an ocean view, plus island-style decor with rattan furnishings, ceiling fans, television, kitchenettes, and private lanais. If you stay here you can still take advantage of the **Kaluakoi Hotel's** activities. ♦ Kaluakoi Rd, off Hwy 460. 552.2721, 800/525.1470; fax 552.2201

22 Ke Nani Kai $$$ Adjoining Colony's Kaluakoi Hotel and Golf Club, the Ke Nani Kai offers 120 large one- and two-bedroom suites that are well-managed, clean, and spread out in clusters of wooden buildings. This isn't exactly a deluxe hotel, but it's comfortable, with ocean and mountain views, large kitchens, and lanais. It's about a five-minute walk from here to the beach. ♦ Kaluakoi Rd, off Hwy 460. 552.2761, 800/552.2761 (HI), 800/888.2791 (U.S.); fax 552.0045

22 Colony's Kaluakoi Hotel and Golf Club $$$ Molokai's top (and only) destination resort is a serene oasis for the traveler who truly wants to get away from it all. Managed

by **Colony Resorts,** the two-story redwood and ohia structures overlook a wide stretch of **Kepuhi Beach.** A championship golf course, 15-kilometer jogging path, horseback riding, four tennis courts, a pool, and a volleyball court are available to guests. For the less energetic, the hotel gives lessons in lei making, coconut-frond weaving, and hula dancing. There are 290 guest rooms with lanais, high-beamed ceilings, and fans to augment the ocean breezes. ♦ Kaluakoi Rd, off Hwy 460. 552.2555, 800/777.1700; fax 552.2821

Within Colony's Kaluakoi Hotel and Golf Club:

Ohia Lodge ★★$$$ The tiered dining room gives every table a panoramic view of the beach and of Oahu in the distance. Molokai bread does wonders for the French toast at breakfast, and don't miss the *paniolo* beef stew for lunch. Dinner menus are rotated nightly; the Continental fare includes fresh fish, Hunan duck, Indonesian herbal chicken, rack of lamb, prime rib, and a few pasta dishes. The bountiful salad bar is a meal in itself. Live music nightly at the adjoining bar. ♦ 552.2555

Paniolo Broiler ★$$ Steaks are the main item here, broiled over *kiawe* charcoal and accompanied by the best salad bar on Molokai. The Broiler opens when the hotel is 60 percent occupied. ♦ 552.2555

Kaluakoi Golf Course There is a joke within Hawaii's hotel circles that people here lower their golf handicap by 10 strokes— meaning there's not much else to do on Molokai. Designed by **Ted Robinson,** the Kaluakoi course is windy yet pleasant, with five of its 18 holes bordering the ocean. Many inveterate golfers from Oahu consider this their getaway course, a place to enjoy the game while taking in panoramas of the Pacific and, if they're lucky, the quail, deer, pheasant, wild turkey, and partridge that roam the 160 acres. Nice putting green and driving range. Par 72, 6,559 yards. ♦ Moderate green fees (ask about specials). Pro shop 522.2739

Restaurants/Clubs: Red   **Hotels:** Blue
Shops/ 🌳 Outdoors: Green   **Sights/Culture:** Black

Hail to the Chiefs

In 1796, after years of civil war, the Hawaiian islands were united under **Kamehameha the Great.** His ascension to the throne gave birth to a dynasty that would last nearly a century and forever change the way of life of his subjects. After his death in 1819 he was succeeded by seven monarchs, the last of which was **Queen Liliuokalani,** the first female ruler of Hawaii, who was overthrown in 1893. What follows is a list of Hawaii's mighty monarchs and the years they ruled the islands.

Kamehameha I (1796-1819)

Kamehameha II (1819-24)

Kamehameha III (1825-54)

Kamehameha IV (1855-63)

Kamehameha V (1863-72)

William C. Lunalilo (1873-74)

David Kalakaua (1874-91)

Liliuokalani (1891-93)

King Kamehameha V and Prince Lunalilo were both bachelors when they died.

Kamehameha the Great

23 Papohaku Beach If you continue on Kaluakoi Road past the Colony's Kaluakoi Hotel and Golf Club, you'll see the sign for Papohaku, Hawaii's longest white sand beach. The three-mile stretch is ideal for beachcombing, sunning, and swimming during the calm summer months. ♦ Off Kaluakoi Hwy, west end of Molokai

24 Hale o Lono Harbor The only reason to come here is for Hawaii's annual **Aloha Week** (which actually lasts several weeks) held in September. Aloha Week is when the world's fastest outrigger paddlers participate in the grueling 42-mile canoe race from Molokai to Oahu (see "Paddlemonium!" on page 134). Founded in 1952 by Oahu canoeing enthusiast **Albert Edward "Toots" Minvielle,** the race is celebrated as the world's first and foremost long-distance, open-ocean canoeing competition. It begins with a ceremony at southwest Molokai's little Hale o Lono Harbor, crosses the treacherous **Molokai Channel,** and ends in a flourish of flowers and shouts at the **Duke Kahanamoku Beach** fronting the Hilton Hawaiian Village in Waikiki. The women race first, and the men compete two weeks later. ♦ One mile west of Halena

Author's Bests

Sights:
Halawa Valley
Molokai Ranch Wildlife Park
Palaau State Park
Purdy's All-Natural Macadamia Nut Farm

Restaurants:
Kanemitsu Bakery ★$
Kualapuu Cookhouse ★$
Ohio Lodge ★★$$$

Hotels:
Paniolo Hale Condominiums $$$
Pau Hana Inn $$

The first automobile in Hawaii was a Wood Electric, delivered to H.A. Baldwin of Honolulu, Oahu, in 1899.

The sea cliffs along the north coast of Molokai are the highest in the world, topping out at 3,000 feet.

Oahu

With its avenues of avarice, high-rise hotels, legendary beaches, historical battleships, and banzai surfers, Oahu (o-AH-hoo) is the nucleus of Hawaii, the island that has it all and then some. Although smaller than Maui and only slightly larger than Kauai, Oahu is where the majority of Hawaii's citizens choose to live—800,000 people, a whopping 80 percent of the state's entire population. Subsequently, Oahu has inherited more problems than any other island. One of the greatest ironies of tourism in Oahu is the J.O.J. (just off the jet) tourists who come to Hawaii expecting to get away from it all, only to find themselves stuck in **Honolulu's** rush-hour traffic and hopelessly lost (the road layout in Honolulu is comical at best). And city planners continue to approve developments, including two new convention centers in Waikiki, the $3 billion **Ko Olina** resort on the Waianae Coast, and a major expansion of the **Honolulu International Airport**. Fortunately, Oahu's undaunted aloha spirit compensates for these oversights. Even in the major metropolis of Honolulu, this remains a friendly island, whose people take great pride in their homeland. Cars here still slow down for yellow lights, warm smiles greet you at the hotels and restaurants, and there is plenty of prime beachfront space for everyone.

In addition to having some of the most exclusive hotels in the state (**Royal Hawaiian, Kahala Hilton**), famous attractions (**Pearl Harbor,** the **Polynesian Cultural Center**), finest restaurants (**Roy's, La Mer**), and largest shopping mal (**Ala Moana, Royal Hawaiian**), Oahu also has "TheBus," the only public transportation system in Hawaii. These seemingly ubiquitous brown-and-yellow behemoths will, for only 60 cents, take you anywhere on the island, such as the **Greater Honolulu** area, which includes Pearl Harbor, **Waikiki,** and the **Diamond Head** and **Koko Head** volcanoes; the scenic **windward side,** from **Kahaluu** to **Makapuu Point,** sight of the popular **Sea Life Park;** the **North Shore,** home of fabled **Sunset Beach,** monster waves, and insane surfer: and **Waianae Coast** on the northwestern side of the island. Aside from the mostly residential Waianae Coast, where locals prefer to remain undisturbed b tourists, all of these areas warrant exploring. The North Shore in particular makes for a pleasant day trip (not to be missed when the mammoth surfing waves come in), while the stunning views across **Pali Highway** and around the southeastern tip of the island offer a break from the cityscape.

There are basically two types of tourists who come to Oahu: the first-timers, who are at the mercy of their travel agents' advice; and the frequent flyers, who know exactly where and where not to go. The former usually end up in Waikiki, which is paradise to some and a bumper-to-bumper and rump-to-rump nightmare to most others. Even after a multimillion-dollar face-lift, Waikiki still suffers from overabundance; there's simply too much of everything in too small a space, occupied by coupon-laden tourists purchasing cheap souvenirs and dining at overrated, overpriced restaurants. But "vacationing" is a relative term, and what some would consider the equivalent of watching paint dry is a great time for others. That's the key to Oahu—there's something here for everyone, you just have to know where to look.

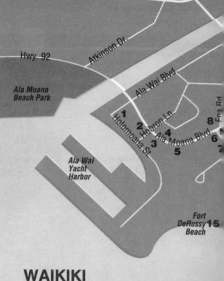

1 Hawaii Prince $$$$ The five-star Prince is crafted in international opulence (though its critics complain it has too much pink marble), boasting English slate, Spanish glass, Italian marble, Japanese tiles, and French accessories. All 521 rooms have floor-to-ceiling windows overlooking the yacht harbor. The Prince is within walking distance of **Ala Moana Beach Park** and **Ala Moana Shopping Mall,** although a free shuttle service will take you there and most other places in Waikiki. ◆ 100 Holomoana St, Honolulu. 956.1111, 800/321.6248; fax 800/338.8763

Within the Hawaii Prince:

Prince Court ★★★$$$ They call the cuisine American-regional, but the extensive menu has many Pacific and local elements, including slipper lobster and Kahuku shrimps on grilled corn bread, Hawaiian salmon and corn cakes, seafood and taro-leaf minestrone, and seared and smoked *ahi* with radish salsa and ginger-lime vinaigrette. American favorites are also featured—*kiawe*-grilled capon with corn-bread pudding, pan-seared duckling breast, and a wide selection of beef, lamb, and veal. The view of the harbor is cheerful by day and romantic at night. Brunch is served on Sunday. ◆ 956.1111

Hakone ★★★$$$$ The dishes served here are both traditional and exquisite: *kaiseki* dinners of soup, pickles, sashimi, broiled fish, and other Japanese favorites; grilled clam and salmon roe appetizers; and noodles, tempura, and assorted sashimi. When in season, the Kona crab is cooked to perfection. ◆ 956.1111

2 El Crab Catcher ★$$$ Yet another fresh seafood restaurant competing for a share of Honolulu's market, El Crab Catcher already has a good track record on Maui (where it originated), Kauai, and the West Coast. The airy interior is filled with lots of plants, wood, and bamboo. Crab-stuffed fish, shrimp scampi, and the catch of the day—especially the *opah* (moonfish)—are favorites. ◆ 1765 Ala Moana Blvd, Waikiki. 955.4911

Oahu's population density is nearly 10 times that of Maui, the second most crowded island in Hawaii.

Restaurants/Clubs: Red   Hotels: Blue
Shops/ 🌳 Outdoors: Green   **Sights/Culture:** Black

WAIKIKI

For nos. 64-136, see pg. 118

For nos. 137-190, see pg. 102

3 Ilikai Hotel $$$ Located on the outer fringe of Waikiki overlooking the **Ala Wai Yacht Harbor,** this 800-room high rise offers a compromise for people who want to be near the action but not consumed by it. Although dramatically eclipsed by the new Hawaii Prince hotel next door, the Ilikai still reigns as Waikiki's acknowledged tennis center, with six courts (including a lighted court with artificial grass) and two resident tennis pros. Nearby you'll find a placid beachfront lagoon and **Ala Moana Beach Park,** plus it's only a five-minute walk from the **Ala Moana Shopping Mall,** a mecca for shopping enthusiasts. The newly renovated rooms include kitchens with refrigerators and minibars, and five executive-meeting suites and a fitness center were recently added in the **Yacht Harbor Tower.** ◆ 1777 Ala Moana Blvd, Waikiki. 949.3811, 800/367.8434; fax 947.5523

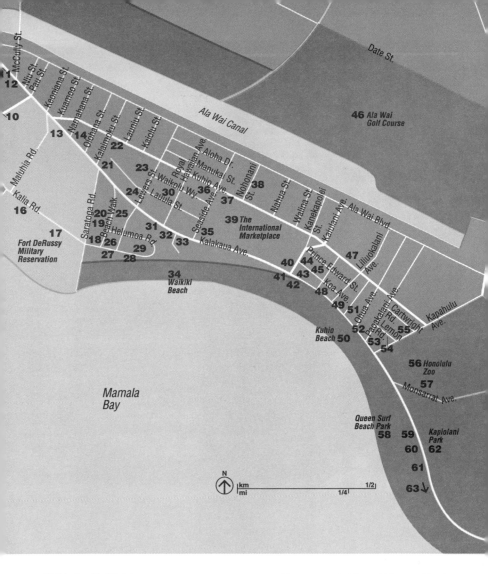

McCully St.
Niu St.
Pau St.
1
12
Keoniana St.
Kuamoo St.
Namahana St.
Olohana St.
Kalaimoku St.
Launiu St.
Kaiolu St.
10
13 **14**
22
Date St.
Ala Wai Canal
46 Ala Wai
Golf Course
Maluhia Rd.
21
23
Royal Hawaiian Ave.
Aloha Dr.
Manukai St.
Kuhio Ave.
Nohonani
Nahua St.
Walina St.
Kanekapolei St.
Kaiulani Ave.
Ala Wai Blvd.
38
37
36
Lewers St.
Waikolu Wy.
Lauula St.
24
30
Seaside Ave.
31
32
33
35
34
Waikiki
Beach
Kalia Rd.
16
Saratoga Rd.
Beach Walk
20
19
25
18 **26**
Helumoa Rd.
27
28
29
17
Fort DeRussy
Military
Reservation
39 The
International
Marketplace
Kalakaua Ave.
40
41
42
44
43
45
Prince Edward St.
Koa Ave.
48
Liliuokalani Ave.
Kanekapolei
Kaiulani Ave.
47
49
51
52
53
54
55
Paoakalani
Cartwright Rd.
Lemon Rd.
Ohua Ave.
Kanahulu
Ave.
Kuhio
Beach **50**
56 Honolulu
Zoo
57
Monsarrat Ave.
Queen Surf
Beach Park
58
59
60
61
62
63 ↓
Kapiolani
Park
Mamala
Bay
N ↑ km
mi   1/4   1/2

Within the Ilikai Hotel:

Yacht Club Restaurant and Bar ★★$$$
Fresh island seafood is the specialty here,
embellished with everything from black-bean
sauce to caviar butter. There's a nice view of
the harbor from the terrace and split-level
dining room, and live entertainment nightly.
♦ 949.3811

The Comedy Club Local and national
comedians, from budding hypnotists to big-
name acts, perform here, many of them
straight from "The Tonight Show" and other
mainland talk shows. ♦ Admission. Shows
Tu-Su 7PM, 10PM. 922.5998

4 Bon Appetit ★★$$$ Tucked away inside
the mammoth **Discovery Bay** condominium
towers, this petite French restaurant looks like
the kind of place you'd find in Beverly Hills or
Carmel. Owner/chef **Guy Banal,** a veteran of
some of the world's finest kitchens, changes
the menu weekly to include tempting entrées

of island fish, duckling, chicken, and lamb.
♦ 1778 Ala Moana Blvd (across from the Ilikai
Hotel), Waikiki. 942.3837

5 Aston Waikikian Hotel $$ The hotel's
most appealing aspect is that it's everything
the rest of Waikiki isn't—small (132 rooms),
friendly, and Polynesian in both appearance
and mood (in other words, don't expect
anything fancy). The original buildings are no
more than two stories high (the separate
seven-story tower was built later), with
ground-level lanai rooms that open onto a
walkway verdant with palms and ferns.
Second-story rooms have lanais with partial
views of the ocean, the mountains, or at least
the walkway. It's an easy stroll from the
hotel's **Duke Kahanamoku Lagoon,** which has
its own beach, to the sands of Waikiki Beach.
Guests who prefer the Waikikian's low
elevation should specify a room in the original
Banyan Wing building, which is slated to be

replaced by an enormous high rise as soon as permits are obtained. ◆ 1811 Ala Moana Blvd, Waikiki. 949.5331, 800/922.7866; fax 946.2843

Within the Aston Waikikian Hotel:

TAHITIAN LANAI

Tahitian Lanai ★★$$$ Old-timers love this balmy poolside setting with its casual Polynesian ambience, superb breakfasts, and popular sing-along piano bar. Come try the legendary eggs Benedict before the place is razed. ◆ 946.6541

6 **Kobe Steak House** ★$$$ Although the chefs, who give flamboyant live performances at the teppanyaki grills, contribute to the festive atmosphere, they're still serving formula Japanese cuisine—good but not worth writing home about. ◆ 1841 Ala Moana Blvd, Waikiki. Valet parking. 941.4444

7 **Hilton Hawaiian Village** $$$ After spending $100 million on architectural renovations in the 1980s, the palatial Hilton has a new look. Several small buildings were torn down and replaced by landscaped gardens and a two-tier swimming pool, and the **Ocean Tower** was gutted and reborn as the upscale **Alii Tower**, an exclusive hotel within the hotel, with its own separate guest reception area, concierge, private pool, and exercise room. Some of the original architecture remains, including the garish 16,000-tile rainbow mural on the **Rainbow Tower's** exterior (the tallest mosaic mural in the world, according to Guinness).

With a total room count of 2,523, the Hilton is the largest hotel in the state, just short of a self-contained village, with more than a hundred shops, 20 restaurants and lounges, three pools, banquet and convention facilities for up to 5,000 people, a six-story parking garage, its own boat dock, and one of Waikiki's largest showrooms, the **Hilton Dome**, home of the "Don Ho" show. It also has a choice location on **Waikiki Beach,** with catamaran sailing, **Pearl Harbor** cruises, and various other outdoor activities. ◆ 2005 Kalia Rd, Waikiki. 949.4321, 800/445.8667; fax 947.7898

Within the Hilton Hawaiian Village:

Benihana of Tokyo ★$$$ Not only is everything cooked here (making Benihana a perfect choice for those with a phobia of Japanese food, especially raw fish), cooking is the main attraction. Chefs perform at the teppanyaki grills, twirling their knives while slashing away—samurai style, with blinding speed and precision—at beef, shrimp, and vegetables. ◆ 955.5955

Golden Dragon ★★$$ Longtime chef **Dai Hoy Chang** has retired, leaving his stellar menu and many doubtful fans hoping that his successor, **Steve Chiang,** can continue the legacy. A festive atmosphere still prevails, as does the Peking duck and Beggar's chicken (24-hour advance notice required), the signature dishes of this vermilion and black Chinese restaurant. The extensive menu includes traditional Cantonese dishes such as lemon chicken, smoked duck, and lobster in curry sauce. ◆ Rainbow Tower. 946.3556

Bali by the Sea ★★$$$ This casually elegant restaurant lives up to its name, with spectacular views of Waikiki Beach and Diamond Head. Chef **Y'ves Menoret** has a knack for fresh seafood and imaginative sauces—*opakapaka* with fresh basil sauce, venison medaillons with cranberry and *poivrade* sauce, roast rack of lamb with black fig-and-peanut sauce, and *coquille* of shrimp and scallops in ginger sauce. The shrimp-and-lobster bisque is not to be missed. ◆ Rainbow Tower. 941.2254

8 **Wailana Coffee House** $ Open 24 hours, this Honolulu institution offers typical coffeehouse fare. Nothing special here, but it's still very popular among residents and tourists. (Hint: parking is a nightmare, so use the garage in the same building and validate your ticket). ◆ 1860 Ala Moana Blvd (across from Hilton Hawaiian Village), Waikiki. 955.1764

9 **California Pizza Kitchen** ★★$$ The immensely popular pizza-and-pasta chain has successfully invaded Honolulu, serving oven-fired pizzas with an eclectic choice of toppings, including rosemary chicken-potato, Caribbean shrimp, Peking duck, Thai chicken, and duck sausage. The ingredients are fresh and the crusts are the real thing (try the honey-wheat dough). Even the pasta dishes stand out. If you can't decide what to order, try the Sante Fe chicken pizza. ◆ 1910 Ala Moana Blvd (at Ena Rd), Waikiki. Validated parking for two hours. 955.5161

10 **Park Plaza Hotel** $$$ The recently opened Park Plaza has certainly stiffened the competition in the luxury-class hotel market. The 313 guest rooms are decorated in a modern yet subdued tone, with meticulous

attention to detail. Costly works of art, including a Picasso, are placed modestly about in the lobby. Amenities include a fitness center, business center, reading room, conference facilities, and room service provided by **Roy's Park Bistro**. If you have to stay in Waikiki and don't mind a short walk to the beach, check yourself into this small, unpretentious hotel. ◆ 1956 Ala Moana Blvd, Honolulu. 941.7275, 800/367.6070; fax 949.099

11 The Wave For Waikiki (or all of Hawaii, for that matter), this is as wild as the nightlife gets. The underground clubs here are tame compared to the big city clubs found on the mainland. The Wave is strictly for the young and the tireless, with live music until late into the night and DJ-spun dance music until much, much later (four in the morning to be exact). ◆ Admission. Daily 9PM-4AM. 1877 Kalakaua Ave (look for the snorkeling mural), Waikiki. 941.0424

12 Eggs 'n Things ★$ An institution for insomniacs, late-night party fiends, and workers getting off the graveyard shift. For a midnight snack or early breakfast, try a spinach, bacon, and cheese omelet, lemon crepes, or pancakes with macadamia nuts, chocolate chips, pecans, raisins, or bananas. Fresh mahimahi, swordfish, and *ono* (straight from the owner's fishing boat) are favorites, too. ◆ 1911 Kalakaua Ave, Waikiki. Validated parking at the Hawaiian Monarch Hotel. 949.0820

13 Kyo-ya ★★★$$$$ The landmark neon pagoda of the old Kyo-ya has been transformed into an ultracontemporary but very Japanese structure: marble, glass, slate, and concrete—a statement in minimalist elegance. A corner of the restaurant is devoted to *soba* (noodles) and the main dining room is downstairs. The breathtaking private tatami rooms are upstairs amid tasteful Zen gardens. Much has changed (including the prices, which have gone up), but the food is still first-rate; the sashimi is always fresh, and the fish *misoyaki* (fish soaked in a savory soybean by-product) is superb. ◆ 2057 Kalakaua Ave, Waikiki. 947.3911

14 Nick's Fishmarket ★★$$$ Nick Nickolas opened the first of his seafood palaces here, then moved on to greater fame and glory with other "Fishmarkets" in Los Angeles, Chicago, and Houston. The luxurious black booths and classic seafood selections make for a pleasant dining experience at one of Honolulu's premier seafood restaurants. Rumor has it that **Tom Selleck** is fond of the bouillabaisse here. ◆ 2070 Kalakaua Ave (in the Waikiki Gateway Hotel), Waikiki. Valet parking. 955.6333

15 Fort DeRussy Beach This Army-owned oasis of green open space is a favorite of residents and the military, with military personnel serving as lifeguards (talk about a cushy assignment). Picnic facilities, volleyball courts, and a snack bar. ◆ Opposite Kalia Rd, Waikiki

16 Hale Koa Hotel $$ The kingpin of the Army's Fort DeRussy reservation—72 acres of prime Waikiki real estate—this military-owned high rise is a sweet deal for military personnel and retired officers. Located next to one of the best beaches in Waikiki, the hotel has 419 units, a pool, and tennis courts. ◆ 2055 Kalia Rd, Waikiki. 955.0555, 800/367.6027

17 Fort DeRussy Army Museum Wartime artifacts and memorabilia are displayed inside a 1911 bunker with 22-foot-thick walls built so solidly that the Army turned it into a museum to avoid having to tear it down. Exhibits include ancient Hawaiian weapons, as well as memorabilia from the Korean and Vietnam wars, World War II, and even the Spanish-American War. Uniforms and tanks, coastal defense artillery, and articles and photos relating to the Army in Hawaii have also been preserved. ◆ Free. Tu-Su 10AM-4:30PM. Guided tours must be booked in advance. Building 32, Kalia Rd, Fort DeRussy, Waikiki. 438.2821

18 Royal Islander Hotel $$ A budget-minded hotel with a hundred nicely decorated rooms, the Royal Islander is within walking distance of Waikiki Beach. ◆ 2164 Kalia Rd, Waikiki. 926.0679, 800/462.6262; fax 922.1961

18 Malakini Hotel $ Okay, so it's not the Ritz-Carlton. There's no pool, TVs, or air-conditioners, and it's not even on the water (though it's near the beach). But for the price, this is a steal. The 28 rooms are spartan but clean, with kitchenettes, ceiling fans, and daily maid service. The low-budget Malakini is very popular, so make reservations well in advance. ◆ 217 Saratoga Rd, Waikiki. 923.9644

Oahu's Iolani Palace was the first building in Hawaii to have an electric light system and an in-house telephone; it was also the first palace in the world to have flush toilets.

Leaving your shoes at the doorstep before entering a guest's home is a common courtesy in Hawaii.

19 The Breakers $$ Those of you who want to be close to the beach without paying the price of a big-name hotel should check out this two-story lodge hidden among the high rises. It's reasonably priced, with 64 air-conditioned rooms (plus kitchenettes) in a setting complete with the requisite palm trees and tropical plants and flowers. Pool and daily maid service. ♦ 250 Beach Walk (between Kalakaua Ave and Waikiki Beach), Waikiki. 923.3181, 800/426.0494

20 The Hawaiiana Hotel $$ A refreshingly unpretentious low rise located half a block from Waikiki Beach and close to the Fort DeRussy Beach. The 95 newly redecorated rooms come with kitchenettes, air-conditioning, and connecting rooms for families. Overall, it's a good deal for Waikiki, and the mostly Hawaiian staff is unforgettable. Two pools and complimentary Kona coffee service. ♦ 260 Beach Walk, Waikiki. 923.3811, 800/367.5122; fax 926.5728

21 South Seas Village $$ On a thoroughfare besieged by fast-food restaurants pushing tacos and burgers, South Seas Village stands out as one of the few establishments plugging "authentic" Hawaiian specialties. For a snack try the *pipikaula* (Hawaiian beef jerky) and poi (pudding made of taro) or the Hawaiian platter of *kalua* pork, *lomilomi* salmon, rice, and *haupia*. The dinner menu also has Japanese *shabu-shabu*, American dishes, and curry. ♦ 2112 Kalakaua Ave, Waikiki. 923.8484

21 Popo's $$ What began as a strange architectural hodgepodge (containing even stranger restaurants) built by Japanese investors quickly folded and was bought out by the **Spencecliff** chain. Now it's a popular Japanese-owned Mexican restaurant (go figure) serving seemingly authentic Mexican dishes, including tacos, burritos, and enchiladas. ♦ 2112 Kalakaua Ave, Waikiki. 923.7355

22 Hamburger Mary's ★$ A landmark institution in Waikiki's gay quarter, this open-air grill and bar serves health-conscious fare ranging from meatless sandwiches to vegetarian eggs Benedict, but their specialty is, of course, hamburgers. The casual atmosphere is ideal for a quick break from the city shuffle. Stop just long enough to knock down a beer and a mushroom burger for less than 10 bucks—a bargain in Waikiki. ♦ 2109 Kuhio Ave, Waikiki. 922.6722

23 Waikiki Joy Hotel $$$ A boutique hotel—petite, catering to business travelers, and big on things like bathrooms with Jacuzzis and state-of-the-art stereo speakers. Some of the nicer touches include: the Corporate Suite Program, which guarantees special rates for business travelers; valet parking; complimentary newspaper, breakfast, and local calls; and many business services. On a small, noisy side street off the beach, the Joy Hotel has a curious charm despite the absence of views from its two towers, one with 11 floors and the other with eight for a total of 52 rooms and 49 suites. Pool, restaurant. ♦ 320 Lewers St, Waikiki. 923.2300, 800/733.5569; fax 924.4010

24 Moose McGillycuddy's Pub & Cafe ★$$ Part of a chain that extends from Maui to the mainland, Moose McGillycuddy's is a blue-collar kind of place, with daily drink specials, cheap breakfasts, and a popular early-bird dinner menu (try the prime rib). Rock music plays every night upstairs and sporting events are shown continuously via satellite. ♦ 310 Lewers St, Waikiki. 923.0751

25 House of Hong ★$$ This restaurant has suffered a severe drop in popularity, but for many years it was the leading Chinese restaurant in Waikiki. The large glittery dining rooms are decorated with ancient art objects and serviced by a huge Cantonese menu of standard fare. ♦ 260-A Lewers St (at Kalakaua Ave), Waikiki. 923.0202

25 Perry's Smorgy $ Still popular with the all-you-can-eat-cheap buffet crowd, Perry's is something of an American phenomenon, where tourists are corralled toward troughs of grub to receive their wafer-thin slice of roast beef. Large windows allow spectators to witness feeding time. ♦ 250 Lewers St, Waikiki. 922.8814

26 Trattoria ★★$$$ A longtime Honolulu favorite located in the **Outrigger Edgewater Hotel,** Trattoria serves a variety of pasta dishes, veal (which is particularly popular), lasagna, fettuccine Alfredo, and other Northern Italian classics. This is one of Waikiki's perennial, reliable restaurants—even locals eat here. ♦ 2168 Kalia Rd, Waikiki. Valet parking. 923.8415

27 Outrigger Reef Hotel $$$ One of the nicest (and most expensive) hotels of the Outrigger chain, the Reef is located directly on Waikiki Beach with 885 air-conditioned rooms (some of which have kitchenettes) in a wide price range. Fort DeRussy Beach, with its volleyball courts and water activities, is nearby. Rates have gone up because of recent renovations but are still more reasonable than at most beachfront hotels. Pool. ♦ 2169 Kalia Rd, Waikiki. 923.3111, 800/462.6262

Halekulani

28 Halekulani Hotel $$$$ The Halekulani (which means "the house befitting heaven") successfully combines the impeccable standards of a first-class establishment with the gracious atmosphere of old Hawaii. When **Robert Lewers** opened the Halekulani in 1907, it consisted of quaint cottages with overhanging eaves, nestled in a coconut grove. In 1981 the hotel was sold to the **Halekulani Corporation,** which razed the aging cottages to make way for the existing medium-rise resort but restored the main building and the **House without a Key** lounge (leaving untouched an impressive beachside *kiawe* tree). Almost all of the 456 rooms look out at the beach, each one tasteful down to the smallest detail—bathrobes, complimentary morning paper, and freshly cut flowers. Another luxury is the in-room check-in service, which eliminates waiting in the lobby to register. If you're in Waikiki and can afford the steep rates, the Halekulani is the place to stay. ♦ 2199 Kalia Rd, Waikiki. 923.2311, 800/367.2343; fax 926.8004

Within the Halekulani Hotel:

Orchids ★★★$$$ For breakfast, lunch, or dinner, Orchids stands out as one of Hawaii's nicest restaurant settings, with a terraced open-air dining room overlooking Diamond Head and the Pacific. The innovative menu complements the casually elegant surroundings. Entrées range from smoked mahimahi to an occasional Asian specialty, including a green papaya salad. Sunday brunch is Orchid's most popular production, though you may have to abuse the credit card a bit to attend. ♦ 923.2311

La Mer ★★★★$$$$ Serious connoisseurs dub La Mer the finest restaurant in Hawaii. Certainly the view from the elegant dining room is uncomparable, with palm trees silhouetted against the darkening ocean at sunset. It's a picture-perfect setting, and chef **George Mavrothalassitis** has created a menu to match it. The signature here is fresh seafood prepared a number of imaginative ways—*onaga* (red snapper) poached with three-caviar sauce; *kumu* (goatfish) *en papillote,* with seaweed and shiitake

mushrooms; and a carefully gleaned selection of meat and fowl. Whatever you do, leave room for dessert—the fruit tulip with passion fruit coulis is amazing. Yes, it's a very expensive meal, especially if you have to buy a jacket to get in, but at least you can say you've dined at the best. ♦ Jacket required. 923.2311

House without a Key ★★$$ A key would actually be useless here considering this is an open-air restaurant and cocktail bar. Full breakfast buffet, sandwiches on whole-wheat bread, and hamburgers, as well as local favorites such as sashimi and saimin (noodles in broth), are served with a view of the ocean and Diamond Head. A romantic hula show under the old *kiawe* tree may inspire you to dance under the stars after knocking back a few mai tais. ♦ 923.2311

Lewers Lounge Plush with leather and teak, Lewers is the perfect cocktail spot for couples and conferring businesspeople. It's quiet except for the tinkling of ivory at the piano bar and the voices of the fine jazz singers who regularly perform here. Play a game of backgammon while enjoying a cup of tea in the enclosed veranda. ♦ 923.2311

29 Waikiki Parc $$$ The **Halekulani Corporation** built this 22-story hotel in 1987 as a less-expensive alternative to the Halekulani Hotel just across the street. If you can live with the limited ocean view and the 30-second walk to the beach, it makes sense to stay here. All 298 rooms have private lanais or balconies, fully stocked refrigerators and minibars, and individual temperature controls. Pool, laundromat. ♦ 2233 Helumoa Rd, Waikiki. 921.7272, 800/422.0450; fax 923.1336

Within Waikiki Parc:

Parc Cafe ★★★$$$ An appealing buffet in terms of price and selection, though certainly not as big as those at the larger, fancier hotels. The selection of Continental and American cuisine is prepared with an island flair, and the dinner buffet is one of Honolulu's best values, with a variety of fresh fish; stir-fried vegetables; duck, leg of lamb, or chicken carved to order; and a fabulous salad bar, with everything from Peking duck salad to Kula tomatoes and charbroiled eggplant. A commendable choice for breakfast, lunch, or dinner. ♦ 921.7272

Kacho ★★$$$ Sushi is the specialty in this small but stunning contemporary restaurant, highlighted by a long granite sushi bar. The more adventurous might try the *kaiseki* dinner (a set-menu affair) or the 11-course traditional Japanese breakfast, which includes miso soup, grilled fish, steamed rice, and a raw egg. ♦ 924.3535

Restaurants/Clubs: Red	**Hotels:** Blue
Shops/ 🌴 Outdoors: Green	**Sights/Culture:** Black

109

30 Duty Free Shops If you have an airline ticket for a destination outside the U.S., you can visit a duty-free shop at the **Honolulu International Airport** or here in Waikiki. Duty-free shops are especially popular among Japanese tourists because the merchandise is generally less expensive than in their homeland, but there aren't many bargains for Americans. ◆ Daily 9AM-11PM. 330 Royal Hawaiian Ave, Waikiki. 931.2700

31 Royal Hawaiian Shopping Center A four-level, 150-store complex with the biggest names in international fashion: **Chanel, Louis Vuitton, Hermès, Lancel, Gianni Versace,** and more, as well as a liberal selection of restaurants. ◆ Kalakaua Ave (at Lewers St), Waikiki. 922.0588

Within the Royal Hawaiian Shopping Center:

Restaurant Suntory ★★$$$ Suntory Ltd., the Japanese liquor producer that has built showcase restaurants in the major capitals of the world, reportedly spent more than $2 million on this one. Elegance abounds from the handsome cocktail lounge to the separate dining rooms, each devoted to a special style of Japanese cuisine: *shabu-shabu,* teppanyaki, sushi, and a traditional Japanese room with tatami seating (sunken areas accommodate extended legs). ◆ Orchid Court, third floor. 922.5511

Cafe Princess $$ A coffee shop with an American menu embellished with several island favorites. Outdoor seating makes for a nice break from shopping. ◆ Orchid Court, ground floor. 926.2000

32 Sheraton-Waikiki $$$$ A giant of a hotel with 1,852 rooms and more than 45,000 square feet of meeting space. Even after the much-touted millions spent on improvements in the 1980s, the lofty ocean views remain the best feature of this monstrosity, the largest resort in the world when it opened in 1971 (**Hilton Hawaiian Village** has since surpassed it). Although advertisements promote the Sheraton-Waikiki as a hotel on the beach (which it is in a structural sense), don't blink or you'll miss the actual beachfront, which seems as tiny as a postage stamp when compared to the size of the hotel. Two pools. ◆ 2255 Kalakaua Ave, Waikiki. 922.4422, 800/325.3535; fax 923.8785

Within the Sheraton-Waikiki:

Hanohano Room ★★$$$$ Take the glass elevator 30 floors to the highest viewing area on Waikiki Beach for a panorama of Diamond Head and the beaches. Your best bet here is breakfast or sunset cocktails, but there's also a large dining room serving Continental cuisine with dancing afterwards. ◆ 922.4422

33 Royal Hawaiian Hotel $$$$ Despite overbearing high-rise neighbors, the Royal Hawaiian (pictured below) clings to its nostalgic glory as the "Pink Palace of the Pacific." The original Spanish-Moorish design, by **Warren & Wetmore,** cost the **Matson Navigation Company** a cool $4 million by the time the hotel opened in 1927 (Matson built it primarily to provide world-class accommodations for passengers sailing on their luxury liners). Before World War II, the Royal Hawaiian was the exclusive playground of the wealthy and famous, who traveled with steamer trunks, servants, and sometimes Rolls-Royces. Hollywood celebrities such as **Mary Pickford** and **Douglas Fairbanks** vacationed here, as did honeymooners **Nelson Rockefeller** and **Henry Ford II** (with their brides, that is). The halcyon days ended abruptly during World War II, when the hotel was leased to the Navy as an R&R spot for sailors from the Pacific fleet.

Sheraton bought the hotel in 1959 and added the 16-story **Royal Tower,** then sold it to

Royal Hawaiian Hotel

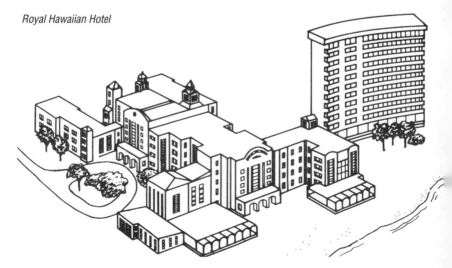

Japanese industrialist **Kenji Osano** (though Sheraton continues to run operations). Entering the ornate porte cochere is impressive; chandeliered walkways leading from the spacious lobby are wide and richly carpeted, and the famous flower tree at the entrance to the **Monarch Room** bursts with hundreds of tropical blossoms. A green lawn ensconced by lush tropical foliage and banyan trees leads to Waikiki Beach, where Royal Hawaiian guests enjoy a private stretch of sand. Though the Royal Tower offers modern levels of comfort, nostalgic guests will prefer to stay in the original stucco structure, still faithfully and regularly repainted to its traditional pink color. There are 526 rooms on the 10-acre property, all with air-conditioning, refrigerators, and pink telephones. ◆ 2259 Kalakaua Ave, Waikiki. 923.7311, 800/325.3535; fax 924.7098

Within the Royal Hawaiian Hotel:

Mai Tai Bar Watch the action on Waikiki Beach from this open-air, beachside bar, open until 1AM. True to its name, the bar makes excellent (and expensive) mai tais. There's also live Hawaiian entertainment by **Keith** and **Carmen Haugen.** ◆ 923.7311

Monarch Room ★★$$$ This large, ornate dining room overlooking the beach opened in 1927. For years the dress code was black-tie (aloha attire is now accepted) and great entertainers from all over the world performed here. The immensely talented **Brothers Cazimeros** put on the current act, with a show that encompasses the best in traditional and modern Hawaiian dance, contemporary Hawaiian music, and humorous "talk-story" routines. The menu offers a wide range of entrées, from veal to lobster, and the service is first-rate. ◆ Shows Tu-Sa 6:30-10PM. 923.7311

Royal Hawaiian Luau $$$ If you want to experience the ubiquitous and classic hotel luau, you might as well go all out and do it here. ◆ Cover. M 6-9PM

34 **Waikiki Beach** The "Mother Superior" of all Hawaii's beaches stretches in broken segments from **Ala Wai Canal** to **Diamond Head,** tirelessly absorbing the throngs of tourists and hotel facades that encroach its golden grains. Despite what hotel markers claim, the two-mile beach is public property up to the high-water mark (and that's what you'll find here . . . plenty of the public). Although parts of the beach were widened in the mid-1980s to ease traffic, congestion is still a problem. Swimming is safe, even for beginners, and surfboards, boogie boards, umbrellas, beach mats, snorkel gear, and more can be rented from concession stands along the beach. You can even take surfing lessons (they guarantee you'll stand on the board) for about $15 an hour, which includes the surfboard. ◆ Off Kalakaua Ave, Waikiki

35 **Waikiki Beachcomber** $$ Set in the very heart of congested Waikiki, the Beachcomber offers easy access to the shopping malls and Waikiki Beach, reasonable rates, and air-conditioned rooms with balconies. There's also a pool, Hawaiian entertainment nightly in the **Surfboard Lounge,** and dining in the **Beachcomber Restaurant.** ◆ 2300 Kalakaua Ave, Waikiki. 922.4646, 800/622.4646; fax 923.4889

36 **Matteo's** ★★$$$ Well-known restaurateur **Fred Livingston,** who also owns **Trattoria** and **Tahitian Lanai,** uses high-backed booths, soft lighting, and amber tones to create an intimate, relaxing ambience. The osso buco, chicken Florentine, and steaks are all popular with the lawyers, yuppies, and show-biz types that frequent here. ◆ 364 Seaside Ave, Waikiki. Valet parking. 922.5551

37 **Maharaja** $$$ Somewhat uppity and self-conscious, Maharaja is a Japanese-owned restaurant and disco with a dress code, a VIP room where members are ushered in for $500 a year in dues, and a varied late-night menu. Decked out in marble and brass, with the full gamut of high-tech bells and whistles on the dance floor, this place fancies itself as Honolulu's hottest nightclub. ◆ In the Waikiki Trade Center, 2255 Kuhio Ave, Waikiki. 922.3030

38 **Sergio's** ★★★$$$ Loyal local patrons frequent this trattoria, considered by many to be the best Italian restaurant in Honolulu. **Sergio Battistetti,** who owned **Trattoria** for 13 years, has applied his seasoned culinary wizardry to the 50-plus Northern Italian dishes on the menu. The osso buco, fresh fish, and lamb are recommended, as is everything with shiitake mushrooms. ◆ 445 Nohonani St (within the Ilima Hotel), Waikiki. 926.3388

39 **The International Marketplace** The fancy name belies the mostly worthless merchandise, much of which looks exactly the same, probably because it is. Located across from the Moana Surfrider Hotel, the open-air grounds are shaded by a huge banyan tree. The only thing remotely international about the place is the bargaining system—make an offer. ◆ Daily 9AM-late at night. 2330 Kalakaua Ave, Waikiki. 923.9871

40 **Princess Kaiulani Hotel** $$$ This **Sheraton** hotel has seriously expanded since 1955, when the 11-story main building opened. A 28-story tower built in 1970 and three wings bring the present total to 1,150 rooms. Located across from the **King's Village** shopping center, it's only one block from Waikiki Beach. The rooms have several price categories, dictated by ocean, city, or mountain views, although note that this is not an oceanfront hotel. Pool, several restaurants, and bars. ◆ 120 Kaiulani Ave, Waikiki. 922.5811, 800/325.3535; fax 923.9912

111

Hang Ten

Surfing was formally introduced to the Hawaiian islands by Polynesians, who brought the ancient sport with them when they migrated from the South Seas around AD 500. Hawaiian chants dating back to the 15th century also refer to surfing exploits and contests. And when **Captain James Cook** arrived on Oahu in 1778, he found Hawaiian men and women riding waves on wooden planks and canoe fragments. At that time, surfing was the sport of Hawaiian royalty, who not only got the best surfboards (made of choice lighter woods) but also enjoyed exclusive rights to the top surfing beaches. In fact, commoners caught trespassing on the "royal" surfing spots faced the death penalty.

The sport all but disappeared during the missionary era and wasn't officially reestablished until the early 1900s, when **Duke Kahanamoku,** a champion Hawaiian swimmer and surfer, formed Waikiki's first surfing club. Kahanamoku was a major force in popularizing surfing throughout the world, demonstrating his prowess in competitions from Atlantic City to Australia.

Stringer   Fiberglass Covering

Foam Core

As new materials were developed, surfboards became lighter and easier to ride. The first "modern" board was made in the mid-1940s from balsa wood sheathed in fiberglass. Today, boards are made of lighter synthetic foam. Professional boards are cut, shaved, and sanded by hand, and are of the highest-quality fiberglass and resin, offering the ultimate in speed and control.

Hawaii's professional surfing events established the foundation for the world circuit, in which the island surfers still reign supreme. In the 1950s the **Makaha International** was the only major worldwide surfing event. Some of Hawaii's prime surfing conditions are still found on Oahu at Makaha Beach, where the annual **Big Board Classic** is held in February or March, depending on when the surf is good. But most of the attention is focused on Oahu's giant North Shore waves and a turbulent ocean strip known as the **Banzai Pipeline.** Every December the North Shore hosts the **Marui Pipeline Masters,** the **Hard Rock Cafe World Cup of Surfing,** and the **Hawaiian Professional Surfing Classic**—collectively known as the Triple Crown—to determine who will reign as the next surfing champion.

Many surfers have declared the Banzai Pipeline the home of the perfect wave. Banzai (a Japanese war cry) refers to the courage required to surf the waves here (a courage reserved for expert surfers only), and Pipeline describes the tube-shaped form a wave creates as it breaks. Larger and other tube-shaped waves exist, but none as ferocious as the pipeline wave during the winter months.

Surfers trying to tackle a pipeline wave have about 5 to 10 seconds to soar from one end of the tube to the other before they're buried under swirling sand or caught by the "guillotine"—the name for the wave's falling edge (also known for breaking some surfers' necks). The only thing surfers can see as they race to get through the pipeline is a trickle of light gleaming at the other end. If a surfer fails to get through the tube and manages to survive the fall, the next 10 to 60 seconds of being hurled through the water can be even more terrifying, and once the water starts to pull back, the coral bottom can be a worse enemy than the crashing tube.

Petroglyphs on lava near the Banzai Pipeline suggest that Polynesian surfers were perhaps the first to ride a pipeline wave.

However, the first known person to ride a pipeline was **Phil Edwards** in 1961, and the filmed event, called *String Hollow Days,* was a forerunner of the movie *Endless Summer.* Edwards used a 10-foot board, although today the most commonly used boards measure seven feet and shorter.

If you're eager to test your prowess on the waves, a good way to start learning is by boogie-boarding—a combination of bodysurfing and surfing. The boogie-boarder lays down on a three-foot board and rides with the waves, which is much easier (and safer) than surfing. If you're ready to try true surfing, however, the widest, longest boards are best for beginners; they catch the waves earlier, allowing more time to get balanced before the wave grows too steep. Most surf shops rent surfboards for beginners and can arrange private lessons.

Boogie Board

The Evolution of the Surfboard

| Olo | Redwood Balsa | Big Gun | Semi Gun | Simmons | Malibu | Pig Board | Modern | Thruster |

---

41 Sheraton Moana Surfrider $$$$ A stately and venerable landmark, the Moana Surfrider was the first hotel on Waikiki Beach. It opened in 1901, a time when Hawaiian beachboys hung out at the 300-foot Moana pier, greeting tourists and playing music as the sun set. Opulent luxuries included a dance floor, saloon, billiards room, roof-garden observatory, and the area's first electric-powered elevator. Subsequent expansions, changes in ownership, and a $50 million restoration resulted in today's impressive hotel. Restored to its original architecture and listed in the **National Register of Historic Places,** the Moana Surfrider is furnished with indigenous woods, four-poster beds, marble-top tables, a grand staircase, Victorian-style lamps, colonial verandas and millwork, and all manner of memorabilia. **Robert Louis Stevenson** penned some of his famous prose under the banyan tree in the courtyard of the hotel. Planted in 1885, the famous tree now towers more than 75 feet high, with a 150-foot limb span. The **Banyan Court** and **Banyan Veranda** feature some of the best Hawaiian music in the islands, with sunset performances. The 793 rooms in three towers have all the modern amenities, including air-conditioning, refrigerators, TVs, and 24-hour room service. ♦ 2365 Kalakaua Ave, Waikiki. 922.3111, 800/325.3535; fax 923.0308

Within the Sheraton Moana Surfrider:

Banyan Veranda ★★★$$ Since the Banyan Veranda instituted a Hawaiian music program, it has become Waikiki's top beach attraction. Sundays with **Emma Veary** and **Charles K.L. Davis** get rave reviews, and **Mahi Beamer's** weekend show draws locals from all over the island. The setting is unbeatable: rattan chairs and polished wood floors with an expansive view of the Banyan Court and the Pacific, all of which is ensconced by an enormous banyan tree. Drinks, be forewarned, are hideously expensive. Breakfast, high tea, cocktails, after-dinner coffee with dessert, and Sunday brunch. ♦ 922.3111

Ship's Tavern ★★$$$$ The newly renovated tavern specializes in steak and seafood, including fresh Maine lobster, poached *onaga,* sautéed scallops, Kahuku prawns, and more in a formal oceanside setting. ♦ 922.3111

W.C. Peacock & Co., Ltd. ★$$$ Dine alfresco in a casual, oceanside restaurant. The emphasis here is on steaks, seafood, and the elaborate salad bar. ♦ 922.3111

42 Wizard Stones Modestly cropping out of the sand in front of a bronze statue of champion Hawaiian surfer/swimmer **Duke Kahanamoku,** the Wizard Stones look like ordinary rocks but, like the memorial, add a quiet majesty to the spot. When you see these boulders, think of the four Tahitian priests, or *kahuna,* said to have journeyed here from Tahiti in the 16th century. Hawaiian lore has it that **Kapaemahu, Kahaloa, Kinohi,** and **Kapuni** gave their *mana* (healing powers) to the stones, and vanished. ♦ Kuhio Beach (off Kalakaua Ave, across from the Hyatt Regency Waikiki), Waikiki

43 Hyatt Regency Waikiki $$$$ Designed by **Wimberly, Whisenand, Tong & Goo** in association with **Lawton & Taylor,** the Hyatt (pictured below) was built in 1976 for $100 million, and sold in 1987 for $300 million. Forty-story twin towers rise on both sides of the elaborately landscaped atrium lobby, designated the Great Hall. There are 1,230 rooms, several restaurants and bars, more than 65 boutiques, and a noisy two-story waterfall. The rooms are decorated in warm earth tones, with private lanais, air-conditioning, and Oriental furnishings. Although impressive, this Hyatt isn't a place to get away from it all. In fact, it's quite the opposite, located in the busiest part of Waikiki. ♦ 2424 Kalakaua Ave, Waikiki. 923.1234, 800/233.1234; fax 923.7839

Within the Hyatt Regency Waikiki:

Musashi ★$$$ As much attention is paid to drama and theater as to food in this Japanese restaurant, named after famous samurai **Miyamoto Musashi.** (His classic study of the warrior code, *A Book of Five Rings,* is the bible of Japanese business schools.) Waitresses dress in kimonos, chefs in samurai garb, and busboys in traditional street-acrobat wear. In the morning, try the traditional Japanese breakfast, and for dinner, order the duckling glazed with herb sauce and the "jewel box," a dessert of five sherbets. Sushi bar, teppanyaki grills, or table dining. ♦ 923.1234

The Colony Seafood and Steak House ★$$$ Fresh seafood entrées include Hawaiian prawns, lobster, scallops, and the catch of the day. Of course, steak, chops, prime rib, and chicken broiled over *kiawe* wood are also available, plus an elaborate dessert bar. ♦ 923.1234

Furusato ★★$$$ The only restaurant within the Hyatt that is independently owned and operated, the Furusato actually predates the

Hyatt Regency Waikiki

hotel, having been a popular restaurant in the old **Biltmore,** which was razed to make room for the Hyatt. It's remarkably good, very authentic, extremely expensive, and caters to Japanese tourists. ♦ 922.4991

44 The Rose and Crown ★$$ Styled after a London pub and somewhat of an anomaly in Waikiki, this spot is very popular with the Aussies, Brits, and New Zealanders, who come for the lusty sing-alongs, island-style pub grub, dart boards, and, of course, imported beer. ♦ 131 Kaiulani Ave (behind the Hyatt Regency Waikiki), Waikiki. 923.5833

45 Odoriko ★$$$ Tanks of lobsters, prawns, crabs, and oysters add living color to this authentically furnished Japanese seafood and steak house. There's a list of specialties, plus a sushi bar. For something out of the ordinary, try the Japanese-style breakfast. ♦ 2400 Koa Ave (just off Kalakaua Ave, behind the Hyatt Regency Waikiki), Waikiki. 923.7368

46 Ala Wai Golf Course A flat, moderately interesting course bordering the murky **Ala Wai Canal.** The inexpensive green fees mean that it's crowded with local players; getting a tee-off time can be difficult. Par 71, 6,065 yards. ♦ Starting times. 404 Kapahulu Ave, Waikiki. 732.7741

47 Hy's Steak House ★★$$$ If this plush bar and dining room give you the feeling of being inside the rich, wood-paneled walls in some baron's library, that's because the interior of Hy's actually came from a private estate in the eastern U.S. The dining room features a stunning brass-broiler gazebo. The menu includes poultry and fresh fish, but steak is the best choice. ♦ 2440 Kuhio Ave, Waikiki. Valet parking. 922.5555

48 Aston Waikiki Beachside Hotel $$$$ The Aston is impressive if you like marble and don't object to the ultra-European, non-Hawaiian decor. It's tiny, with 79 rooms (also tiny but well-appointed) in a narrow 10-floor tower drenched in travertine marble. **André** and **Jane Tatibouet** made this their dream project, decorating it lavishly with careful attention to details. The entrance looks like Tiffany's, with moldings galore, Oriental art and furnishings, and expensive wall coverings. Three of the eight rooms on each floor have fabulous ocean views over bustling Kalakaua Avenue, and all feature Chinese lacquered furniture, Oriental screens, and black-chrome-and-gold shower heads that cost more than a room for the night. ♦ 2452 Kalakaua Ave, Waikiki. 931.2100, 800/922.7866; fax 931.2129

49 Pacific Beach Hotel $$$ The 38-story **Ocean Tower** and 17-story **Beach Tower,** across from **Kuhio Beach,** have 850 rooms with ocean, city, and mountain views. Each room has a private lanai, air-conditioning, refrigerators, and full bathrooms. Other amenities include a swimming pool, two tennis courts, a fitness center, and a Jacuzzi. ♦ 2490 Kalakaua Ave, Waikiki. 922.1233, 800/367.6060; fax 922.8061

Within the Pacific Beach Hotel:

Oceanarium Restaurant ★$$$ The big attraction is dining alongside what the proprietors claim is Hawaii's largest indoor oceanarium—three stories of glass holding 250,000 gallons of water. Otherwise, it's your basic, unexciting American menu, featuring steaks and seafood (served buffet style). ♦ 922.1233

Shogun ★$$ Especially popular among seafood lovers, this Japanese restaurant is a good value for the money. The trade-off is its pedestrian environment. ♦ 922.1233

50 Kuhio Beach Swarming with hundreds of people, this section of Waikiki doesn't boast the clearest water in the world, but it's still great for strolling and wading. Use caution while swimming, though; large underwater holes pose an invisible danger. ♦ Off Kalakaua Ave, Waikiki

51 Damien Museum Granted the museum is a dive, but it still houses some interesting pictures, artifacts, and other possessions of **Father Damien,** the martyr of Molokai. Damien dedicated his life to the physical and spiritual needs of patients with Hansen's disease (leprosy). Even if you aren't interested in the displays, it's a great place to park your car for nothing. ♦ Free. M-F 9AM-3PM; Sa 9AM-noon. 130 Ohua Ave, Waikiki. 923.2690

The Charlie Chan mysteries of the '20s and '30s, written by Earl Derr Biggers, were inspired by Honolulu detective Chang Apana, who used to relax under the ancient *kiawe* tree at Halekulani's House without a Key restaurant in Waikiki, Oahu.

In 1988 Oahu's highways averaged 6.8 abandoned vehicles per every thousand miles of road, which is down from 23.6 in 1981.

Restaurants/Clubs: Red   **Hotels:** Blue
Shops/ 🌳 **Outdoors:** Green   **Sights/Culture:** Black

52 Hawaiian Regent Hotel $$$ A decent but hardly dazzling hotel, except for the impressive lobby and courtyard. The Hawaiian Regent (pictured below), which is managed by **Otaka Hotels and Resorts,** is a sister property to the nearby Hawaiian Waikiki Beach Hotel. There are 1,346 rooms, many with ocean views, in two towers on more than five acres. Request an oceanside room; the view is spectacular. Six restaurants, two pools, a tennis court, and a shopping arcade. ♦ 2552 Kalakaua Ave, Waikiki. 922.6611, 800/367.5370; fax 921.5222

Within the Hawaiian Regent Hotel:

The Secret ★★★$$$$ Lavish displays of fruits and vegetables mark the entrance to a brilliantly designed dining area, decorated in wood, copper, crystal, and bright overhanging banners. The effect is of intimate, understated luxury, with high-backed rattan chairs and parquet tables. The lamb and venison dishes are unforgettable, and the nightly specials, especially the fresh fish, are reliably good, as is the service and wine selection. All dinners begin with complimentary *naan* bread, a legendary house ritual, delivered warm from clay ovens and served with goose liver pâté. ♦ 922.6611

53 Hawaiian Waikiki Beach Hotel $$$ For the price and location (near the Honolulu Zoo, Kapiolani Park, and Waikiki Aquarium), this is one of the better deals in town, with 715 rooms in two towers. After you've visited the nearby attractions, relax in the hotel's pool. ♦ 2570 Kalakaua Ave, Waikiki. 922.2511, 800/877.7666; fax 923.3656

53 Park Shore Hotel $$ Smack dab on a busy corner, with Kuhio Beach across one street and Kapiolani Park across the other. The 227 guest rooms, some with kitchenettes, feature private lanais and views of Diamond Head, the park, or the ocean. Pool. ♦ 2586 Kalakaua Ave (at Kapahulu Ave), Waikiki. 923.0411, 800/367.2377; fax 923.0311

54 Waikiki Grand Hotel $$ Taking into consideration the rooms (recently refurbished in a pleasant tropical decor), the location, and the affordable price, the Waikiki Grand is a bargain if you can live with the noises from the nearby Honolulu Zoo. It's relatively small (170 rooms), with a rooftop sun deck and pool. ♦ 134 Kapahulu Ave, Waikiki. 923.1511, 800/535.0085; fax 922.2421

55 Queen Kapiolani Hotel $$ A Waikiki veteran located across the street from Kapiolani Park and the Honolulu Zoo, and only a block from Kuhio Beach. The 315 rooms overlook the park, Diamond Head, and the ocean. Pool. ♦ 150 Kapahulu Ave, Waikiki. 922.1941, 800/367.5004; fax 922.2694

56 Honolulu Zoo Building a zoo in Waikiki is like taking coals to Newcastle, but there's one here nonetheless. The usual animals peer out through cages that are covered with vegetation for a tropical jungle effect. The **Children's Zoo** lets kids pet the lemurs, ponies, goats, chickens, and the like. Kids also

Hawaiian Regent Hotel

have a chance to feed **Mari,** the zoo's only elephant, under the supervision of zookeepers. The **Education Pavilion** features puppet shows on Saturday and hands-on demonstrations in weaving, basketry, and other crafts. The main attraction during summer months is the weekly **"Wildest Show in Town,"** featuring the best local entertainment, from **Hookena** to **Gabe Baltazar** and the **Pandanus Club.** The show is immensely popular and, even better, it's free. ♦ Admission; children 12 and under free when accompanied by an adult. Daily 8:30AM-4PM; summer shows Wednesday at 6PM. 151 Kapahulu Ave, Waikiki. 971.7171

57 Weekend Art Mart Every weekend local artists of varying degrees of expertise set up card tables and prop their wares against the zoo's fence, hoping to make a sale. The proverbial ocean sunsets and palm-fringed beaches cover most canvasses, although snowy New England scenes occasionally find their way to the mart. It's a pleasant outing, with souvenir potential. ♦ Free. Tu 9AM-1PM; Sa-Su 10AM-4PM. Kapiolani Park along Monsarrat Ave, Waikiki

58 Queen's Surf Beach Park Local families often picnic here. ♦ Off Kalakaua Ave, just north of Kapiolani Park

59 Waikiki Aquarium The newly renovated and expanded Walkiki Aquarium is scheduled to open in the fall of '93, with new exhibits such as: a 40,000-gallon shark tank; a theater featuring a 10-minute video program; an improved monk seals exhibit; an exhibit of Hawaiian jellyfish; and the Reef Machine. Also in the making is a mahimahi hatchery, a working aquaculture research center where you can observe mahimahi bred on site, not caught in the wild. Other tanks display stingrays, butterfly fish, turtles, octopi, live coral, lionfish, a seahorse, and a giant clam— a total of 280 marine species. In 1990 the aquarium became the first in the U.S. (and second in the world) to successfully hatch a chambered nautilus. The **Nautilus Nursery** tank opened that year and furthered the aquarium's renown as a national resource on the rare mollusk. Children's programs, summer reef explorations, music festivals, field trips, workshops, travel programs, guided tours, and many other types of programs make this a lively experience for adults and children. ♦ Donation. Daily 9AM-5PM. 2777 Kalakaua Ave, Waikiki. 923.9741

60 Waikiki War Memorial Natatorium Located on the oceanside of Kapiolani Park, this deteriorating cement structure has seen better days since it was built in 1927. Once the site of gala swimming meets, the saltwater pool has become a living laboratory of refuse, algae, and grime. Nostalgia, not to mention its dedication as a war memorial, have saved it from destruction but not from disrepair. ♦ Closed to public, but can be viewed at the Diamond Head end of Kalakaua Ave, Waikiki

61 The New Otani Kaimana Beach Hotel $$$ A favorite among many repeat visitors, this modest high rise is found in the best part of Waikiki—on historic **Sans Souci Beach,** where **Robert Louis Stevenson** sunned himself in the 1890s. The small white sand beach offers a refreshing alternative to Waikiki congestion. Hikers and joggers have easy access to Kapiolani Park and to the road winding around the base of Diamond Head, where a lookout offers sweeping views of the surfers and windsurfers below. In fact, Kaimana manager **Steve Boyle** founded the very popular **Diamond Head Climbers Hui,** a club for hikers who've made it to the top of the crater. Following a $10 million renovation, the hotel was reintroduced in 1989 with a slightly more upscale feel. Choose from 125 guest rooms (and beautiful suites). Some rooms are quite small, but they all have air-conditioning and refrigerators; corner suites have the best views. ♦ 2863 Kalakaua Ave, Waikiki. 923.1555, 800/733.7949; fax 922.9404

Within the New Otani Kaimana Beach Hotel:

Hau Tree Lanai ★★$$ A great spot for breakfast, lunch, or dinner, especially at sunset, with a giant *hau* tree serving as a canopy for the open-air dining room. The restaurant, which is set right on the ocean's edge, has an extraordinary view of the Pacific. Local grinds worth trying on the French-Polynesian menu include poi pancakes and fresh fish. ♦ 923.1555

Miyako ★$$$ Fine food is served in a pleasant setting, with family-style seating on tatami mats at low tables. The menu includes *shabu-shabu* (cook-it-yourself soup), good tempura, teppanyaki items grilled at the table, and a wide variety of other Japanese favorites. ♦ 923.1555

Sans Souci Beach (French for "without a care"), located near the volcanic crater Diamond Head on Oahu, was the favorite haunt of author Robert Louis Stevenson. He also penned some of his famous prose under the Moana Hotel's old banyan tree on Waikiki Beach.

About 90,000 tourists bump elbows daily in Waikiki, Oahu.

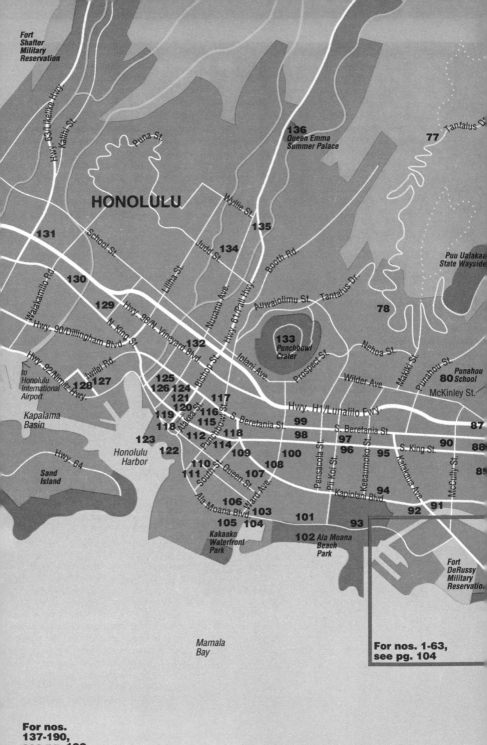

Fort
Shafter
Military
Reservation

136
Queen Emma
Summer Palace

77 Tantalus Dr.

Hwy. 63/Likelike Hwy.

Kaihii St.

Puna St.

Wyllie St.

HONOLULU

135

Judd St.

134

131

School St.

Lilha St.

Nuuanu Ave.

Booth Rd.

Auwaiolimu St.

Tantalus Dr.

Puu Ualakaa
State Wayside

130

129

Waiakamilo Rd.

Hwy. 96/N. Vineyard Blvd.

N. King St.

Hwy. 61/Pali Hwy.

78

Nehoa St.

Hwy. 90/Dillingham Blvd.

132

Bishop St.

Iolani Ave.

133
Punchbowl
Crater

Prospect St.

Wilder Ave.

Makiki St.

Punahou St.

Nehoa St.

Punahou
School

80

McKinley St.

Hwy. 92/Nimitz Hwy.

Iwilei Rd.

to
Honolulu
International
Airport

128**127**

125

126**124**

121

117

116

115

Alakea St.

Punchbowl St.

S. Beretania St.

Hwy. H1/Lunalilo Fwy.

99

S. Beretania St.

Pensacola St.

Pii Koi St.

Keeaumoku St.

S. King St.

90

McCully St.

87

Kapalama
Basin

119

120

118

112

118

114

109

98

97

96

95

88

Hwy. 64

123

122

Honolulu
Harbor

South St.

Queen St.

100

108

94

Kalakaua Ave.

89

110

107

111

106

Ward Ave.

103

Kapiolani Blvd.

92

91

Sand
Island

Ala Moana Blvd.

105 **104**

Kakaako
Waterfront
Park

101

102 Ala Moana
Beach
Park

93

Fort
DeRussy
Military
Reservatio.

For nos. 1-63,
see pg. 104

Mamala
Bay

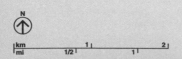

For nos.
137-190,
see pg. 102

N

km
mi
1/2   1   1   2

Pacific
Ocean

76

75

WOODLAWN

Monoa
Valley
Park

Manoa Rd.

E. Manoa Rd.

79

University Ave.

Bertram St.

Waahila
74 State Park

82
University
of Hawaii
(UH)

81

Dole St.

86
5
4
3

Chaminade
University

Paiolo Ave.

10th Ave.

Wilhelmina Rise

6th Ave.

Waialae Ave.

70

69

Halekoa Dr.

Kilauea Ave.

Keaiaolu Ave.

Ainakoa Ave.

Laukahi St.

KAHALA

73

Hwy. H1/Lunalilo Fwy.

6th Ave.

71

Pahoa Ave.

Hunakai St.

72

Date St.

Ala Wai Canal

'AIKIKI

Vaikiki
each

Kilauea Ave.

Kapahulu Ave.

68
67

Alohea Ave.

Waialae
Beach Park

Maunalua
Bay

Honolulu
Zoo

66

Cambell Ave.

Monsarrat Ave.

18th Ave.

Elepaio St.

Waikiki
Shell

Kapiolani
Park

Sans Souci
Beach

Paki Ave.

65
Diamond
Head

Kahala Ave.

Kupikipkio
Point

Diamond Head Rd.

64
Diamond Head
Beach Park

Sweet Talk

When the Polynesians first sailed to Hawaii some 1,500 years ago, they used the thick stalks of sugarcane to hold water for the long journey. The rich lava soil and wet climate, coupled with abundant sunshine, proved fertile ground for the sugarcane, but it wasn't until the end of Hawaii's whaling era in the 1860s that sugar was relied upon as a cash crop. The islands' unrefined sugar was first exported to America during the gold rush, when Northern California's sudden population boom made sugar a profitable commodity.

In its heyday, from 1953 to 1986, Hawaiian fields yielded about a million tons of sugar a year (more than 12 percent of the sugar produced in the entire country) and strengthened Hawaii's economy to the tune of $353 million annually. The sugar industry was also primarily responsible for Hawaii's diverse racial mixture. Native Hawaiians weren't interested in the hard labor required to harvest sugar, so peasants were imported from China, Japan, Korea, Portugal, South America, and many other foreign lands.

But times are changing in Hawaii, and the sugar industry is destined to follow the pineapple industry's fate—unprofitable operational costs and stiff competition has led to the phasing out of pineapple production. Soon Hawaii's economy will be based almost exclusively on military operations and tourism, and the verdant cane fields that for generations symbolized Hawaiian prosperity will be plowed under for good.

Colony Surf

61 Colony Surf Hotel $$$$ The 21-story hotel looks unimpressive from the outside, but its choice location (right on the beach) and first-rate accommodations have convinced many discriminating travelers to adopt it as their exclusive Hawaiian hideaway (it's not exactly hidden but certainly far enough removed from Waikiki to afford some feeling of remoteness). Look out on Kapiolani Park, with Diamond Head in the background, or on the ocean. Of more importance to most guests, however, is the almost-private beach in front of the hotel. The large and elegantly appointed one- and two-bedroom suites are equipped with full kitchens, and the one-bedrooms feature floor-to-ceiling windows. The adjacent **Colony East** tower, set farther back from the beach, has kitchenettes and substantially lower rates, but anyone who prefers true luxury should request a room in the main building. ◆ 2895 Kalakaua Ave, Waikiki. 923.5751, 800/252.7873 (U.S.), 800/423.7781 (Canada); fax 922.8433

Within the Colony Surf Hotel:

Michel's ★★★$$$$ The award-winning Michel's (that's pronounced with a soft "c") has a setting few restaurants can match. Literally on the beach, the oceanside half of the three large dining rooms is kept completely open except during storms, and diners fortunate enough to secure the best tables are within a linen napkin's toss of the beach. The decor is lavish, with candlelight shimmering off the crystal and chandeliers. The background piano music, along with front-row views of the sunset and Waikiki's glittering lights, can prove mesmerizing. The cuisine is supposed to be French, but the menu actually emphasizes local seafood (their specialty) and a legendary rack of lamb. Because of crowded dinner conditions, you might enjoy Michel's more at lunch, and it's unquestionably the most elegant location for breakfast and brunch in Hawaii. ◆ Jacket requested for dinner. 923.6552

McGee's Conglomeration $$ McGee's is part of a dinner and dancing chain that's been extremely successful selling silliness, with waiters dressed in cartoon character costumes, salad bars in bathtubs, and generally corny decor. Everyone, celebrities included, seems to love it. Comedians **Don Rickles** and **Bob Newhart** once got so caught up in the spirit of the restaurant that they did table-hopping insults of guests, gratis. It's located on the ground floor of the Colony East tower and serves steak, fish, and pasta. ◆ Disco daily until 2AM. 922.1282

62 Kapiolani Park Hawaii's first public park has been a popular recreational hub since it opened in 1877—a gift from **King Kalakaua** to the people of Honolulu (in return, he asked that the park be named after his wife, **Queen Kapiolani**). Sprawled across 220 acres in Diamond Head's shadow—conveniently close to Waikiki yet away from the roar of the crowd—the park is a mecca for joggers, softball games, barbecues, and picnics. It also encompasses the **Waikiki Aquarium,** the **Honolulu Zoo,** and the landmark **Waikiki Shell Amphitheater,** home of the **Kodak Hula Show.** And if you're in town in early December, stop by to see the finish of the annual **Honolulu Marathon,** one of the world's largest races. ♦ Between Kalakaua and Monsarrat Aves, Waikiki. 971.2500

Within Kapiolani Park:

Kodak Hula Show A Waikiki institution, the Kodak Hula Show premiered in 1937, and some of its original dancers, now in their eighties, are still performing. Three mornings a week, nearly 3,000 people wait in line an hour or more for the chance to plop themselves down on bleachers and watch a show they've probably already seen a dozen times on TV: Hawaiians in G-rated native garb dancing to ukuleles played by *tutus* (grandmothers) wearing bright muumuus and floppy hats. Spectators who volunteer to dance with the performers inevitably provide the most entertainment. ♦ Free. Tu-Th 10-11:15AM. 833.1661

63 Diamond Head Beach Hotel $$$ A small European-style establishment with just 22 suites and a limited number of luxury rooms, the Diamond Head Beach Hotel features fully equipped kitchens and lanais overlooking the Pacific. It's a charming hotel run by **Colony Resorts,** occupying a minuscule wedge of white sand on Diamond Head Beach. Guests can jog, play tennis and soccer, or fly kites in Kapiolani Park, which is just across the street. ♦ 2947 Kalakaua Ave, Waikiki. 922.1928, 800/367.2317; fax 924.8980

64 Diamond Head Beach Park A narrow, rocky beach stretching for two acres along Diamond Head Road, with unlimited access but tricky parking. A dangerous beach for swimming and surfing, it's best used for meditating or fishing. Check out the view from the overlook. The trail leads to interesting tide pools. ♦ Diamond Head Rd, Waikiki

65 Diamond Head If you fly into Hawaii, chances are the first thing you'll see (at least if you're seated on the right side of the plane) is this landmark, a volcanic crater that's been dormant for an estimated 150,000 years. Early Hawaiians called it **Leahi** (referring to the forehead of an *ahi* tuna) because its lines resemble the profile of a fish. But when sailors found diamondlike crystals here in the 1800s, the nickname "Diamond Head" was coined (the crystals, however, turned out to be calcite). The crater's walls are 760 feet high; an hour's climb (roughly one mile) up the inside slopes to the top is rewarded by a stunning view of Honolulu. ♦ Diamond Head Rd, Waikiki

66 Queen Kapiolani Rose Garden Pathways meander around dozens of varieties of fragrant roses free for the looking but not for picking. Many are named after public figures such as **Princess Grace** of Monaco and **Lady Bird Johnson.** This showcase garden thrives on conscientious care from its curator and manure from the nearby Honolulu Zoo. ♦ Free. Between Paki and Monsarrat Aves, Waikiki

67 Irifune ★★$$ One of the best local-style Japanese restaurants in town, for the money. Although the decor is a tad eccentric, there are certainly no complaints about the simple yet exquisite cuisine, which is prepared without MSG. The mixed kushiyaki (chicken and vegetables barbecued on a skewer) is always a big hit, as are the breaded tofu appetizers. ♦ 563 Kapahulu Ave (at Campbell St, across from Zippys), Honolulu. 737.1141

68 Keo's ★★★$$$ The proprietors of **Mekong** in Honolulu created such a following for their little dining room that they converted this former strip joint into a large, orchid-drenched establishment. (Owner **Keo Sananikone** decorates the ornate room with fresh orchids and stalks of jungle greens.) A magnet for celebrities and the otherwise chic, Keo's is regularly voted in magazine polls as one of Hawaii's most popular restaurants. The menu is enormous, but the food can be inconsistent. Highlights include Evil Jungle Prince (a blend of chicken, lemongrass, coconut milk, Chinese cabbage, and red chiles), green papaya salad, prawns in a sweet peanut sauce, and delicious spring rolls. Sananikone grows his own herbs, bananas, and produce on the North Shore. Keo's is a star in the island's ethnic dining scene and deserving of its fame. ♦ 625 Kapahulu Ave, Kapahulu. 737.8240

69 Azteca Mexican Restaurant ★$$ The ambience may need some help, but Azteca still has the spiciest salsa and richest guacamole in town. Hefty burritos (meat or vegetarian) and other Mexican favorites are served in a colorful but gaudy setting. ♦ 3569 Waialae Ave, Kaimuki. 735.2492

69 Hale Vietnam ★★$$ The specialty here is *pho,* a steamy Vietnamese soup that's prepared in nearly two dozen versions. Pho lovers come here from all over the island to linger over the hot bowls of soup or light, piquant spring rolls. ♦ 1140 12th Ave, Kaimuki. 735.7581

70 3660 On The Rise ★★$$$ Following on the successful heels of other trendy establishments is this small yet elegant restaurant specializing in "Euro-Island" cuisine. The constituency is mainly composed of wealthy locals who come for the well-rounded menu of uniquely prepared veal, steak, lamb, and seafood, including farm-raised catfish tempura with *ponzu* sauce and pan-seared fillets of salmon with a Chinese black bean and lime sauce. The location is somewhat removed from the tourist scene, but it's certainly worth the short drive for lunch or dinner. ♦ 3660 Waialae Ave, Honolulu. 737.1177

71 Kahala Mall The Ala Moana Shopping Mall may be larger, but this shopping center has more character. Located in Oahu's wealthiest neighborhood, Kahala Mall houses the standard merchandisers (Liberty House, The Gap, Banana Republic, Benetton, and Woolworth), as well as a host of unique specialty shops that warrant serious browsing from visitors and residents alike. ♦ M-Sa 10AM-9PM; Su 10AM-5PM. 4211 Waialae Ave, Honolulu. 732.7736

Within Kahala Mall:

California Pizza Kitchen ★★$$ It's the same exact slice as the Waikiki restaurant, and likewise packs 'em in with pizza and pasta specials. ♦ 737.9446. Also at: 1910 Ala Moana Blvd (at Ena Rd), Waikiki. 955.5161

Yen King ★$$ The specialty is northern China cuisine, with nearly a hundred items on the menu, most of which are reasonably priced. If you like spicy dishes, try the garlic chicken, lemon beef, or sizzling rice shrimp. ♦ 732.5505

72 Hajji Baba's ★$$$ Caftanned waiters and waitresses serve Moroccan dishes while the belly dancers shake their things. The dancing is good, the food moderate, and the seating awkward, with some people in chairs and others on the floor while the waiters reach and hop around them. ♦ 4614 Kilauea Ave, Kahala. 735.5522

73 Waialae Country Club One of Hawaii's most exclusive and private country clubs is home to the Hawaiian Open golf tournament, held every January. Built in 1927 in a then-remote part of Oahu, the flat course borders the ocean and offers vicious doglegs, deep bunkers, and nearly 2,000 palm trees—many of them centuries old—to challenge even the toughest golfers. The club is adjacent to the Kahala Hilton, but hotel guests don't have playing privileges. Par 72, 6,651 yards. ♦ Members and guests only. 4997 Kahala Ave, Kahala. Pro shop 734.2151

Restaurants/Clubs: Red   Hotels: Blue

Shops/ 🌴 Outdoors: Green   **Sights/Culture:** Black

73 Kahala Hilton Hotel $$$$ One of Oahu's finer hotels, the Kahala Hilton commands an exclusive setting—six and a half acres of oceanside luxury well removed from the congestion of Waikiki. The landscaping is lush: quiet pathways wind among tropical foliage, tiny streams, miniature waterfalls, and flowering gardens. Guests also enjoy a wide private beach (excellent for swimming) surrounded on three sides by the greenery of the Waialae Country Club. Designed by Edward Killingsworth, the 10-story hotel opened in 1964 with 369 rooms and suites, some of them right at the edge of a lagoon filled with large sea turtles, tropical fish, and cavorting dolphins (lagoon units must be booked far in advance). Hoku, born in the lagoon in 1991, is the star dolphin, swimming beside its mother in front of adoring fans. Many of the guests are Hollywood stars, producers, agents, and writers who appreciate the privacy here. The hotel keeps a record of repeat guests and their partialities, including room preferences. ♦ 5000 Kahala Ave, Kahala. 734.2211, 800/367.2525; fax 737.2478

Within the Kahala Hilton Hotel:

Hala Terrace ★★$$ A wonderful choice for a leisurely breakfast or Sunday brunch, this pleasant open-air room offers ocean views, excellent service, and fine food. The eggs Benedict and the pancakes with coconut syrup are both divine. There's also a large breakfast buffet, and a lunch menu that includes fresh island fish, pasta, salads, and sandwiches. ♦ 734.2211

Maile Restaurant ★★★$$$$ One of Honolulu's finest restaurants, Maile features elegant Continental cuisine in a gardenlike setting, complete with fountains, pools, and soft background music. The signature roast duckling Waialae is embellished with bananas, lychees, mandarin oranges, spiced peaches, and Grand Marnier. Another house specialty is a Hawaiian trio: *opakapaka* (pink snapper) with mushroom sauce, mahimahi (golden dolphinfish) with spinach sauce, and *onaga* (red snapper) with Chardonnay sauce. Indulge yourself, but save room for the Grand Marnier soufflé. Live music and dancing are offered from 8PM to 12:30AM in the adjoining lounge. ♦ Jacket required. 734.2211

Plumeria Cafe ★★$$ A courtyard cafe with a tropical atmosphere, the Plumeria serves morning pastries, afternoon tea, and Continental cuisine for dinner. Special menus are featured monthly. ♦ 734.2211

Danny Kaleikini Show Danny Kaleikini has been the Kahala Hilton's resident star since 1967. He and his talented cast of dancers and Hawaiian entertainers perform inside the **Hala Terrace,** a romantic setting with the nearby surf glowing in the moonlight. ♦ Cover. M-Sa 9PM; dinner seatings at 7PM and 7:30PM. 734.2211

74 Waahila State Park Residents who want to escape the heat drive to this cool, elevated retreat at the top of residential **St. Louis Heights.** Picnic facilities (including barbecue grills) are available under the Norfolk pines and ironwoods, and there's a great strawberry guava grove that's yours for the picking when in season. ♦ St. Louis Dr, Kahala

75 Lyon Arboretum Taro, orchids, bromeliads, ferns, cinnamon, coco, koa, kava, palms, coffee, yams, bananas, and hundreds of other species can be found in these lush botanical gardens, only a short drive from downtown Honolulu. The 124-acre arboretum is closely associated with **Beatrice Krauss,** an ethnobotanist who has taught here for decades. Crafts and cooking workshops, plant sales, special outings, and many other activities are offered here. Bring along mosquito repellent. ♦ M-Sa 9AM-3PM for self-guided tours. One-hour guided tours at 1PM the first Friday and third Wednesday of each month, and 10AM every third Saturday. 3860 Manoa Rd, Honolulu. Reservations required. 988.3177

76 Manoa Falls Tired of the Waikiki hustle? Escape to this cool, quiet forest fragrant with ginger and tropical blooms. It's the perfect place for a long picnic followed by a swim in the freshwater pool underneath the falls. To get here, take the trail that begins at the end of Manoa Road (look for the brown trail marker and park just past it). It's about a 30-minute hike (one mile) to the falls. ♦ End of Manoa Rd (just past Paradise Park)

77 Tantalus Drive If you start to get the feeling that the entire Honolulu area is void of any natural beauty, make your way down this scenic route. Start on Puowaina Drive (on the north side of Punchbowl Crater), which eventually turns into Tantalus Drive and winds through some incredible real estate, with pull-offs every mile or so to admire the view of Honolulu. At the top of Tantalus Drive, pull over and wander through the trails that

meander through the valley, then head back down Round Top Drive, stopping at Puu Uualakaa Park's lookout point for a photo shoot. ♦ Makiki Heights

78 The Contemporary Museum A cultural oasis in a city where fine art consists of cartoonlike portraits of flippers, fins, and sunsets, this stunning 3.5-acre setting exhibits works by artists of international reputation, including **David Hockney** and **George Rickey.** The main building consists of five interconnected galleries and a separate pavilion, although some of the most interesting works are displayed on the impeccably landscaped grounds, a former estate of **Mrs. Charles Montague Cooke.** The prints sold at the adjacent **Museum Shop** make wonderful gifts. ♦ Admission. Tu-Sa 10AM-4PM; Su noon-4PM. 2411 Makiki Heights Dr, Honolulu. 526.1322

Within The Contemporary Museum:

The Contemporary Cafe ★★$$ If you're anywhere near the Makiki Heights area, stop at this chic cafe and choose from a wide selection of salads, gourmet sandwiches, daily specials, and homemade desserts. On a sunny day, the outdoor seating is unbeatable. ♦ Reservations recommended. 523.3362

79 Coffee Manoa ★$ A popular local gathering place for university students, this small cafe sells dozens of coffee beans, or you can take home a bag of your favorite gourmet blend ground on the premises. Oat cakes, muffins, breads, scones, and assorted pastries are also available. ♦ 2752 Woodlawn Dr (in the Manoa Marketplace, between E. Manoa Rd and Woodlawn Dr), Manoa. 988.5113

80 Punahou School Hawaii's most famous private school opened in 1841 for the education of children whose parents were Congregationalist missionaries and Hawaiian *alii* (royalty). The grounds were donated by **Queen Kaahumanu, Kamehameha I's** favorite wife and one of the mission's noteworthy converts. Punahou's alumni list reads like a *Who's Who* of Hawaii, and new generations of missionary descendants, joined by Honolulu's nouveau riche, perpetuate the exclusivity of the kindergarten through high-school enrollment. ♦ 1601 Punahou St, Honolulu. 944.5711

81 Manoa Valley Inn $$ Under the direction of preservationist **Rick Ralston,** this two-story 1920s structure was designated a historical home and survived impending destruction. Ralston furnished the inn, which consists of seven bedrooms and a cottage, from his extensive collection of antiques and period furnishings, including brass beds. The **Hawaiian Hotel Corporation** (which purchased the inn from Ralston in 1989) continues to offer guests Continental breakfasts, afternoon cheese and fruit, and other pleasant amenities. Although precariously close to the bustling university, the Manoa Valley Inn is a good choice for the price and the ambience. ♦ 2001 Vancouver Dr, Honolulu. 947.6019, 800/634.5115; fax 946.6168

82 University of Hawaii (UH) Probably the ugliest collection of unrelated architectural styles in Hawaii can be found on the university's 300-acre campus, although the extensive landscaping provides some relief. The center for higher education opened in 1908 with 12 teachers and 5 full-time students. Now nearly 19,000 full-time students attend the Manoa campus, with another 26,000 enrolled at the Hilo campus and in the university's statewide community college system. UH earned its reputation with strong international studies, marine biology, tropical agriculture, and oceanography programs, along with specialized programs in the travel industry and hotel management. It's also in the forefront of astronomy research and a leader in the world search for alternative energy sources. ♦ University Ave, Manoa Valley. 956.8111

Within the University of Hawaii:

East-West Center In 1960 this institution and the surrounding 21 acres were dedicated by Congress to promote better relations, both cultural and technical, between the United States and the countries of Asia and the Pacific. Funded by various nations and private companies, the center contains several artistic treasures from the Far East, including murals, paintings, sculptures, and tapa hangings from China, Korea, Thailand, and Japan. The landscaped grounds around **Jefferson Hall** are also worth strolling. ♦ M-F 8AM-4:30PM. 944.7111

the Willows

83 The Willows ★$$$ Founded in 1944 as a neighborhood family establishment, the Willows offers exactly the kind of restaurant experience most tourists hope to find in Hawaii but rarely do. The thatched-roof dining pavilions overlook lagoons filled with colorful carp and the outdoor **Garden Court,** thus enhancing the tropical mood. The Polynesian cuisine, if unremarkable, is at least highlighted by Willows traditions—Hawaiian curries and a sky-high coconut cream pie. You may not remember your meal (well, maybe if it's one of the poi suppers, where the more courageous can try *lomilomi* salmon, *lau lau,* and other Hawaiian dishes), but you'll enjoy the restaurant's distinctively Hawaiian ambience. A strolling trio entertains with traditional

Hawaiian songs during dinner hours, and **Puamana, Genoa Keawe,** and other popular local musicians meander among the ohia pillars during the "Poi Thursday" luncheons. Inevitably, their friends and relatives in the audience will join in and you'll be treated to family-style Hawaiian entertainment. Rumor has it that the Willows is closing, so you might want to call ahead. ♦ 901 Hausten St (between S. King St and Kapiolani Blvd), Honolulu. 946.4808

84 Down to Earth Natural Foods Store Everything from fresh organic produce to "Tom of Maine" toothpaste is stocked in this natural foods store, including a fine selection of vegetarian vitamins, pasta, Indian chutney, grains, nuts, greeting cards, health-conscious cosmetics, cheese, and other things sold in bulk. Within the store is the **Down to Earth Deli,** a vegetarian mecca with salads, chili, tabbouleh, pastries, and pastas. Be sure to bring your own bag for groceries—it's de rigueur these days. ♦ Daily 8AM-10PM. 2525 S. King St (1 block west of University Ave), Honolulu. 947.7678

85 Buzz's Original Steak House ★$$$ Yet another appendage of the always reliable Buzz's steak-house empire, conveniently located across the street from the **Varsity Theater.** Come here only if you can't think of anywhere else to eat. ♦ 2535 Coyne St, Honolulu. 944.9781

86 Philip Paolo's ★★$$$ One of Honolulu's better Italian restaurants is found in a remodeled colonial-style house with wood floors, high ceilings, and a patio overlooking the garden. The menu includes pasta, seafood (the specialty is lobster parmigiana), and salads. ♦ 2312 S. Beretania St, Honolulu. Reservations recommended. 946.1163

87 Anna Bannana's ★$ During the day you'll still see the occasional Harley-Davidson motorcycle parked in front of this unpretentious social pub. In the '60s and '70s, it was *the* hangout for beer-guzzling students from the nearby university campus. Now, Anna Bannana's is better known for serious dart-board tournaments and substantial Mexican food. Honolulu's No. 1 reggae band, **Pagan Babies,** plays to a crowded house Friday and Saturday nights, and there's live blues and rock music Wednesday, Thursday, and Sunday evenings (there's a cover charge). It's also a great place to use the restroom (you'll see). ♦ 2440 S. Beretania St (at University Ave), Honolulu. 946.5190

88 Quilts Hawaii Hawaiian quilts are the specialty here, most of them in the four-digit price range. There's also a smattering of other Hawaiiana items, including fine koa furniture and bowls, handbags, jewelry, pillows, and quilt kits. ♦ M-Sa 9:30AM-5PM. 2338 S. King St, Honolulu. 942.3195

88 India Bazaar Madras Cafe ★$ You've probably had better Indian food, but at least this is a decent deal (it's popular with college students if that's any indication). The six entrées, ranging from vegetarian to chicken and seafood, come with a choice of two vegetable dishes. ♦ 2320 S. King St, Honolulu. 949.4840

89 Maple Garden ★★$$$ A longtime favorite for spicy Mandarin and Szechuan cuisine, the Maple Garden is usually crowded and noisy with chatter and platter-clatter. Specialties include smoked Szechuan duck and eggplant with a hot spicy sauce. ♦ 909 Isenberg St (3 blocks west of University Ave), Honolulu. 941.6641

90 King Tsin ★★$$ The **Joseph Wang** family oversees the kitchen, which specializes in remarkably creative Szechuan dishes. Try the beggar's chicken baked in clay pots (half-day advance notice is required). ♦ 1110 McCully St, Honolulu. 946.3273

91 Hard Rock Cafe ★★$$ Like all other Hard Rock Cafes, this place seems to sell more T-shirts than dinners. It's all here—the loud music, central bar, wood and brass decor—but with a Hawaiian twist: surfboards are mixed in with the rock 'n' roll memorabilia (including **John Lennon's** Starfire 12 guitar). The all-American menu, heavy on the Texas-style ribs, barbecued chicken, chili, sandwiches, apple pie, and strawberry shortcake, is served carhop style. Don't bother trying to find free parking; it's not worth the trouble. ♦ 1837 Kapiolani Blvd (at Kalakaua Ave), Honolulu. 955.7383

92 Ala Moana Hotel $$$ The newly renovated Ala Moana, at 36 stories high, is the tallest building in the state. Better yet, it's linked by a footbridge to the **Ala Moana Shopping Mall.** A host of services are provided, including a massage and medical clinic, executive business center, and a shopping arcade. Pool and sun deck. ♦ 410 Atkinson Dr, Honolulu. 955.4811, 800/367 6025; fax 944.2974

Within the Ala Moana Hotel:

Royal Garden ★$$$ For lunch, the waitresses here cart dim sum around from table to table, and dinner is served until *very* late at night. A popular place for dinner parties thrown by local Chinese-Americans. ♦ Third floor. 942.7788

Nicholas Nickolas ★★$$$$ Treat yourself to fabulous views of Waikiki while dining on steak and seafood. Nicholas Nickolas is among the most popular places in town for sophisticated after-dining dancing. ♦ 36th floor. 955.4466

93 Ala Moana Shopping Mall The granddaddy of all shopping centers, the Ala Moana is the largest mall in the state, with more than 200 stores and restaurants. When it opened in 1959, it was the largest shopping center in the world, with four levels of open-air walkways alongside carp-filled streams. More than 56 million shoppers come here every year. **Palm Boulevard,** on the upper level, is its snobby subsection, a mini-version of Beverly Hills' Rodeo Drive, with **Chanel, Gucci, Escada, Dior, Tiffany & Co.,** and **Cartier.** Other stores include **The Nature Company, Sharper Image, Ralph Lauren, Laura Ashley, Adrienne Vittadini, Benetton,** and **Crazy Shirts,** a locally owned chain of T-shirt shops. **Liberty House,** the major local department store, and **Sears** are the anchors. ♦ Free parking. M-Sa 9:30AM-9PM; Su 10AM-5PM. 1450 Ala Moana Blvd (across from Ala Moana Beach Park), Honolulu. 946.2811

Within the Ala Moana Shopping Mall:

Makai Market A carnival of fast-food establishments, Makai Market features outstanding pizza at **Sbarro's,** Korean plate lunches at **Yummy's,** Cantonese cuisine at **Patti's Chinese Kitchen,** Szechuan fare at **Panda's,** and much more, including Japanese and Thai food to go, hot dogs, hamburgers, deli items, baked potatoes, and salads.

Bryon II Steak House ★$$$ Steak is the best choice on the menu at this business-lunch hangout. It's the only true restaurant at the shopping center and stays open even after the stores have closed. ♦ 949.8855

94 Cafe Cambio ★★$$ The creative Italian menu focuses on pasta and antipasto, and the bright Art Deco dining room is usually full of people enjoying good food and conversation. A wall of scribbles and great thoughts spans the length of the restaurant. BYOPen. ♦ 1680 Kapiolani Blvd (in the Kapiolani Business Center), Honolulu. 942.0740

95 Sada Restaurant ★★$$$ You can order off the Japanese menu, but most folks come for the sushi, prepared with the freshest fish and seafood. The food can be inconsistent, but when it's on, it's one of the best sushi bars in town. ♦ 1473 S. King St, Honolulu. 949.0646

96 Wisteria ★$$ A longtime local favorite, the Wisteria is one of those word-of-mouth places you'd never discover on your own. The cuisine is Japanese (and some American). Don't try to get in on a Friday night without reservations. ◆ 1206 S. King St, Honolulu. 531.5276

97 Mekong I ★★★$$ The first of a now well-established chain, this tiny restaurant offers a long list of Thai specialties prepared by **Keo Sananikone** and his talented family. Mekong I's reputation led to the immediate success of **Keo's,** its far more glamorous sister restaurant; those who come to Meking I are strictly interested in the food, including curries, spring rolls, satays, and Evil Jungle Prince, a house specialty. Alcohol isn't served, but you're welcome to bring beer or wine. ◆ 1295 S. Beretania St, Honolulu. 521.2025

98 Auntie Pasto's ★$ If you're in the mood for a quiet, relaxing dinner, keep looking. But if you want decent Italian food at very reasonable prices and are willing to endure the noise, Auntie Pasto's is the place. Start with an order of basil bread, then try the eggplant Parmesan or fish stew. Save room for the delicious mud pie. ◆ 1099 S. Beretania St, Honolulu. 523.8855

99 Honolulu Academy of Arts
The 30 galleries here display world-renowned European and American masterpieces, a permanent Oriental collection, as well as the best of Hawaii's art. Landscaped courtyards filled with plants and sculptures are housed in the handsome, tile-roofed structure, which opened as a museum in 1927. The academy was founded by avid art collector **Mrs. Charles Montague Cooke,** whose family home had been on this site. New York architect **Bertram Goodhue** designed the structure, a blend of Hawaiian, Oriental, and Western styles. ◆ Donation requested. Tu-Sa 10AM-4:30PM; Su 1-5PM. Tours are offered Tuesday through Saturday at 11AM, and Sunday at 1PM. 900 S. Beretania St, Honolulu. 532.8700

Within the Honolulu Academy of Arts:

Garden Cafe ★$ This canopied cafe serves commendable but curtailed soups, salads, and sandwiches for lunch, but since it's a fund-raising venture for the academy, operated entirely by volunteers, who would dare complain about quantity, especially in such a pleasant garden setting? (A bonus: the volunteers often share family recipes with the cafe.) ◆ 532.8734

100 Neal S. Blaisdell Center (NBC) Formerly the **Honolulu International Center (HIC)** and now known as the NBC, this $12.5 million complex was renamed in the '70s for a popular Honolulu mayor, **Neal S. Blaisdell,** who served from 1955 to 1968.

The 8,000-capacity arena plays host to basketball, boxing, and sumo-wrestling events, as well as conventions, rock concerts, and circuses. The NBC's 2,158-capacity concert hall is home to the **Honolulu Symphony Orchestra.** Ballet and major theatrical productions are also performed here. ◆ 777 Ward Ave, Honolulu. 521.2911

101 Ward Centre A trendy shopping mall on the Diamond Head side of **Ward Warehouse,** Ward Centre has restaurants and fast-food establishments upstairs and shops downstairs. ◆ M-F 10AM-9PM; Sa 10AM-5PM; Su 11AM-4PM. 1200 Ala Moana Blvd, Honolulu

Within the Ward Centre:

Keo's Thai Cuisine ★★$$$ Another offshoot of **Keo Sananikone's** restaurant dynasty. Dine in an air-conditioned room or in the open-air courtyard amid orchids and Thai art. The menu offers a limited selection compared to Sananikone's popular Kapahulu establishment, but it's still a pleasant place to enjoy Evil Jungle Prince (a popular entrée), spring rolls, and spicy curries. ◆ 533.0533

Honolulu Chocolate Company The owners, who have stores in several other locations, fill their largest shop with toys, gift boxes, preserves, and teas, as well as sinful sweets. Indulge in the apricots or ginger dipped in white, dark, or milk chocolate, truffles, liqueur-flavored cordials, macadamia turtles, and much more. ◆ 531.2997

Il Fresco ★★$$$ The menu at this people-watching mecca offers California cuisine with an Italian accent (grilled eggplant with chile peppers and goat cheese, for instance). The desserts are heavenly; try the chocolate cake with strawberry sauce. ◆ First level. 523.5191

Mocha Java Espresso & Fountain ★$ The best coffeehouse in the area, with a wide selection of gourmet blends and pastries. The espresso milk shakes are great for an afternoon boost. ◆ First level. 521.9023

Mary Catherine's Bakery One of Honolulu's finest bakeries, whether you're looking for a richer-than-rich chocolate cake, cookies for your sweetie (try the Ishler Hearts, two heart-shaped cookies with raspberry preserves between them, dipped in chocolate), or breakfast pastries (the scones and croissants are exceptional). You can also enjoy a cappuccino with dessert at one of the pleasant indoor or outdoor patio tables. ◆ First level. 521.5749

Andrew's ★$$$ Locals come here for the generous servings. The best buy is the complete dinner, which includes a respectable minestrone soup, salad, and dessert. The traditional Italian menu offers a wide selection of seafood, veal, and chicken. ◆ Second level. 523.8677

COMPADRES

Compadres Mexican Bar and Grill $$ Enjoy a pitcher of margaritas with complimentary tortilla chips and salsa. A few fish entrées have slipped onto the basically Mexican menu, and you can't go wrong ordering items such as the all-American burger and the *pollo* burger (broiled chicken sandwich), which come with a huge pile of Maui chips. Specialties include baby back ribs and *pollo barracho* (chicken cured in tequila, rock salt, and herbs for 24 hours and grilled to a crisp). ♦ Second level. 523.1307

Ryan's Parkplace Bar & Grill ★$$ Extremely popular for the affordable menu, which includes fish, salads, pastas, and *pupus* (appetizers), Ryan's is also a well-known singles bar, with a wide selection of beer and fresh oyster shooters. ♦ Second level. Reservations recommended. 523.9132

102 Ala Moana Beach Park Protected by an offshore reef, this beach is safe for swimming year-round, with lifeguards on duty during peak hours. Picnic and public facilities, snack stand, and tennis courts. ♦ Opposite the Ala Moana Shopping Mall, Honolulu

103 Ward Warehouse A variety of family restaurants (everything from pizza, sandwiches, and seafood), boutiques, and specialty stores are found in this two-story mall. ♦ M-F 10AM-9PM; Sa 10AM-5PM; Su 11AM-4PM. Between Ala Moana Blvd and Ward Ave, Honolulu. 531.6411

Within the Ward Warehouse:

Spaghetti Factory ★$ Part of the popular mainland chain, this is the perfect place for feasting on inexpensive carbohydrates. ♦ 531.1513

Dynasty II Restaurant ★$$$ The Dynasty serves gourmet Chinese food in an elegant setting with rosewood furniture and pink tablecloths. There are two Dynasty restaurants, the other a smaller and simpler establishment, so don't confuse them when making reservations. ♦ 531.0208

Nohea Gallery Located on the ground floor, this eclectic gallery features crafts by Hawaiian artists. You'll find Japanese-influenced woodblocks by **Hiroki Morinoue** and woodwork by **Ron Kent**, as well as ceramics, sculpture, glasswork, prints, wearable art, and jewelry. ♦ 599.7927

Pomegranates in the Sun Innovative island clothing and jewelry designs are carried here, plus a small selection of children's clothes. ♦ 531.1108

104 Pearl Harbor Tours The three-hour cruises from **Kewalo Basin,** the hub of the Honolulu fishing fleet, follow the coastline, sailing slowly through Pearl Harbor. The cruises include narrations on the details of infamous Japanese bombing raids, but you won't be able to tour the **Arizona Memorial** unless you take the official Navy tour (see page 146). ♦ Admission. Daily 9:30AM, 12:30PM. 536.3641

105 John Dominis ★★$$$$ Named after an early governor of Oahu, the oceanside restaurant beckons from a spectacular point in **Kewalo Basin;** floor-to-ceiling windows showcase the exceptional view (if you can get over gawking at the lobster-filled indoor lagoon). Favorites include the fish-and-prawns dish and the macadamia cream pie. John Dominis is also a fabulous, albeit high-priced, choice for Sunday brunch, with omelets, pasta, or waffles prepared to order at different food bars. Loyal customers return for the wide variety of fish and seafood, which chef **Greg Paulson** personally selects from the nearby **Honolulu Fish Market.** ♦ 3 Ahui St (off Ala Moana Blvd), Honolulu. 523.0955

106 Hawaiian Bagel ★$ It blends in a little too well with the rest of the small businesses in the **Kakaako District,** most of which are auto shops and warehouses, but this modest bagel factory bakes them as fresh as they get. Sandwiches, quiches, and a limited selection of deli items are also available. ♦ 753-B Halekauwila St, Honolulu. 523.8638

107 Columbia Inn ★$$ Every city has a bar that caters to the media, and this is Honolulu's. Adjacent to the **News Building,** which houses both of the state's daily papers, the original Columbia Inn opened the day the Japanese bombed Pearl Harbor. Journalists and flacks choose from the mixed menu, which offers basic American and Japanese cuisine with assorted local favorites thrown in for good measure. Try the peach Bavarian cake or the sizzling steak platter. ♦ 645 Kapiolani Blvd, Honolulu. 531.3747

108 Yanagi Sushi ★★★$$$ *Shoji*-screened Yanagi serves some of the freshest sashimi and sushi in Hawaii, packing in the locals as well as tourists and celebrities (photos and autographs of the latter adorn the walls). ♦ 762 Kapiolani Blvd, Honolulu. 537.1525

109 News Building Home of Hawaii's two daily newspapers, this green building with a red-tile roof is also a museum and gallery. The **Twigg-Smith** family runs the *Honolulu Advertiser,* the morning newspaper, and **Gannett Corporation** owns the *Honolulu Star-Bulletin,* the afternoon publication. ♦ 605 Kapiolani Blvd, Honolulu. 525.8000

Restaurants/Clubs: Red	**Hotels:** Blue
Shops/ 🌴 Outdoors: Green	**Sights/Culture:** Black

Nature's Necklaces

Around AD 500, when Polynesians first came to the Hawaiian islands, leis were among the most precious keepsakes from their homeland. The exotic garlands were used in many aspects of Hawaiian daily life, not only as ornaments but to indicate rank in religious and spiritual rites. Royalty usually preferred *lei hulu mans* (leis made of feathers, especially bright yellow ones). The various designs reflected different backgrounds, and historians studied them to help define emigration patterns. Today, the art of making leis continues to flourish.

Not all leis are made of flowers or feathers; many are fashioned from shells, seeds, or animal teeth and are either strung together by hand, braided with flowers or greens, sewn to heavy fabric, or wound with cord. Feather leis are more expensive than shell or nut leis because they take more time to construct, especially when the feathers are from exotic birds. Nowadays pheasant, geese, peacock,

or duck feathers are generally used to make feather leis, and these handcrafted leis last for years, if not generations.

More temporary leis are made with fruit, vines, berries, leaves, and, of course, flowers, with jasmine, plumeria, orchids, carnations, and ginger as the blossoms of choice. Leis made from the *pandanus* shrub have been worn since ancient times; they're considered an aphrodisiac, as well as a symbol of love and the end of bad luck.

Mokihana (pictured on the opposite page) and maile leis are often worn at important ceremonies. Leis made of maile are traditionally untied, rather than cut, at opening ceremonies, and if green mokihana berries (grown in the mountains of Kauai) are added to a lei, that signifies a special honor—one reserved for newly married couples or special guests. Illustrated here are a few other samples of popular Hawaiian necklaces.

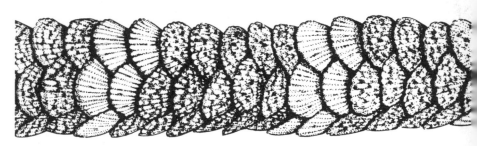

Lei olepe

Tonga

Peacock lei

Lei awapuhi melemele

Lei mauna-loa

Lei of mamane, lehua, a ali i, ukae-nene, oa, and palapalai

Lei mokihana

Lei pupu o Niihau

110 Royal Brewery People have been trying to tear down this redbrick building for years, while others, armed with duct tape and bubble gum, are equally determined to keep it up. The local **Primo** beer was once brewed here, but the building (circa 1900) is now unoccupied. ♦ 533 S. Queen St, Honolulu

111 Restaurant Row Thanks to its selection of trendy restaurants and bars near the Honolulu waterfront, Restaurant Row is the "in" place for discriminating singles and yuppies. ♦ Between South St and Ala Moana Blvd, Honolulu

Within Restaurant Row:

Sunset Grill ★★$$$ The noise level tends to get out of hand in this high-ceilinged restaurant, but that hasn't made it any less popular, especially for lunch. The menu offers a pleasant selection of pasta, salads, grilled fish, and meat, with tempting appetizers to begin. Try the mozzarella cakes, Anaheim peppers, and roasted garlic and goat cheese. And if you've room for dessert, treat yourself to an ice-cream concoction. Sunday brunch is bright and cheery with eggs, waffles, pancakes, and pasta. ♦ Reservations recommended. 521.4409

Rex's Black Orchid ★★★$$$$ When actors **Tom Selleck** and **Larry Manetti** decided to open the Black Orchid, they had the foresight to put veteran restaurateur **Rex Chandler** at the helm with chef **Martignago,** born and trained in Venicia, as his right-hand man. Their restaurant has since established itself as a fine dining experience in its own right. The space has been divided so that diners eat in different rooms, all of which feature stylish Art Deco interiors. The gourmet American cuisine can be inconsistent, although fish is generally a reliable choice; the black-and-blue *ahi* (Selleck's personal favorite), which is pan-seared rare and Cajun style, is the signature dish. ♦ Alohawear is recommended. 521.3111

Rose City Diner ★$$ The decor, jukebox, and framed photos of '50s heartthrobs are cute, but don't expect more from the malt-shop menu than hamburgers and milk shakes. ♦ 524.7673

Ruth's Chris Steak House ★★$$$ Hefty steaks and charbroiled fish are served in a pleasant decor (for a steak house, that is). Everything is à la carte, so dinner can get pricey real quick. ♦ 599.3860

112 King Kamehameha I Statue The gold-and-black monument of the spear-carrying chief wearing a feather cloak and helmet stands outside **Aliiolani Hale** (the **State Judiciary Building**). **King Kamehameha I,** who conquered and then united the islands into one kingdom, is regarded as Hawaii's greatest warrior. This statue is a replica, however; the original stands in front of the Kapaau Courthouse in Kohala on the Big Island, where Kamehameha was born, reared, and first came to power. Visit here in June during the **King Kamehameha Day** celebration, when the statue's outstretched arms are filled with dozens of leis. ♦ 417 S. King St, Honolulu

113 Kawaiahao Church Completed in 1842, more than 20 years after the first New England missionaries arrived aboard the *Thaddeus,* this handsome structure took five years to build, using 14,000 coral blocks that the congregation cut from ocean reefs. The walls of Kawaiahao, which means "freshwater pool of Hao" (the ancient spring), have witnessed royal marriages, coronations, and funerals. The 10:30AM Sunday service is noted for its stirring sermons, first-rate choir, and organ music. ♦ Punchbowl St (at S. King St), Honolulu

On the grounds of the Kawaiahao Church:

King Lunalilo's Tomb The tomb can be seen near the entrance to the church (Lunalilo was the only Hawaiian monarch who refused to be interred in the Royal Mausoleum in Nuuanu Valley, requesting on his deathbed to be buried closer to his people at Kawaiahao), and the churchyard serves as the cemetery for several missionaries and converts. ♦ Sunday services conducted in English and Hawaiian. Visitors are usually welcome to tour the church following the 10:30AM Sunday service. 538.6267

113 Mission Houses Museum The first frame house in the islands was built in 1821 for newly arrived Congregationalist missionaries who were suffering from culture shock. Two coral-block buildings were added to the prim white-frame structure soon after. One, the **Coral House,** is where printer **Elisha Loomis** established Hawaii's first press. The other, the **Chamberlain House,** was for the mission's purchasing agent. Now operated as a museum by the **Hawaiian Mission Children's Society** (descendants of the missionaries), Mission Houses is a repository of mementos from the state's early history. ♦ Admission includes guided tour. Tu-Sa 9AM-4PM; Su noon-4PM. 953 S. King St, Honolulu. 531.0481

114 Skygate When **Isamu Noguchi's** sculpture was unveiled in 1977 it was hardly a popular piece; people generally moaned or chuckled. Now, however, the black-steel abstract has been assimilated, if not accepted—all 15 tons of it. Families picnic under its 24-foot arches, and on special occasions, concerts are held nearby. ♦ Off S. King St

114 Honolulu Hale (Honolulu City Hall) Built in 1929, Honolulu City Hall's gracious California Spanish-style design provides a nice contrast to Iolani Palace and the State Capitol. Italian sculptor **Mario Valdastri** designed the bronze-sheeted front doors, which weigh 1,500 pounds each; the 4,500-pound chandeliers in the terracotta-tile courtyard, which is patterned after the 13th-century Bargello Palace in Florence, Italy; and the columns and balconies made of coral and crushed Hawaiian sandstone. Two three-story wings in the original style were added to Honolulu Hale in the early 1950s. A belt of green space links the city hall to the colonial-style Mission Memorial buildings and the gray concrete Honolulu Municipal Building. ♦ 530 S. King St, Honolulu. 523.4385

115 Iolani Palace In an attempt to keep the highly polished Douglas fir floors scuff-free, America's only royal palace (pictured below) provides guests with booties to cover their shoes. Iolani, which means "the hawk of heaven," epitomizes **King Kalakaua's** preoccupation with emulating the royal courts of Europe. Aptly nicknamed **"The Merry Monarch,"** Kalakaua's penchant for surrounding himself with material goods was unsurpassed by other Hawaiian kings and queens. Iolani cost $360,000 to build and was completed in 1882, eight years after Kalakaua was crowned king. The Florentine design, the work of architects **Thomas J. Baker, Isaac Moore,** and **C.J. Wall,** provided the perfect backdrop for Kalakaua's elaborate court life. The palace was filled with period furniture shipped around Cape Horn or painstakingly copied by local artisans. Royal guards were outfitted in dazzling uniforms that weighed entirely too much for the tropics.

Following Kalakaua's death in 1891 and the coup that toppled **Queen Liliuokalani** and the monarchy in 1893, the palace became Hawaii's seat of government. Until 1969, when the new State Capitol was built, the Senate met in the palace's royal dining room and the House of Representatives in the throne room. Since then, some $6 million has been spent restoring the palace to its former glory. The nonprofit **Friends of Iolani Palace** conducts 45-minute tours. ♦ Admission. Tours W-Sa 9AM-2:15PM, every 15 minutes. Reservations recommended. Between S. King and Richards Sts, Honolulu. 522.0822

115 Iolani Banyan What appears to be a massive tree is really two banyans that have been intertwined for a century. Said to have been planted by **Queen Kapiolani,** the banyan provides a shady canopy for passersby. ♦ In the parking lot between Iolani Palace and the State Archives Building

115 Coronation Bandstand King Kalakaua wanted a fitting site for his coronation, so in 1883 he built this gazebo and crowned himself and **Queen Kapiolani** in a lavish ceremony. The copper dome of the wedding cake-like pavilion is the original, but the rest of the structure was rebuilt of concrete after termites had weakened it. Eight pillars symbolizing Hawaii's major islands support the dome. Kalakaua was the only king crowned here, but the bandstand occasionally serves as a stage for gubernatorial inaugurations, weddings, and, most recently, the **Hawaiian Sovereignty rally,** which drew

Iolani Palace

thousands of spectators in 1993. Each Friday, the **Royal Hawaiian Band,** established in 1836 by **King Kamehameha II,** gives a free concert at noon. ♦ On the grounds of Iolani Palace, between S. King and Richards Sts, Honolulu

116 Queen Liliuokalani Statue Hawaii's last monarch is memorialized in a bronze sculpture at the entrance to the **State Capitol** near **Iolani Palace,** where she was imprisoned following her overthrow. Unveiled in 1982, the eight-foot statue by Boston artist **Marianne Pineda** shows the queen standing erect, her left hand holding the proposed constitution of 1893 (which cost her the throne) and a page of the composition to "Aloha Oe," the islands' traditional song of farewell. Her right hand is extended in friendship. ♦ S. Beretania St (between Punchbowl and Richards Sts), Honolulu

116 State Capitol Designed to take advantage of the views of the ocean, city, and mountains, the capitol (illustrated below) features a four-story atrium that enables natural light to fill the center of the structure. The interior trim, paneling, and furnishings are all koa wood, and the courtyard is paved with Molokai sand, a nice Hawaiian touch. The state legislature and the governor moved into the dramatic $24.5 million building in 1969, after being headquartered in Iolani Palace. The sign on the governor's double doors reads *E komo mai* (Please come in). Visitors are also free to sit in on regular sessions of the Senate and the House of Representatives, which are held from January through April. While the laws of parliamentary procedure are followed on the floor, proper English tends to crumble in favor of local pidgin (Hawaiian slang) during the more heated debates.

The capitol's most festive occasion is the traditional opening of the legislature the third Wednesday of every January. On that day, both the legislators and their desks are covered with flowers and leis. Morning festivities include hula dancing, songs, and even comedy routines by leading island entertainers. At noon, everyone adjourns to lavish buffets. ♦ Courtyard open daily 24 hours. Elevators: M-F 8AM-4:30PM. Bounded by S. Beretania, Punchbowl, and Richards Sts, Honolulu. 548.2211

State Capitol

116 Father Damien Statue Belgian priest **Damien Joseph de Veuster,** who has since been nominated for sainthood, lived and worked among the lepers of Molokai for 16 years before dying of the disease in 1889. He is memorialized in this bronze statue by **Marisol Escobar,** a work that ignited a great deal of public criticism for portraying the priest in his dying days, when he was a victim of leprosy. The controversial statue depicts a short, squat man with a cape and brimmed clerical hat, his features deformed and bloated. ♦ State Capitol courtyard, Honolulu

117 Washington Place When the American naval captain who built this estate in 1846 was lost at sea, his son, **John Dominis,** moved into the mansion with his wife, **Lydia Kapaakea,** the future **Queen Liliuokalani.** After Dominis' death and the overthrow of the monarchy in 1893, Liliuokalani returned to Washington Place (named after **George Washington** by a U.S. commissioner who once rented rooms here), and lived in the stately white mansion until her death in 1917. The governor of Hawaii now resides in the two-story residence, and the ground floor, most of which has been restored to look as it did then, is often used for state receptions. Past governors have hosted dinners here for visiting dignitaries, including **Queen Elizabeth** and the late **Emperor of Japan.** The upstairs rooms are private quarters for the governor and his family. ♦ Not open to the public. S. Beretania St, across from the State Capitol, Honolulu

117 St. Andrew's Cathedral Shortly after the traumatic death of his four-year-old son, **Albert, King Kamehameha IV** converted to the Church of England and founded St. Andrew's. The king died a year later at age 29, but construction of this Episcopalian headquarters began in 1867 under the direction of his widow, **Queen Emma.** The uniformed students on the premises go to **St. Andrew's Priory,** at the back of the cathedral. ♦ Daily 6:30AM-6PM. Queen Emma Sq (between S. Beretania and Alakea Sts), Honolulu. 524.2822

118 Yong Sing ★$$ Lunch conversations reverberate off the high ceiling of this popular and crowded Chinese restaurant. The extensive menu includes outstanding dim sum (Chinese dumplings of beef, pork, and seafood). ♦ 1055 Alakea St, Honolulu. 531.1366

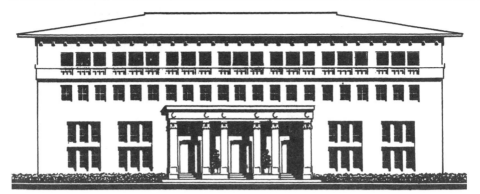

Alexander & Baldwin Building

119 Alexander & Baldwin Building A memorial to **Samuel T. Alexander** and **Henry P. Baldwin,** this distinctive headquarters (pictured above) opened in 1929. Alexander and Baldwin founded the youngest of the "Big Five" companies, a group of corporations that ruled the islands economically until Hawaii became a state, which included **Alexander & Baldwin, C. Brewer & Company, Theo. H. Davis & Company, Amfac Inc.,** and **Castle & Cooke Inc.** Architects **C.W. Dickey** and **Hart Wood** designed the structure with Dickey's trademark Hawaiian roof (double-pitched with a high peak and low, widespread eaves); the subtle Chinese influence was Wood's signature. At the time, the building was one of only two Honolulu structures made completely of concrete and steel. Critics praised its excellent workmanship and unique details, particularly the murals, terracotta ornamentation, and black Belgian marble in the first-floor reception area. A floating mezzanine has since been added, but many of the original details remain. ♦ 822 Bishop St, Honolulu

120 Tamarind Park Bring a brown-bag lunch and enjoy one of the frequent noontime concerts held in this green, open space fronting the **Pauahi Tower. Henry Moore's** *Upright Motive No. 9,* an 11-foot bronze statue in the reflecting pool, was executed in 1979 and cast in six editions. Loosely derived from the human figure, it draws its inspiration from the prehistoric monoliths at Stonehenge, North American Indian totem poles, and Polynesian sculpture. ♦ Bishop St (between Hotel and King Sts), Honolulu

121 C. Brewer Building Constructed in 1930, this last and smallest of the "Big Five" headquarters built in downtown Honolulu looks more like a mansion than a corporate office. Chief architect **Hardie Phillips** gave the two-story structure a Mediterranean flavor with Hawaiian motifs, most notably the double-pitched tile roof with a wide overhang, commonly referred to as a "Dickey" roof. Details include wrought-iron rails and

grillwork that represent sugarcane, as well as light fixtures designed to recall the form of sugar cubes. ♦ 827 Fort St, Honolulu

122 Hawaii Maritime Center Trace the role of the sea in life on the islands, from Polynesian migration by canoe to the whaling days and the era of Matson steamships. The ship docked outside, *Falls of Clyde,* is part of the tour. ♦ Admission. Daily 9AM-5PM. Pier 7, Honolulu Harbor, Honolulu. 536.6373

At the Hawaii Maritime Center:

Falls of Clyde A square-rigged, four-masted ship, the last of its kind in the world, the *Falls of Clyde* used to sail into Honolulu Harbor more than a century ago, when the docks were lined with similar vessels and sailors could virtually step from one ship to another. Built in Scotland, the wooden ship was purchased in 1898 by the Matson cruise line to serve on the route between San Francisco and Hawaii. Now the *Falls of Clyde* is a restored museum and a popular site for private parties.

123 Aloha Tower Passengers who sailed Matson steamships to Hawaii decades ago will remember the Aloha Tower as an imposing architectural landmark, probably because it was the tallest structure on the waterfront. But the 10-story, 184-foot tower, designed in 1921 by **Arthur Reynolds,** has long since been dwarfed by the steel-and-glass high rises in downtown Honolulu. ♦ Pier 9 (adjacent to Irwin Park and Nimitz Hwy), Honolulu. 537.9260

Honolulu, Oahu, is the largest city in the world, with municipal boundaries stretching across 540,000 square miles of the Pacific, most of which is underwater.

Honolulu means "sheltered bay" in Hawaiian.

Restaurants/Clubs: Red   Hotels: Blue
Shops/ 🌿 Outdoors: Green   **Sights/Culture:** Black

124 Chinatown Galleries Low rents and interesting storefronts and spaces first attracted art dealers to Honolulu's Chinatown, resulting in a number of galleries clustered within several blocks of **Nuuanu Avenue**.

Some favorite galleries include:

Lai Fong Inc. You could easily mistake Lai Fong for a thrift shop, what with the musty mounds of Chinese bric-a-brac from who knows when or where. But real treasures lurk in the shadows of the store: carved jade buttons, *cheongsams* (fitted Chinese dresses), funky ivory jewelry from pre-statehood days, and garish Chinese statues of folk gods. ♦ M-Sa 10AM-4:30PM. 1118 Nuuanu Ave, Honolulu. 537.3497

Pegge Hopper Gallery One of Hawaii's best-known artists, Pegge Hopper's trademark is huge Hawaiian women painted in Gauguin colors. Their various poses create a feeling of calm serenity. You can also buy novelty items of her work, including greeting cards, calendars, and T-shirts. A small, koa-framed print might sell for about $75. ♦ M-F 10AM-5PM; Sa 11AM-3PM. 1164 Nuuanu Ave, Honolulu. 524.1160

Cathedral of Our Lady of Peace The first Catholic priests came to Hawaii in 1827 from France, but it wasn't until 1843 that opposition to Catholicism had died down and this cathedral could be dedicated. It was here, three years later, that the first pipe organ on the islands was played. ♦ Daily 5:30AM-6:30PM. Fort Street Mall, next to S. Beretania St, Honolulu. 536.7036

125 Maunakea Street Lei Stands Along a few short blocks on Maunakea Street you'll find little storefronts selling leis, with workrooms behind the large, refrigerated flower cases. The scents of carnation, maile, ginger, pikake, and tuberose fill the air as women string the leis with long, thin needles. Leis are sold all over the islands, but these shops offer some of the best prices and selections. **Cindy's Lei Shoppe** (1034 Maunakea Street) is a family-run landmark that's been around for generations. Also recommended are **Lita's Leis** (59 North Beretania Street), **Aloha Leis and Flowers** (1145 Maunakea Street), and **Jenny's** and **Sweetheart's** (South Beretania Street, near Maunakea Street).

Paddlemonium!

What soccer is to Mexico and hockey is to Canada, outrigger canoe paddling is to Hawaii: a sport of heritage. Not only is it Hawaii's official team sport, it's one of the oldest organized sporting events in the Pacific.

Outrigger canoe paddling may seem somewhat simple and straightforward to the spectator, but it actually takes years for individual paddlers to develop and execute the perfect stroke and rhythm, then incorporate it into a team effort (which is why an individual's paddle is as respected as a shortstop's favorite glove). Competition among—and even within—teams is fierce, especially at advanced levels, but sportsmanship and camaraderie always prevail.

Although outrigger canoes have played a role in Hawaiian history since the first Polynesians arrived centuries ago, competition paddling didn't formally begin until 1908, when **Alexander Hume Ford** founded the **Outrigger Canoe Club.** Ford's club led to the first regatta solely devoted to canoe racing, which was held in 1933 on the Big Island. Since then, paddling popularity has exploded, and each major island has its own association and member clubs competing on local, state, and international levels.

The Superbowl of all races is the **Bankoh Molokai Hoe** (which means "The Bank of Hawaii Molokai Paddle"), the annual Molokai to Oahu men's world championship, held on the second Sunday of October. Hundreds of athletes from around the world paddle the 40.8 miles from Hale O Lono Harbor on Molokai to Waikiki Beach on Oahu, braving canoe-splitting waves and treacherous currents. (**Eddie Aikau,** one of Hawaii's most revered surfers, drowned after paddleboarding away from his swamped canoe in the 1977 race.) The women's championship competition, **Bankoh Na Wahine O Ke Kai** (which stands for "Women Against the Sea"), is held on the last Sunday of September.

126 Hotel Street Although gentrification is right on its heels, Hawaii's version of skid row isn't what it was during World War II, when servicemen frequented the area's red-light establishments. **James Jones** documented the seediness of these few downtown blocks in his novel *From Here to Eternity*. You can still buy a cold beer at any of the Hotel Street bars, and ladies of the night continue to beckon from the street corners, but the city is making an effort to clean up the area (as is indicated by the police station on one of the side streets). Restaurants and groceries operated mainly by immigrants from Southeast Asia are gradually replacing the bars and X-rated businesses. ◆ Between Bishop and River Sts, Honolulu

126 Chinatown In 1900, a fire was intentionally started in a group of shacks in Chinatown in an attempt to stop the spread of bubonic plague. Instead, the wind-whipped flames razed most of the area. From its ashes rose a new Chinatown of two-story wooden buildings with Chinese-operated laundries, grocery stores, bakeries, and tailor and herb shops on the ground floors, and family quarters upstairs.

The first Chinese arrived in Hawaii around 1850 as contract laborers for sugar plantations. Those who stayed saved their money and started their own businesses. Within 10 years, 60 percent of the stores in downtown Honolulu were owned by *pakes* (pah-KAYS), as Hawaiians called the Chinese. Some of the wealthiest people in Hawaii today are among their descendants. Chinatown's population has never been pure Chinese, however. Its multiracial complexion includes Filipinos, Hawaiians, and a recent influx of Vietnamese and Laotian refugees. Urban renewal has given the area a face-lift, although the lived-in look is far from gone. But the seedy bars, pool halls, and rooming houses aren't as plentiful as the noodle factories, open-air markets, herb shops, bakeries, clothing and jewelry stores, and restaurants.

Rather than randomly exploring the streets of Chinatown, you might want to take a walking tour, an entertaining and informative way to absorb the ethnic flavor. A few of the groups that offer tours: **Hawaii Heritage Center** (1128 Smith Street, 521.2749) on Friday at 9:30AM and 12:30PM, for a fee; **Chinatown Historic Society** (1250 Maunakea Street, 521.3045) Monday through Friday at 10AM and 1PM, no charge; and **Chinese Chamber of Commerce** (42 North King Street, 533.3181) Tuesday at 9:30AM, for a fee; reservations required. ◆ Bounded by Nuuanu Ave, Beretania and River Sts, and Nimitz Hwy

126 Wo Fat ★$$ Hawaii's oldest restaurant, established in 1882, is a landmark and an institution. In its heyday, the monumentally ornate restaurant was the choice locale for banquets and celebrations among the Chinese community. It's still worth a try for lunch or dinner, especially if you're experienced at ordering from a Cantonese menu. ◆ 115 N. Hotel St, Honolulu. 533.6393

126 Maunakea Marketplace If you're cruising through Chinatown, don't miss the Maunakea Marketplace and don't eat before you come here. A permanent conglomeration of stands, set up here county-fair style, sells food from all over the world—the Philippines, Japan, Singapore, Malaysia, China, Hawaii, Thailand, Korea, Italy, India, and Vietnam. After you're filled to the brim, waddle through the huge Asian market and gaze upon the myriad foodstuffs. ◆ Maunakea St (between N. Hotel and N. Pauahi Sts), Honolulu

126 Wong and Wong Restaurant ★★$$ Wonderful down-home cooking characterizes this small and modest restaurant. The trick is to order the specials, which are touted on signs hanging from the walls. The steamed fish, especially the mullet, is prepared Chinese style with a soy sauce, ginger, and green-onion sauce. You may be able to walk right in for lunch, but dinner reservations are a good idea. ◆ 1023 Maunakea St, Honolulu. 521.4492

126 Doong Kong Lau-Hakka Restaurant ★★$$ The food here is as superb as the decor is simple. Hakka cuisine isn't as spicy as Szechuan, but it's just as good. Some of the more popular selections arrive at your table on sizzling platters. ◆ 100 N. Beretania St, Suite 111 (in the Chinese Cultural Plaza, directly across from the canal), Honolulu. 531.8833

126 Oahu Market Every morning but Sunday this large, bustling market illustrates how busy Chinatown was before supermarkets came into existence. The regular customers obviously prefer to select their fresh fish and roast pork from butchers who know their names. You'll hear Cantonese, Vietnamese, and other Asian dialects as prices are agreed upon. When in season, mangoes and lychees are on sale, but you'll have the most fun buying *char siu* (barbecued pork). The butcher will chop the meat into bite-size pieces so you can nibble as you browse through the stalls. ◆ M-Sa 6:30AM-4:30PM; Su 6:30AM-noon. 145 N. King St, Honolulu. 528.2879

126 Ba-le Sandwich Shop 1 ★$ Some of the best French baguettes in the islands (and great French coffee, too) are made and sold by the Vietnamese owners of the Ba-le concessions around Honolulu. This little coffee shop, the headquarters, serves Vietnamese dim sum, spring rolls, noodle dishes, and sandwiches that hint of the flavors of Saigon. ◆ 150 N. King St, Honolulu. 521.3973

127 Dole Pineapple Cannery Back in the old days, the cloying smell of pineapple filled the air as you neared the pineapple cannery in the Iwilei District. Two million pineapples a day were processed in the cannery, each one inspected by women in white aprons, gloves, and caps. Now the machines and workers are only there seasonally. A short film depicting the history of pineapple production in Hawaii is shown every half hour from 9:30AM-3:30PM. ♦ Admission. 650 Iwilei Rd (look for the kitschy pineapple-topped water tank on stilts), Honolulu. 548.6600

127 Hawaii Children's Museum Bring your kids by for a range of hands-on exhibits in arts, crafts, and science. ♦ Admission. Tu-F 9AM-1PM; Sa-Su 10AM-4PM. 650 Iwilei Rd (at Dole Cannery Square), Honolulu. 522.0040

128 Hilo Hattie Garment Factory Every month, more than 30,000 aloha garments (shirts, dresses, shorts, etc.) are cranked out at this factory outlet, Hawaii's largest. Busloads of tourists come to watch the garments being made by the dozens of workers toiling at their machines. It's a great place for alohawear souvenirs. ♦ Daily 8:30AM-6PM. 700 N. Nimitz Hwy (at Pacific Hwy). 537.2926

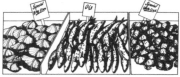

129 Tamashiro Market Look for a hot-pink building and the faded landmark sign (a pinkish-orange crab), and start hoping for a parking space. The market is worth a visit, especially if you love seafood, offering a wide selection of fresh island fish as well as favorites from the mainland and other parts of the world. The kids will be kept entertained looking at the live crabs, frogs, and lobsters crawling around in tanks. A huge board hanging over one of the fish counters lists the Hawaiian and mainland names for fish. If you're not squeamish, Tamashiro has a first-rate selection of *poke* (raw fish and seafood appetizers). ♦ M-F 9AM-6PM; Sa 8AM-6PM; Su 8AM-4PM. 802 N. King St, Honolulu. 841.8047

130 Helena's Hawaiian Food ★$ The customer seated next to you may have driven miles just to order one of **Helena Chock's** down-home specialties: *pipikaula* (spicy smoked beef), *lau lau* (*imu*-roasted pig), *opihi* (shellfish), and *poke* (raw fish). This simple diner is a longtime favorite among the islanders. The paintings on the walls are gifts from leading Hawaiian artists, who adore Helena and her prices. It's impossible to spend more than $10 here. ♦ 1364 N. King St, Honolulu. 845.8044

131 Bishop Museum and Planetarium When **Charles Reed Bishop** founded the Bishop Museum in 1889 in honor of the Hawaiian heritage of his wife, **Princess Bernice Pauahi,** he hoped it would rank among the great museums on earth. No doubt he would be proud to know that it not only houses the world's greatest collection of Hawaiian cultural and natural-history artifacts but is a highly regarded center for Pacific area studies. The Bishop Museum's success is largely attributable to the dedication of museum director **W. Donald Duckworth,** who came to Honolulu from the Smithsonian in Washington, DC, in the early '80s, and continues to expand the exhibition and publication programs.

The museum's centerpiece is **Hawaiian Hall**—three floors of carved war gods and feather cloaks, mementos of the 19th-century monarchs, valuable Polynesian artifacts, and more. The **Hall of Hawaiian Natural History** offers fascinating displays on the islands' fiery geological origin, including a lava tube with its own ecosystem. Children are free to feel lava or try their hands at making a grass hut in the **Hall of Discovery,** just across the lawn from the main gallery building. Next door is the **Planetarium and Science Center** and the **Shop Pacifica,** which stocks an exhaustive inventory of books on Hawaiian and Polynesian history. You can also purchase Niihau shell leis, authentic reproductions of museum pieces such as *lauhala* bags and hats, and Hawaiian quilts. ♦ Admission. Daily 9AM-5PM. Tours daily 10AM, noon. Planetarium shows M-Th 11AM, 2PM; F-Sa 11AM, 2PM, 7PM. Observatory F-Sa 7:30-9PM, weather permitting. 1525 Bernice St, Honolulu. 847.3511. For information about current programs, call 848.4129. For planetarium reservations, call 847.8201

132 Foster Botanic Gardens A tranquil setting at the edge of downtown Honolulu. Feel free to picnic and wander this 20-acre green domain, enjoying the plethora of orchids and other plants (4,000 species of tropical flora in all). ♦ Admission. Daily 9AM-4PM. Tours Wednesday at 1PM (reservations required). 180 N. Vineyard Blvd, Honolulu. 522.7060

133 Punchbowl Crater Centuries ago, human lives were sacrificed here to appease the gods (hence the dormant volcano's Hawaiian name, **Puowaina,** which means **"Hill of Sacrifice"**). And, ironically enough, the crater's 114-acre floor is now the final resting place for veterans of World Wars I and II, the Korean and Vietnam wars, and the Persian Gulf War, as well as their dependents. Some 34,000 white pillars in neat rows line the velvet expanse—officially known as the **National Memorial Cemetery of the Pacific**—creating a powerful effect when the first rays of sun probe the rim of the crater at dawn, especially during the sunrise service on Easter Sunday. World War II journalist **Ernie Pyle** is buried here among the soldiers he immortalized, as is **Ellison Onizuka**, the astronaut from Hawaii who was killed in the *Challenger* space-shuttle disaster in 1986. ♦ Free. Daily 8AM-6:30PM Mar-Aug; daily 8AM-5:30PM Sept-Apr. 2177 Puowaina Dr (follow the green-and-white signs), Honolulu. 541.1430

134 Alexander Cartwright Tomb The man who invented baseball died in Honolulu on 12 July 1892, and his pink granite tomb is in **Oahu Cemetery** (just off to the right of the road, a few hundred feet from the entrance). **Alexander Cartwright** not only created baseball, he umpired in the first official game, which was held 19 June 1846 between the **New York Knickerbockers** and the **New York Nine** in Hoboken, New Jersey. Later, during a trip to the islands, he became so enamored of Honolulu that he moved here and proceeded to teach baseball. (He also founded the city's first volunteer fire department.) **Cartwright Playground** in Makiki is where he supposedly laid out Hawaii's first baseball diamond. ♦ 2162 Nuuanu Ave, Honolulu

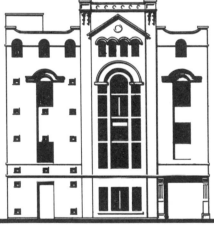

135 Royal Mausoleum The most important burial place in the islands, the Royal Mausoleum (pictured above) holds the remains of **King Kamehameha II** through **King Kamehameha V, King Kalakaua, Queen Liliuokalani,** and other royalty and favored friends of their courts. (**King Kamehameha I's** bones have never been discovered, though historians presume they're hidden in secret burial caves on the Big Island, where he died in 1891.) The other Hawaiian monarch who isn't buried here is **King Lunalilo,** who requested a private tomb on the grounds of **Kawaiahao Church.** King Kamehameha V selected the mausoleum's three-acre site in 1865, and royal remains were brought here from an old, overcrowded tomb on the **Iolani Palace** grounds. The cross-shaped chapel was designed by the islands' first professional architect, **Theodore Heuck.** ♦ Free. M-F 8AM-4:30PM. 2261 Nuuanu Ave, Honolulu. 536.7602

136 Queen Emma Summer Palace This cool summer retreat in Nuuanu Valley belonged to **Queen Emma** and her husband, **King Kamehameha IV.** When the **Duke of Edinburgh** visited Hawaii in 1869, Emma had the elegant Edinburgh Room built to accommodate a lavish gala for him (a party that she, unfortunately, failed to attend). The Hawaiian government purchased the palace in 1890, after Emma's death, and the **Daughters of Hawaii** have maintained it as a museum since 1915. The grand rooms contain many personal belongings of the royal family, including the koa wood cradle of Emma and Kamehameha's son, **Albert,** heir to the throne and **Queen Victoria's** godson, who died at the age of four. ♦ Admission. Daily 9AM-4PM. 2913 Pali Hwy, Honolulu. 595.3167

137 Swiss Inn ★★$$$ Fans of **Martin Wyss'** cooking love the Swiss Inn for its affordable menu and first-rate cuisine. The veal dishes (Wiener schnitzel, veal medaillons, Holstein schnitzel) are very popular, and there's also pasta, chicken, seafood, and fondue. ♦ 5730 Kalanianaole Hwy (in the Niu Valley Shopping Center), Honolulu. 377.5447

137 Al Dente ★★$$$ The seasoned hands of chef **Jean Pierre Germaine** orchestrate the French and Italian fare. A small, excellent wine list accompanies a menu featuring linguine with clams, osso buco, fresh salmon steamed in lettuce leaves, and many other delicacies. It's an intimate, pleasant restaurant. ♦ 5730 Kalanianaole Hwy (in the Niu Valley Shopping Center), Honolulu. 373.8855

138 Roy's Restaurant ★★★★$$$ **Roy Yamaguchi** was a leader in establishing a regional Hawaiian/California cuisine, and his consistently innovative creations keep it interesting. He calls his version "Euro-Asian" cuisine, and specialties include seafood potstickers; ravioli of lamb, goat cheese, and pesto; lobster in macadamia nut butter sauce; rack of Niihau lamb; and grilled Lanai venison in a basil and port sauce. The hundreds of other selections change regularly, depending on the produce and seafood in season. Although Roy's is for the adventurous palate, even tried-and-true conservatives will walk away satisfied. The noise level in the dining room may prove distracting to conversationalists and it's in an odd location on the outskirts of the **Hawaii Kai** suburb, but Roy's is wildly successful nonetheless. ♦ 6600 Kalanianaole Hwy, Hawaii Kai. 396.7697

Restaurants/Clubs: Red   **Hotels:** Blue
Shops/ ♣ Outdoors: Green   **Sights/Culture:** Black

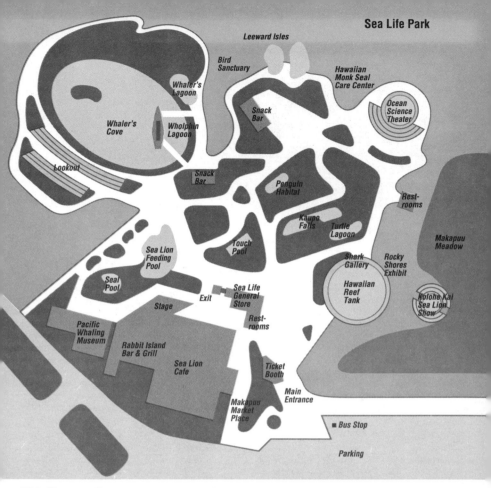

Leeward Isles

Bird Sanctuary

Hawaiian Monk Seal Care Center

Whaler's Lagoon

Snack Bar

Ocean Science Theater

Whaler's Cove

Wholphin Lagoon

Lookout

Snack Bar

Penguin Habitat

Rest-rooms

Kaupo Falls

Turtle Lagoon

Makapuu Meadow

Sea Lion Feeding Pool

Touch Pool

Shark Gallery

Rocky Shores Exhibit

Kolohe Kai Sea Lion Show

Seal Pool

Hawaiian Reef Tank

Stage

Exit

Sea Life General Store

Pacific Whaling Museum

Rest-rooms

Rabbit Island Bar & Grill

Sea Lion Cafe

Ticket Booth

Makapuu Market Place

Main Entrance

■ **Bus Stop**

Parking

139 Hanauma Bay Nestled against a volcanic crater that's missing a chunk on one side, Hanauma Bay is a beautiful snorkel spot, with waves so gentle even nonswimmers feel safe. The fish in this underwater state park are protected by law from spearhunters and fishers, which means snorkelers often find themselves nose-to-nose with brilliantly colored reef fish boldly going about their business (they're accustomed to stares). The downside is that it gets pretty crowded; try to avoid the afternoon rush. Once you get to the bay, it may look familiar. This is where **Elvis Presley** filmed *Blue Hawaii,* and directors used it for beach scenes in *From Here to Eternity* (the **Burt Lancaster-Deborah Kerr** clincher, however, was shot near Makapuu Beach for the surging waves).

And so you'll know, fish food can't be brought in but must be purchased at the concession stands, where snorkel gear is rented, too. ♦ Off Kalanianaole Hwy

140 Halona Blowhole A powerful gush of water spews into the air whenever ocean waves shooting through the lava tube here cause enough pressure to build. (You may hear a honking sound, too.) The lookout over the geyser is so spectacular that the city council is pushing to turn it into a national park. On clear days, the islands of Molokai and Lanai are visible on the horizon, and on those rare, exceptionally fine days, you may see Maui between them. ♦ Off Kalanianaole Hwy, east of Hanauma Bay, at the Hawaii Visitors Bureau marker

141 Sandy Beach (Koko Head Beach Park) Despite the people you'll see playing in the surf, this shorebreak is extremely dangerous because the waves break in shallow water— many swimmers and bodysurfers have suffered broken necks here throughout the years. Also known as Koko Head Beach Park, this beach is popular for kite-flying, and offers the best tubes for bodysurfing (only experts should attempt). Picnic and public facilities, and a lifeguard. ♦ Off Kalanianaole Hwy, northeast of Hanauma Bay

142 Makapuu Beach Park A dangerous swimming spot, but there is excellent bodysurfing for experts. The lookout point above Makapuu offers a breathtaking view of the windward coastline, outlying Sharkfin and Rabbit islands, and bodysurfers in the waves below. Public facilities and lifeguards are available here, too. ♦ Off Kalanianaole Hwy, east of Sea Life Park

143 Sea Life Park Paying to see fish and sea
mammals in land-based tanks and pools
seems ridiculous in Hawaii, surrounded as it
is by water full of these saltwater denizens.
But Sea Life Park (see the map on the
opposite page) is well worth the price of
admission to budding oceanographers and
anyone else who likes to watch dolphins soar
through hoops, not to mention schools of
tropical fish, monk seals, penguins, and all
manner of marine life—more than 4,000
creatures. The **Touch Pool** is a great attraction
for kids, who can reach into a shallow pool
and run their fingers across the sea
cucumbers, starfish, shells, giant worms, and
other slippery, spineless creatures. The **Rocky
Shores Exhibit** re-creates the surfswept
intertidal zone of Hawaii's shoreline, and the
Hawaiian Reef Tank simulates an offshore
reef three fathoms below sea level, with live
sharks, eels, sea turtles, and fish. A Pacific
bottlenose dolphin rides a boogie board at the
Ocean Science Theater, where you can also
meet **Kekaimalu,** the world's only "wolphin"
(a cross between a whale and a dolphin). The
park's setting, in beautiful Makapuu, lends
itself to a leisurely day of swimming,
sunbathing, and picnicking. On Friday nights,
some of Hawaii's best entertainers and local
bands liven up the **Sea Lion Cafe** and
Makapuu Meadow. ♦ Admission. M-Th, Sa
9:30AM-5PM; F 9:30AM-10PM. Off
Kalanianaole Hwy, southeast of Waimanalo
Bay, Honolulu. 259.7933

Within Sea Life Park:

Pacific Whaling Museum The largest
collection of whaling artifacts and scrimshaw
in the Pacific is housed in this privately owned
museum. The 36-foot-long skeleton
suspended from the ceiling is from a sperm
whale that became stranded and died off
Barber's Point on Oahu in 1980. ♦ 259.7933

144 Bueno Nalo ★★$ Don't be surprised to find
a line outside this humble establishment; the
Mexican food here is *muy bueno.* If you don't
mind eating early, you can avoid the wait. But
otherwise, join the party outside the
restaurant (they can only seat 20 or so at a
time). Specials include the Baja chowder and
chicken chimichangas. Bueno Nalo has no
liquor license, so BYOB. ♦ 41-865
Kalanianaole Hwy, Waimanalo. No credit
cards. 259.7186

145 Dave's Ice Cream Sleepy Waimanalo
doesn't make it into the national press much
(if ever), but it *did* get mentioned once in

People magazine. When Dave sent his
coconut-macadamia concoction to *People's*
ice-cream competition, his entry ranked
among the top five scoops in America—pretty
heady stuff for a local boy. The 40-plus flavors
change depending on stock, but on a good
day you can get a cone of carrot cake, mango,
or lychee. There are 10 branches of Dave's
scattered around the island. ♦ 41-1537
Kalanianaole Hwy, Waimanalo. 259.8576

146 Bellows Field Beach Park You can ride
 the gentle bodysurfing waves at this rural
beach, which is part of the **Bellows Air Force
Station,** but only from noon Friday to Sunday
evening, since war games are played here the
rest of the week. ♦ Off Kalanianaole Hwy (look
for the Bellows AFS sign), Waimanalo

147 Olomana Golf Links Waimanalo sports a
short, relatively easy course on Oahu's
northeast shore. Par 72, 6,081 yards.
Inexpensive green fees. ♦ 41-1801
Kalanianaole Hwy, Waimanalo. Pro shop
259.7926

148 Mid-Pacific Country Club The club offers
a long, tight, and challenging course on the
windward side of the island. Par 72, 6,848
yards. ♦ Walk-ons allowed Monday and
Tuesday afternoons, and Wednesday through
Friday before 11AM. 266 Kaelepulu Dr (off
Kalaheo Ave), Kailua. Pro shop 261.9765

149 Buzz's Original Steak House ★$$ One of
Oahu's first surf 'n' turf restaurants, this
Buzz's is the *original* Original Steak House. At
lunch you order off the menu, and for dinner
there's a selection of specials, including the
usual fresh fish, steaks, and a salad bar that's
better than most. ♦ 413 Kawailoa St (across
from Kailua Beach Park), Kailua. 261.4661

150 Kailua Beach Park A family-oriented
 windwardside beach with generous stretches
of white sand, this spot is safe for swimming
and bodysurfing, but look out for windsurfers
recklessly zipping about. Picnic and public
facilities and a lifeguard are available here.
♦ Off Kalaheo Ave, Kailua

151 Los Arcos ★$$ Old wine bottles decorate
this tiny restaurant, a commendable choice
for Mexican dishes. Recommendations
include the stuffed squid and the not-very-
Mexican but superb *lilikoi* (passion fruit) pie
and Black Forest torte. ♦ 19 Hoolai St (off
Kailua Rd near Burger King), Kailua. 262.8196

152 Koolau Farmers Stop at this nursery just
outside of Kailua for freshly cut flowers and
potted plants. Colorful hibiscus, bougainvillea,
heliconia, anthuriums, and orchids contribute
to the fragrances in the air. Longtime
customers rave about the personal service
(e.g., if cut gardenias are one of your favorite,
Koolau Farmers will call you when a delivery is
made). They ship to the mainland daily. ♦ M-
Sa 8AM-5PM; Su 8AM-4PM. 1127 Kailua Rd,
Kailua. 263.4414

153 Pali Golf Course This verdant course is located at the foot of the Koolau Mountains. Par 72, 6,493 yards. Inexpensive green fees for both residents and visitors. ♦ Call a week ahead for reservations. 45-050 Kamehameha Hwy, Kaneohe. 261.9784

154 Nuuanu Pali Lookout Follow the signs or the busloads of tourists along the Pali Highway to this lookout and hold on to your hat as you step out of the car. It's one of the most blustery spots in Hawaii—a place where gentle trade winds turn into formidable gusts. Civilization hasn't improved the panorama much, but at one thousand feet, it's still a great vantage point to view windward Oahu. Legend has it that the **Battle of Nuuanu Valley** was fought here in 1795, with **Kamehameha the Great** and his forces pushing the opposing army over the palisades to their deaths. ♦ From Pali Hwy, take the Nuuanu Pali Lookout turnoff (watch out, it comes up quick), Kaneohe

Haiku Gardens

155 Haiku Gardens The **Chart House** (★$$) restaurant overlooks this luxuriant tropical garden at the base of the misty Koolau Mountains. Pathways wind through the landscaped grounds and around a pond for pleasant after-dinner walks and the occasional wedding. ♦ 46-336 Haiku Rd, Kaneohe. 247.6671

156 Byodo-in Temple A replica of a 900-year-old Buddhist temple in Japan, Byodo-in was built in 1968 to honor Hawaii's first Japanese immigrants. It's situated serenely in the **Valley of the Temples Memorial Park,** a huge cemetery at the foot of the Koolau Mountains. A Buddha statue (illustrated above) near a pond filled with swans and carp watches the peacocks roam and listens to the visitors ringing the three-ton bronze bell. ♦ Admission. Daily 8AM-4PM. 47-200 Kahekili Hwy (Hwy 83), Kaneohe. 239.8811

157 Kahaluu Drive Highway 836, from Kaneohe to Kahaluu, is a pleasant coastline detour around Kahekili Highway (Highway 83). If you don't wish to see the Haiku Gardens or Byodo-in Temple, take this alternate scenic route when heading north.

158 Senator Fong's Plantation and Gardens Former **U.S. Senator Hiram Fong** retired to devote more time to cultivating this botanic garden, which opened to the public a few years ago. There are more than a hundred varieties of fruits and flowers, and sweeping ocean views from certain sections of the garden. The gift shop offers a discriminating selection of Hawaiian-made souvenirs. ♦ Admission. Daily 10AM-4PM. Last tour 3PM. 47-285 Pulama Rd (off Hwy 83, north of Kahaluu), Kahaluu. 239.6775

159 Paniolo Cafe $ Mosey on down this way for some Texas-style grub, including the Texas-size genuine rattlesnake burgers. There's no guarantee on the quality of the grinds, which can go either way, but after a couple of their mason-jar margaritas, you won't really care. ♦ 53-146 Kamehameha Hwy, Punaluu. 237.8521

160 Polynesian Cultural Center If you haven't been to the South Seas, this is a good introduction to the cultures of Polynesia: Hawaii, Fiji, Tonga, Samoa, Tahiti, and the Marquesas. It's a kind of Disney-goes-Pacific, with village replicas and traditions demonstrated by students from the nearby **Brigham Young University** (BYU) campus, many of them natives of Polynesia. Watch as they pound poi, string leis, husk coconuts, and make tapa cloth from mulberry bark. Set aside an entire day to make the round-trip drive from Waikiki, tour the various villages, and take in all the demonstrations. You may be exhausted and overwhelmed, but the narration is as entertaining as it is corny. Each half-hour there's a song-and-dance revue, and in the evening a buffet dinner show. (You can purchase a general admission ticket, which includes daytime activities and the dinner show, or an admissions-only ticket, which doesn't include the evening buffet.)

With more than 23 million guests, the center has been one of Hawaii's leading visitor attractions since the **Church of Jesus Christ of Latter-day Saints** opened it in 1963. And though there's a bit of controversy about the integrity of the whole production, which has provided a whopping $105 million for BYU, it's still an educational experience. ♦ Admission. M-Sa 12:30-9PM. Kamehameha Hwy, Laie. 293.3333, 800/367.7060

Restaurants/Clubs: Red   **Hotels:** Blue
Shops/ 🌳 **Outdoors:** Green   **Sights/Culture:** Black

Taking the Plunge

To only see Hawaii from above the sea is to only see half of paradise. Below the turquoise-blue depths is an unearthly, dreamlike world that, thanks to Jacques Cousteau and his Self-Contained Underwater Breathing Apparatus (also known as SCUBA gear), is widely accessible to just about anyone. In fact, more than 20,000 visitors and residents are happily blowing bubbles around Hawaii's islands every day—and among tourists it's an even more popular pastime than surfing.

Hawaii offers some of the best—and least expensive—dive programs in the world. And if you aren't sure whether diving is the sport for you, it's now possible to test the waters by signing up for a one-time introductory dive with an instructor without having to take classes or purchase gear. Most hotels either have their own dive program or will recommend a nearby dive center. Hotel-run programs usually offer free 30-minute pool lessons in an attempt to sell an introductory dive (for $50 to $70) and eventually a SCUBA certification course (prices for certification range from $150 to $400, depending on where the dives take place). Five-day certification courses usually last a few hours each morning, whereas three-day courses take all day. Both are equally educational, although five-day courses tend to be more fun and relaxed.

Diver's Dress Code

- **Buoyancy Control Device (BCD)** This inflatable/deflatable vest enables you to maintain neutral buoyancy underwater, and keeps you afloat when you're at the water's surface. Can be inflated manually (by mouth) or from the air tank.

- **Dive Knife** It's hardly ever used, but a knife is good for banging on the tank to get your partner's attention.

- **Fins** The fins provide a diver with his or her sole means of propulsion. The large surface area and stiff material increases swimming efficiency and decreases effort, making arm movement unnecessary.

- **Gauges** This important piece of equipment shows you how much air remains, the depth of the water, the direction in which you're headed (compass directions), and how much nitrogen you've absorbed (via a dive computer).

- **Mask** A properly fitted mask is essential to safe diving because it allows your eyes to focus underwater. Almost all masks are made of silicon,

which lasts longer than rubber. For those who have sight problems, prescription masks are available, too.

- **Regulator** This crucial device automatically regulates air flow and pressure from tank to lungs. You have complete control over the amount of air you breathe.

- **Tank** Made from aluminum, steel, or alloy, a full size-80 tank holds enough air (at ±3000 psi) to fill a phone booth. Rate of air consumption depends on various conditions (depth, current, experience), but beginning certified divers can normally stay 60 feet underwater for about 40 minutes.

- **Weightbelt** Literally a belt with weights attached to it, this piece of equipment compensates for the buoyancy of the tank and wet suit. It's easily removable in case of emergency.

- **Wet Suit** A full- or half-body dive suit is necessary for maintaining warmth (yes, even in Hawaii's warm waters) and for protection against cuts and scrapes.

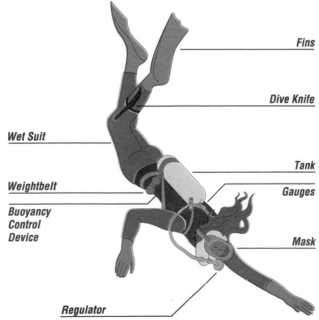

Fins

Dive Knife

Wet Suit

Tank

Weightbelt

Gauges

Buoyancy Control Device

Mask

Regulator

161 Mormon Temple Since 1864, the Mormon headquarters has occupied 6,000 acres in the community of Laie, where 95 percent of the population is Mormon. The **Church of Jesus Christ of Latter-day Saints** built the temple here in 1919, a comely white edifice on impeccably landscaped grounds. Visitors are not allowed to enter the temple, but you're welcome to tour the surroundings, which feature reflecting pools. ♦ Grounds open daily 9AM-8PM. 55-600 Naniloa Loop (off Kamehameha Hwy), Laie. Visitor's Center 293.9297

161 Ura Behling's Pareas Just down the street from the Mormon Temple is the home and business of **Ura Behling,** a charming and talented designer and fabricator of colorful *pareas* (wraparounds). You can't miss the place when it's in full operation, with dozens of brightly colored sheets stretched across the driveway, utilizing solar power and patterned cutouts to create tropical impressions through fading. The prices here are the best around and the service can't be beat, which explains the occasional tourist bus unloading at the doorstep. ♦ 55-533 Naniloa Loop, Laie. 293.5893

162 Malaekahana State Recreation Area

Just past Laie, right before you reach the former plantation town of Kahuku, you'll find postcard-perfect Malaekahana. On weekdays the arc-shaped beach is usually empty except for a fisher or two waiting to cast a net. There's good swimming and bodysurfing, but no lifeguard on duty. Remember to lock your car and keep valuables out of sight, then take your time strolling down the wide white sand beach or picnicking under the ironwood trees on the south end. There's a bathhouse with cold showers, and camping with permit. ♦ Daily 7AM-6:45PM. Off Kamehameha Hwy, 3 miles north of Laie

163 Huevos Restaurant ★$ As you enter Kahuku from the southeast on Kamehameha Highway, watch for the pole (which used to be a sign) by the roadside indicating where to turn off and turn right (immediately after the **Kahuku Superette**). About a hundred yards down the dirt road is this little country restaurant, serving breakfast only—down-home cooking that includes generous portions of omelets with fresh veggies, short stacks, and French toast. It's worth starting off the morning here if you're planning a day at the Polynesian Cultural Center or at a beach on this side of the island. ♦ Closed on Thursday. Kahuku. No phone

164 Royal Hawaiian Shrimp & Prawn If it weren't for the cars and folks queued at the side of the highway, you'd drive right past this roadside stall. The attraction is fresh prawns and shrimp prepared any number of ways, including steamed and tempura style. Behind the small stand is the aquaculture farm where

the goods were raised, which is about as fresh as you can get. No bargains here, though. ♦ Off Kamehameha Hwy, west of Kahuku

165 Turtle Bay Hilton and Country Club $$$ More than an hour's drive from Waikiki, the Turtle Bay Hilton is for people who really want to get away. There's not much to do here but golf on the 27-hole **Arnold Palmer** championship course, sunbathe by the two pools, or hit the beach. It can get pretty windy on **Kuilima Point,** where the hotel's 485 guest rooms and cottages are located, but that's one reason the beach next door is popular with surfers. Sit back and watch them ride the waves, or motivate yourself to play tennis, ride horses, windsurf, or try dune cycling. If you rent a car, Waimea Bay, Sunset Beach, or the town of Haleiwa are nice day trips. ♦ 57-091 Kamehameha Hwy, Kahuku. 293.8811, 800/445.8667; fax 293.9147

Within the Turtle Bay Hilton and Country Club:

Sea Tide Room ★$$ The Sunday brunch buffet here draws the local residents for the bountiful selection, including sashimi and sushi, and the fine beach view. ♦ 293.8811

Turtle Bay Hilton Golf Course This oceanside course, run by the **Arnold Palmer Management Company,** is known for its ferocious winds, but that doesn't keep golfers away. Legend has it that **Mickey Mantle,** with the wind at his back, drove a ball over the 357-yard fourth hole using a No. 4 wood, even though **George Fazio** supposedly designed the course to compensate for the wind. Par 70, 6,411 yards, with a 70 championship rating. ♦ Preferred starting times and rates for Turtle Bay Hilton guests. 293.8811

166 Sunset Beach It's a world-famous North Shore site for winter surfing contests, but year-round high waves and strong currents make Sunset Beach dangerous for swimmers. When the *Big Wednesday* sets come in, head this way, pull over somewhere, and join the mesmerized crowd. It's a good beach for strolling and sunbathing during spring and summer, but don't ever turn your back on the winter waves. ♦ Off Kamehameha Hwy, 7 miles north of Haleiwa

Tourism was introduced to Oahu in the late 1920s, when Matson Navigation Company steamships dropped off the first mainlanders in Waikiki.

167 **Ke Iki Hale** $$ This is the Hawaii everyone dreams of—palm trees silhouetted against the sunset, golden beaches stretching for miles, whales cavorting in the winter, and cozy little cottages with large picture windows to take it all in. Ke Iki is one of Oahu's best beaches, a broad expanse of white sand and palm trees that partially recedes during the winter, when thundering 10-foot waves crash on the reefy shoreline. Rinse off under a shower that's been fastened to a palm tree, then lay in a hammock or picnic at tables near the sand: the place is glorious.

Only a dozen cottages occupy this acre and a half of oceanfront property, from single bedrooms on the street side to one- and two-bedroom adjoining units facing the ocean. Simplicity and serenity are the operative words here, with a deliberate absence of modern-day luxuries: no Jacuzzi, room service, restaurant, TVs, or even telephones (there's a pay phone nearby, though), and the amenities of Haleiwa are only minutes away. The exterior of the Hale could use a new coat of paint, but the cottages are immaculate inside, with clean linens, full kitchens, tables, sofas, plants, and patios—you could easily stay in your swimsuit all day, "talking story" with aloha-spirited owner **Alice Tracy** and not giving one whit about the rest of the world. ♦ 59-579 Ke Iki Rd, Haleiwa. 638.8229

168 **Puu-o-Mahuka Heiau** For an incredible view of the North Shore and Waimea Bay, drive up Pupukea Road to this *heiau* (ancient temple), where humans were once sacrificed as part of the Hawaiian religion. Puu-o-Mahuka is a sacred place, where offerings of ti leaves and stones are still made. ♦ Off Kamehameha Hwy (take Pupukea Rd east to the Hawaii Visitor's Bureau marker)

169 **Waimea Falls Park** In 1990 a tropical storm devastated the 1,800-acre park across the street from Waimea Beach, but it was remodeled and opened to the public within a year. The lush grounds include an arboretum and more than 30 botanical gardens, with thousands of tropical and subtropical species. Ride through the park in an open-air minibus or take a guided walking tour. Be sure to see the cliff divers jumping from the 45-foot falls that give the park its name, and **Halau O Waimea,** the park's resident hula troupe, which performs the *kahiko* (ancient hula) in the upper meadow several times a day. The **Proud Peacock Restaurant** ($$) features nightly entertainment, and there's also a snack bar and picnic grounds. ♦ Admission. Daily 10AM-5:30PM. 59-864 Kamehameha Hwy, 7 miles north of Haleiwa. 638.8511

170 **Waimea Beach Park** The waters are calm during the summer, when you'll see local kids playing "king of the mountain" on the huge rock in the bay. But you'd never recognize this beach in November, when enormous waves pound the shore. Waimea Beach is one of the world's premier surfing spots, lined with spectators in the winter, when the expert surfers are out. Lifeguards and public facilities. ♦ Off Kamehameha Hwy, just north of Haleiwa

171 **Haleiwa Beach Park** There's good swimming and snorkeling here during the spring and summer, but surfing should be left to the experienced. ♦ 62-449 Kamehameha Hwy, just north of Haleiwa

172 **Jameson's by the Sea** ★★$$$ At sunset Jameson's is *the* roadside stop for seafood and pasta. Scampi and fresh *opakapaka* are served in the upstairs dining room. Downstairs, at the informal open-air lanai, *pupus* (appetizers) and drinks flow all day. ♦ 62-540 Kamehameha Hwy, Haleiwa. 637.4336

172 **Chart House at Haleiwa** ★★$$$ The popular seafood-and-steak chain opened on the site of the old **Seaview Inn** and immediately became the local hot spot, with indoor and outdoor dining right next to Haleiwa Harbor. Service may be spotty, but the salad bar is always good (especially the Caesar salad) and the fish menu is ample. Try the opah or moonfish. ♦ 66-011 Kamehameha Hwy, Haleiwa. 637.8005

172 **H. Miura Store & Tailor Shop** Walking into the H. Miura Store is like stepping back in time to the days when Haleiwa was a plantation town. The Miuras can tell you about that era because they opened the store in 1918. They're a friendly family, and the secret to their success is making swim trunks and walking shorts for the surfers who frequent the North Shore every winter. The names and measurements of their regular customers are kept in a ledger, but the Miuras never forget a face. ♦ M-Sa 8AM-5PM. 66-057 Kamehameha Hwy, Haleiwa. 637.4845

172 **S. Matsumoto Store** For generations, Haleiwa has been the home of a local favorite: finely shaved ice flavored with fruit syrups, served modestly in a paper cone. Comparing "shave ice" to a snow cone would be an injustice, though; even the best snow cone couldn't compete. The best establishments, like Matsumoto's, make their own syrups and offer variations with vanilla ice cream (delicious) and sweet *azuki* beans. Multiple flavors on one cone is the norm. ♦ Daily 8:30AM-5:30PM. 66-087 Kamehameha Hwy, Haleiwa. 637.4827

172 Rosie's Cantina $$ Surfers meet here for the hefty breakfasts, good margaritas, standard Mexican cuisine, and friendly environment. ◆ Haleiwa Shopping Plaza, Haleiwa. 637.3538

172 Pizza Bob's $$ Your typical beer and pizza joint, with small booths and a bustling surfer atmosphere. ◆ Haleiwa Shopping Plaza, Haleiwa. 637.5095

172 Kua Aina Sandwich Shop ★★$ The hamburgers here are so juicy they'll literally drip down your elbows, the french fries actually taste like potatoes, and the sandwiches are *onolicious*, especially those with creamy avocados. The only thing that needs work is the less-than-amiable service. ◆ 66-214 Kamehameha Hwy, Haleiwa. 637.6067

172 Coffee Gallery ★★$ Not that it's worth it to drive from Honolulu for a cup of java, but if you're anywhere near the Coffee Gallery you'd be insane not to stop here for the olfactory rush, an "aesthetically correct cup of coffee" (according to the business card), and a pesto veggie sandwich. Soup, desserts, sandwiches, waffles, and bagels are served in a covered patio setting, with Grateful Dead music in the background. ◆ 66-250 Kamehameha Hwy, Haleiwa. 637.5571

172 Kaala Art Artist/owner **John Costello** paints his dreams on canvases while brother **Kevin** keeps the racks stocked with T-shirts and scads of imported casualwear from Thailand and Bali. Flapping sheets of colorful *pareus* (Polynesian wraparounds) line the walls—the perfect tropical gift. ◆ Daily 9AM-6PM. 66-456 Kamehameha Hwy, Haleiwa. 637.7065

172 Raising Cane Check out the beachwear and island crafts, designed by local artists. Everything from hand-painted children's clothing to the **Tutuvi** line of T-shirts and Polynesian wraps is carried here. ◆ M-F 10AM-6PM; Sa-Su 10AM-5PM. 66-521 Kamehameha Hwy, Haleiwa. 637.3337

173 Sugar Bar A cool, blue oasis in a desert of tourist traps, Sugar Bar may be Oahu's last bastion of local beer-guzzling solidarity. Described as your basic down-home country bar by owner **Peter Birnbaum**, a patron of the arts and possessor of what must be Hawaii's only bust of Beethoven, this place is a second home to the people of sleepy Waialua. Packs of bikers tether their hogs here on the weekends and proceed to gorge on the cheap food and drinks, always under the watchful, scowling eye of ol' Ludwig V. And rumor has it that somewhere on the memorabilia-lined walls, if you look hard enough and drink long enough, is the answer to the meaning of life. ◆ 67-069 Keaalohanui St, Waialua. 637.6989

174 Dole Pineapple Pavilion Try a piece of pineapple while viewing the pictorial display on the history of the fruit. The pavilion is located in the heart of Hawaii's pineapple country, surrounded by neatly trimmed pineapple fields and red soil so rich it'll stain your white sneakers. The gift shop carries replicas of old Dole labels, now a collector's item. ◆ Daily 9AM-5:30PM. Off Hwy 99 (Kamehameha Hwy), north of Wahiawa. 621.8408

175 Schofield Barracks The U.S. Army's 25th Infantry Division headquarters are here, right beside the sugarcane and pineapple fields that Japanese bombers flew over during the raid on Pearl Harbor. The barracks is named for **Major General John M. Schofield,** the Army's Pacific military division commander, who came to Hawaii in the 1870s on the pretext of vacationing but spent more time around the **Pearl River Lagoon**—as Pearl Harbor was then called—investigating its suitability as an American military enclave. ◆ Off Hwy 99 (Kamehameha Hwy), Wahiawa

176 Keawaula Bay It's easy to find—just keep driving until you run out of road, and you'll come to a popular surf spot (called **"Yoke's"**) with a great beach for soaking in the rays. ◆ End of Hwy 930 (Farrington Hwy)

177 Makaha Beach Park Professional surfing originated here and then shifted to the North Shore, but Makaha still hosts the annual **Buffalo Keaulana Big Board Classic,** a championship tournament for surfers who use the long, elegant boards that first put the sport on the map. The competition is held every February or March, depending on when the surfing conditions are best. As with most other beaches along the Waianae Coast, this isn't the most hospitable place for tourists, so keep a low profile and lock you car. ◆ Off Hwy 930 (Farrington Hwy), Makaha

178 Sheraton Makaha Resort & Country Club $$$ If you want to be far from the action—an hour's drive from Waikiki— with nothing much to do except play tennis or golf, ride horses, cool off in the Olympic-size pool, and explore Makaha Beach, this may be the place for you. Guest rooms and suites are in low-rise cottage clusters, with lanais and views of the Pacific or the golf course. ◆ 84-626 Makaha Valley Rd (look for the market off Farrington Hwy), Makaha. 695.9511, 800/325.3535

Within the Sheraton Makaha Resort & Country Club:

Sheraton Makaha West Course An 18-hole championship golf course set against the green cliffs of the Waianae range, the fairways here have great views of the Pacific coastline, especially at sunset. Expensive green fees but uncrowded play. Par 72, 7,091 yards. Shuttle service from Sheraton hotels in Waikiki also available. ♦ Starting times. 695.9544

179 Pokai Bay Beach Park The only fully sheltered beach along the Waianae Coast. Unfortunately, this part of the island doesn't cater to tourists. To avoid vandalism, be sure to lock your car. Picnic and public facilities, lifeguards. ♦ Off Hwy 930 (Farrington Hwy), south of Waianae

180 Mililani Golf Club Located in the suburbs of leeward Oahu, the Mililani course is shaded by trees on former sugarcane fields. Par 72, 6,800 yards, 70 rating. Moderate green fees. ♦ Starting times. Kamehameha Hwy (Hwy 99), north of Waikiki. 623.2254

181 Arakawa's Watch for the sugar-mill smokestack once you get to the town of Waipahu and eventually you'll run into this weathered anachronism, more a museum than a store. A cross between a Woolworth and a Hawaiian thrift mart, Arakawa's carries an eclectic mix of cross-cultural necessities and plain old junk. Some of the merchandise includes Japanese dishes for sashimi and soup, *palaka* (plaid) aloha shirts that have more cachet among the local residents than the garish prints you'll find in Waikiki, coconut husk lamps, and jade pendants. ♦ M-Sa 9:30AM-5:30PM; Su 11AM-4PM. 94-333 Waipahu Depot Rd (off Farrington Hwy), in downtown Waipahu. 677.3131

182 Pearl City Tavern If it's still in business, stop by this tavern, order a brew, and contemplate the glass cage filled with squirrel monkeys that's behind the bar. ♦ 905 Kamehameha Hwy, Pearl City. 455.1045

183 Pearl Country Club A country club in name only, this public golf course overlooks Pearl Harbor; a small forest of trees patiently awaits your hooks and slices. Par 72, 6,230 yards. ♦ Starting times. Expensive green fees. 98-535 Kaonohi St (just off H1 toward the mountains), Pearl City. 487.3802

184 Pearlridge Center The two sections of this air-conditioned mall are connected by monorail. **Liberty House, JCPenney,** and **Sears** anchor the boutiques and specialty shops, movie theaters, and restaurants, including **Bravo** ($) for pizza, and **Monterey Bay Canners** ($$) for grilled fish at affordable prices. On the corner of the busy intersection leading to Pearlridge is **Anna Miller's** (★$), a coffee shop with winning pies; look for a circular building separate from the center. ♦ M-Sa 10AM-9PM; Su 10AM-5PM. 98-1005 Moanalua Rd (off Kamehameha Hwy, across from Pearl Harbor), Pearl City. 488.0981

185 Aloha Stadium **Charles Luckman & Associates** designed the 50,000-seat stadium, home of the **University of Hawaii Rainbows,** the state's only college football team. It's also used for high-school football games and rock concerts. But the real excitement is when the **Hula Bowl** and **Pro Bowl** football games are televised from here every January. The movable stands can be converted from a football to a baseball field. Unfortunately, it's been discovered that Aloha Stadium is slowly rusting from the inside-out because of the salty environment. ♦ 99-500 Salt Lake Blvd (near Pearl Harbor). 486.9300

185 Aloha Stadium Flea Market Wednesdays and weekends the stadium parking lot becomes a giant flea market, with new and secondhand goods. Scores of vendors sell jewelry, kids' clothes, food, muumuus, aloha shirts, slippers, and toys, among other things. Shuttles to the flea market pick up at the major hotels. ♦ W, Sa-Su 6AM-3PM. 99-500 Salt Lake Blvd (near Pearl Harbor). 955.4050

186 Pacific Submarine Museum The 10,000-square-foot museum, which opened in 1988, is operated by the **Pacific Fleet Submarine Memorial Association.** Exhibits include sections of American and captured enemy submarines (including an ominous one-man suicide torpedo), an intact World War II sub, defused torpedoes, and related military knickknacks. ♦ Admission. Daily 8AM-5PM. 11 Arizona Memorial Dr. 423.1341

Check out Oahu's North Shore in November and December, when some of the gnarliest surfers in the world come to ride the choicest waves in Hawaii. Radical.

Garbage collectors in Honolulu, Oahu, have a clause in their contract that allows them to go fishing as soon as they're done with their route, which is usually just before dawn..

Restaurants/Clubs: Red   **Hotels:** Blue

Shops/ **Outdoors:** Green   **Sights/Culture:** Black

187 USS Arizona Memorial It was early Sunday morning, 7 December 1941, and most of Honolulu was still sleeping when United States' defense outpost in the Pacific was savaged by a wave of Japanese bombers. Several ships were hit, and the USS *Arizona* sank at its mooring blocks in 40 feet of water, all in about five minutes. The remains of 1,102 officers and sailors are entombed inside its rusting hull.

In 1962, after a benefit concert by **Elvis Presley,** a gracefully arched white structure was built over the USS *Arizona.* Designed by Honolulu architect **Alfred Preis,** the memorial became a national shrine, with the names of the 1,177 U.S. Navy men and Marines killed in the attack engraved on a marble plaque. This is one of Hawaii's most popular tourist attractions. Before boarding one of the Navy shuttleboats that carry passengers to the memorial, walk through the $5 million **Visitors Center,** where the "Day of Infamy" is recounted. The entire tour, including a documentary film and shuttle to the memorial, lasts about 75 minutes. ◆ Free, although tickets to the day's launches are issued on a first-come first-serve basis. Before noon there's often a one- to three-hour wait. Visitors Center daily 7:30AM-5PM. Shuttleboat 7:45AM-3PM (weather permitting). From Honolulu and Waikiki, drive west on H1, past the Honolulu International Airport, take the USS *Arizona* Memorial exit, and follow signs to the Visitors Center. Shirts and shoes required. 422.0561

188 Pearl Harbor Naval Ship Tours On the first Saturday of every month, the U.S. Navy opens one of its ships in Pearl Harbor to the public from noon to 4PM. ◆ Free. Enter through the Nimitz Gate at the end of the Nimitz Hwy, Pearl Harbor. 474.6156

189 Honolulu International Country Club Designed in part by **Arnold Palmer,** this golf course opened for play in the late '70s. Par 71, 5,995 yards. ◆ Members and guests only. 1690 Ala Puumalu, Salt Lake. Pro shop 833.4541

190 Moanalua Gardens The huge monkeypod trees on this sprawling 26-acre playground first capture the attention of westbound motorists on Highway 1. The expansive park is open to the public, although it's usually empty. The **Prince Lot Hula Festival** is held here each spring to honor the prince (who became **King Kamehameha V**) for reviving the ancient hula during his 1863-72 reign, after more than four decades of a missionary-imposed ban. The only buildings that remain are an old cottage where Kamehameha V used to entertain his friends and the Chinese Hall built in the early 1900s by **Samuel Mills Damon.** Nearby **Moanalua Valley** features petroglyphs and other historic sights.

◆ Donation. Daily 7:30AM-6PM. Nature hike into valley twice monthly; call for dates and reservations. From Moanalua Fwy, take Moanalua Gardens exit near Tripler Army Hospital. 839.5334

Bests

George Mavrothalassitis
Executive Chef, La Mer, Halekulani Hotel, Honolulu

On Lanai:

My favorite hotel (after the Halekulani, of course) is **The Lodge at Koele.** Go with the love of your life. It is the most romantic place in the world, and the food is great.

On Oahu:

My favorite restaurant (after **La Mer,** of course) is **Uraku** on Kapiolani Boulevard in Honolulu.

Strolling down the ocean sidewalk along the South Shore between the **Kaimana Beach Hotel** and **Kapahula Avenue.** Try it at sunset.

The **Contemporary Museum** in Honolulu. Visit the pavilion displaying a set from Mozart's opera *L'Enfant et les Sortilèges.* Good lunch spot; bring your own wine.

Do not miss the **Brothers Cazimeros'** annual outdoor concert on 1 May at the Waikiki Shell. It's a glimpse of *real* Hawaii on the stage and in the audience.

Roy Yamaguchi
Chef/Restaurateur; Roy's Restaurant, RJ's Ranch House, Roy's Kahana Bar & Grill, Roy's Tokyo, Roy's Guam, Honolulu

Hiking **Upper Tantalus,** and visiting the **Bishop Museum and Planetarium,** the **East-West Center,** and the **Lyon Arboretum,** all on Oahu.

Haleiwa and **Waimea Bay** on Oahu's North Shore.

A romantic dinner at the beautiful **La Mer** restaurant at the Halekulani Hotel in Waikiki, Oahu, or at the **Canoe House** in the Mauna Lani Bay Hotel on the Big Island.

Visiting the **Hawaii Volcanoes National Park** on the Big Island with a picnic lunch from **Sam's Restaurant.**

Driving to the **Parker Ranch** in Kamuela on the Big Island, and enjoying the **Kona coffee country** along Route 180.

Windsurfing near **Hookipa Park** on Maui, and driving up **Haleakala Crater.**

Lunch at the **Haliimaile General Store** on Maui.

Roy's Kahana Bar & Grill on Maui, where you can see David Abella in action.

Visit Jean-Marie at **A Pacific Cafe** on Kauai; stay at the **Hyatt Regency Kauai.**

Enjoy a weekend at **The Lodge at Koele** on Lanai and let chef Darin Schultz go wild with creativity.

Joyce Matsumoto

Public Relations Director, Halekulani Hotel, Honolulu

Whale-watching off **Wailea** on Maui.

On Oahu:

May Day Twilight Celebration with the **Brothers Cazimeros** at the Waikiki Shell (don't miss the lei exhibition, either).

Sunset cocktails and traditional Hawaiian entertainment at the Halekulani Hotel's **House without a Key** in Waikiki.

A rainbow-colored shave ice at **Matsumoto's** on the North Shore.

Celebrating Christmas with the **Honolulu Boys Choir.**

Brett A. Uprichard

Editor, *Hawaii Drive Guides*
Associate Editor, *Honolulu Magazine*

On Oahu:

Sunset drinks at the Sheraton Moana Surfrider's **Banyan Veranda**—very relaxing and beautiful, with views of surfers and canoes.

A morning hike to the top of **Diamond Head Crater**—the very best view of Waikiki and the beach.

Any **Hawaiian luau** at an old beachside house. *Kalua* pig never tastes as good anywhere else, and the amateur entertainment is usually terrific.

A midnight stroll on **Lanikai Beach** during a full moon—very romantic when the moon lights up Mokulua Island.

Teriyaki steak on a stick at the **Punahou** or **McKinley high-school carnivals.**

Hiram L. Fong

Retired U.S. Senator/Attorney/Chairman of the Board, Finance Enterprises, Ltd., Honolulu

Having been born and raised in Hawaii and having traveled to many parts of the world, I must say there's no place like Hawaii. Nature created the Hawaiian islands in a series of volcanic eruptions, leaving great mountain ranges, cliffs, lush valleys with tropical vegetation, seawalls, spectacular landscapes, and dramatic panoramas. A drive around each island is a must. Here are some of my favorite places:

Oahu—Take a scenic drive, stopping at the **USS Arizona Memorial,** a monument built in tribute to those who died aboard the USS *Arizona* on 7 December 1941. The U.S. Navy offers a free boat tour of Pearl Harbor and the memorial. Also visit **Waimea Falls Park,** a 1,800-acre arboretum on the North Shore; the **Polynesian Cultural Center** in Laie, which features re-created villages representing seven ancient cultures; **Senator Fong's Plantation and Gardens,** a 725-acre garden estate with lush tropical forests and exotic flowers and fruit trees; and **Sea Life Park** in Makapuu, an oceanside display of marine life.

To become king, Kamehameha I drove his enemies over what is now the **Nuuanu Pali Lookout.** The

National Memorial Cemetery of the Pacific, located in Punchbowl Crater, is the final resting place for Americans who served in either of the World Wars, the Korean War, or the Vietnam War.

Take Tantalus Drive to the **Puu Ualakoa State Wayside** for a spectacular view by day or night; walk through a natural rain forest at **Paradise Park** in Manoa Valley.

Walk along our famous **Waikiki Beach;** see the animals and collections of tropical birds at the **Honolulu Zoo;** take a historic walking tour of downtown Honolulu and visit **Iolani Palace,** the only palace in America, the **Mission House, Kawaiahao Church, Washington Place,** and our **State Capitol;** or walk through **Chinatown,** where you can shop at the open markets.

Visit **Hawaii Volcanoes National Park** and see the **Kilauea Volcano,** which is still active, and go to **Nani Mau Gardens** in Hilo for the fragrant flowers.

Maui—The view of the sunrise from **Haleakala Crater** is unforgettable; take a stroll along the waterfront of **Lahaina,** an old whaling port, now home to many artists and galleries; visit **Iao Valley,** known as the "little Yosemite of Hawaii," with its famous **Iao Needle,** a 2,250-foot product of erosion rising sharply amidst the background of mountain cliffs; or tour the **Maui Tropical Plantation,** a 120-acre agricultural showcase.

Kauai—This is the lushest and greenest island. **Mount Waialeale** is considered the wettest spot on earth with an average rainfall of nearly 500 inches per year. Take a drive to the **Waimea Canyon Lookout** for a spectacular panoramic view of the valley gorge and then travel on to **Kalalau Valley Lookout** for a view of the valley and the ocean. Drive to **Hanalei Valley,** which was once a bustling Hawaiian settlement with rice fields and taro patches.

Author's Bests

Sights:

Bishop Museum and Planetarium

The Contemporary Museum

Chinatown

Hanauma Bay

Nuuanu Pali Lookout

Restaurants:

Bueno Nalo ★★$

Eggs 'n Things ★$

Irifune ★★$$

La Mer ★★★★$$$$

Roy's Restaurant ★★★★$$$

Hotels:

Kahala Hilton Hotel $$$$

Ke Iki Hale $$

Malakini Hotel $

Manoa Valley Inn $$

Sheraton Moana Surfrider $$$

147

Kauai

On the morning of 11 September 1992, Kauai (kuh-WHY) as a tourist destination ceased to exist. Still licking the wounds of **Hurricane Iwa**, which leveled **"The Garden Island"** more than a decade ago, the residents and resort owners found themselves staring into the eye of the worst hurricane to hit Hawaii in this century—**Hurricane Iniki**. What started as a tropical storm became a billion-dollar nightmare, turning lush, verdant Kauai into, as one resident put it, "a big garbage dump." Winds gusting up to 180 miles per hour pruned the entire island, leveling sugarcane fields and macadamia orchards, and literally stripping the foliage from trees and bushes.

Man-made structures fared no better. Telephone poles were toppled like matchsticks, leaving residents without electricity for months (blown back to the Roman era, people resorted to communicating with runners), and every structure received some damage, ranging from a few lost roofing tiles to doors, walls, and entire houses that were completely blown away. Families ran from room to room as sections of their homes were ripped apart, and many were forced to retreat to their cars for safety. Of the island's 55,000 residents, there were (miraculously) only three deaths and about a hundred nonserious injuries.

What didn't escape near-fatal injuries, however, was the tourist industry, which accounted for 80 percent of Kauai's economy. Parts of the exclusive **Poipu Coast** washed away, including multimillion-dollar homes and luxury resorts (cement foundations and "For Sale" signs now dominate the landscape). Many hotel employees packed their bags and went elsewhere looking for work, while eager construction workers arrived by the planeload. Some of the major resorts that await insurance settlements are actively seeking buyers. The problem is compounded by the tourism infrastructure itself, which remains too weak to support the dozens of hotels and resorts that will soon reopen. Even when the physical structures are completely rebuilt, it will take nearly a decade for the island's main attraction—its dazzling natural beauty—to fully recover. While the beaches and canyons remain mostly untouched, the rest of Kauai needs at least a few years to rebuild and recuperate.

Ironically, some residents praise the hurricane as nature's way of purging the island of its "mainlandish" qualities, weeding out the transient, profit-oriented population and strengthening the spirit of Kauai's true *ohana* (family). In contrast to many survivors of Florida's Hurricane Andrew, who had to struggle with looting and homelessness, the islanders of Kauai instead exchanged hugs, shared food and water, and housed anyone who chose to stay and help rebuild what will soon regain its title as Hawaii's most beautiful island.

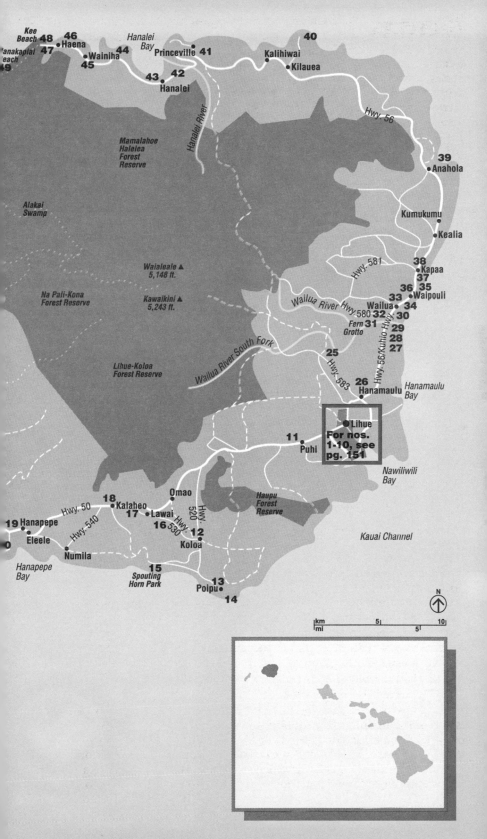

Kee
Beach
48 **46**
Haena
Kanakapiai
Beach
47
49

Hanalei
Bay
44
Wainiha
45

Princeville **41**

43 **42**
Hanalei

Kalihiwai
Kilauea

40

Hanalei River

Mamalahoe
Halelea
Forest
Reserve

Hwy. 56

Alakai
Swamp

39
Anahola

Kumukumu

Kealia

Na Pali-Kona
Forest
Reserve

Waialeale ▲
5,148 ft.

Kawaikini ▲
5,243 ft.

Hwy. 581

38
Kapaa **37**

36 **35**
33 Waipouli
Wailua
34
Wailua River Hwy. 580 **32** **30**
Fern **31** **29**
Grotto **28**
27

Wailua River South Fork

Lihue-Koloa
Forest
Reserve

25

Hwy. 583

26
Hanamaulu

Hanamaulu
Bay

Lihue
**For nos.
1-10, see
pg. 151**

11
Puhi

Nawiliwili
Bay

Hwy. 50
18
Kalaheo
Omao
17 Lawai
19 Hanapepe **16**
Eleele
Hwy. 540
Numila
Koloa
12

Haupu
Forest
Reserve

Kauai Channel

Hwy. 520

Hwy. 530

Hanapepe
Bay

15
Spouting
Horn Park

13
Poipu
14

N

km
mi
5
10
5

149

1 Hamura's Saimin Stand ★$ If you haven't experienced the saimin sensation, hunker over a bowl of the traditional Hawaiian noodle soup (the ethnic equivalent of burgers and fries) here with the locals. With its narrow Formica counters and steaming slices of teriyaki beef, Hamura's spoons out some of the best noodles on Kauai. ♦ 2956 Kress St, Lihue. 245.3271

2 Barbecue Inn ★$$ A popular cheap-eats joint for more than 25 years, the Barbecue Inn built its reputation on complete dinner plates from the American/Japanese menu. It's certainly nothing fancy, with screens for windows and an ambience set by plywood, but drop by for an inexpensive lunch. ♦ 2982 Kress St, Lihue. 245.2921

3 Restaurant Kiibo ★$$ Teriyaki steak, sashimi, sushi, tempura, sukiyaki, and other authentic Japanese specialties are served in a rustic Oriental setting. ♦ 2991 Umi St, Lihue. 245.2650

4 Kauai Museum The story of the islands of Kauai and Niihau, from the first volcanic eruptions more than six million years ago through the 19th century, is told in a permanent exhibit in the **William Hyde Rice Building,** named in honor of the last appointed governor of Kauai under the Hawaiian monarchy. In the **Albert Spencer Wilcox Building** (illustrated above), which was named for the son of missionary teachers, you'll find changing exhibits of Kauai art and historic artifacts. To see some of the generally inaccessible sights of the island without boarding a chopper, watch the film that was shot from a helicopter tour. ♦ Admission. M-F 9AM-4:30PM; Sa 9AM-1PM. 4428 Rice St, Lihue. 245.6931

5 Eggbert's ★★$$ One of Lihue's best diners, Eggbert's was known for excellent food, friendly service, and reasonable prices before the hurricane shut it down. Omelets were the specialty, along with a lengthy list of salads, sandwiches, burgers, and local seafood. ♦ 4483 Rice St, Lihue. 245.6325

6 Tip Top Motel, Cafe & Bakery Noted by locals and visitors from the outer islands as *the* breakfast place in Lihue for a stack of macadamia nut or banana pancakes, side orders of spicy Portuguese sausage, and papaya with morning eggs, this favorite meeting place of Kauai's politicians, journalists, and other movers and shakers is also well known for its fresh-baked cookies, cakes, and pies. Back in the old days, Tip Top was the only bakery with macadamia cookies, now the ubiquitous gift among islanders. ♦ 3173 Akahi St, Lihue. 245.2333

7 Si Cisco's ★$$ Basic south-of-the-border fare, plus a few house specialties, including tamales, fajitas, and "Kauai's largest margaritas." The food isn't great, but for the money and the generous portions, Si Cisco's is one of the better deals in town. ♦ Off Hwy 58, Kukui Grove Center, Lihue. 245.8561

8 Grove Farm Closed for repairs until at least November 1993, Grove Farm represents a slice of the real Kauai. Engineer **George N. Wilcox,** a New England missionary descendant, founded the self-contained sugar plantation in 1864. When his niece, **Mabel Wilcox** (the last Wilcox to live on the plantation), died in 1978, it became a nonprofit educational organization dedicated to preserving the history of plantation life on Kauai. Well-versed guides conduct tours of the main plantation home, the cottages in which George lived and guests stayed, and the workers' camp houses. Miss Mabel's clothes still hang in her closet, her sister **Elsie's** silver-handled hairbrushes remain on her dresser, their uncle's collection of canes and hats are in his cottage, and two housekeepers regularly dust the furniture, replace the flowers, bake cookies, and make mint iced tea for the visitors. This is one of the most genuinely unique attractions on Kauai; in all of Hawaii, for that matter. ♦ Admission. Tours M, W-Th 10AM, 1:15PM. No children under age five. Reservations required (sometimes one week in advance). Tours are cancelled on rainy days. Nawiliwili Rd, Lihue. 245.3202

9 Westin Kauai $$$$ Kauai's largest hotel took the brunt of **Hurricane Iniki,** suffering blown-out windows, flooding, and considerable damage to the grounds. Preliminary estimates are that $20 million will be needed to rebuild the resort, with completion scheduled for the beginning of 1994.

Along with the Hyatt Regency Waikoloa on the Big Island and the Westin Maui, the Westin Kauai was one of three big **Chris Hemmeter** projects to open on the islands in the late 1980s. Whether you call them "experiences," as Hemmeter does, or simply hotels, they are all flamboyant and very controversial. Take the Westin Kauai, the result of a $350 million metamorphosis of the Kauai Surf Hotel. It features a stable filled with purebred Clydesdales, Belgians, and Percherons, waiting to pull you in one of the hotel's 35 carriages along eight miles of paths. And for guests who have something more serious in mind, a team of white horses harnessed to a white carriage stands ready to whisk them off to the resort's own seaside wedding chapel. The horse theme is carved in stone in the Versailles-like palace court, a 2.1-acre reflecting lagoon with seven white marble steeds charging from the fountain in the center. Within this lagoon are islands where kangaroos, wallabies, gazelles, zebras, monkeys, turkeys, and llamas live.

The Westin Kauai's main swimming pool is one of the largest in Hawaii, with 26,000 square feet of water surface and a lining of 1.8 million blue-and-white mosaic tiles. If you prefer the sea, however, Hemmeter designed an elevator inside a hundred-foot cliff to take you to the sandy beach below. The hotel features five towers with 847 well-appointed guest rooms. The bathrooms are marble, the towels fluffy, and the beds comfortable. The resort is linked to Lihue Airport by its own two-mile road. ♦ Kalapaki Beach, Lihue. 245.5050, 800/228.3000; fax 246.5097

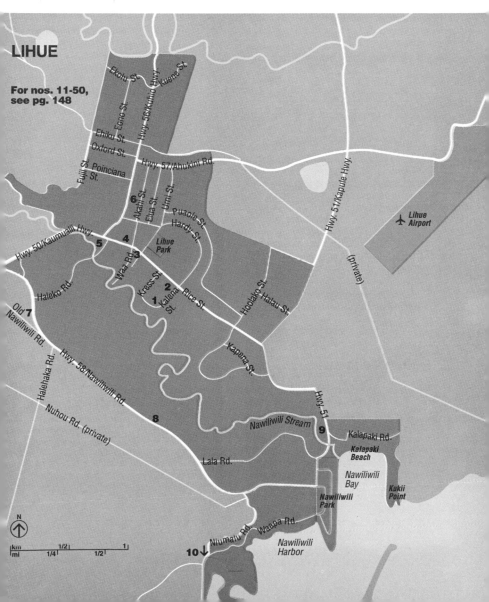

9 Westin Kauai Lagoons Golf and Racquet Club The championship **Kiele Course** is created for tournament play, and the **Kauai Lagoons Course,** designed in the traditional links style, is for all levels; all 36 holes were designed by **Jack Nicklaus.** The club also has a swimming pool, health spas, and eight tennis courts, including a stadium court. Par 72, 7,070 yards. ♦ Expensive green fees. 245.5050

9 Nawiliwili Park The swimming at **Kalapaki Beach** in Nawiliwili Park is superb because of its sheltered cove and sandy bottom, and the waves are suitable for novice surfers. Old-timers will remember the days when Hawaiian beachboys steered their canoes through the surf here. ♦ Hwy 51, Nawiliwili

9 JJ's Broiler $$$ The Broiler received extensive damage along with the entire **Anchor Cove** complex, and rumor has it that whether it reopens depends on the insurance settlement. Even *Gourmet* magazine couldn't pry apart owner **Jim Jasper's** lips for the secret sauce on his famous garlic-flavored Slavonic steak. Mahimahi and lobster join the beefy stars served in this handsome establishment. ♦ Anchor Cove, Lihue. 246.4422

9 Kauai Chop Suey ★★$$ The enormous menu here has a following among the lunchtime crowd hungry for chow mein, shrimp with black beans, and the dozens of other Cantonese offerings. Kauai Chow Mein —a steaming plate of noodles, chicken, shrimp, *char siu* (barbecue pork), and lots of vegetables—is the house specialty. ♦ Pacific Ocean Plaza. 3501 Rice Street, Lihue. 245.8790

9 Cafe Portofino ★★$$$ Wood beams, ceiling fans, and an open-air terrace overlooking Kalapaki Bay all lend to Portofino's charming ambience. The gourmet Italian menu is centered around fresh fish, shellfish, veal, rabbit, and pasta. Treat yourself to an afternoon cocktail or an espresso at the full bar. ♦ Pacific Ocean Plaza. 3501 Rice Street, Lihue. 245.2121

Electronic windows that change from clear to frosted at the flick of a switch are installed in every room at the Princeville Resort on Kauai. When the power is off, a thin layer of crystals sandwiched between two plates of glass diffuse light rays, creating a "frosted" effect. By flipping the switch, the crystals align themselves and voilà—instant room with a view.

10 Alakoko Fish Pond (Menehune Fish Pond) According to folk legend, the Menehune were two-foot-tall people who occupied Kauai long before the Polynesians and accomplished enormous physical feats, the remains of which are still visible. The Menehunes are credited with making this mullet pond at **Niumalu Beach Park** by building a 900-foot-long wall to cut off a bend in the Huleia River. Legend has it that a princess and her brother asked the Menehune to undertake this task, and they agreed as long as the two didn't watch them build it. Naturally, they did watch, and, quite unnaturally, they were turned to stone as a result. The twin pillars near the fish pond are said to be the dearly departed. ♦ Overlook on Niumalu Rd, south of the Westin Kauai Hotel

11 Kilohana Estate When **Gaylord Parke Wilcox,** the head of the Grove Farm plantation and relative of Grove Farm founder **George N. Wilcox,** built his Tudor-style dream house in 1935, he probably never imagined it would be turned into a shopping complex, and that his office would one day become a jewelry store. Although the Kilohana complex (pictured above) was heavily damaged by **Hurricane Iniki,** plans are under way to restore the great old plantation house to its former splendor by 1993. Along with the original woodwork, Gump's furnishings, and an Art Deco gallery are shops and restaurants. The former library exhibits the **Hemmeter Collection,** fine art from Asia and the Pacific, and the master bedroom is now a gallery featuring the works of leading Hawaiian artists. ♦ M-Sa 9:30AM-9:30PM; Su 9:30AM-5PM. Hwy 50, just outside Lihue in Puhi. 245.5608

Within Kilohana Estate:

Gaylord's Restaurant $$$ Named after **Gaylord Wilcox** of the prominent missionary family, this restaurant offered alfresco dining in one of the most pleasing surroundings on the island before **Hurricane Iniki** hit town. A courtyard overlooked the sprawling lawns of the plantation estate while a private dining room retained the luxury and splendor of the plantation heyday. Continental specialties included fresh seafood, prime rib, and lamb with exotic chutneys. Gaylord's is scheduled to reopen in 1993. ♦ 245.9593

12 Old Koloa Town Bodysurfing isn't the only attraction in the Poipu area, especially since Old Koloa Town was restored in 1984. This $2 million project was the idea of **Robert H. Gerell** of Koloa Town Associates, who negotiated a 67-year lease from the **Mabel P. Waterhouse Trust** and acquired three acres and about one thousand feet of frontage road in Koloa. Gerell then set to work refurbishing the weathered, termite-ridden storefronts that creaked from one end of Koloa to the other, dressing them in an 1800s look. Some of the historical structures that were restored are a stone mill stack from **Grove Farm;** the **Koloa Hotel** (Kauai's first hotel), an 1898 one-story building; and the 1900 **Yamamoto Store.** Among the dozens of other businesses that have opened behind the renovated storefronts are **Lappert's Aloha Ice Cream, Pancho & Lefty's Mexican Cantina** (★$$), and a **Crazy Shirts** store. Unfortunately, several *kamaaina* (longtime residents) couldn't afford the steep rents and so had to leave their cozy hometown storefronts. ◆ Maluhia Rd (Hwy 520), turn 5 miles west of Lihue

12 Koloa Broiler ★$$ Save some money and broil your own steaks and burgers at this casual and rather quaint little restaurant (illustrated above). Fish and chicken are also reasonably priced and include the salad bar and baked beans. (Part of the **Chuck's Steak House** chain.) ◆ Old Koloa Town, Koloa. 742.9122

13 Poipu If you're looking to buy inexpensive beachfront property, Poipu is the place to go. The area was the hardest hit by **Hurricane Iniki.** What wasn't demolished by 30-foot waves was blown apart by 180 mph winds; entire houses, some priced in the millions, were either gutted or ripped off their foundations. Poipu will take years to restore, especially rebuilding the washed-out roads. Before the hurricane, the most popular drive from the Wailua or Lihue areas was to the sunny south shore and **Poipu Beach.** The **Tunnel of Trees** (now the Tunnel of Trunks), a grove of eucalyptus trees that forms a natural archway along Highway 520, is a distinctive landmark along the way. **Poipu Beach Park** is a choice picnic area and all of Poipu Beach is generally reliable for sunbathing, swimming, and snorkeling, with quality bodysurfing at **Brennecke Beach.** The Poipu area's most famous natural attraction, beyond the fine beaches, is **Spouting Horn,** a geyserlike lava tube with a reputation that exceeds its eruptive performance. ◆ Approximately 14 miles from Lihue

14 Kiahuna Plantation Golf Course Poipu's first championship 18-hole course, designed by **Robert Trent Jones, Jr.**, was completed in 1983. It was bought by a Japanese sports company in 1986 and plans are in the works to add nine holes. Par 70, 6,440 yards. ◆ 2545 Kiahuna Plantation Dr, Koloa. 742.9595

14 Kiahuna Plantation Condominiums $$$ Scheduled to reopen in early 1994, this first-class resort has plantation-style buildings right beside Poipu Beach. It is an excellent place to settle while enjoying Kauai's sunniest shoreline. The rambling property is generously landscaped with broad, manicured lawns, trees, and bougainvillea, with pathways and tiny Japanese-style bridges leading to the beach. While the most popular units are those on the shore, the ones fronted by lawns are equally pleasant. Pool, tennis, TVs. ◆ 2253 Poipu Rd, Koloa. 742.6411, 800/367.7052; fax 742.1047

14 Sheraton Kauai $$$$ Once the heavily damaged shoreline units and the road leading to them are repaired, the Sheraton is scheduled to reopen (hopefully sometime in early 1994). For all practical purposes, there are now two Sheraton Kauai hotels: the original two-story **Ocean Wing,** anchored on a crescent-shaped white sand beach (perhaps the best beach location of any Poipu hotel), with all 220 rooms overlooking the ocean; and the 238-room **Garden Wing,** opened in 1982, with four-story pitched-roofed buildings arranged amid fragrant tropical foliage, meandering lagoons, and a large pool area.

The Garden Wing is a superior bargain, with rooms about half the price of the Ocean Wing rooms. Although they have garden or mountain views instead of ocean views, the Garden Wing rooms have private lanais, clock radios, and excellent wheelchair access. All of the rooms in both wings have refrigerators and minibars, and each wing has its own pool, plus a wading pool for children. The hotel also features three new tennis courts and a nearby golf course. ◆ 2440 Hoonani Rd, Koloa. 742.1661, 800/325.3535; fax 742.9777

14 Poipu Beach Park What used to be the best swimming beach on the island and one of the most beautiful on Kauai is now devastated and abandoned, thanks to **Hurricane Iniki.** Even all the king's horses and men couldn't put this park back together again, and it's going to take Mother Nature a long time to restore Poipu Beach to its original state. ◆ Take Hoowili Rd from Poipu Rd

Kauai didn't get its first traffic lights until 1973, when they were installed in the town of Lihue at the intersection of Rice, Umi, and Kalena streets, near the Kauai Museum.

Restaurants/Clubs: Red   **Hotels:** Blue
Shops/ ♣ Outdoors: Green   **Sights/Culture:** Black

14 Poipu Beach Hotel $$ Located on one of the island's loveliest and most popular beaches (before Hurricane Iniki, at least), this **Stouffer** hotel has 138 rooms in three-story buildings arranged horseshoe fashion around a courtyard and pool, opening toward the ocean. The rooms have Japanese shoji sliding doors, tropical decor, and are equipped with kitchenettes and refrigerators. The hotel's neighbor, also managed by Stouffer, is the comfortably luxurious Waiohai Beach Resort, which shares tennis facilities with the Poipu Beach Hotel. ♦ 2249 Poipu Rd, Koloa. 800/468.3571

14 Poipu Kai Condominiums $$$ Expected to resume operations in the summer of 1993, the comfortably appointed condominium resort has 250 units on 110 lavishly landscaped acres along the beach. Swimming pools, tennis courts, and Poipu's first championship golf course are nearby. A **Colony Resorts** establishment. ♦ 1941 Poipu Rd, Koloa. 742.6464, 800/777.1700; fax 742.7865

14 Stouffer Waiohai Beach Resort $$$$ Hearts were broken when the 47 charming cottages of the original Waiohai were replaced with a $60 million luxury resort in 1981—Kauai's first luxury hotel. But it didn't take long for visitors to fall in love with **Amfac Hotels'** showcase property. The Stouffer-managed resort continues to reign as one of the best on Kauai (it used to be *the* best before the Hyatt Kauai opened in 1991).

The setting is luxurious but not pretentiously so, with a brass and marble lobby (where mint iced tea is served when you check in), 11 acres of gorgeously landscaped gardens, ocean-view rooms and suites, and high-class restaurants. The resort also has three swimming pools, a fitness center, six tennis courts, and a quiet, inviting library generously stocked with books on Hawaii. The rooms are filled with special amenities, such as minibars and refrigerators.

The W-shaped design, by **Arthur Y. Mori & Associates** of Honolulu, was criticized at first because many of the 434 rooms face each other. But the configuration maximizes the number of ocean-view rooms, and the lateral views improved as the interior gardens matured. Unfortunately, the Stouffer Waiohai and the adjacent Poipu Beach Hotel were among the most heavily hit of the major

hotels on Kauai, with all ground floors virtually destroyed by high waves. Both hotels hope to reopen sometime in 1994. ♦ 2249 Poipu Rd, Koloa. 742.7214, 800/468.3571; fax 742.6799

14 Hyatt Regency Kauai $$$$ Although Kauai's second-largest resort received rather brutal treatment from Iniki, which washed away the saltwater lagoons, gutted the **Tidewater** restaurant, and damaged about 100 guest rooms, the completely restored hotel reopened in March 1992 (a heroic achievement, considering many other hotels in the area are still in ruins).

Built at a cost of $220 million, the south shore's newest resort sits on 50 acres of choice oceanfront property. Designed by Honolulu architect **Wimberly Allis** of **Tong & Goo** (exterior) and Santa Monica designers **Hirsch-Bedner & Associates** (interior), the Hyatt is splendidly landscaped with a re-created shipwreck and a five-acre lagoon that faces Keoneloa Bay, commonly called "Shipwreck's Beach." The remarkable architecture draws inspiration from island homes, with gorgeous, handcrafted koa wood furnishings. Scuba diving, snorkeling, tennis, and windsurfing are among the many sports, plus there's a 27-hole **Robert Trent Jones, Jr.,** golf course and driving range. Facilities for sailing, horseback riding, kayak excursions, and helicopter tours are all nearby, or you can take advantage of the hotel's "**Discover Kauai**" program, run under the auspices of the **Kauai Historical Society** and **Na Hula O Kaohi Kukapulani.** The program's activities (free to guests) include the history and lore of hula (with demonstrations), the history of the Koloa area, and a dune walk featuring the endemic plants and sea life of the Poipu Beach area. ♦ 1571 Poipu Rd, Koloa. 742.1234, 800/233.1234; fax 742.1557

15 Spouting Horn Park Poipu's starring attraction (actually, the only attraction left in Poipu for the time being) is a gush of ocean water that explodes through a lava tube when the waves roll in, sometimes causing a moaning sound. Legend has it that the groan is from a lizard trapped in the tube. Spouting Horn's reputation far exceeds its actual performance, which often sounds more like an exhausted humpback whale than a horn. ♦ West end of Lawai Rd, Poipu

The maximum ocean depth between any two adjacent Hawaiian islands is 9,950 feet (between Kauai and Oahu).

Making Waves: Smart Steps to Snorkeling Safely

Thanks to the warm, clear, and relatively shallow coastline, Hawaii boasts some of the top snorkeling beaches in the world. Snorkeling is also one of the cheapest and most rewarding activities Hawaii has to offer. For less than three dollars a day, anyone who can float or swim can rent snorkel gear and spend hours gawking at the colorful sea life that inhabits the offshore coral reefs.

Optimum snorkeling conditions change daily depending on the weather and surf, so your best bet is to ask a rental-shop employee where to go (try to avoid overrated spots such as Molokini Island, unless you don't mind swimming over and under other bodies to get a glimpse of some fish). If you're fearful of taking the plunge, keep in mind that those who are afraid to try snorkeling (and you *know* who you are) usually are the ones who enjoy it the most. And no matter where you decide to jump in, remember that the number one safety rule is to snorkel with a partner.

Tips for Staying on Top

1. Make sure your mask fits properly. Check it by trying to inhale through your nose—you shouldn't be able to. (If you have a mustache, water may leak through your mask; apply Vaseline to your upper lip to help form a seal that will keep the water out.)

2. To test the fit of a full-foot fin, lean forward while standing up. The back of your foot should not slip out.

3. A wet suit isn't necessary in Hawaii's warm waters and will only inhibit your ability to dive underwater.

4. Apply waterproof sunblock to your face, ears, neck, arms, back, and legs.

5. Defog your mask properly to avoid condensation (De-Fog, which is sold as a liquid spray or drops, works best, but saliva will suffice in a pinch). Thoroughly rinse your mask with water immediately after using it; never let it dry out with saltwater on it.

6. Put your fins on just before you enter the water (otherwise they may sink, and you'll never find them), leaning on your buddy for support.

7. Enter the water walking backwards, with your mask on and the snorkel in your mouth, keeping a constant eye on the waves. When you're chest-deep into the water, turn and face the waves and start kicking.

8. Do not use your arms to swim. It's best to keep them at your sides and let your legs and fins do the work.

9. Avoid looking straight down or your snorkel will fill with water; instead, look slightly ahead. If water enters your snorkel, don't panic. Just tilt

your head back and blow out the water. If you're caught without any breath, lift your head above water, remove the snorkel from your mouth, and drain it.

10. Don't touch the marine life unless you're absolutely sure it's safe, and stay off the coral. Coral is a fragile, living animal that can die easily from careless human contact. Furthermore, coral may look soft, but it isn't. Not only can it easily scrape off your skin, it can also cause a nasty infection, so make sure each scrape is scrubbed and rinsed thoroughly with fresh water.

11. Periodically check the shoreline to confirm that you're not on your way to Tahiti. Currents can be very deceiving.

12. If you're nervous, bring along a boogie-board to hold on to. Holding hands with your partner is also calming.

13. Toting a small plastic fish chart (available at most snorkel shops) is a great way to identify the various species.

14. If you feel adventurous and want to swim underwater, remember to pinch your nose and blow into it *gently* whenever you feel even the slightest pressure in your ears. It is very easy to blow a hole in your eardrum by failing to do this.

15. To exit the water, walk out backwards (so you're always facing the waves).

16. Clean and rinse all of the rental equipment in fresh water before returning it.

16 National Tropical Botanical Garden The garden has survived hurricanes, storms, and floods in the past, and **Hurricane Iniki** will prove no exception, though repairs are expected to last through 1993. The 186-acre botanical jewel protects and propagates plants that otherwise might become extinct, adding some 1,000 plants to its inventory each year. In a tradition established by the early Polynesians, who carried plants to the islands in their canoes, modern botanists and serious gardeners have brought cuttings from throughout the tropical regions of the world to Hawaii, where they've flourished and multiplied. Since the world's large tropical research gardens in the old Dutch and English colonies had begun to deteriorate, this tradition became of significant importance to the field of tropical botany.

In 1964, when Congress chartered what was then the **Pacific Tropical Botanical Garden** in Hawaii, no one was more supportive than **Robert Allerton,** the son of a pioneer Chicago cattleman. By 1938, he and his adopted son, **John Gregg Allerton,** had transformed a hundred-acre estate (formerly a vacation domicile of **Queen Emma,** wife of **Kamehameha IV**) in Lawai-Kai, Kauai, into a garden showplace. With the help of hired gardeners, Allerton and his son spent 20 years clearing jungle growth to create sweeping gardens around reflecting pools, fountains, and statues. Kauai's *kamaaina* (old-timers) gave them cuttings and seeds, and the Allertons scoured the islands of the South Pacific for varieties never before seen on Kauai. With substantial funding from the late Robert Allerton, the Pacific Tropical Botanical Garden opened next door to his estate in 1971. And when John Gregg Allerton passed away, he left the beachside estate to the botanical garden. Today visitors are able to tour the garden and Allerton estate, guided by the volunteers of **Na Lima Kokua** (Helping Hands). If you can bear riding in the back of a slightly warm van with eight or nine other people, you will learn a great deal about the plant life of the tropics. ♦ Admission. Call well in advance for reservations (sometimes six months is required). Tours daily 9AM, 1PM. Write to: Box 340, Lawai, Kauai, Hawaii 96765. From Hwy 50 take the turnoff to Lawai Valley. 332.7361

Restaurants/Clubs: Red   Hotels: Blue
Shops/ 🌿 Outdoors: Green   **Sights/Culture:** Black

17 Mustard's Last Stand ★★$ If you're anywhere near the area, stop at this red-and-yellow kiosk for hot dogs, hamburgers, sausage, and fish-and-chips. Surfboard seating, daily specials, and friendly service win over the adults, but the real crowd-pleaser is the playground and mini-miniature golf park behind the stand, where you can let the kids go wild for a while. ♦ Hwy 50 and Koloa Rd, Lawai. 332.7245

18 Brick Oven Pizza ★$$ It's the best-known name in pizza on the island and one of the few places to eat on the way to Waimea Canyon. Selections include pineapple and vegetarian pizza on whole-wheat dough (made fresh daily). Sandwiches, salads, and to-go orders available. ♦ Off Hwy 50, Kalaheo. 332.8561

19 Lappert's Aloha Ice Cream The hula pie ice cream—a concoction of coffee and fudge with a hint of coconut and macadamia—is one of the irresistible flavors created by ice-cream wizard **Walter Lappert,** who came to Kauai to retire in 1981 and instead found himself churning out batches of this creamy dessert. Soon the hobby snowballed into a 13,000-gallon-a-month business. His sweet success is spreading to local merchants as well, who supply him with crates of papayas, guavas, coconuts, pineapples, and mangoes, and about 8,000 pounds of macadamia nuts a month, not to mention the pure cane sugar, which he whips into more than 70 flavors of ice cream. You can buy Lappert's from this small white factory and shop, as well as throughout the islands. ♦ 1-3555 Hwy 50, just past Hanapepe. 335.6121

19 Green Garden Restaurant ★★$$ **Sue Hamabata** and her daughter **Gwen** continue the family tradition that started in 1948 by serving abundant amounts of delicious Asian, American, and Hawaiian food in the greenery-filled dining room that was once the family's home. Draped in her signature cascade of Niihau shell leis, Sue greets guests, helps with the serving, and offers advice on meals tailored to your taste and budget. Start with a fresh *lilikoi* (passion fruit) daiquiri and don't dare leave without finishing a piece of the famous lilikoi chiffon pie. ♦ Hana Rd, off Hwy 50, Hanapepe. 335.5422

20 Salt Pond Beach Park Named for the nearby ancient ponds where the Hawaiians harvested salt from drying beds, the beach is unmistakably bruised by Iniki but otherwise intact. Every year the **Hui Hana Paakai O Hanapepe** (The Hanapepe Association to Work with Salt) lets ocean water dry in the ponds, collecting the prized salt crystals for use at home or for gifts. Sometimes referred to as "Hanapepe salt," it has a reddish tint and is coveted by Hawaiians, who consider the colored salt the best for healing and seasoning. However, because of state health regulations, it can't be sold commercially.

There's also good swimming, fishing, and shelling at this beach. Picnic and public facilities.·♦ From Hwy 50 take Lele Rd, west of Hanapepe

21 Russian Fort (Fort Elizabeth) In 1817, a German doctor named **George Anton Scheffer** arrived in Kauai on business as an agent of Russia but immediately got other ideas. Convincing Kauai's **King Kaumualii** that Russia could bring the other islands under its subjugation, a Russian-style fort named after the Czar's daughter was built in the shape of a star on the banks of the Waimea River, and the Russian flag flew over it. However, **Czar Nicholas** didn't share Scheffer's enthusiasm (he preferred to concentrate on conquering Alaska), and the ambitious Russian doctor eventually left. Remnants of the lava stone fort remain buried in the brush. ♦ Trail to the fort on the beachside of Hwy 50, west of Waimea

22 Menehune Ditch Kauai schoolchildren learn shortly after they can talk that if they don't want to be held responsible for something that goes wrong, they can always blame it on the Menehune. Some say the Menehune were a pygmy-size class of Polynesian laborers brought to Kauai by the old Hawaiians. True romantics credit the mysterious, mischievous people with magical powers and maintain that the ones who left Kauai did so on a floating island. The Menehune Ditch is a prodigious work, probably their most famous. What's left of the interlocking stones, a unique form of fitted stonework not found anywhere else in Hawaii, was at one time an aqueduct built by the Menehune at the request of a Kauai king who wanted to irrigate nearby taro patches. Legend holds that the king was so pleased with their work he rewarded them with a feast of shrimp, along with their favorite foods: sweet potatoes and *haupia* (coconut pudding). ♦ From Hwy 50 in Waimea, follow Menehune Rd 1.5 miles to what used to be a swinging footbridge (another victim of Iniki) and look for a plaque to your left

23 Waimea Canyon Plummeting 3,657 feet at its deepest point, 10-mile Waimea Canyon is a rough, inhospitable cut—only goats and birds can withstand the jagged terrain. For lack of a better comparison, it is called the "Grand Canyon of the Pacific"—a worn-out exaggeration. That Waimea is no match for the Grand Canyon, however, does not lessen its importance as one of Hawaii's most photographed attractions. The main overlook offers a sprawling landscape, where white-tailed tropic birds soar overhead and the echoes of bleating feral goats can often be heard. Colors range from gold to purple, red, and green, and when the canyon depths are clouded by mist, the effect is even more dramatic.

Hardy hikers may want to tackle the trails that zigzag down the canyon's wall, and the **Iliau Nature Loop** north of the lookout is a nice path for casual strollers. Treat Waimea as an all-day excursion because interesting towns invite exploring along the way and slow-moving traffic occasionally causes delays. Once there, you'll want to continue on to **Kokee State Park** for a peek into the verdant and mysterious Kalalau Valley. Check your gas gauge before heading up to the canyon, and bring a sweater for the higher elevation. ♦ From Hwy 50, take Waimea Canyon Dr. From Kekaha, take Kokee Rd (Hwy 550) up to the canyon lookout, which is marked by a Hawaii Visitors Bureau sign. From Lihue, it's about a 35-mile trip.

Hawaii's Helicopters: A Hovering Controversy

Nothing ruins a peaceful, serene nature hike like a Bell Jet Ranger helicopter flying a few hundred feet over your head. Unless you're an aviation enthusiast, such encounters will give you a newfound appreciation for the controversy surrounding chopper tours. Proponents rightly argue that helicopters give tourists an opportunity to see breathtaking topography that would undoubtedly be missed by car, boat, bus, or even on foot, and that, aside from the noise pollution, choppers have less impact on the environment than hikers. Fed-up locals, however, claim the noise is getting out of hand and that the helicopter-touring industry is saturated and unsafe (particularly near Kilauea on the Big Island, where one company keeps slamming its helicopters into the mountainside). For sleepy Hawaii, chopper crashes make the front-page news almost routinely these days (everywhere but in the tourist publications, that is).

As the debate rages on, the helicopter-tour industry continues to soar. After all, it's a multimillion-dollar business, charging up to $300 a person for a single flight in a million-dollar craft. Whether this is a fair price for the controversial airborne adventure is open to interpretation; however, very few people return from the experience with any complaints. For more information about helicopter tours, visit any of the hundreds of information booths scattered throughout the islands.

23 Kokee State Park and Kokee Lodge

Situated eight miles from the canyon lookout in the northern reaches of Waimea, the park's cool temperatures attract islanders who tire of the same perfect weather day in and day out. At a 4,000-foot elevation, the 4,345-acre park is a cool, crisp nature-lover's bonanza, with rare honeycreepers, native flora, streams, and trails aplenty. Twelve rental cabins, completely furnished, must be booked well in advance. The hiking trails (45 miles worth) are abundant, with one for just about every level of expertise. From the end of June through August, the park's island-famous plums are free for the picking, and anglers will be delighted to know that (with a license) they can fish for rainbow trout in Kokee's cool streams from August through September. The fish eggs were flown in from the mainland, hatched on Oahu, and released for sportfishing at Kokee. You'll also find a lodge, gift shop, bar, restaurant, and information center in this idyllic forest setting. ♦ End of Hwy 550. Write to: Kokee Lodge, Box 819, Waimea, Kauai, Hawaii 96796. 335.6061

23 Kokee Natural History Museum

Informative and well-managed, the Kokee museum is open year-round with displays, videos, and photographs about Waimea Canyon and Kokee State Park. Trail information also is available. ♦ Free. Daily 10AM-4PM. End of Hwy 550. 335.9975

23 Kalalau Valley Lookout

Timing is everything at this 4,000-foot-high lookout, where the vista is usually clear in the early morning but obscured by mist and clouds by afternoon. Sightseers often make the long ascent to Kalalau only to find the fabled view hidden by the clouds. But when the clouds part, even if just for a moment, the effect is startling. Honeycreepers feed on lehua blossoms; waterfalls and fluted cliffs stand before you. Until early this century, the valley—the largest on the **Na Pali Coast**—was occupied by hundreds of Hawaiians who lived on the abundant fruits and vegetables grown here (no one lives here now). Experienced hikers can reach Kalalau from Haena on the north shore, but there is no trail from the lookout because of the dangerous terrain. ♦ End of Hwy 550

Restaurants/Clubs: Red   **Hotels:** Blue
Shops/ ♣ Outdoors: Green   **Sights/Culture:** Black

24 Polihale State Park

This is the most remote beach on Kauai that can be reached by car. Take the road just beyond the turnoff to Waimea Canyon that winds through the cane field. There's good summer swimming, but it's rough the rest of the year. Restrooms, showers, and barbecue grills. ♦ End of Kaumualii Hwy (Hwy 50)

25 Wailua Falls

If there's been substantial rain, you'll see two exquisite falls (Wailua means "twin waters") tumbling over the 80-foot cliff that Hawaiian chiefs used to dive from to prove their courage. Pass on the lookout for the falls, which is four miles west of Kapaa, unless you don't mind the monotonous ride to get there. ♦ From Hwy 56 north of Lihue, take Hwy 583 (Maalo Rd) near Kapaa to the end of the road

26 Hanamaulu Cafe & Tea House ★★$$

Kick the Kauai salad-bar habit and spend a unique island evening in one of the garden rooms (by reservation only) at this Japanese/Chinese restaurant, a local favorite for more than 60 years. The nine-course dinners (including snow crab claws, spare ribs, and ginger-seasoned fried chicken) are memorable, and Hanamaulu adds special flavor to lobster, baking it in a rich butter sauce with bread crumbs. ♦ Hwy 56, old Hanamaulu Town. 245.2511

27 Outrigger Kauai Beach Hotel $$$

Blessed in that it rode out **Hurricane Iniki** relatively unscathed, and cursed in that it rests on a Hawaiian burial sight, the Outrigger suffers from bad vibrations (no joke, folks, this place will give you the willies). Rife with controversy since the day it opened (supposedly, a few political kickbacks were involved), the hotel has a long history of mediocre success. The series of four-story buildings are oriented toward a long strip of the ocean and the sandy beach (which is only suitable for sunning because of the undertow). Three swimming pools more than compensate, though, with caves, trickling waterfalls, fountains, and lots of greenery around the main pool. The main hotel has 350 guest rooms with lanais, as well as 150 older one- and two-bedroom villas with kitchens and laundry facilities (a terrific bargain, especially for families). The **Wailua Golf Course** is a short, free shuttle ride away. ♦ 4331 Kauai Beach Dr, Kapaa. 245.1955, 800/733.7777; fax 246.9085

28 Wailua Golf Course

Rated one of the top 10 public courses in America by *Golf Digest,* Wailua's inexpensive green fees make it the best golf bargain in Hawaii. Extending more than a mile along Wailua Beach, the course was built in 1920 among sand dunes and

ironwood trees. The ocean comes into play on three holes, and the demanding back nine is highlighted by the famous **Sea Beach Hole** at the par-three 17th, where too much club will guarantee a Pacific-bound ball. Par 72, 6,665 yards, 71.9 rating. ♦ Off Hwy 56, Wailua. 245.2163

29 Kaha Lani Condominiums $$$ Closed for repairs until the summer of 1993, the Kaha Lani is secluded on the beach at Wailua. The 74 units have ocean-view lanais and are managed by the always-reliable **Aston Resorts**. Pool, tennis, and a nearby golf course. ♦ Off Hwy 56, Wailua. 822.9331, 800/922.7866; fax 922.8785

30 Lydgate State Park What's left of Lydgate Park is a favorite among local families and others who enjoy the pleasant combination of beach, protected pools, picnic pavilions, and a tree-shaded park beside the Wailua River. Public facilities. ♦ Off Hwy 56, Wailua

31 Fern Grotto The **Wailua River,** the best-known river in Hawaii, leads to Fern Grotto, a visitor attraction that has achieved the supreme status of being a must-do (a must-not-do if you don't like crowds or a circuslike atmosphere). Boxy cruise boats glide upriver as entertainers do the hula and perform standard Hawaiian tunes to ukulele accompaniments.

After the boats land, you'll walk through jungle to a cool cave filled with giant cascading ferns. Inside, the hired help recount legends with more island background music. The return trip is highlighted by a Hawaiian sing-along. The grotto is a popular site for weddings, replete with the traditional "Hawaiian Wedding Song," a guaranteed tear-jerker. Owing to **Hurricane Iniki,** the operation is only running limited service. Call ahead. ♦ Cruise fee. Boats leave from Wailua Marina off Hwy 56, Wailua. Smith's Motor Boat Service 822.4111; Waialeale Boat Tours 822.4908

31 Wailua Marina Restaurant $$ Crowded with Fern Grotto tourists during the day, this huge, very touristy restaurant has a little more breathing room during dinner hours. Fish, steak, chicken, and pork dishes carry reasonable price tags, and there's pickup for dinner guests staying at Wailua area hotels. ♦ Wailua Marina, off Hwy 56. 822.4311

32 Coco Palms Resort Hotel $$$ The long, 390-room structure (closed until early 1994 owing to hurricane damage) blends into the carefully preserved grove of 200-year-old coconut trees. Room decor carries out the Polynesian theme with

huge clamshell wash basins in the **Sea S[...] Rooms** and wrought iron and rattan in the [...] Kai wing. The schmaltzy evening show at th[...] Coco Palms is legendary. Every night, a hus[...] settles over the lily-dotted lagoon (which is surrounded by thatched-roof honeymoon cottages) as the history of the torchlighting ceremony is recited. During the dramatic narration, conch shells sound, drums beat, and barefoot youths run along the banks of the lagoon leaving a trail of lighted torches. A big disappointment is that **Grace Guslander,** the general manager since 1953 and acknowledged founder of the torchlighting ceremony in Hawaii, has retired, leaving a certain spirit and excitement at the gate. Her vision of what a resort hotel in Hawaii should be like helped make the Coco Palms Kauai's most successful hotel for many years. A sandy beach is located across the road (watch out for speeding traffic), but it's often windswept and not very suitable for swimming. A mile-long jogging path runs through the coconut grove, and clay tennis courts (the first on the island) invite recreation. ♦ 4-241 Hwy 56, Wailua. 822.4921, 800/338.1338; fax 822.7189

33 Kintaro ★★$$$ Sleek, elegant, and authentically decorated with kimonos and Japanese screens, Kintaro offers an impressive selection of sashimi, sushi, *zaru soba* (buckwheat noodles), *nabemono* (seafood soup), teppanyaki, and other exquisite delicacies. Be adventurous and try freshwater eel grilled with sweet sauce over rice. ♦ Hwy 56, near Wailua. 822.3341

34 Colony's Kauai Beachboy Hotel $$ Built within the Coconut Plantation development, this 243-room hotel occupies a mile-long stretch of **Waipouli Beach,** which is better suited for wading and beachcombing than for swimming. The hotel closed when Iniki hit the beach, though the game plan is to reopen in the summer of 1993. The lackluster, no-nonsense rooms have refrigerators and lanais with ocean or mountain views. Serious shoppers are well located here, within walking distance of the **Coconut Plantation Marketplace,** a complex with some 70 shops, restaurants, and movie theaters, most of them touristy. Pool, tennis. ♦ 484 Hwy 56, Kapaa. 822.3441, 800/922.7866; fax 822.0843

34 Kauai Coconut Beach Resort $$ Set amidst nearly 11 acres of coconut trees along Waipouli Beach, all 309 rooms in this resort have lanais, most with ocean views. Stained-glass windows and tapestries in the public areas are highlighted by a 40-foot waterfall cascading into a reflecting pool. The beach is scenic but often windy, and swimming isn't recommended because of the rocky conditions. ♦ Coconut Plantation Marketplace, Kuhio Hwy, near Kapaa. 822.3455, 800/222.5642; fax 822.1830

ne Daily Grinds

...waii has never been hailed as one of the country's premier culinary destinations, yet thanks to the influence of Asiatic and Polynesian cultures, Hawaiian cuisine is a virtual smorgasbord of unique foods—some you'll never want to sample more than once, and some you'll remember favorably long after you've returned to the mainland. Unfortunately, what the locals eat and what's on a restaurant's menu are often two different things; most restaurants cater to Western tastes, despite their exaggerated claims of serving "island specialties." The best way to experience authentic local dishes is to get an invitation to a private luau, party, or picnic (a rare treat for tourists) or to visit a county fair or an "authentic" public luau (where you'll find a smattering of local dishes among the platters of barbecued chicken and ribs). Whichever way you sample the cuisine, prepare yourself for some surprises, whether you indulge in such favorites as grilled parrot fish (which tastes amazingly similar to lobster) or *poi* (a Hawaiian staple with a consistency and flavor akin to wallpaper paste). Here's a guide to the more popular local dishes:

Adobo (ah-DOUGH-bo) A generic Filipino term for anything (usually pork or chicken) stewed in vinegar and garlic.

Beef Tomato Chunks of beef, onions, tomatoes, and peppers simmered quickly and served with rice.

Char Siu (char-SOO) Chinese sweet roast pork.

Chicken Long Rice Long, transparent noodles boiled with shredded chicken.

Crackseed Preserved and sweetened fruit and seeds, including papaya, watermelon, mango, and coconut. An acquired taste, crackseed makes for great road munchies. Sold at most stores.

Haupia (how-PIE) Custard made from fresh coconut milk and cornstarch.

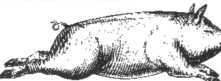

Kalua Pork (kah-LOO-ah) The centerpiece of any luau, the meat from an entire pig wrapped in ti and banana leaves and baked in a pit (*kalua* refers to any dish baked underground). The cooked meat is so tender it can be cut with a plastic fork.

Kimchi (kim-CHEE) A Korean creation of fermented cabbage and tangy spices chopped up into a slaw.

Kona Coffee Gourmet coffee from hand-picked beans grown on the Kona coast of the Big Island. It's the only coffee grown in the United States.

Laulau (LAU-lau) Butterfish, pork, taro leaves, and sometimes sweet potato, all mixed and steamed in a bag of ti leaves.

Lilikoi (LEE-lee-koy) Passion fruit, usually made into juice, pies, or sherbert.

Limu (LEE-moo) Seaweed mixed with ground kukui nuts, salt, and sliced octopus or fish for a seafood salad called *poki* (PO-kee).

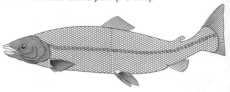

Lomilomi Salmon (LOW-mee-LOW-mee) Salted salmon that's been shredded and kneaded with tomatoes and green onions. Served chilled.

Malasadas (mah-lah-SAH-das) Portuguese doughnut holes, served hot and covered with sugar. Sold at most bakeries.

Manapua (mah-nah-POO-ah) The Hawaiian version of the Chinese *bao* (BOW), a steamed dough bun filled with pork, bean paste, and other stuffings. Sold at roadside stands all over the islands.

Maui Onions Large, mild, sweet onions grown on Maui, considered by teary-eyed onion enthusiasts to be the *no ka oi* (best) of all onions.

Opihi (oh-PEE-hee) Limpets (which cling like barnacles to rocks in the surf zone) that are picked, shelled, and immediately eaten (they sell for about $150 a gallon).

Poa Dolce (pawn-DEUCE) A Portuguese sweet dough loaf. Great for French toast.

Poi (POY) Taro root that's been cooked and pounded into a purple paste. Water is then added, the amount depending on how pasty or watery you want it, and the poi is traditionally eaten using one's fingers. The taste ranges from wallpaper paste to cardboard, but finger-licking locals swear by it, claiming it gives the "fo' real" carbo-buzz.

Portuguese Bean Soup Rich soup made of various beans, vegetables, and Portuguese sausage.

Saimin (sigh-MIN) Noodle soup, usually served with barbecued skewers of chicken or beef in little cafes.

Shave Ice A Hawaiian-style snow cone, with dozens of syrup flavors to choose from. Try the triple flavor combo with sweetened black azuki beans and a tiny scoop of ice cream at the bottom of the cone.

Tako (TAH-koh) Octopus.

Taro Chips (TAR-oh) Sliced and deep-fried taro root; sold at most stores.

35 The Bull Shed ★$$$
Many swear by it and others swear at it, but there's no argument over The Bull Shed's choice location on the windy eastern shore, with the surf marching toward the windows. A heroic cut of prime rib stands out on the short menu of beef, lamb, chicken, fish, and a salad bar. A local favorite since 1973, The Bull Shed is usually crowded and service can be haphazard. ♦ 796 Kuhio Hwy (across from McDonald's), Kapaa. 822.3791

36 Aloha Diner ★$ Strictly local-style, this small diner serves the best saimin and Hawaiian food on the island. The small family operation is an institution, where folks line up for fried *akule* (scad), *lomilomi* salmon, *lau lau* (pork in taro and ti leaves), and poi. Don't get your hopes up if you're a *malihini* (newcomer), as Hawaiian food is usually an acquired taste. ♦ 971-F Hwy 56 (in the Waipouli Complex), Kapaa. 822.3851

36 Zippy's $ A fast-food chain founded on Oahu, Zippy's fortifies islanders with chili, saimin (noodles in broth), and the usual burgers, fries, and shakes. ♦ 4-919 Hwy 56, Kapaa. 822.9866

36 Kauai Village The Village houses a sorely needed **Safeway**, plus a **Waldenbooks, Pay-n-Save, Wyland Galleries,** and a host of restaurants including **Ginger's Grill** (★$$) and **Panda Garden Chinese Restaurant** (★$$). ♦ Off Hwy 56, Kapaa

Within Kauai Village:

A Pacific Cafe ★★★$$$ Owner/chef **Jean-Marie Josselin,** formerly of the Hotel Hana-Maui and the Coco Palms Resort, opened this stylish restaurant in 1990 and lost no time adding to his already considerable reputation. Pacific Rim cuisine takes on new life in his able hands; try the grilled Hawaiian *aku* (tuna) with papaya-black bean relish, deep-fried sashimi with *wana* (sea urchin) sauce, sautéed crab cakes with mango-ginger sauce, or Kauai-grown clams in coconut milk and red curry. Local farmers truck in the fresh produce daily—more than 90 percent of the vegetables he serves are grown on the island.

The Chinese peas in black-bean sauce are a must, and vegetarians will love the potato-tofu lasagna. The decor is tropical, with ceramic plates made by Josselin's wife, **Sophaonia.** ♦ 822.0013

37 Ono Family Restaurant $$ Famous first for their charburgers, Ono has expanded into a fancy three-meals-a-day restaurant, which often has a line to get in for dinner. The prices are low (compared to in the resort areas) and the food is solid American—from fresh snapper to pork chops with mushroom gravy. Or you can choose from the one-of-a-kind buffalo burgers and buffalo steaks, made from bison raised in Hanalei on the north shore. There's a take-out window, too. ♦ 4-1292 Hwy 56, Kapaa. 822.1710

38 Kountry Kitchen ★$$ From the Polynesian omelet with Portuguese sausage and kimchi (spicy, pickled cabbage) to the quarter-pound burgers on sesame-seed buns and the complete steak, chicken, and fish dinners, this dependable little diner keeps big eaters happy without devouring the wallet. ♦ 1485 Kuhio Hwy, Kapaa. 822.3511

39 Anahola Beach Park Because of Anahola's shallow waters, the swimming is excellent here. It's a popular spot for families and fishers, and the northern end is part of the **Hawaiian Homestead** (land set aside for people who are 50 percent Hawaiian). Picnic facilities. ♦ Take Aliomanu Rd from Hwy 56 near Anahola and turn left on any of the dirt roads, all of which lead to the beach

40 Kilauea Point National Wildlife Refuge Lighthouses are usually found in rugged, unspoiled areas, and this windswept corner of the island is no exception. When the **Kilauea Lighthouse,** which is on the **National Register of Historic Places,** was built in 1913, it could be seen 20 miles from shore. The U.S. Coast Guard stopped operating it when an automated light was installed in 1967, and now the **U.S. Fish and Wildlife Service** runs the 169-acre preserve.

Look for red-footed boobies and wedge-tailed shearwaters soaring above; and from the lookout point, try to spot sea turtles and porpoises. From December through April, this nature-lover's refuge is a wonderful vantage point for humpback-whale watching. Although the visitor's center is closed for repairs, the lookout is still open and worth checking out. ♦ Take the Kolo Rd turnoff on Hwy 56 in Kilauea, then left on Kilauea Rd. 828.1413

Metal was such a novelty to stone-age Hawaiians that when Captain Cook first landed on Kauai he was able to swap a single nail for enough fresh pork, potatoes, and taro to feed his ship's entire crew for a day.

41 Chuck's Steak House ★$$$ This Chuck's is a few notches above the Surfer Joe ambience of the chain's earlier restaurants, with a smart design and a more interesting menu. Ask for a table out on the lanai and settle down for a fish sandwich or a hot entrée at lunch; seafood, steak, ribs, and salad are served at night. ◆ Princeville Shopping Center, Princeville Resort. 826.6211

41 Princeville Condominiums $$$ The **Princeville Hotel,** a newcomer within the 2,000-acre **Princeville Resort,** garners more attention, but some of the condominiums on the bluffs above Hanalei Bay are exceptionally roomy. The main attractions are the **Makai** and the **Prince golf courses,** as well as the gorgeous beaches and mountains of the Hanalei area. The **Prince Golf and Country Club,** which serves the Prince Course, has its own restaurant and lounge.

All of the condominiums have pools, plus there are tennis courts, horseback riding, and good beaches nearby (though access is somewhat difficult). Many real-estate companies handle vacation rentals of condos and homes in the Princeville area; a good one to call for information is **Princeville Travel Services. Hawaiian Islands Resorts** manages rentals for Pali Ke Kua (one of the finest projects in Princeville) and Puu Poa. ◆ Off Hwy 56, east of Hanalei Bay. Princeville Travel Services 826.9661, 800/445.6253; Hawaiian Islands Resorts 531.7595, 800/367.7042

41 Princeville Hotel $$$$ In 1985 **Sheraton** decided to venture where no major hotel had dared to go before: to the extraordinary setting and sometimes unreliable climate of Kauai's north shore. Situated on the Hanalei Bay lookout point, the hotel holds the plum location in the Princeville development. After damage from **Hurricane Iniki,** the hotel plans to be in full operation by the spring of 1994.

The architects originally designed a simple hotel, which descended the face of **Puu Poa Point** in a series of three terraces. But the Sheraton corporation wanted more upscale accommodations and more ocean views, so the architects went back to the drawing board for a $100 million renovation, which was completed in 1991.

All of the public areas, including the lobby, lounge, and restaurants, now offer a clear view of the 23-acre site. The **Prince Suites,** about one-and-a-half times larger than the

king and double rooms, accommodate a formal entry hall, an oversize bathroom with a spa tub, 18th-century Italian-style furniture, floor-to-ceiling bronze mirrors in the bedroom, and an additional living room. Special services and amenities include butler and valet service, 24-hour room service, and complimentary transportation to the golf course and tennis courts. Facilities include a luxurious pool, exercise room, beauty salon, and beach kiosks for snorkeling and windsurfing. Guests also have preferred starting times and charge privileges at the adjacent Princeville Resort facilities, including the **Makai Golf Course** and tennis courts. ◆ 5520 Kahaku Rd (within the Princeville Resort), Hanalei. 826.9644, 800/826.4400; fax 826.1166

41 Hanalei Bay Resort Condominiums $$$ Originally built as an exclusive condominium project, the 200 units were converted into a hotel-style operation complete with a full-service restaurant, eight tennis courts, and an on-site tennis pro. Two- and three-story buildings with one- to three-bedroom suites overlook Hanalei Bay, with stunning landscaping and all the romance of Bali Hai. With the Princeville courses nearby, this is an attractive choice for golf and tennis buffs. Spacious units offer quality accommodations, including kitchens. There's a pool, but access to the beach is difficult. ◆ 5380 Honoiki Rd (within the Princeville Resort), Hanalei. 826.6522, 800/827.4427; fax 826.6680

Within the Hanalei Bay Resort Condominiums:

Bali Hai ★★$$$ The light and airy dining room, beautifully embellished with batik banners, overlooks Hanalei Bay Resort's tennis courts, with the Pacific Ocean in the distance. Poached salmon, rack of lamb, scampi, ginger chicken, and cannelloni are among the selections on the extensive menu. Entertainment nightly. ◆ 826.6522

 Princeville Golf Courses Scheduled to reopen in August 1993, these sensationally scenic 45 holes of golf (27 holes at the **Makai Course;** 18 holes at the **Prince Course**) were designed by **Robert Trent Jones, Jr.** (who owns a home in nearby Hanalei). The courses are spread out on a lush plateau high above Hanalei Bay with a view of Mount Waialeale, plunging waterfalls, and the ocean. The ocean holes are the most spectacular, but the lake and woods holes offer superb blends of golf and scenery. Princeville's only drawback is the threat of rain, especially during winter and spring months. Makai Course: par 72, 6,600 yards. Prince Course: par 73, 7,000 yards. ◆ Expensive green fees; preferred starting times and rates for Princeville Resort guests. Pro shop 826.3580

Waioli Mission House Museum Closed until further notice thanks to **Hurricane Iniki,** this two-story cottage was brought to Hawai in prefabricated sections in 1836 by New England missionaries who didn't want to go native. It's a pleasant sojourn into the past, replete with furniture of that period. There used to be a pole-and-thatch meeting house on this site in the early 1830s, when traditional, prehistoric tools were still made and used in Hanalei. The church's present frame, built in 1841, represents the first time plaster, nails, and Western frame construction were used in Hawaii. Lovely gardens flourish in the back. ◆ Donations welcome. Call for hours. Hanalei. 245.3202

42 Hanalei to Haena Drive The drive begins when you cross the Hanalei River on the **Hanalei Bridge** (built in 1912) and dead-ends nine miles later at **Haena Beach Park** (also called **Kee Beach**). Along the way you'll rumble across the 10 little bridges of **Hanalei Valley**, some of them wooden and most only one lane wide. Taro fields fan out across the valley, then the road swings closer to the steep cliffs, which are attempting to regain their tropical foliage after **Hurricane Iniki** stripped them clean. The **Na Pali Coast** is rich with eucalyptus, paperbark, giant tree ferns, and banana and coconut trees.

You'll also see a succession of sandy beaches nuzzled by foamy waves, and waterfalls plunging hundreds of feet down the mountain slopes. Cattle graze in green valleys that extend from the base of the mountains, and side roads dart off through tunnels of trees leading to silent beaches. There are wet caves and dry caves, green clapboard tumbledown houses with saddles straddled across porch rails, and chalet-style vacation homes trying to hide in the thickly wooded areas that guard the long, empty beaches. The only consolation in reaching the end of the road is that you'll get to turn around and drive the same beautiful route all over again.

43 Captain Zodiac Raft Expeditions A Zodiac raft ride is a unique and thrilling experience that offers a spectacular view of the soaring **Na Pali Coast** cliffs. You'll also weave in and out of sea caves and ride around (and sometimes through) waterfalls that spill into the ocean. **Captain Zodiac** (a.k.a. **Clancy Greff**) and his band of enthusiastic guides know every inch of the coast and narrate the expedition with Hawaiian history, legends, and even gossip about the local celebrities. Dolphins or sea turtles might swim alongside the raft, or you can get even closer to the marine life on one of their snorkel-and-raft

trips. Be forewarned that the front hits all the bumps, so sit at the rear want a smoother ride. Zodiac also off. drop-off and pickup raft service to backpackers from May through Septen. for the beautiful 11-mile hike through the **Pali Coast State Park** from Haena to Kala. Valley. Raft trips are sometimes canceled when the weather's rough, particularly durir the winter months. ◆ Fee. Excursions leave from Bali Hai Beach (also called Tunnels Beach), Haena. Reservations required. 826.9371, 800/422.7824

43 Hanalei Bay A stunning, picture-perfect arc of sand cradled by the sharp flanks of Waialeale, Hanalei Bay is popular for picnics, sunbathing, and local beach gatherings, and sought after by Hollywood, which caught it in all its splendor in the movie *South Pacific*. Swimming is dangerous here during the winter. Public facilities. ◆ Weke Rd (off Hwy 56), Hanalei

44 Lumahai Beach Stop and take your own snapshot of the beach that starred in the movie *South Pacific*. It's one of the most photographed beaches in Hawaii. There are two beaches, the farther one more dangerous, especially if the surf is up. ◆ To get to the first swimming area, turn after Hanalei Bay, then follow the trail; the second spot is down the road by the river. Hwy 56, near Hanalei

45 Wainiha General Store "The Last Store on the North Shore" is alive and well and still selling snacks and sodas at "last store" prices. Check out the T-shirts. ◆ Daily 9AM-7PM. 5-6607 Hwy 56. 826.6251

46 Charo's ★$$ The effervescent entertainer of "cuchi cuchi" and **Xavier Cugat** fame bought a house on the north shore and liked it so much that she set up her own restaurant here, a lovely little place on the beach at Haena with a view of the surf. Although it's closed for repairs thanks to **Hurricane Iniki, Charo** plans to reopen her restaurant, although no specific date is set. Drop in for a fresh-fish burger, *pupus,* and *chi chi,* or paella (her secret blend of seafood, chicken, and aromatic Spanish saffron). ◆ Next to the Hanalei Colony Resort, near Haena. 826.6422

Kauai was the first Hawaiian Island discovered by Captain James Cook, who anchored there in 1778.

Restaurants/Clubs: Red   Hotels: Blue
Shops/ 🌳 Outdoors: Green   **Sights/Culture:** Black

...alei Colony Resort Condominiums
. The Colony Resort plans to be back in
...siness by the end of 1993. It's the only
...esort in the majestic Hanalei Valley, which is
spread along the coastline from the town of
Hanalei to Haena. This scenic, isolated
hideaway has 46 two-bedroom
condominiums, a pool, and a beach, but no
TVs, phones, or air-conditioning. Minimum
stay is three days. ◆ Hwy 56, near Haena.
826.6235, 800/628.3004

**47 Waikapalae and Waikanaloa Wet
Caves** According to Hawaiian legend, the
fire goddess **Pele** made a vain attempt to find
a home on the north shore of Kauai, but all
she found were these wet caves. Water was
the last thing she needed, so she packed her
flames and went to Kilauea on the Big Island.
Some people swim in the caves, but it can be
dangerous. It's worth a quick visit to see the
exterior. ◆ Hwy 56, 1 mile west of Haena
State Beach Park

47 Maniniholo Dry Cave The first of a trio of
caves past Haena Beach Park, Maniniholo is
actually a mile-long lava tube running under
a cliff. ◆ Hwy 56, Haena

According to the 1987 state census, the
population of "full-blooded" native Hawaiians
(defined as those with four pure Hawaiian
grandparents) on Kauai is 51.

Because Kauai is the only island without a
carnivorous mongoose population, it's also
the only island "foul with fowl." The ubiquitous
moa, or Hawaiian chicken, is a descendant of
domesticated birds brought to Hawaii by
Polynesian settlers centuries ago. Although
the moa is fair game for anyone's dinner table,
most residents don't care for the taste of it.

47 Haena State Beach Park A set designer
couldn't create a more beautiful beach than
this one, curving sensuously among palm
trees backed by mountains. Haena Beach is a
Kauai legend, used for the Bali Hai setting in
the movie *South Pacific*. Swimming is unsafe
here because of strong currents. Picnic and
camping facilities. ◆ Hwy 56, Haena

48 Haena Point Kauai's famous "end of the
road" also marks the beginning of the hiking
trail into spectacular **Kalalau Valley** and **Kee
Beach,** which is usually a safe place to swim
(but be cautious). During summer months,
when the waters are calm, the snorkeling is
excellent. ◆ End of Hwy 56

49 Hanakapiai Beach Before **Hurricane Iniki**
came to town, the mildly arduous two-mile
hike from **Haena Point** offered spectacular
views at every turn. Pandanus, wild
watercress, guava, fragrant *lauae* ferns,
kukui, and countless other flora were fed by
mountain streams and tiny springs. White-
tailed tropic birds still circle against the cliffs
and porpoises can sometimes be seen when
the trail is close to sea level, but it's going to
be a long while before the area returns to
normal. This trail reveals the marvels of
erosion and the beauty of Na Pali, one of
Hawaii's stellar and unforgettable natural
sights. Be careful of the strong riptides at the
beach; swimming is not recommended here.
◆ Park your car at the end of Hwy 56, and
hike 2 miles from the start of Kalalau Trail

50 Na Pali Coast State Park The history of
the area is as fascinating as the hike to it.
From 1380 until 1919, a small group of
Hawaiians lived in **Nualolo,** a part of the
rugged yet captivatingly beautiful Na Pali
Coast State Park. Remains of their pole-and-
thatch houses and *heiau* (ancient temple) can
be seen along the historic **Kalalau Trail,**

Na Pali Coast

which is open, though a little battered from the hurricane. The former residents worked the agricultural fields of **Nualolo Aina,** then traveled to the reefs by way of a cliff trail to collect fish. Also, **Na Pali Zodiac** (826.6804) offers a hiker's drop-off raft service for an 11-mile hike to Kalalau. Be forewarned, the Kalalau Trail isn't a cakewalk—even the first two miles require a lot of uphill walking.
♦ Trail begins at the end of Hwy 56, and no permit is required to hike the first 2 miles to Hanakapiai Beach. Hiking remaining 9 miles and camping require a permit. For more information about hiking and required camping permits, call the Department of Land and Natural Resources at 241.3444.

Bests

JoAnn A. Yukimura
Mayor, County of Kauai

On Kauai:

A guided hike up **Crater Hill,** which is part of the **Kilauea Point National Wildlife Refuge,** will reveal some of the most spectacular coastline in the world.

Experience the essence of the island by spending a week at the **Mokihana Festival,** which features a statewide hula competition and a remarkable songfest showcasing the best local composers.

A walk through old **Hanapepe Town,** one of the small-town treasures of our west side, filled with the history and spirit of Kauai's people.

The view of **Hanalei Bay** as you descend into the Hanalei Valley. Picnic areas at **Black Pot Park** make this a favorite spot for local family gatherings. The **Hanalei Pier** is a picturesque landmark on the bay.

The **Wailua** area on the east coast of the island is a storehouse of Hawaiian history and culture. Several *heiaus* (ancient temples) are located within the area,

and many legends and events of historical significance are centered here.

If you're interested in Hawaiian history: The **Kauai Museum** is located in Lihue; the **Waioli Mission,** built and furnished by missionaries in 1834, is in Hanalei Valley; and **Grove Farm,** with an operating diesel engine and other plantation artifacts, is in Lihue.

Sheila Donnelly
Public Relations Counselor, Sheila Donnelly & Associates, Honolulu

Mauna Lani Bay Hotel on the Big Island—stay in a bungalow.

Dining at **La Mer** in Honolulu, Oahu, and at **A Pacific Cafe** on Kauai.

Staying at **The Lodge at Koele** on Lanai, and at the **Stouffer Wailea Beach Resort** on Maui.

Author's Bests

Sights:
Hanalei Bay
Kilauea Point National Wildlife Refuge
Na Pali Coast State Park
Waimea Canyon

Restaurants:
Hanamaulu Cafe & Tea House ★★$$
Mustard's Last Stand ★★$
A Pacific Cafe ★★★★$$$

Hotels:
Hanalei Bay Resort Condominiums $$$
Hyatt Regency Kauai $$$$
Poipu Beach Hotel $$

M. BLUM

hau The mysterious island of Niihau (NEE-ee-how), located 17 miles off the leeward coast of Kauai, holds as much intrigue ~~e~~ residents of Hawaii's neighboring islands as it does for tourists, both of ~~m~~ are denied visitation rights. Strict controls on access to this 73-square-~~e~~ island and even on information about Niihau have given rise to its ~~c~~kname, **"The Forbidden Island."**

~~N~~iihau operates by a very simple tenet, established to maintain the island's ~~r~~ole as a haven for indigenous Hawaiians: no one is allowed on the island unless invited, and though residents are free to travel as they please, those who leave the island to marry may never return to live here again.

By modern standards, life on Niihau would best be described as backward, and that's how the residents intend to keep it. The island's 225 inhabitants, most of them pure-blooded Hawaiians, have an abundance of transistor radios and a couple of generators, but few modern appliances and no hotels, telephones, indoor plumbing, or jails. They spend their days fishing, swimming, shelling, and herding cattle or sheep on horseback. A few pickup trucks provide the only modern modes of transportation, and entertainment occasionally includes gathering around a portable television. Most of the residents born and raised on Niihau speak fluent Hawaiian, and the children attend the island's one public school, then move to Kauai for the upper grades. Ironically, despite attempts to keep Niihau an all-native island, few of its students return to live here permanently once they've experienced the modern world.

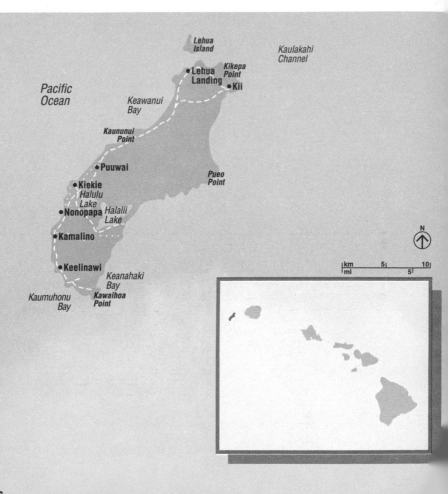

The history of Niihau reads like a James Michener novel. In 1863, Eliz[abeth] Sinclair, the daughter of a wealthy Scottish merchant and widow of a [New] Zealand rancher, loaded her family and all their possessions (including [sheep,] cattle, and prize Arabian horses) aboard a 300-ton bark and set out to fin[d an] island for her clan. After turning down an offer to purchase a swampy are[a] later known as Waikiki, she persuaded **King Kamehameha IV** to sell Niiha[u] to her for $10,000 and proceeded to build a rambling 20-room house, as we[ll] as barns for her animals. Her ranch flourished, and Hawaiian laborers hired from nearby Kauai quickly established a small community. These ranch hands are the ancestors of Niihau's current residents.

Sinclair's descendants, the **Robinson** family (which resides on nearby Kauai but still owns Niihau), has refused all offers by outside agencies, including the state, to sell the island (in the general plebiscite of 1959, Niihau was the only precinct in Hawaii to reject statehood). Aside from a few modest bungalow-type dwellings, the island remains in its natural state, with miles of white sand beaches, mostly arid land, and two large natural lakes. The people of Niihau are employed by the Robinsons to work on the ranch lands. In return, there is no rent to pay, no grocery shopping to do (food and other supplies are brought to the island regularly by boat), and little to worry about. A traditional pastime among the women is the gathering of tiny, rare shells that wash up only on Niihau's windward beaches and are fashioned into the famous Niihau shell leis. These delicate, ornate, and very expensive leis are often of museum quality, insured by **Lloyds of London,** and coveted by private collectors. In fact, Niihau shell leis are one of the most treasured possessions of the Hawaiian people.

Since the profit the ranch produces is inconsequential compared to the amount the Robinsons could make selling the island for commercial development, it is apparent they have an ulterior, perhaps familial, motive for sustaining such a unique lifestyle on this island. Yet, because no newcomers are allowed to settle on Niihau and the children seldom return to live out their lives on this archaic isle, the future of Niihau is uncertain at best. It's widely believed the Robinsons will never bow to commercial interests and sell their rights to Niihau, but a change seems inevitable—even on an island whose people are dedicated to resisting it.

Pass the Pork, Please

The only thing rarer in Hawaii than an authentic Hawaiian native is an authentic luau, where family and friends bearing food arrive as the host puts the finishing touches on the *imu* (an underground oven), where a whole pig is slowly baked. In ancient times such cause for celebration was the crowning of a chief, the victorious end of a battle, or a tribute to the gods for a bountiful harvest. Today, family luaus are held on all of the major Hawaiian islands to celebrate the birth of a first child or bless a new house or marriage. Besides giving everyone a reason to get together, a luau reinforces community friendships and is viewed as a gift from the luau host to his or her neighbors and family.

The modern commercial luau bears little semblance to the genuine event, but this doesn't [nec]essarily make it any less entertaining. Most tourists probably wouldn't enjoy themselves at a real luau anyway, since the festivities primarily consist of conversing with strangers while dining on raw seafood and the ubiquitous *poi* (cooked taro root, which is a popular Hawaiian staple). To compensate for different tastes and tongues, tourist-oriented luaus provide constant entertainment (such as scantily clad male and female dancers and singers); a wide range of very non-Hawaiian food and a smattering of local dishes, including the famous baked pig; plus a nonstop flow of watered-down mai tais to help move things along. A luau costs between $35 and $45, and it's a good idea to research who is currently offering the best show, since quality varies. Truth be known, however, everyone almost always seems to have a good time, even at the tackiest Hawaiian luau.

L

N

O

Z

Restaurants

Only restaurants with star ratings are listed below and at right. All restaurants are listed alphabetically in the main (preceding) index. Always call in advance to ensure a restaurant has not closed, changed its hours, or booked its tables for a private party. The restaurant price ratings are based on the average cost of an entrée for one person, excluding tax or tip.

★★★★	An Extraordinary Experience
★★★	Excellent
★★	Very Good
★	Good

$$$$	Big Bucks ($25 and up)
$$$	Expensive ($15-$25)
$$	Reasonable ($10-$15)
$	The Price Is Right (less than $10)

Hotels

The hotels listed below and at right are grouped according to their price ratings; they are also listed in the main index. The hotel price ratings reflect the base price of a standard room for two people for one night during the peak season.

$$$$ Big Bucks ($225 and up)
$$$ Expensive ($150-$225)
$$ Reasonable ($75-$150)
$ The Price Is Right (less than $75)

$$$$

$$$

Index

Features

Bests

Maps

Page	Entry #	Notes

ACCESS® Travel Diary

Page **Entry #** **Notes**

ACCESS® Travel Diary

Page	Entry #	Notes

ACCESS® Travel Diary

Page	Entry #	Notes

ACCESS® Travel Diary

Page	Entry #	Notes

ACCESS® Visitor's Maps

Promo # RØ1211

NEW An easy-to-carry foldout guide and map

Using a foldout-map format, **ACCESS**® Visitor's Guides focus on the sights people really want to see. Here you'll find the signature features of the successful **ACCESS**® series—color-coded entries and maps organized by neighborhood. Easily stored in your purse or pocket, these guides are also ideal for visitors planning a short stay.

Distinctive features of the **ACCESS**® Visitor's Maps include:

- Convenient size and format
- Top 10 not-to-be-missed attractions
- Easy-to-read maps
- Numbered entries that correspond to numbers on the map
- Color-coded entries that distinguish easily between restaurants, hotels, shops, and other places of interest

---

Order by phone, toll-free: 1-800-331-3761

Name _____   Phone _____

Address _____

City _____   State _____ Zip _____

Please send me the following **ACCESS**® Visitor's Maps:

☐ **BOSTON**ACCESS®
VISITOR'S GUIDE $4.95
0-06-277082-9

☐ **CHICAGO**ACCESS®
VISITOR'S GUIDE $4.95
0-06-277084-5

☐ **HAWAII**ACCESS®
VISITOR'S GUIDE $4.95
0-06-277087-X

☐ **LOS ANGELES**ACCESS®
VISITOR'S GUIDE $4.95
0-06-277088-8

☐ **NEW YORK CITY**ACCESS®
VISITOR'S GUIDE $4.95
0-06-277092-6

Prices subject to change without notice.

☐ **PHILADELPHIA**ACCESS®
VISITOR'S GUIDE $4.95
0-06-277094-2

☐ **SAN DIEGO**ACCESS®
VISITOR'S GUIDE $4.95
0-06-277097-7

☐ **SAN FRANCISCO**ACCESS®
VISITOR'S GUIDE $4.95
0-06-277098-5

☐ **WASHINGTON DC**ACCESS®
VISITOR'S GUIDE $4.95
0-06-277102-7

☐ **WINE COUNTRY**ACCESS®
Northern California
VISITOR'S GUIDE $4.95
0-06-277104-3

Total for **ACCESS**® Visitor's Maps:	$
For PA delivery, please include sales tax:	
Add $2.00 for first Visitor's Map S&H, $1.00 per additional map:	
Total payment:	$

☐ Check or Money Order enclosed. Offer valid in the United States only.
Please make payable to HarperCollins*Publishers*.

☐ Charge my credit card   ☐ American Express   ☐ Visa   ☐ MasterCard

Card no. _____   Exp. date _____

Signature _____

Send orders to:
HarperCollins*Publishers*
P.O. Box 588
Dunmore, PA 18512-0588

Send correspondence to:
ACCESS®PRESS
10 East 53rd Street, 7th Floor
New York, NY 10022